MY HERO ACADEMIA

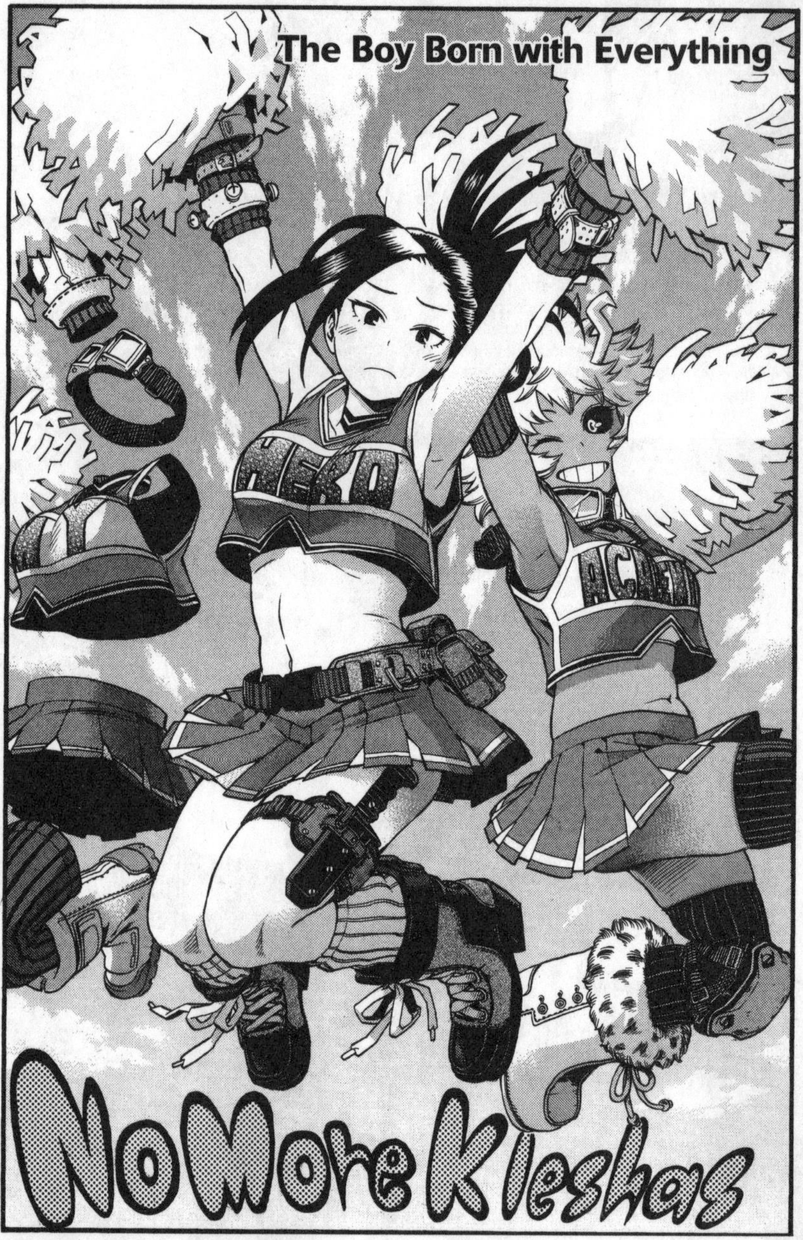
The Boy Born with Everything
No More Kleshas
HERO
ACADEMIA

KOHEI HORIKOSHI

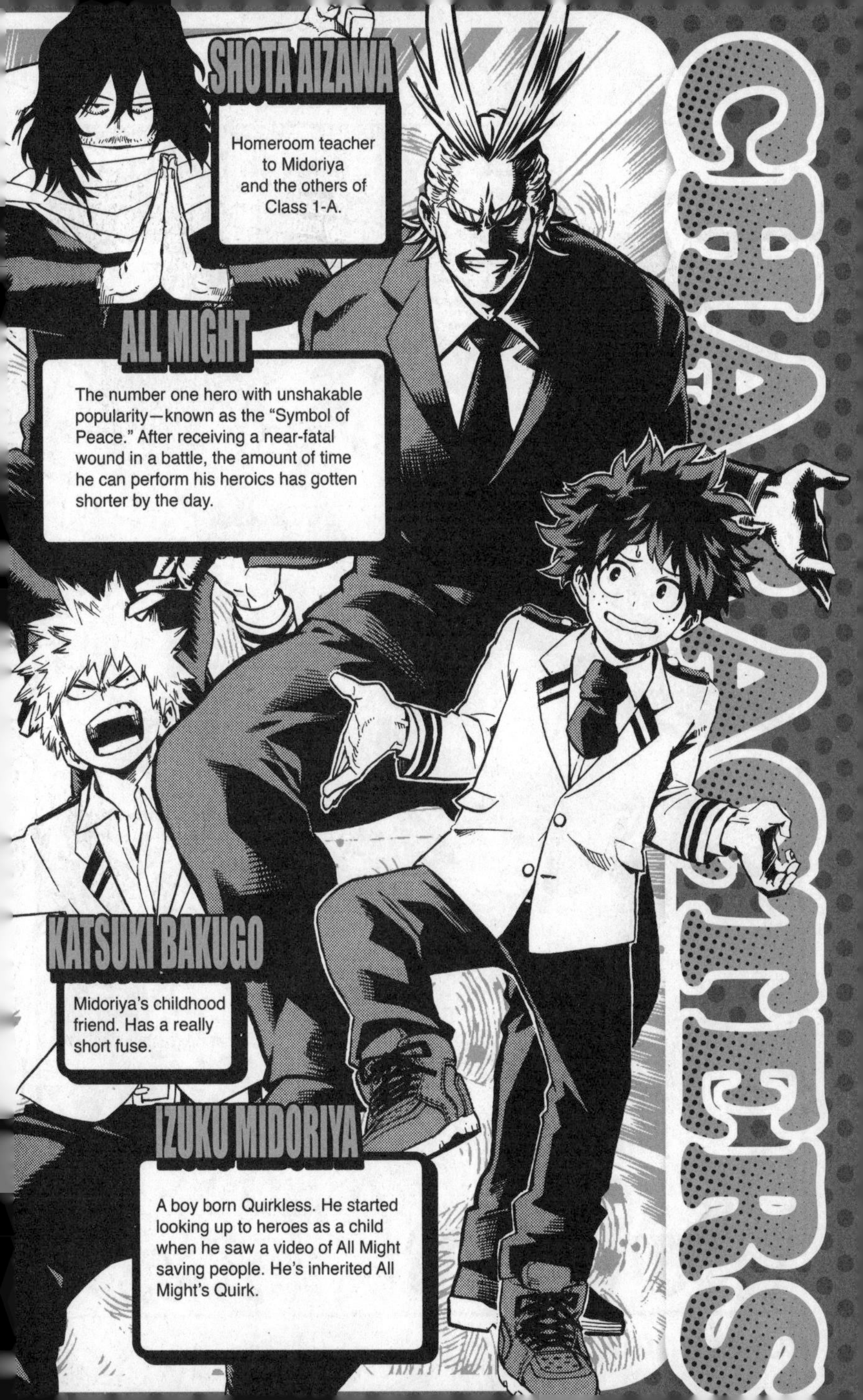
CHARACTERS
SHOTA AIZAWA
Homeroom teacher to Midoriya and the others of Class 1-A.
ALL MIGHT
The number one hero with unshakable popularity—known as the "Symbol of Peace." After receiving a near-fatal wound in a battle, the amount of time he can perform his heroics has gotten shorter by the day.
KATSUKI BAKUGO
Midoriya's childhood friend. Has a really short fuse.
IZUKU MIDORIYA
A boy born Quirkless. He started looking up to heroes as a child when he saw a video of All Might saving people. He's inherited All Might's Quirk.

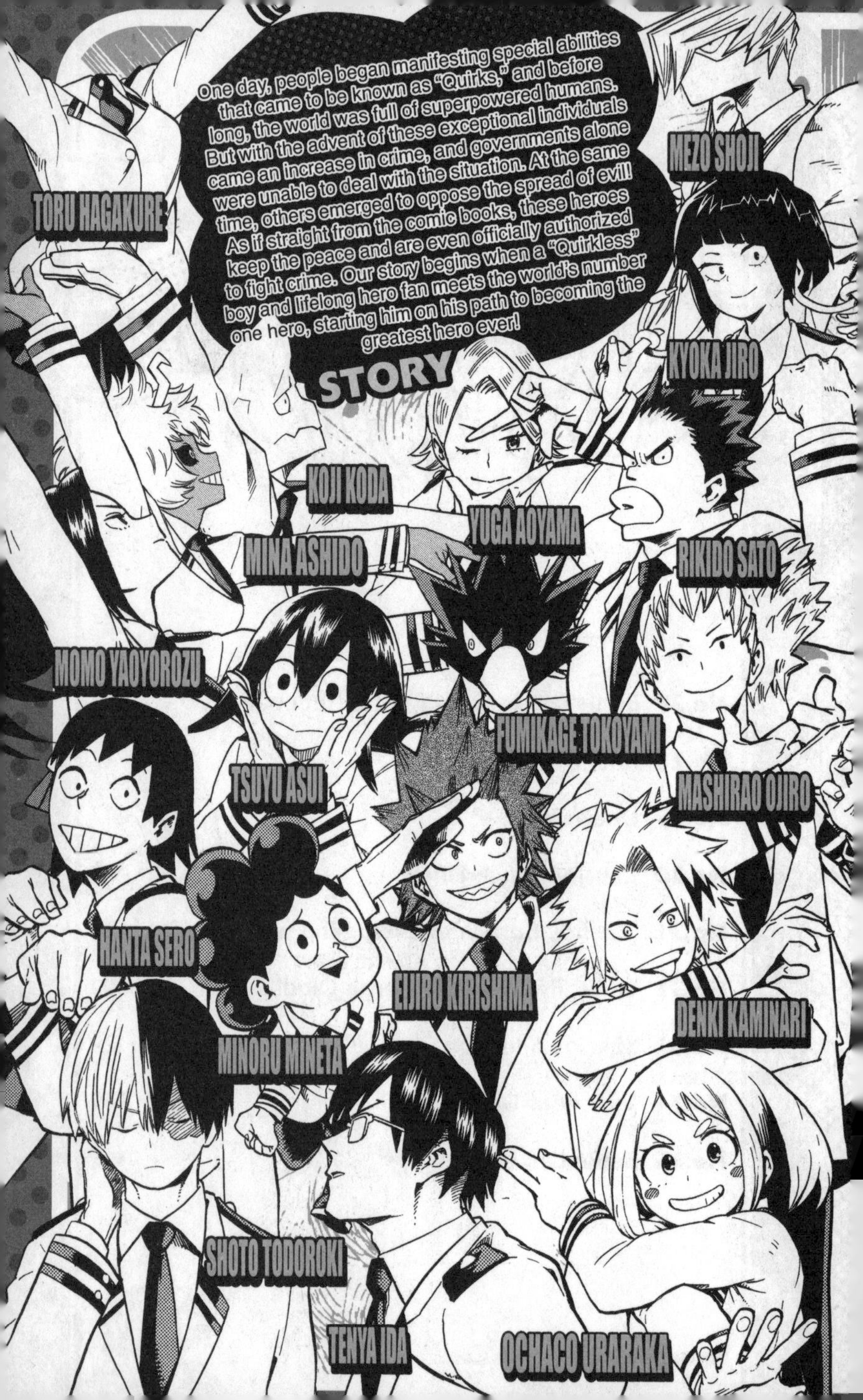
One day, people began manifesting special abilities that came to be known as "Quirks," and before long, the world was full of superpowered humans. But with the advent of these exceptional individuals came an increase in crime, and governments alone were unable to deal with the situation. At the same time, others emerged to oppose the spread of evil! As if straight from the comic books, these heroes keep the peace and are even officially authorized to fight crime. Our story begins when a "Quirkless" boy and lifelong hero fan meets the world's number one hero, starting him on his path to becoming the greatest hero ever!
STORY
MEZO SHOJI
TORU HAGAKURE
KYOKA JIRO
KOJI KODA
YUGA AOYAMA
RIKIDO SATO
MINA ASHIDO
MOMO YAOYOROZU
FUMIKAGE TOKOYAMI
MASHIRAO OJIRO
TSUYU ASUI
HANTA SERO
EIJIRO KIRISHIMA
DENKI KAMINARI
MINORU MINETA
SHOTO TODOROKI
TENYA IDA
OCHACO URARAKA

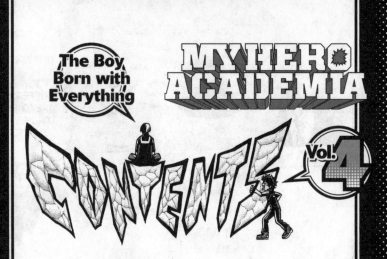

The Boy Born with Everything

MY HERO ACADEMIA

CONTENTS

Vol. 4

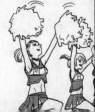

No.27 - Earth-Shatteringly Fateful Negotiations

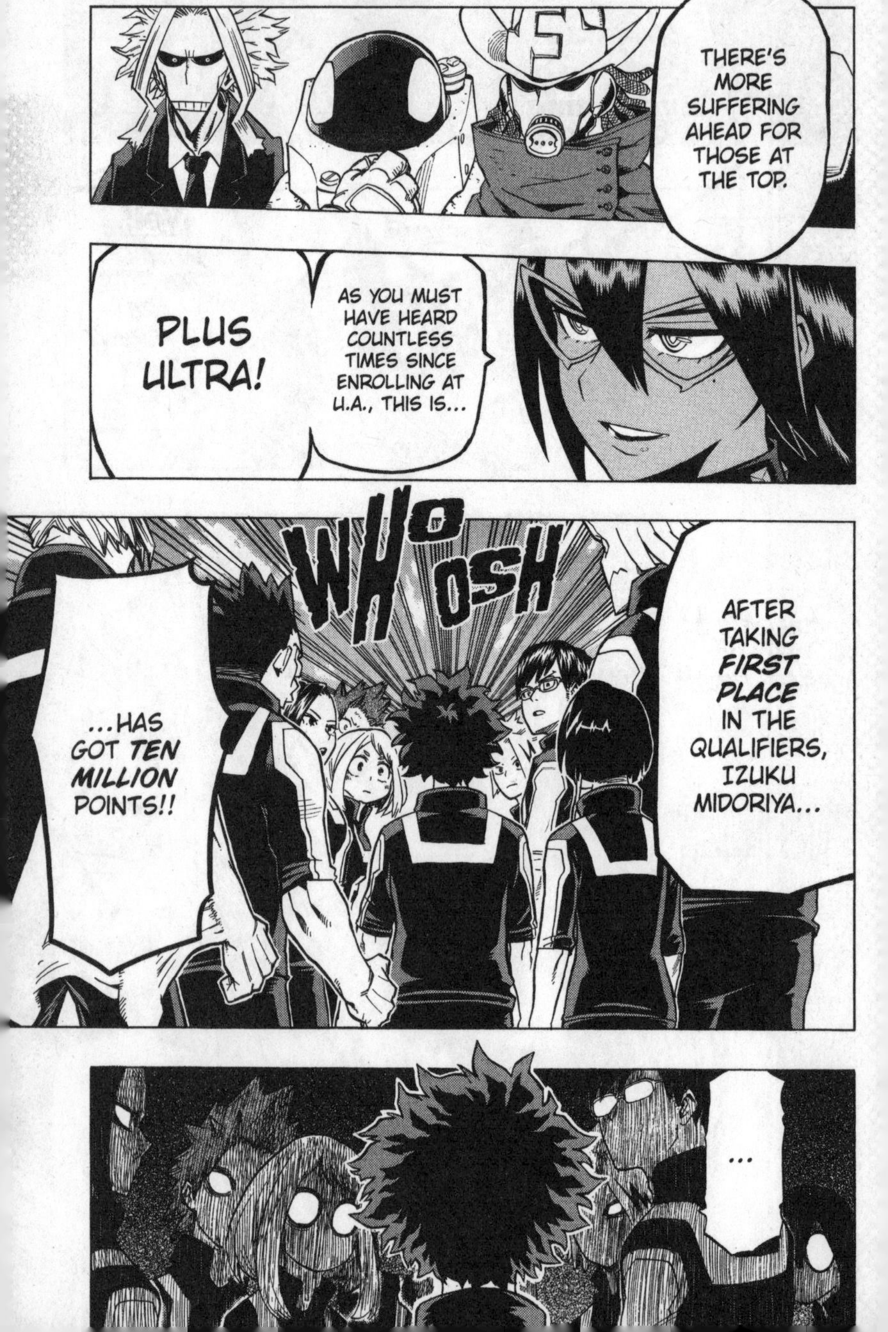
THERE'S MORE SUFFERING AHEAD FOR THOSE AT THE TOP.
AS YOU MUST HAVE HEARD COUNTLESS TIMES SINCE ENROLLING AT U.A., THIS IS...
PLUS ULTRA!
AFTER TAKING FIRST PLACE IN THE QUALIFIERS, IZUKU MIDORIYA...
WHOOSH
...HAS GOT TEN MILLION POINTS!!
...

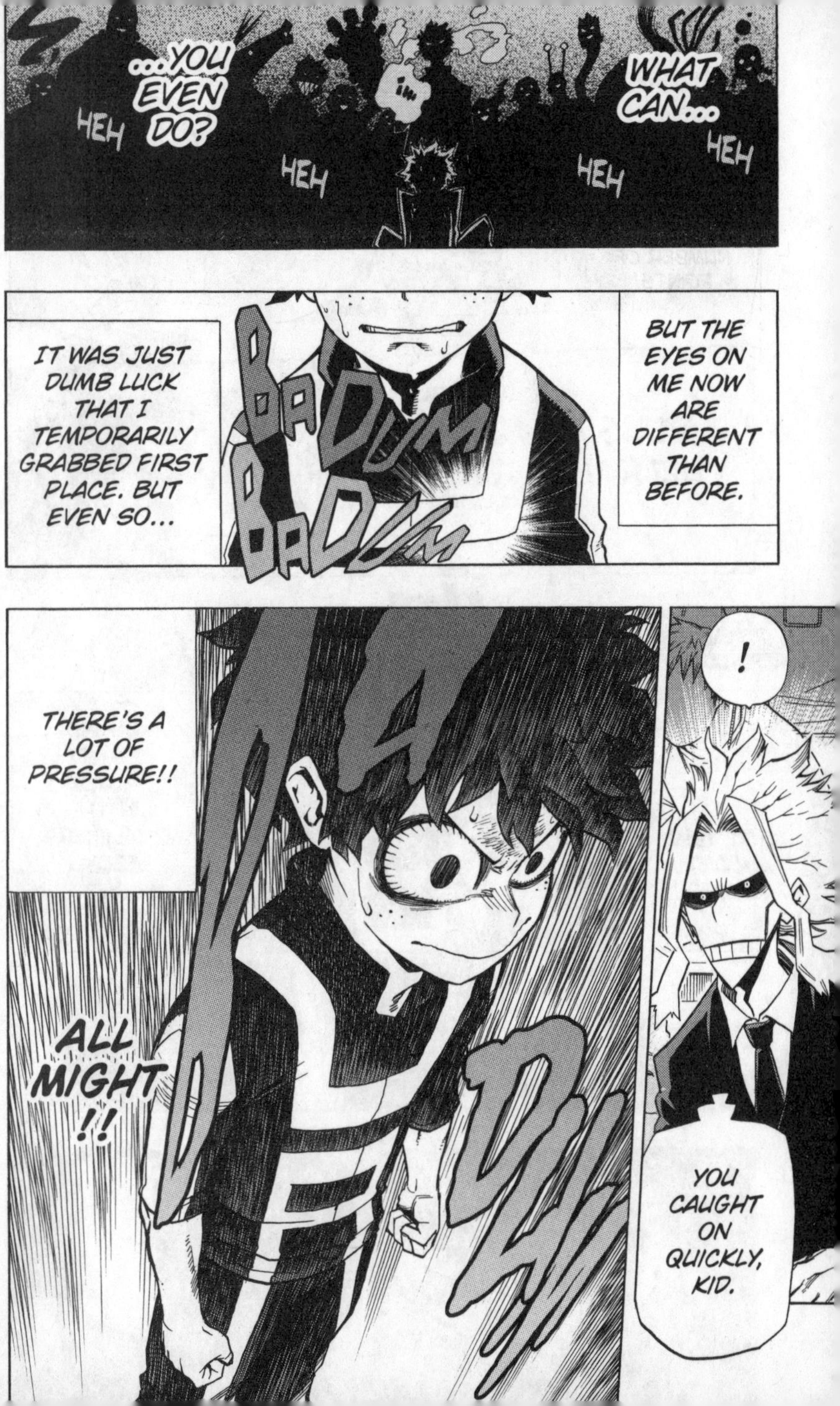
WHAT CAN...
HEH
HEH
...YOU EVEN DO?
HEH
HEH
BUT THE EYES ON ME NOW ARE DIFFERENT THAN BEFORE.
BADUM
BADUM
IT WAS JUST DUMB LUCK THAT I TEMPORARILY GRABBED FIRST PLACE. BUT EVEN SO...
!
YOU CAUGHT ON QUICKLY, KID.
THERE'S A LOT OF PRESSURE!!
ALL MIGHT!!

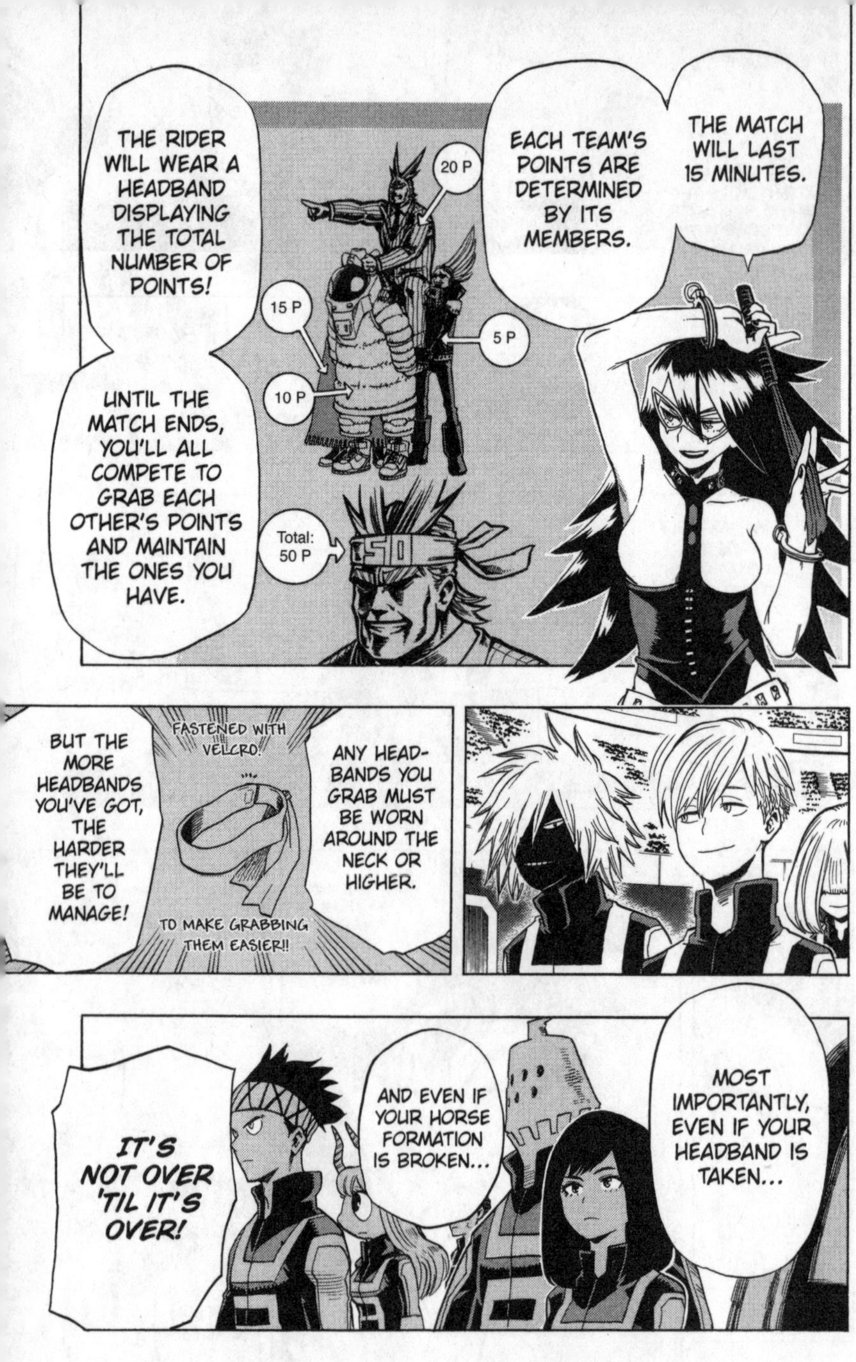
THE MATCH WILL LAST 15 MINUTES.
EACH TEAM'S POINTS ARE DETERMINED BY ITS MEMBERS.
20 P
THE RIDER WILL WEAR A HEADBAND DISPLAYING THE TOTAL NUMBER OF POINTS!
5 P
15 P
10 P
UNTIL THE MATCH ENDS, YOU'LL ALL COMPETE TO GRAB EACH OTHER'S POINTS AND MAINTAIN THE ONES YOU HAVE.
Total: 50 P
ANY HEAD-BANDS YOU GRAB MUST BE WORN AROUND THE NECK OR HIGHER.
FASTENED WITH VELCRO.
...
BUT THE MORE HEADBANDS YOU'VE GOT, THE HARDER THEY'LL BE TO MANAGE!
TO MAKE GRABBING THEM EASIER!!
MOST IMPORTANTLY, EVEN IF YOUR HEADBAND IS TAKEN...
AND EVEN IF YOUR HORSE FORMATION IS BROKEN...
IT'S NOT OVER 'TIL IT'S OVER!

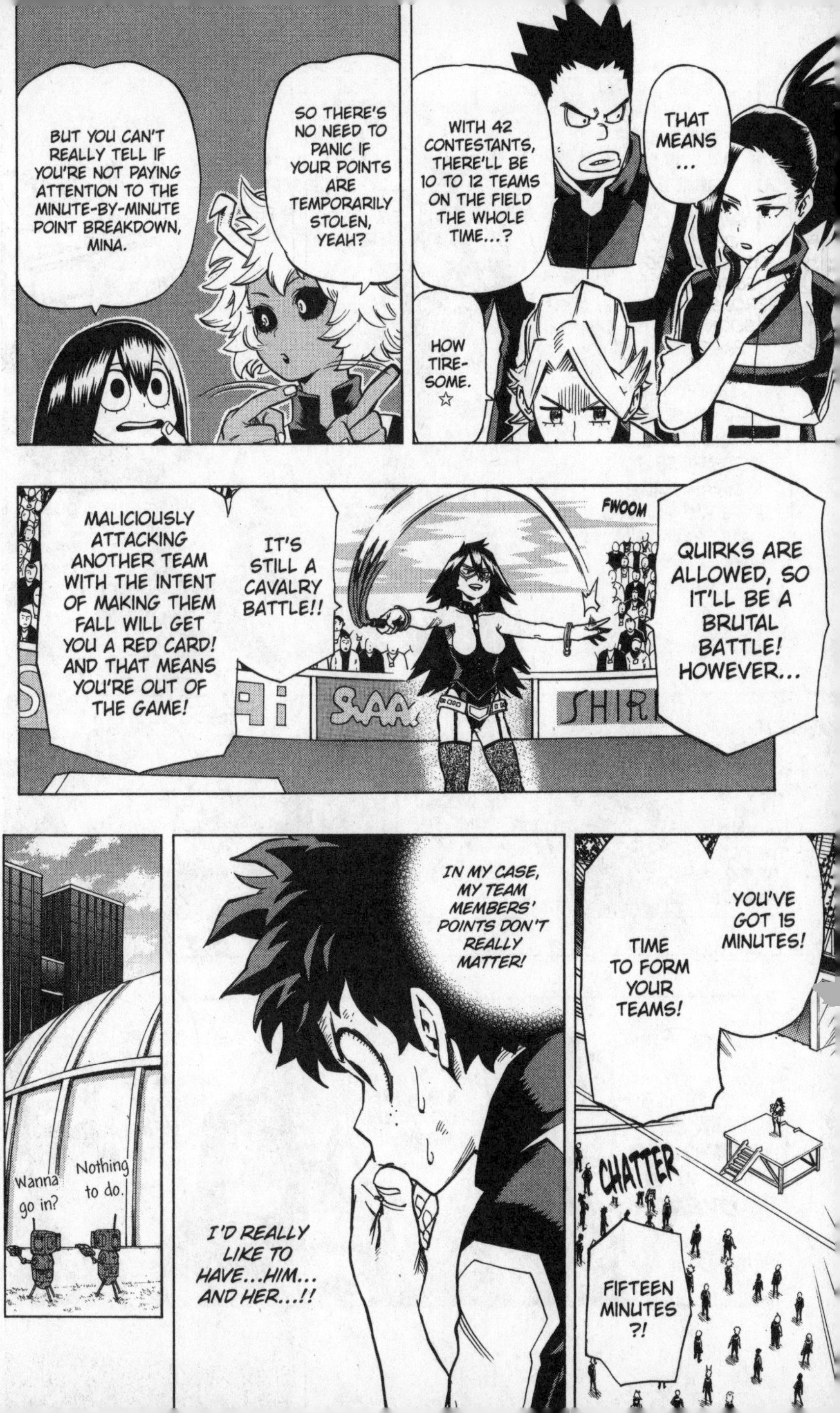
THAT MEANS...
WITH 42 CONTESTANTS, THERE'LL BE 10 TO 12 TEAMS ON THE FIELD THE WHOLE TIME...?
HOW TIRESOME. ☆
SO THERE'S NO NEED TO PANIC IF YOUR POINTS ARE TEMPORARILY STOLEN, YEAH?
BUT YOU CAN'T REALLY TELL IF YOU'RE NOT PAYING ATTENTION TO THE MINUTE-BY-MINUTE POINT BREAKDOWN, MINA.
FWOOM
QUIRKS ARE ALLOWED, SO IT'LL BE A BRUTAL BATTLE! HOWEVER...
IT'S STILL A CAVALRY BATTLE!!
MALICIOUSLY ATTACKING ANOTHER TEAM WITH THE INTENT OF MAKING THEM FALL WILL GET YOU A RED CARD! AND THAT MEANS YOU'RE OUT OF THE GAME!
YOU'VE GOT 15 MINUTES!
TIME TO FORM YOUR TEAMS!
CHATTER
FIFTEEN MINUTES?!
IN MY CASE, MY TEAM MEMBERS' POINTS DON'T REALLY MATTER!
I'D REALLY LIKE TO HAVE...HIM... AND HER...!!
Nothing to do.
Wanna go in?

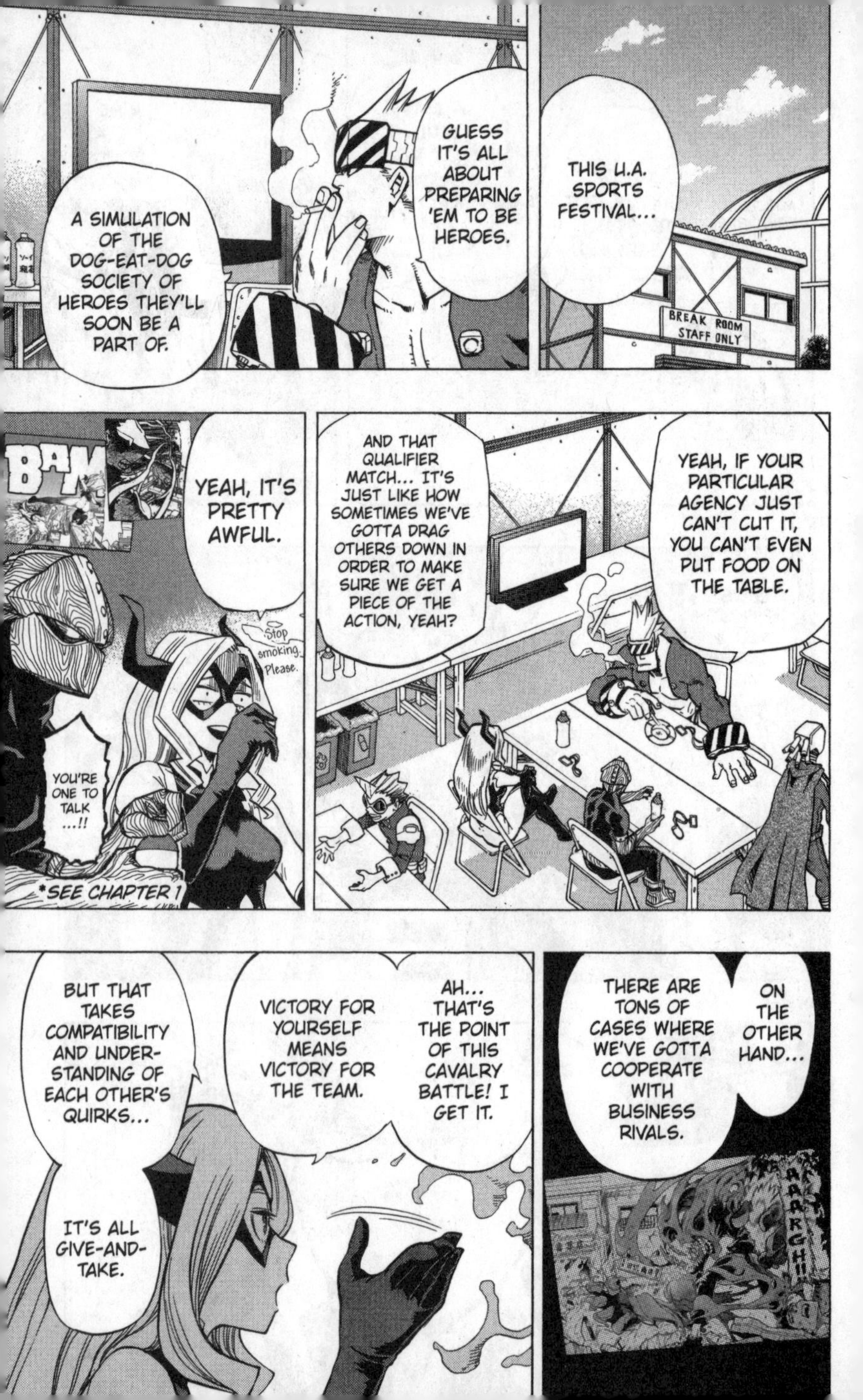
THIS U.A. SPORTS FESTIVAL...
BREAK ROOM STAFF ONLY
GUESS IT'S ALL ABOUT PREPARING 'EM TO BE HEROES.
A SIMULATION OF THE DOG-EAT-DOG SOCIETY OF HEROES THEY'LL SOON BE A PART OF.
YEAH, IF YOUR PARTICULAR AGENCY JUST CAN'T CUT IT, YOU CAN'T EVEN PUT FOOD ON THE TABLE.
AND THAT QUALIFIER MATCH... IT'S JUST LIKE HOW SOMETIMES WE'VE GOTTA DRAG OTHERS DOWN IN ORDER TO MAKE SURE WE GET A PIECE OF THE ACTION, YEAH?
YEAH, IT'S PRETTY AWFUL.
Stop smoking. Please.
YOU'RE ONE TO TALK ...!!
BAM
*SEE CHAPTER 1
ON THE OTHER HAND...
THERE ARE TONS OF CASES WHERE WE'VE GOTTA COOPERATE WITH BUSINESS RIVALS.
AAARGH!!
AH... THAT'S THE POINT OF THIS CAVALRY BATTLE! I GET IT.
VICTORY FOR YOURSELF MEANS VICTORY FOR THE TEAM.
BUT THAT TAKES COMPATIBILITY AND UNDER-STANDING OF EACH OTHER'S QUIRKS...
IT'S ALL GIVE-AND-TAKE.

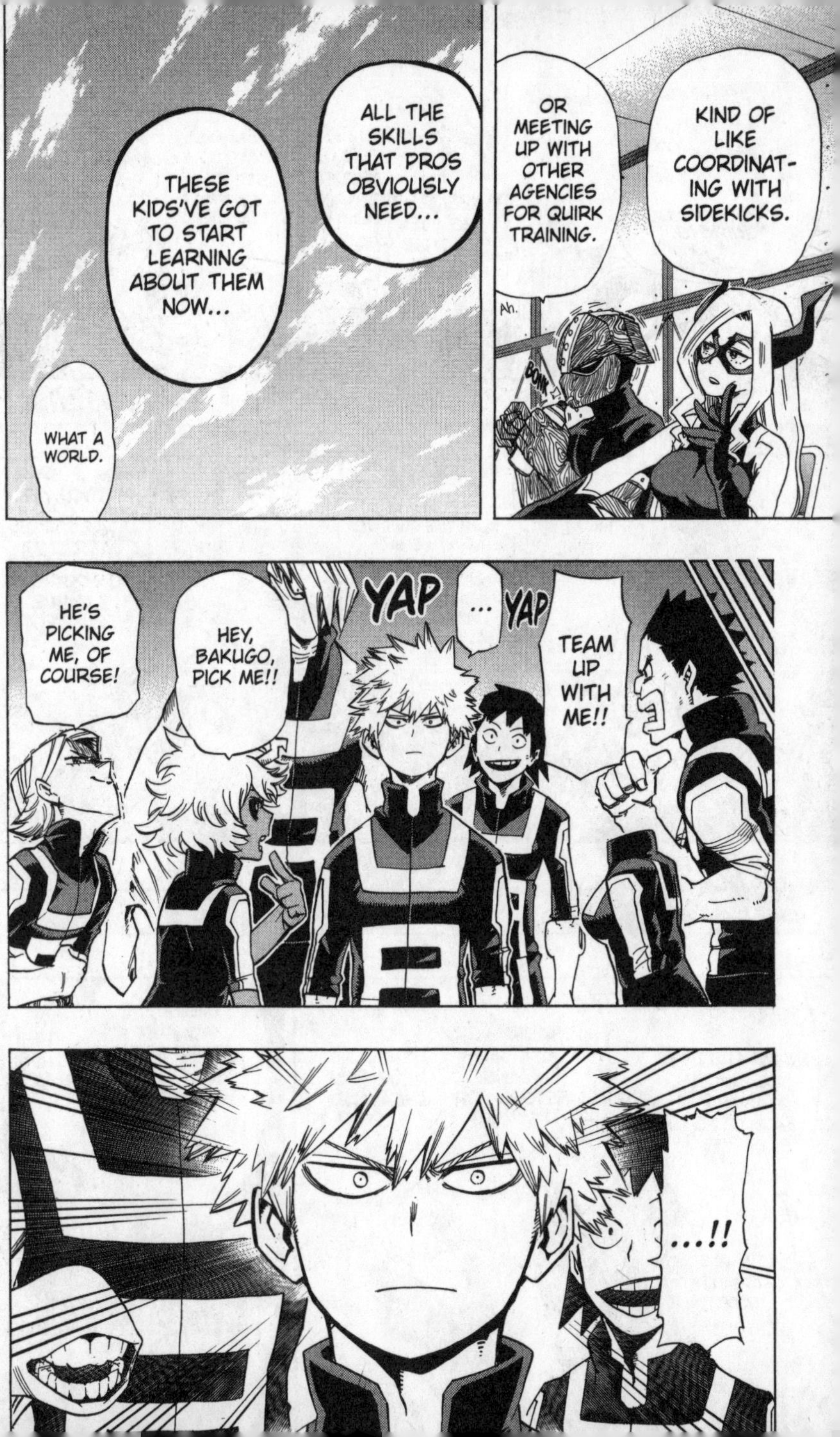
KIND OF LIKE COORDINATING WITH SIDEKICKS.
OR MEETING UP WITH OTHER AGENCIES FOR QUIRK TRAINING.
Ah.
ALL THE SKILLS THAT PROS OBVIOUSLY NEED...
THESE KIDS'VE GOT TO START LEARNING ABOUT THEM NOW...
WHAT A WORLD.
TEAM UP WITH ME!!
YAP
...
YAP
HEY, BAKUGO, PICK ME!!
HE'S PICKING ME, OF COURSE!
...!!

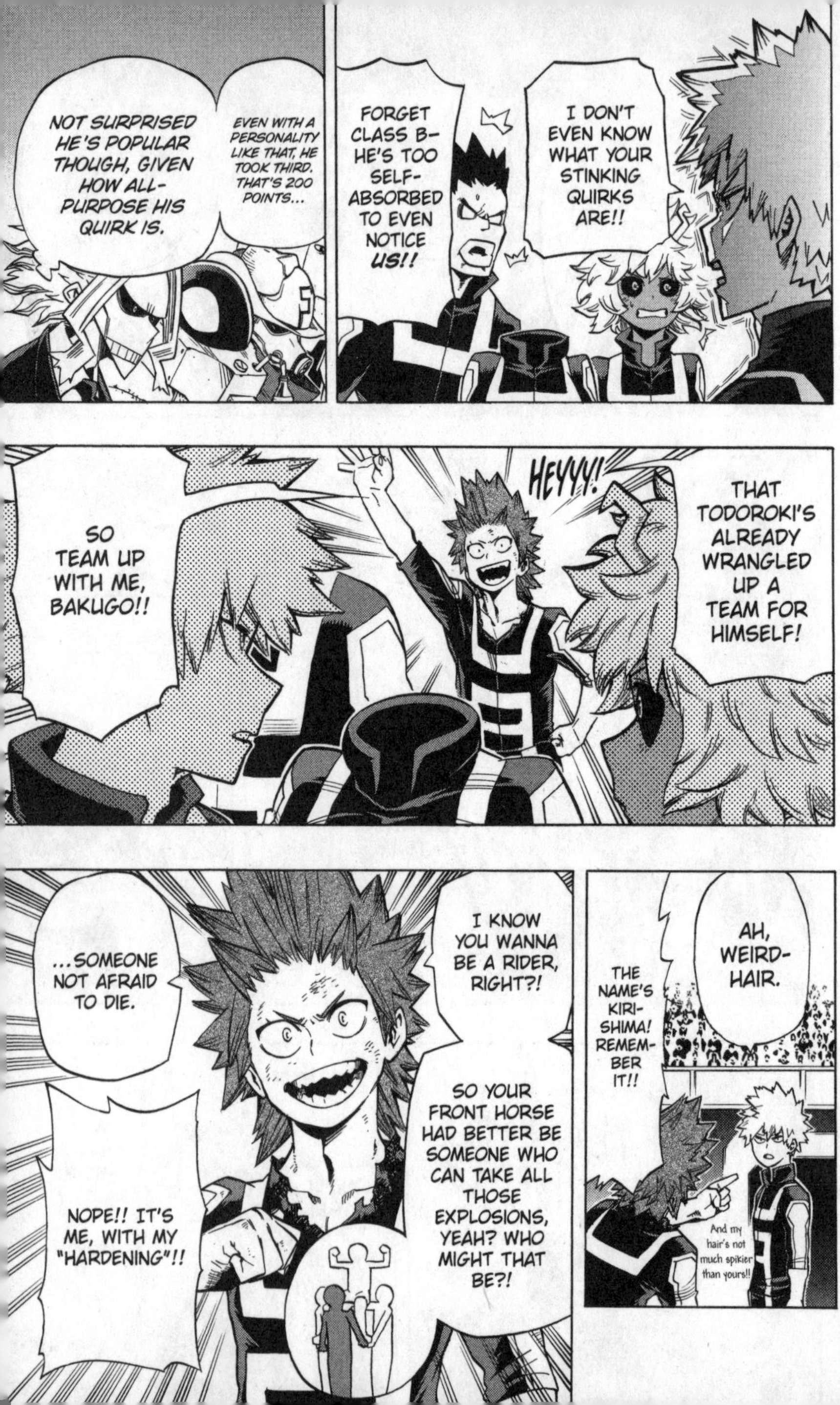
I DON'T EVEN KNOW WHAT YOUR STINKING QUIRKS ARE!!
FORGET CLASS B— HE'S TOO SELF-ABSORBED TO EVEN NOTICE *US!!*
EVEN WITH A PERSONALITY LIKE THAT, HE TOOK THIRD. THAT'S 200 POINTS...
NOT SURPRISED HE'S POPULAR THOUGH, GIVEN HOW ALL-PURPOSE HIS QUIRK IS.
THAT TODOROKI'S ALREADY WRANGLED UP A TEAM FOR HIMSELF!
HEYYY!
SO TEAM UP WITH ME, BAKUGO!!
AH, WEIRD-HAIR.
THE NAME'S KIRI-SHIMA! REMEMBER IT!!
And my hair's not much spikier than yours!!
I KNOW YOU WANNA BE A RIDER, RIGHT?!
SO YOUR FRONT HORSE HAD BETTER BE SOMEONE WHO CAN TAKE ALL THOSE EXPLOSIONS, YEAH? WHO MIGHT THAT BE?!
...SOMEONE NOT AFRAID TO DIE.
NOPE!! IT'S ME, WITH MY "HARDENING"!!

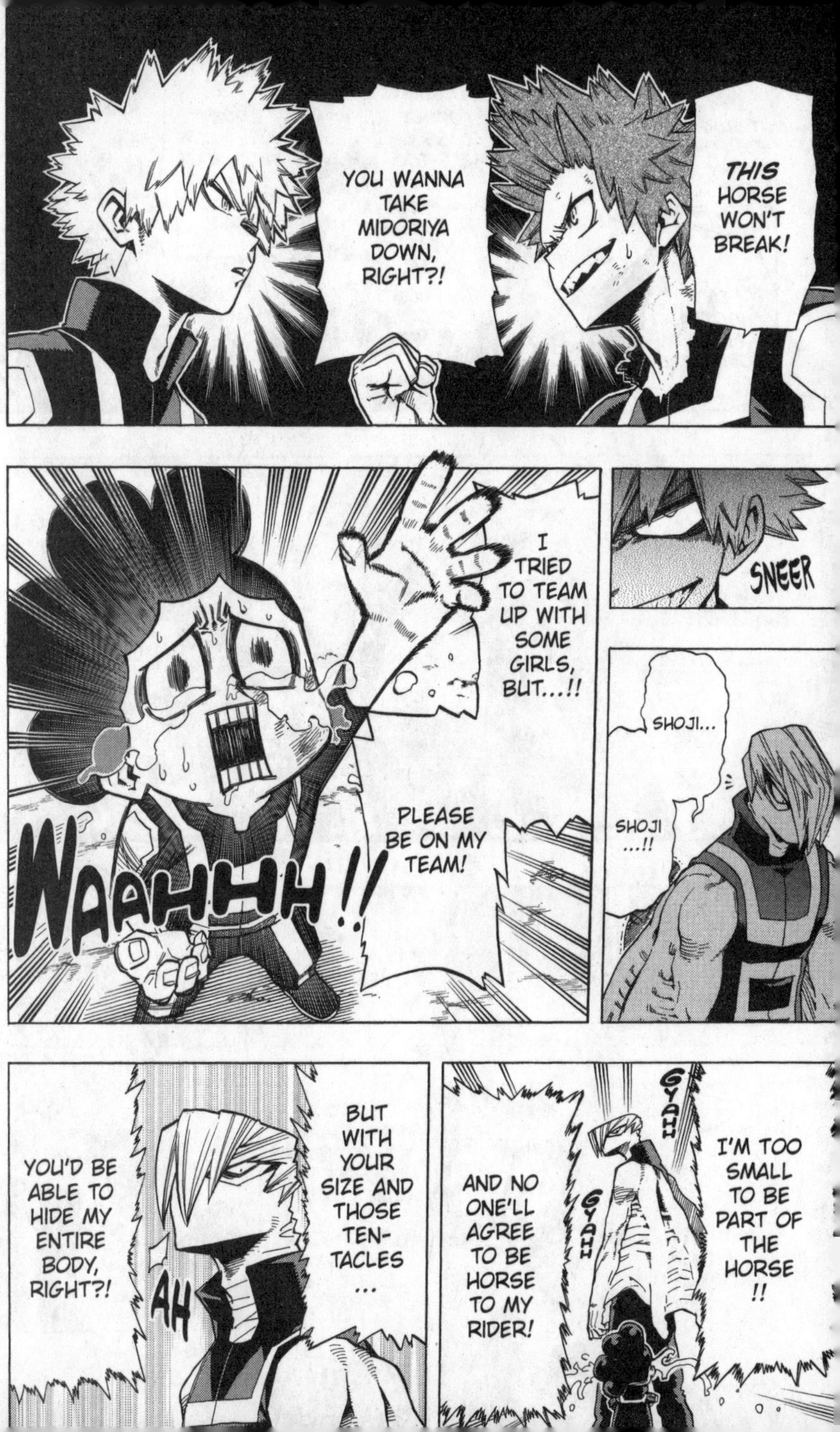
THIS HORSE WON'T BREAK!
YOU WANNA TAKE MIDORIYA DOWN, RIGHT?!
SNEER
SHOJI...
SHOJI ...!!
I TRIED TO TEAM UP WITH SOME GIRLS, BUT...!!
WAAHHH!!
PLEASE BE ON MY TEAM!
GYAHH
GYAHH
I'M TOO SMALL TO BE PART OF THE HORSE!!
AND NO ONE'LL AGREE TO BE HORSE TO MY RIDER!
BUT WITH YOUR SIZE AND THOSE TEN-TACLES...
YOU'D BE ABLE TO HIDE MY ENTIRE BODY, RIGHT?!
AH

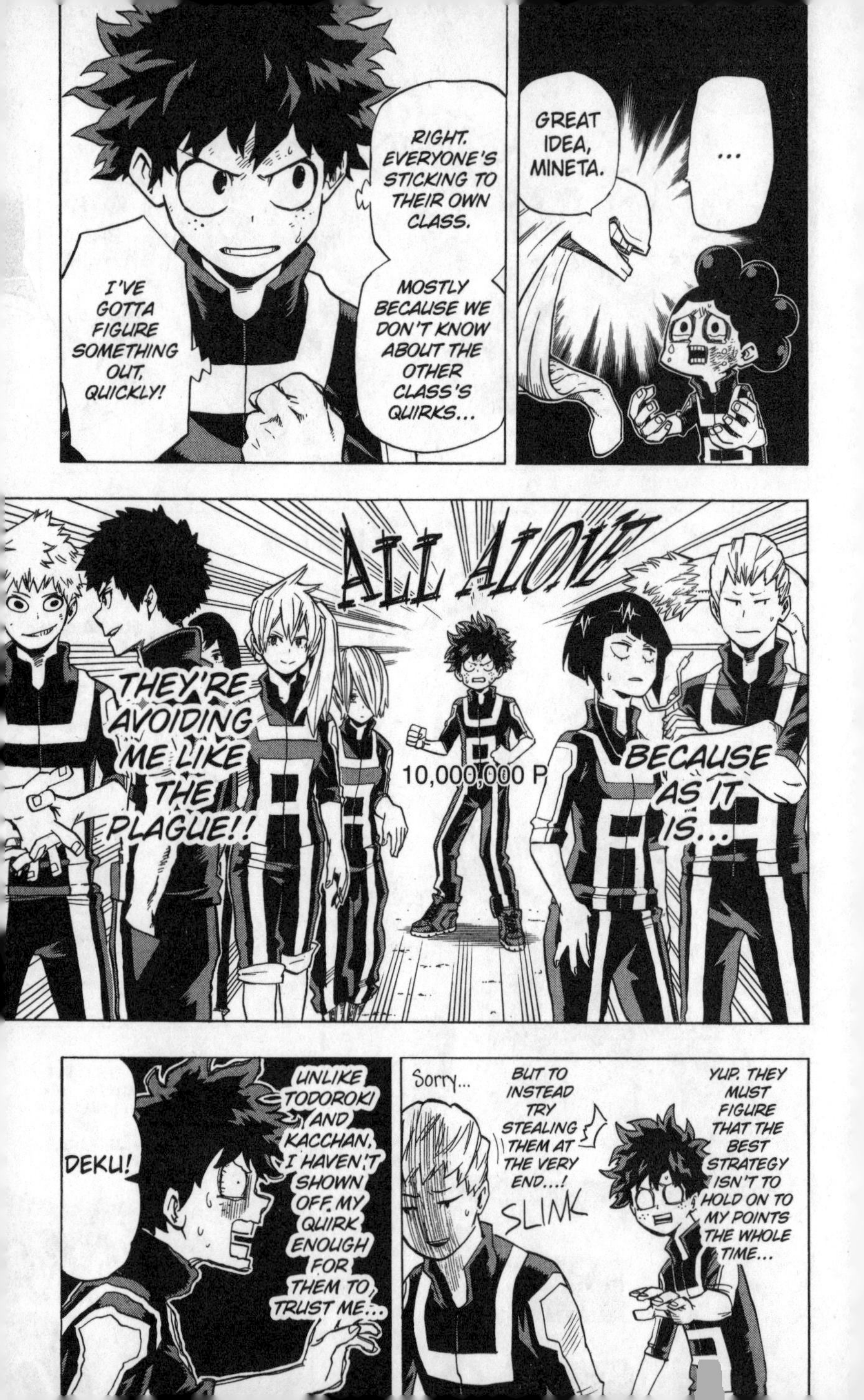
...
GREAT IDEA, MINETA.
RIGHT. EVERYONE'S STICKING TO THEIR OWN CLASS.
MOSTLY BECAUSE WE DON'T KNOW ABOUT THE OTHER CLASS'S QUIRKS...
I'VE GOTTA FIGURE SOMETHING OUT, QUICKLY!
ALL ALONE
BECAUSE AS IT IS...
10,000,000 P
THEY'RE AVOIDING ME LIKE THE PLAGUE!!
YUP. THEY MUST FIGURE THAT THE BEST STRATEGY ISN'T TO HOLD ON TO MY POINTS THE WHOLE TIME...
BUT TO INSTEAD TRY STEALING THEM AT THE VERY END...!
Sorry...
SLINK
UNLIKE TODOROKI AND KACCHAN, I HAVEN'T SHOWN OFF MY QUIRK ENOUGH FOR THEM TO TRUST ME...
DEKU!

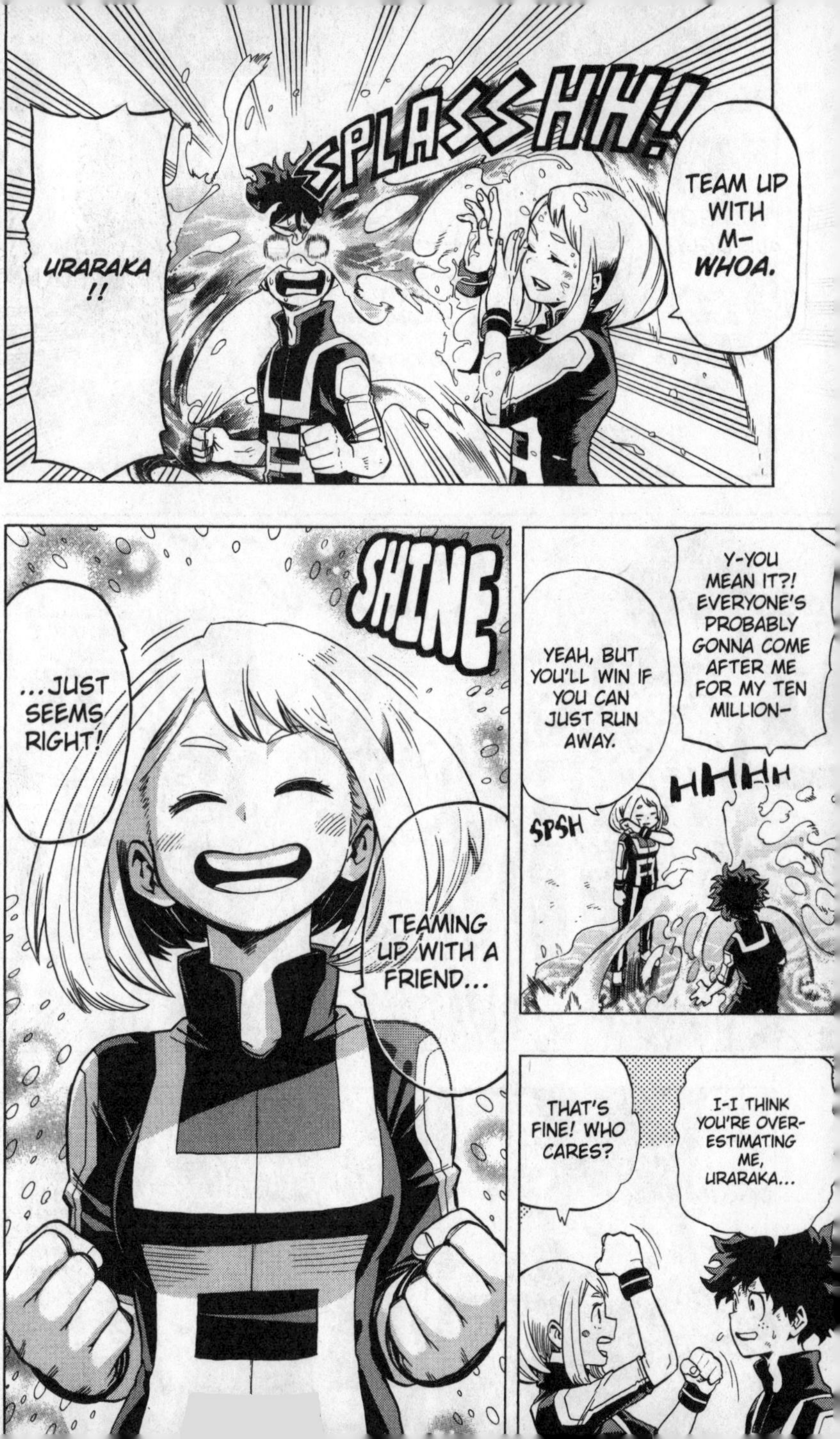
TEAM UP WITH M- WHOA.
SPLASSHH!
URARAKA!!
Y-YOU MEAN IT?! EVERYONE'S PROBABLY GONNA COME AFTER ME FOR MY TEN MILLION-
YEAH, BUT YOU'LL WIN IF YOU CAN JUST RUN AWAY.
HHHHH
SPSH
I-I THINK YOU'RE OVER-ESTIMATING ME, URARAKA...
THAT'S FINE! WHO CARES?
SHINE
TEAMING UP WITH A FRIEND...
...JUST SEEMS RIGHT!

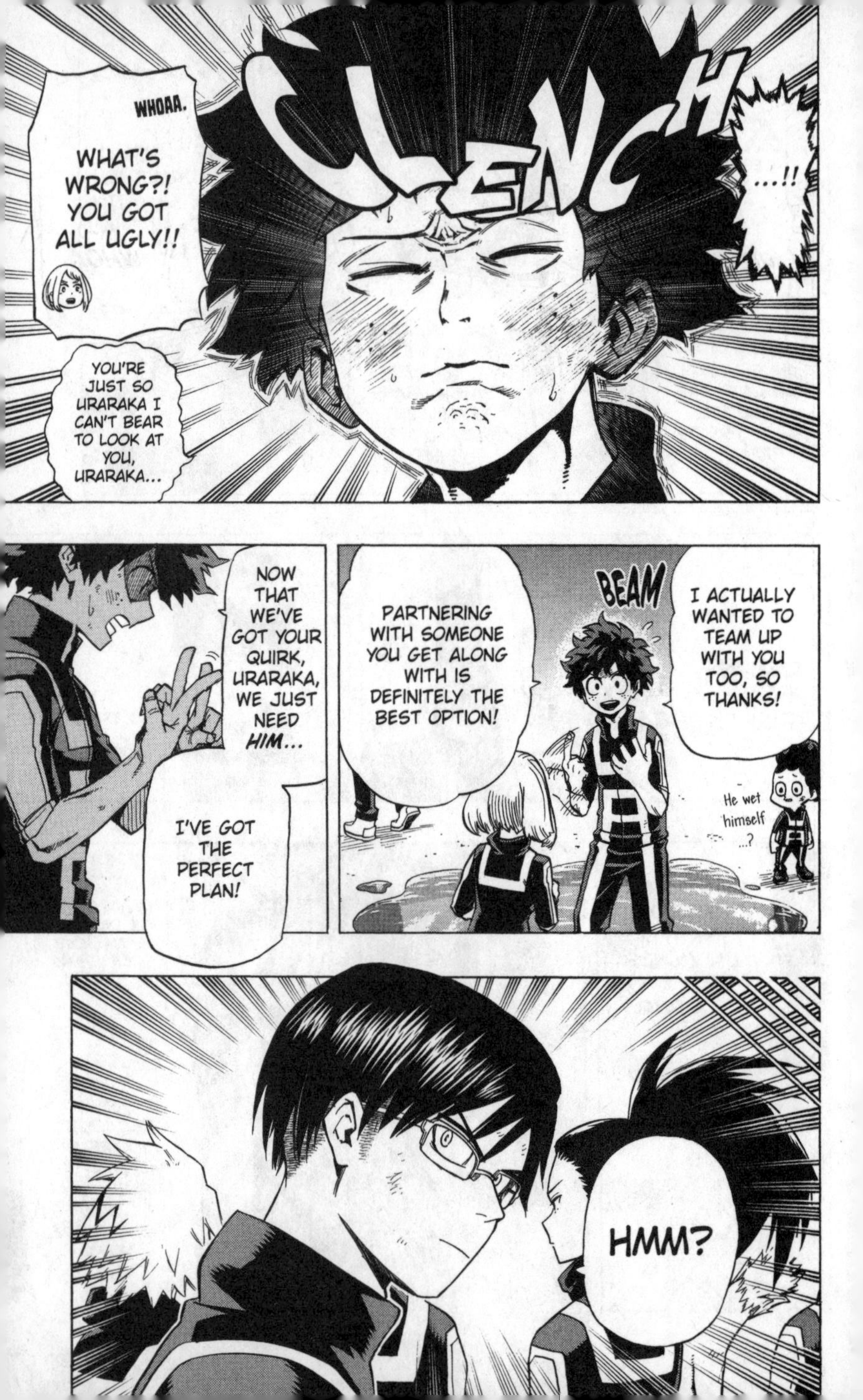
...!!
CLENCH
WHOAA.
WHAT'S WRONG?! YOU GOT ALL UGLY!!
YOU'RE JUST SO URARAKA I CAN'T BEAR TO LOOK AT YOU, URARAKA...
I ACTUALLY WANTED TO TEAM UP WITH YOU TOO, SO THANKS!
BEAM
PARTNERING WITH SOMEONE YOU GET ALONG WITH IS DEFINITELY THE BEST OPTION!
He wet himself ...?
NOW THAT WE'VE GOT YOUR QUIRK, URARAKA, WE JUST NEED *HIM*...
I'VE GOT THE PERFECT PLAN!
HMM?

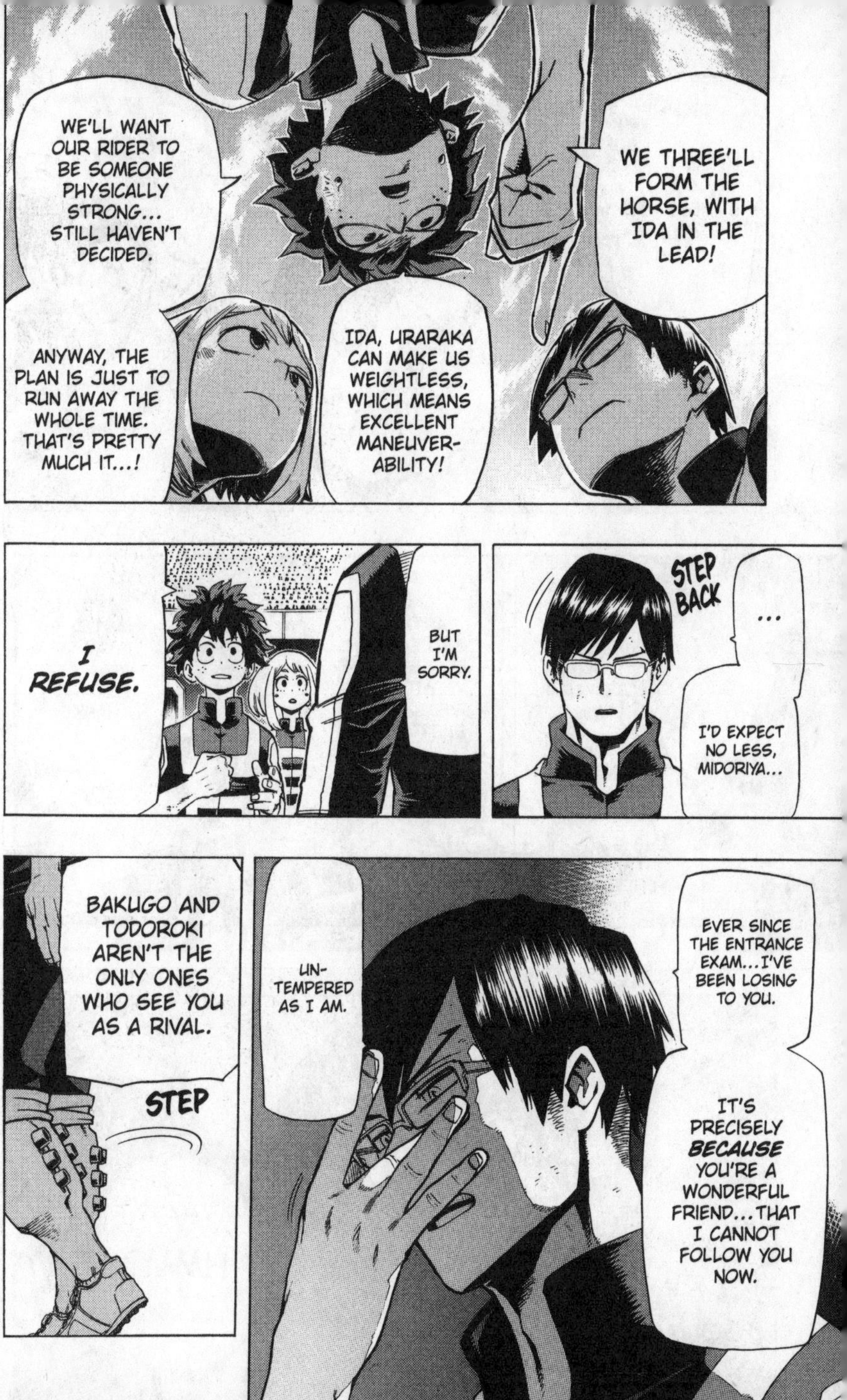
WE THREE'LL FORM THE HORSE, WITH IDA IN THE LEAD!
IDA, URARAKA CAN MAKE US WEIGHTLESS, WHICH MEANS EXCELLENT MANEUVER-ABILITY!
WE'LL WANT OUR RIDER TO BE SOMEONE PHYSICALLY STRONG... STILL HAVEN'T DECIDED.
ANYWAY, THE PLAN IS JUST TO RUN AWAY THE WHOLE TIME. THAT'S PRETTY MUCH IT...!
STEP BACK
...
I'D EXPECT NO LESS, MIDORIYA...
BUT I'M SORRY.
I REFUSE.
EVER SINCE THE ENTRANCE EXAM...I'VE BEEN LOSING TO YOU.
IT'S PRECISELY BECAUSE YOU'RE A WONDERFUL FRIEND...THAT I CANNOT FOLLOW YOU NOW.
UN-TEMPERED AS I AM.
BAKUGO AND TODOROKI AREN'T THE ONLY ONES WHO SEE YOU AS A RIVAL.
STEP

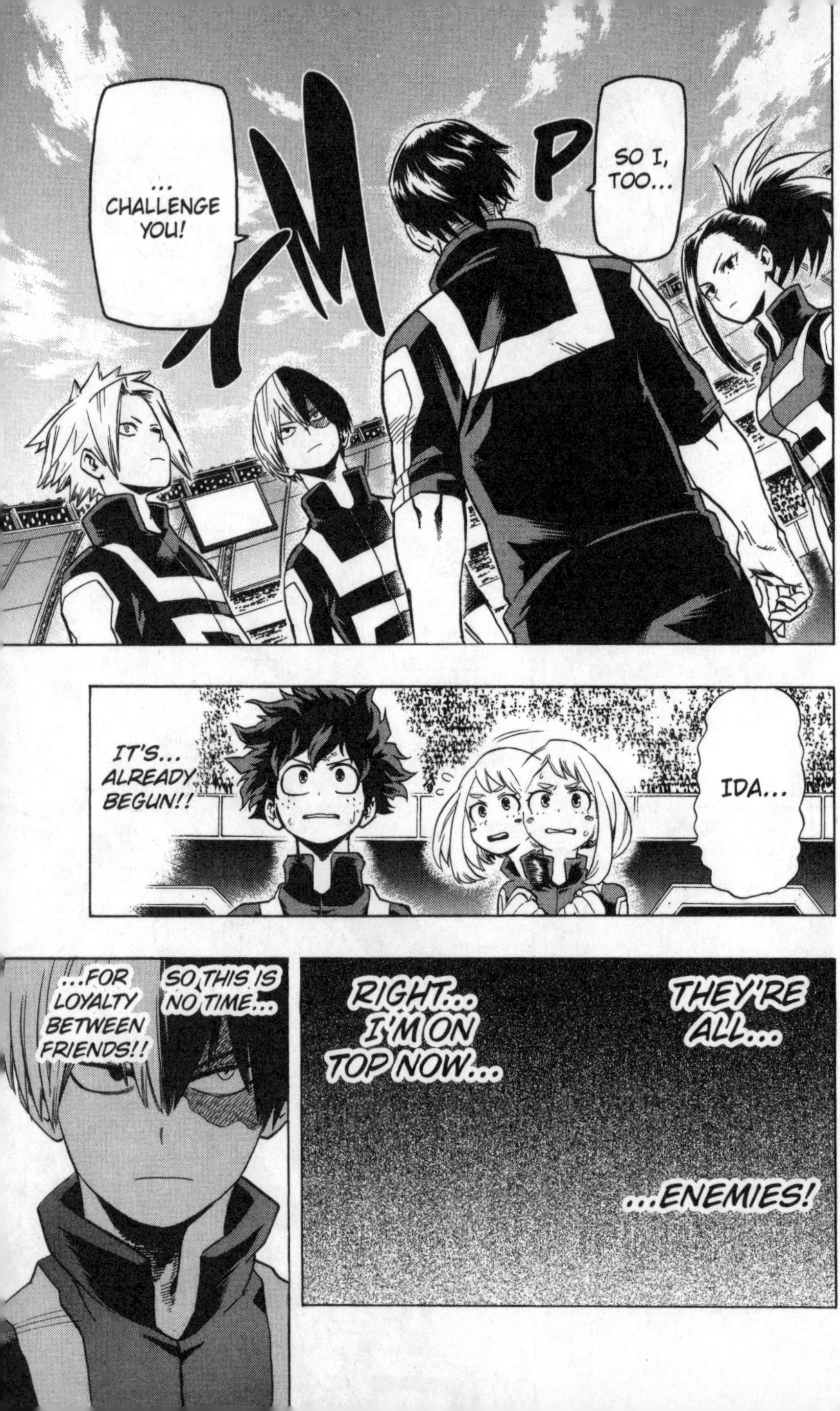
SO I, TOO...
...CHALLENGE YOU!
IDA...
IT'S... ALREADY BEGUN!!
THEY'RE ALL...
RIGHT... I'M ON TOP NOW...
...ENEMIES!
SO THIS IS NO TIME...
...FOR LOYALTY BETWEEN FRIENDS!!

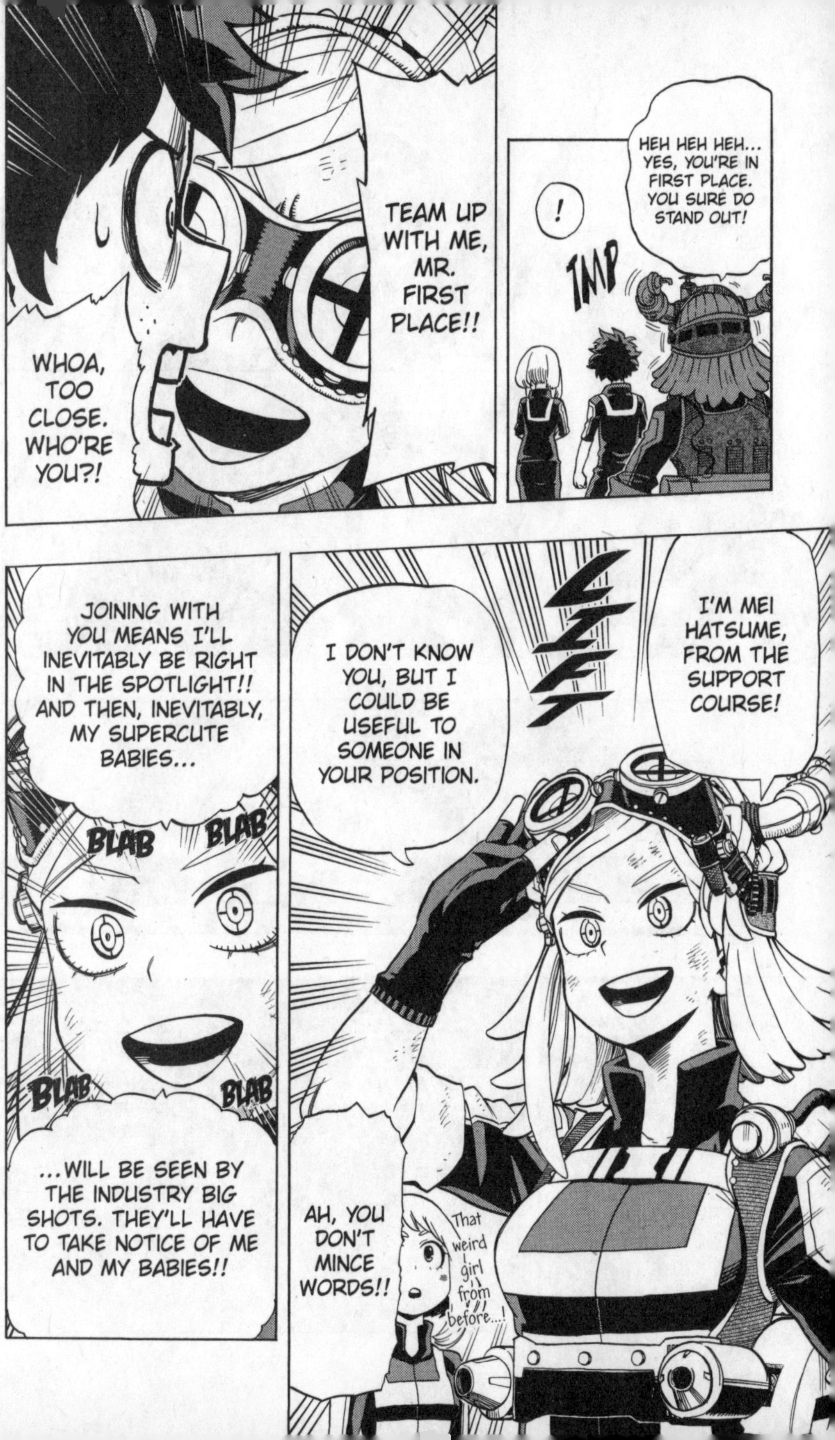
HEH HEH HEH... YES, YOU'RE IN FIRST PLACE. YOU SURE DO STAND OUT!
!
TMP
TEAM UP WITH ME, MR. FIRST PLACE!!
WHOA, TOO CLOSE. WHO'RE YOU?!
I'M MEI HATSUME, FROM THE SUPPORT COURSE!
I DON'T KNOW YOU, BUT I COULD BE USEFUL TO SOMEONE IN YOUR POSITION.
That weird girl from before...!
AH, YOU DON'T MINCE WORDS!!
JOINING WITH YOU MEANS I'LL INEVITABLY BE RIGHT IN THE SPOTLIGHT!! AND THEN, INEVITABLY, MY SUPERCUTE BABIES...
BLAB BLAB
BLAB BLAB
...WILL BE SEEN BY THE INDUSTRY BIG SHOTS. THEY'LL HAVE TO TAKE NOTICE OF ME AND MY BABIES!!

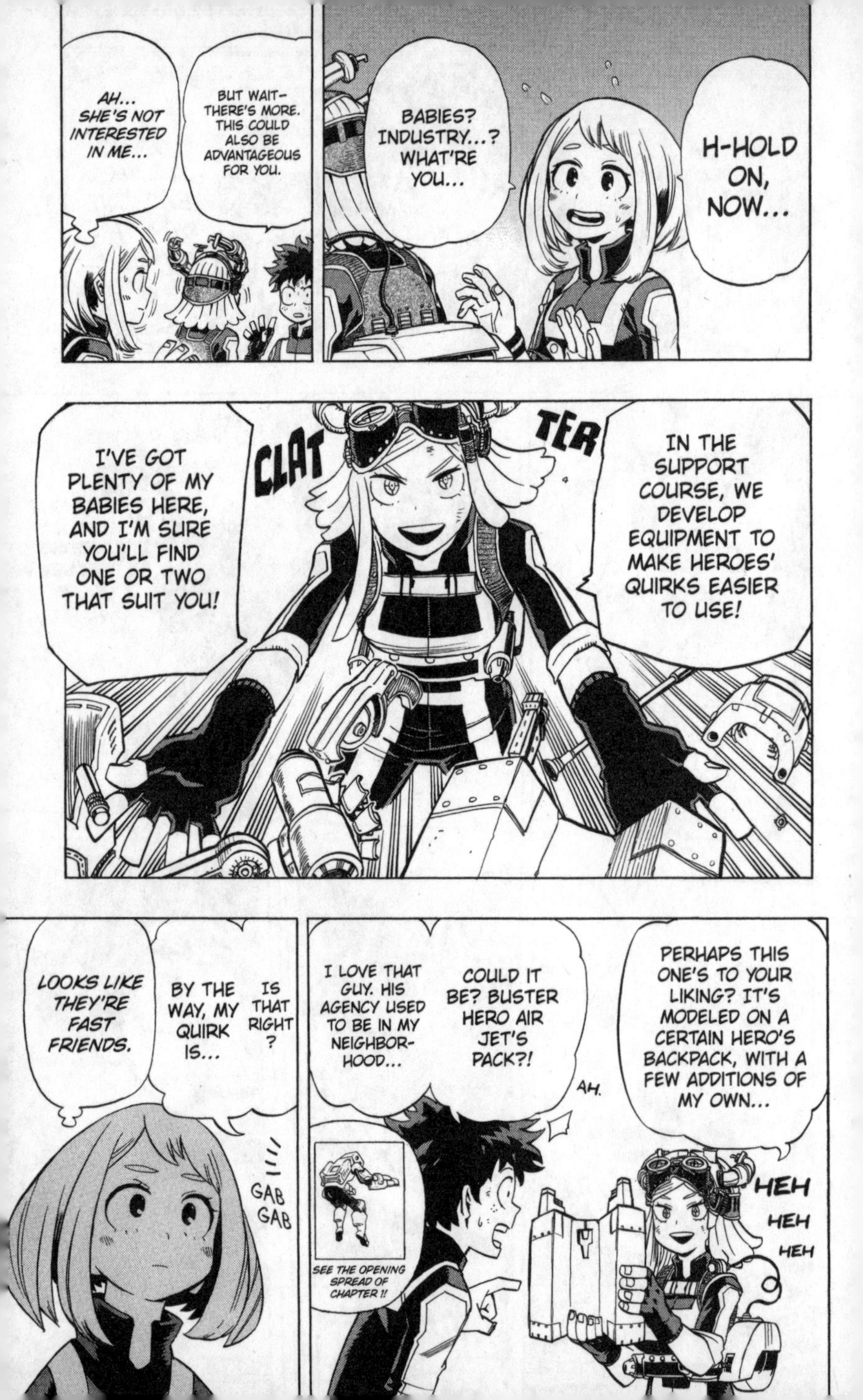
H-HOLD ON, NOW...
BABIES? INDUSTRY...? WHAT'RE YOU...
BUT WAIT— THERE'S MORE. THIS COULD ALSO BE ADVANTAGEOUS FOR YOU.
AH... SHE'S NOT INTERESTED IN ME...
IN THE SUPPORT COURSE, WE DEVELOP EQUIPMENT TO MAKE HEROES' QUIRKS EASIER TO USE!
CLAT TER
I'VE GOT PLENTY OF MY BABIES HERE, AND I'M SURE YOU'LL FIND ONE OR TWO THAT SUIT YOU!
PERHAPS THIS ONE'S TO YOUR LIKING? IT'S MODELED ON A CERTAIN HERO'S BACKPACK, WITH A FEW ADDITIONS OF MY OWN...
HEH
HEH
HEH
AH.
COULD IT BE? BUSTER HERO AIR JET'S PACK?!
I LOVE THAT GUY. HIS AGENCY USED TO BE IN MY NEIGHBOR-HOOD...
SEE THE OPENING SPREAD OF CHAPTER 1!
IS THAT RIGHT?
BY THE WAY, MY QUIRK IS...
GAB GAB
LOOKS LIKE THEY'RE FAST FRIENDS.

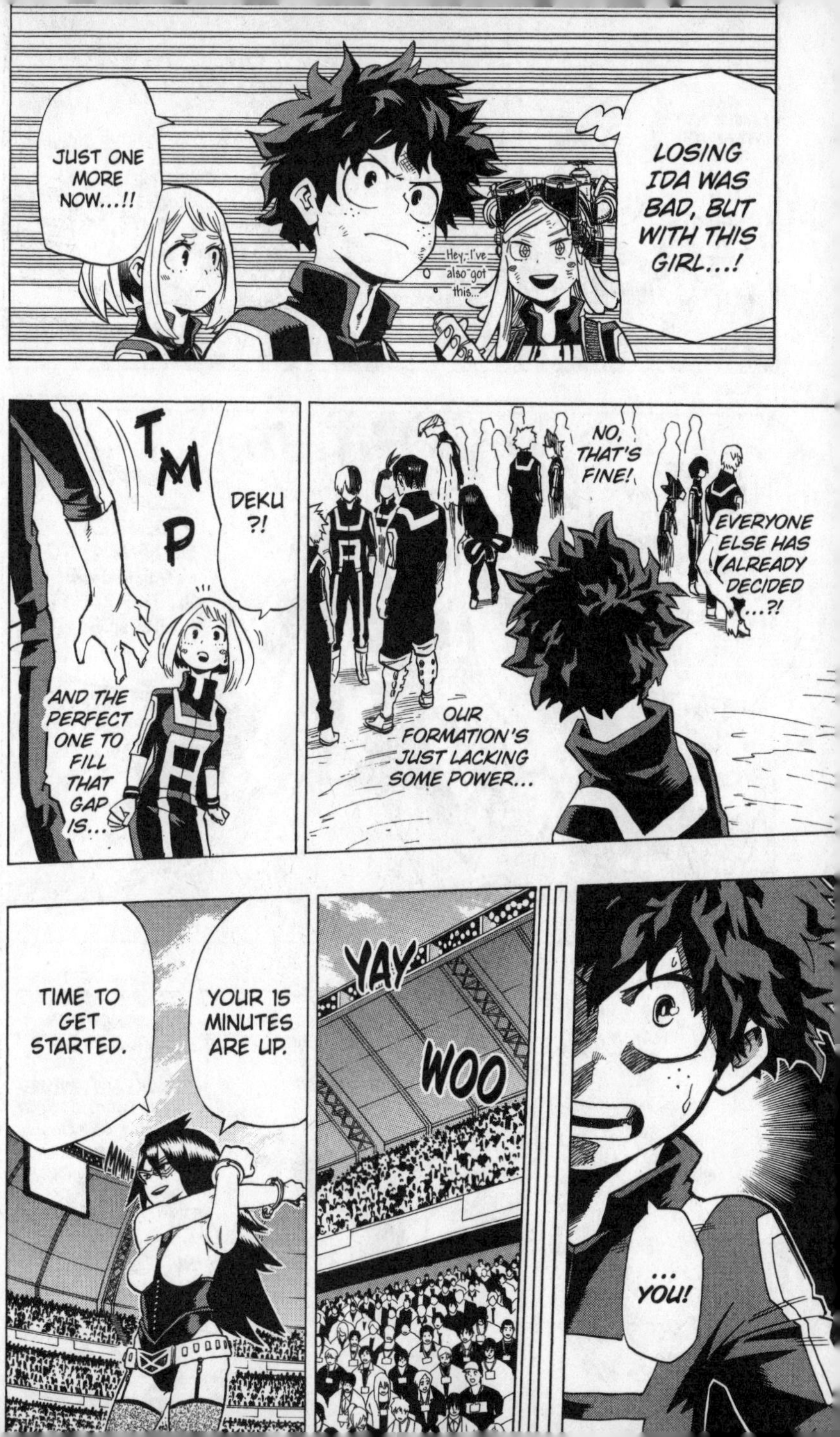
LOSING IDA WAS BAD, BUT WITH THIS GIRL...!
Hey, I've also got this...
JUST ONE MORE NOW...!!
NO, THAT'S FINE!
EVERYONE ELSE HAS ALREADY DECIDED...?!
OUR FORMATION'S JUST LACKING SOME POWER...
TMP
DEKU ?!
AND THE PERFECT ONE TO FILL THAT GAP IS...
...YOU!
YAY
WOO
YOUR 15 MINUTES ARE UP.
TIME TO GET STARTED.

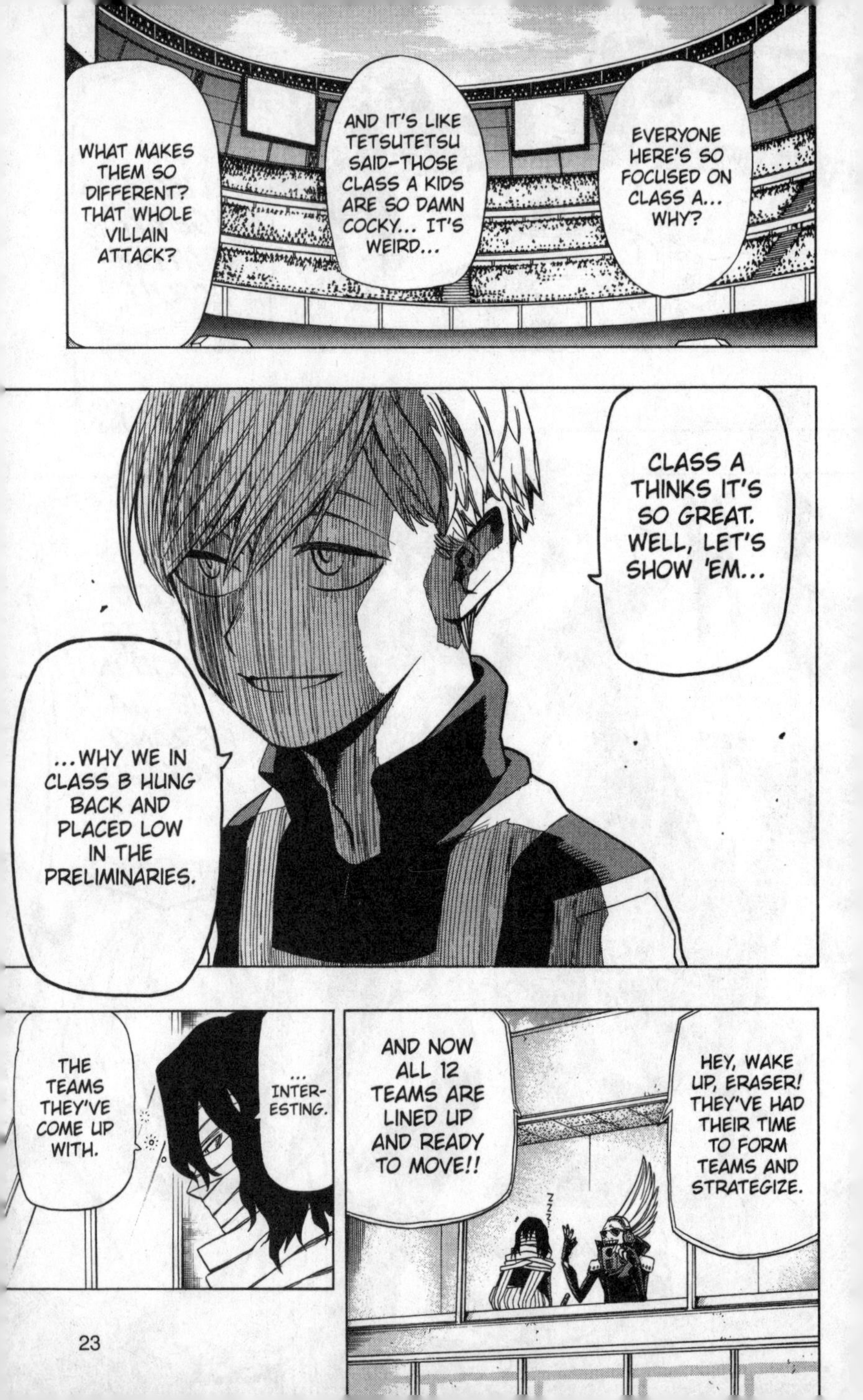
EVERYONE HERE'S SO FOCUSED ON CLASS A... WHY?
AND IT'S LIKE TETSUTETSU SAID–THOSE CLASS A KIDS ARE SO DAMN COCKY... IT'S WEIRD...
WHAT MAKES THEM SO DIFFERENT? THAT WHOLE VILLAIN ATTACK?
CLASS A THINKS IT'S SO GREAT. WELL, LET'S SHOW 'EM...
...WHY WE IN CLASS B HUNG BACK AND PLACED LOW IN THE PRELIMINARIES.
HEY, WAKE UP, ERASER! THEY'VE HAD THEIR TIME TO FORM TEAMS AND STRATEGIZE.
AND NOW ALL 12 TEAMS ARE LINED UP AND READY TO MOVE!!
... INTER-ESTING.
THE TEAMS THEY'VE COME UP WITH.

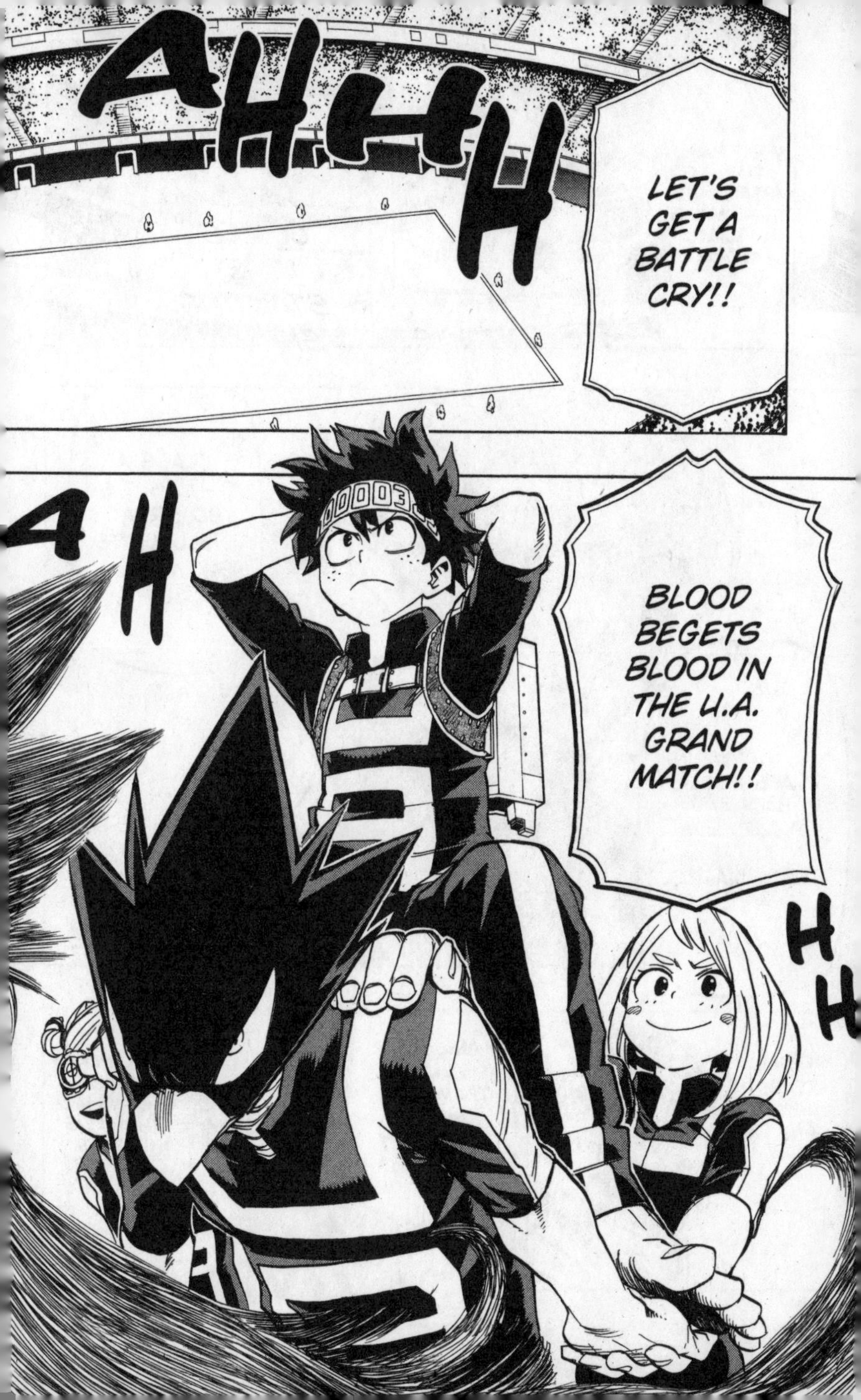
AHHH
LET'S GET A BATTLE CRY!!
AH
BLOOD BEGETS BLOOD IN THE U.A. GRAND MATCH!!
HH

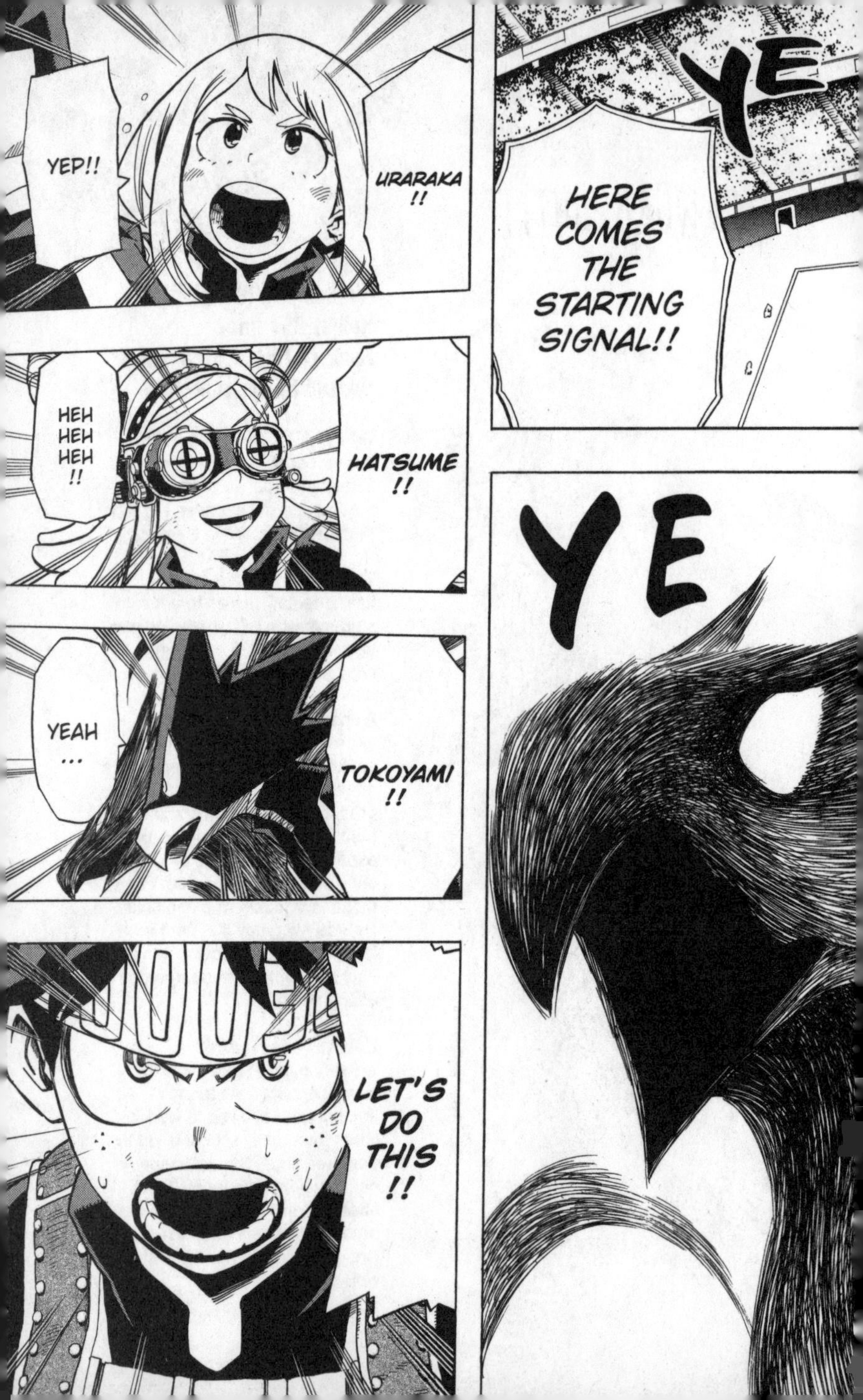
YE
HERE COMES THE STARTING SIGNAL!!
YE
URARAKA!!
YEP!!
HATSUME!!
HEH HEH HEH!!
TOKOYAMI!!
YEAH...
LET'S DO THIS!!

MEI HATSUME (16)

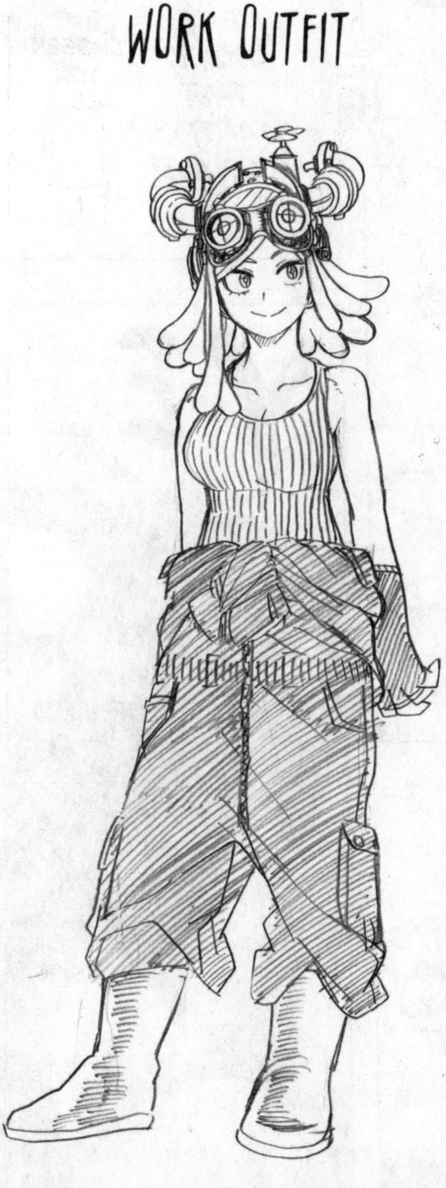
WORK OUTFIT

Birthday: 4/18
Height: 157 cm
Favorite Things: Steampunk-related things, chocolate

BEHIND THE SCENES
A member of the support course. She started out as a guy, but I made her a girl because I thought that seemed more interesting.

The support course fundamentally exists to educate students who will work in design agencies, making items and costumes for heroes.

A special license is needed to produce those items and costumes, and it's granted after a government inspection. Using the produced items usually requires hero qualifications, but running experiments and tests in a lab is okay even for non-heroes. For those individuals whose Quirks impede everyday life, permits for special life-improving items may be granted after a rigorous examination.

U.A. has an on-campus workshop, and students who submit applications to their teachers are allowed to work on items there after school or during their free time. That Hatsume has developed so many items after just one month of school is proof that she's a born inventor who practically never leaves the workshop.

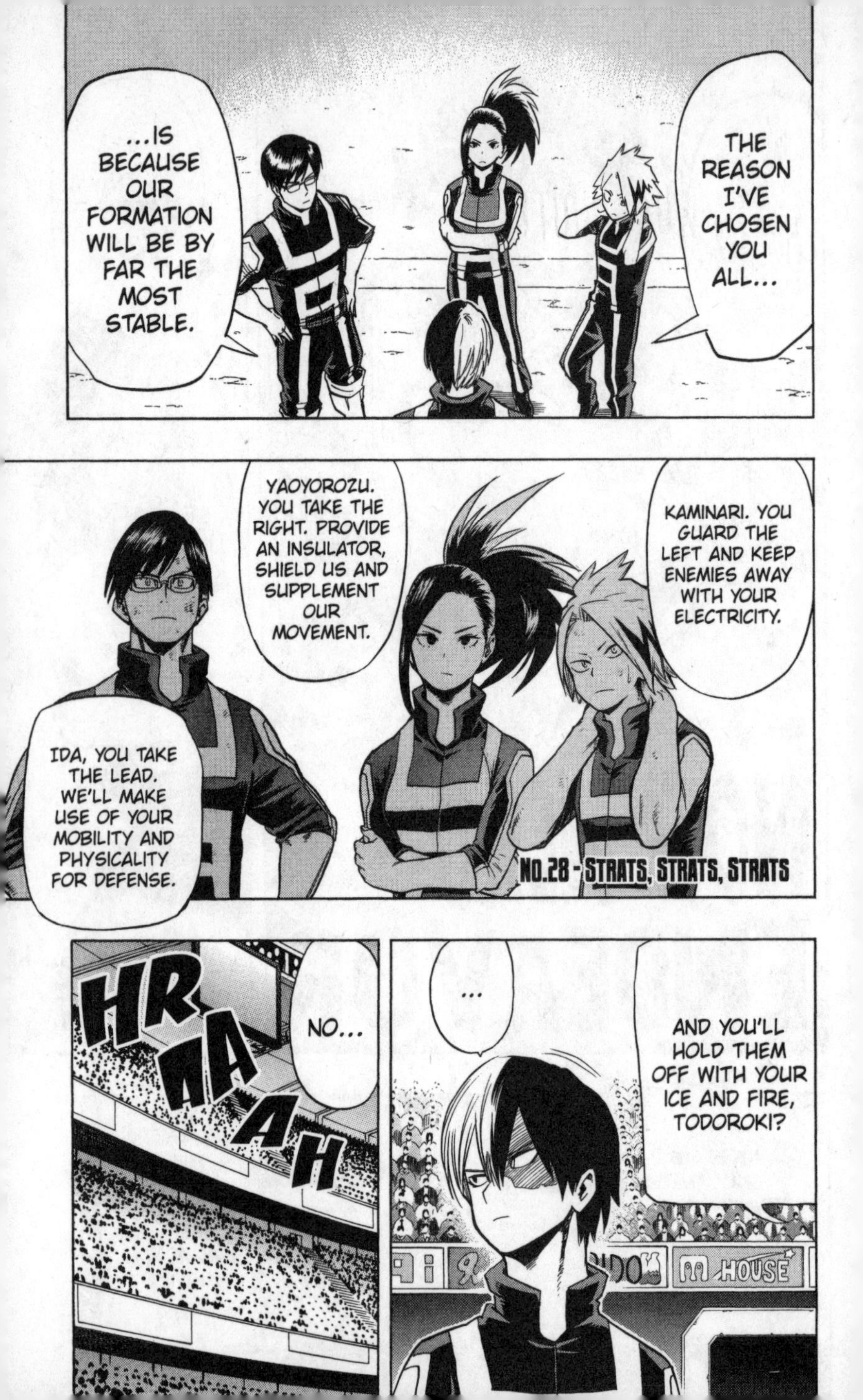
THE REASON I'VE CHOSEN YOU ALL...
...IS BECAUSE OUR FORMATION WILL BE BY FAR THE MOST STABLE.
KAMINARI. YOU GUARD THE LEFT AND KEEP ENEMIES AWAY WITH YOUR ELECTRICITY.
YAOYOROZU. YOU TAKE THE RIGHT. PROVIDE AN INSULATOR, SHIELD US AND SUPPLEMENT OUR MOVEMENT.
IDA, YOU TAKE THE LEAD. WE'LL MAKE USE OF YOUR MOBILITY AND PHYSICALITY FOR DEFENSE.
NO.28 - STRATS, STRATS, STRATS
AND YOU'LL HOLD THEM OFF WITH YOUR ICE AND FIRE, TODOROKI?
...
HOUSE
NO...
HRAAAH

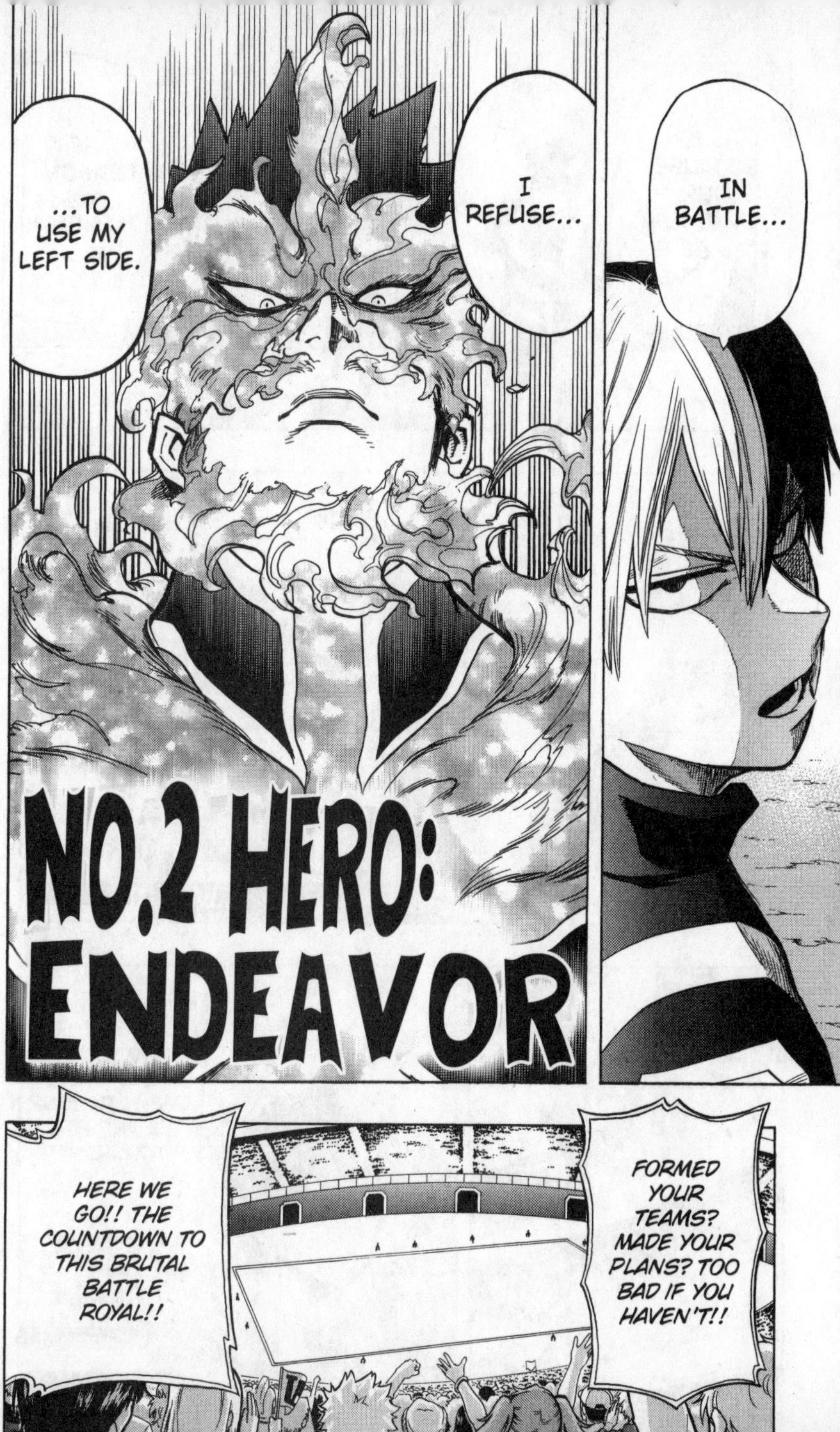
IN BATTLE...
I REFUSE...
...TO USE MY LEFT SIDE.
NO.2 HERO: ENDEAVOR
FORMED YOUR TEAMS? MADE YOUR PLANS? TOO BAD IF YOU HAVEN'T!!
HERE WE GO!! THE COUNTDOWN TO THIS BRUTAL BATTLE ROYAL!!

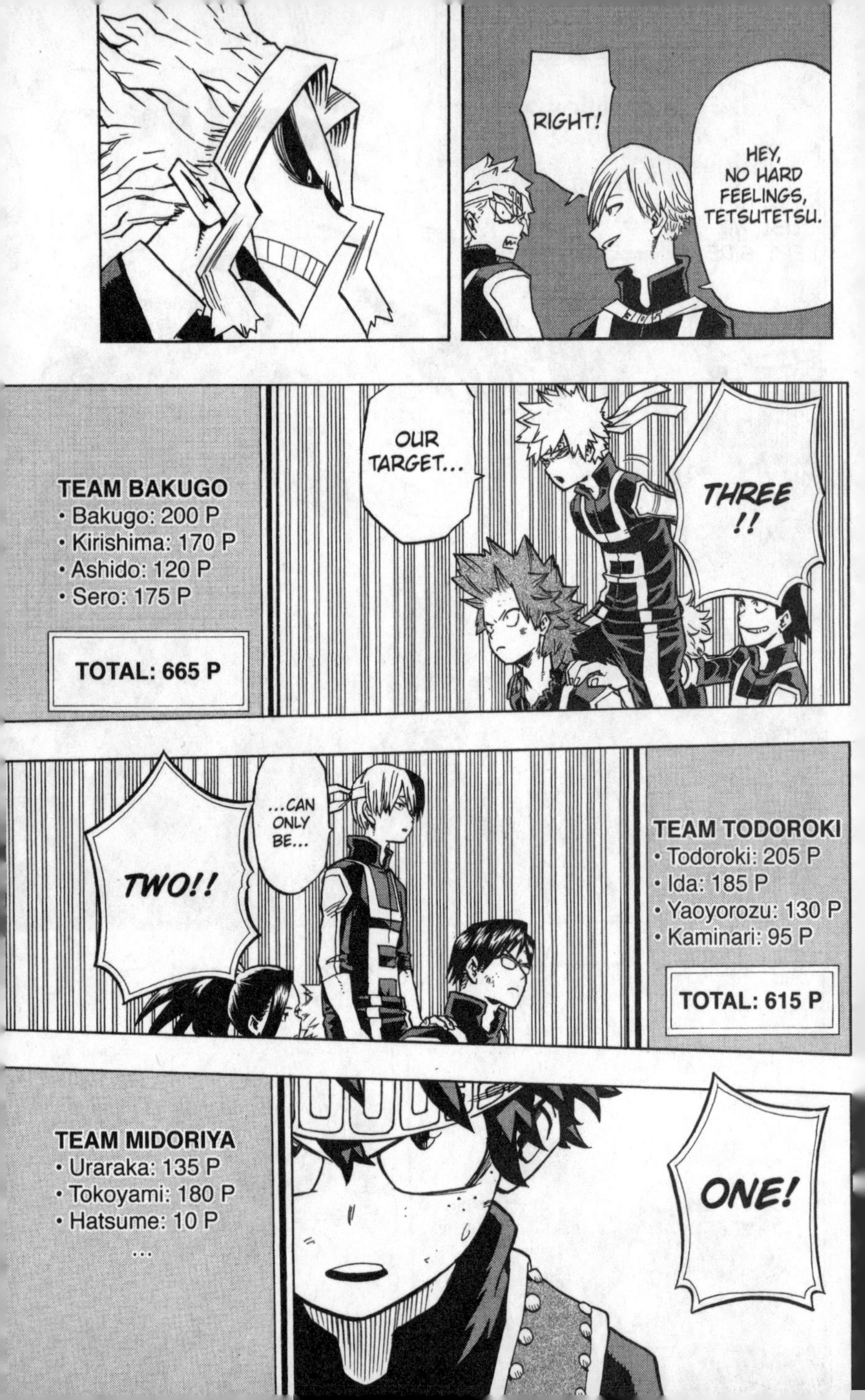
HEY, NO HARD FEELINGS, TETSUTETSU.
RIGHT!
THREE !!
OUR TARGET...
TEAM BAKUGO
• Bakugo: 200 P
• Kirishima: 170 P
• Ashido: 120 P
• Sero: 175 P
TOTAL: 665 P
TEAM TODOROKI
• Todoroki: 205 P
• Ida: 185 P
• Yaoyorozu: 130 P
• Kaminari: 95 P
TOTAL: 615 P
...CAN ONLY BE...
TWO!!
ONE!
TEAM MIDORIYA
• Uraraka: 135 P
• Tokoyami: 180 P
• Hatsume: 10 P
...

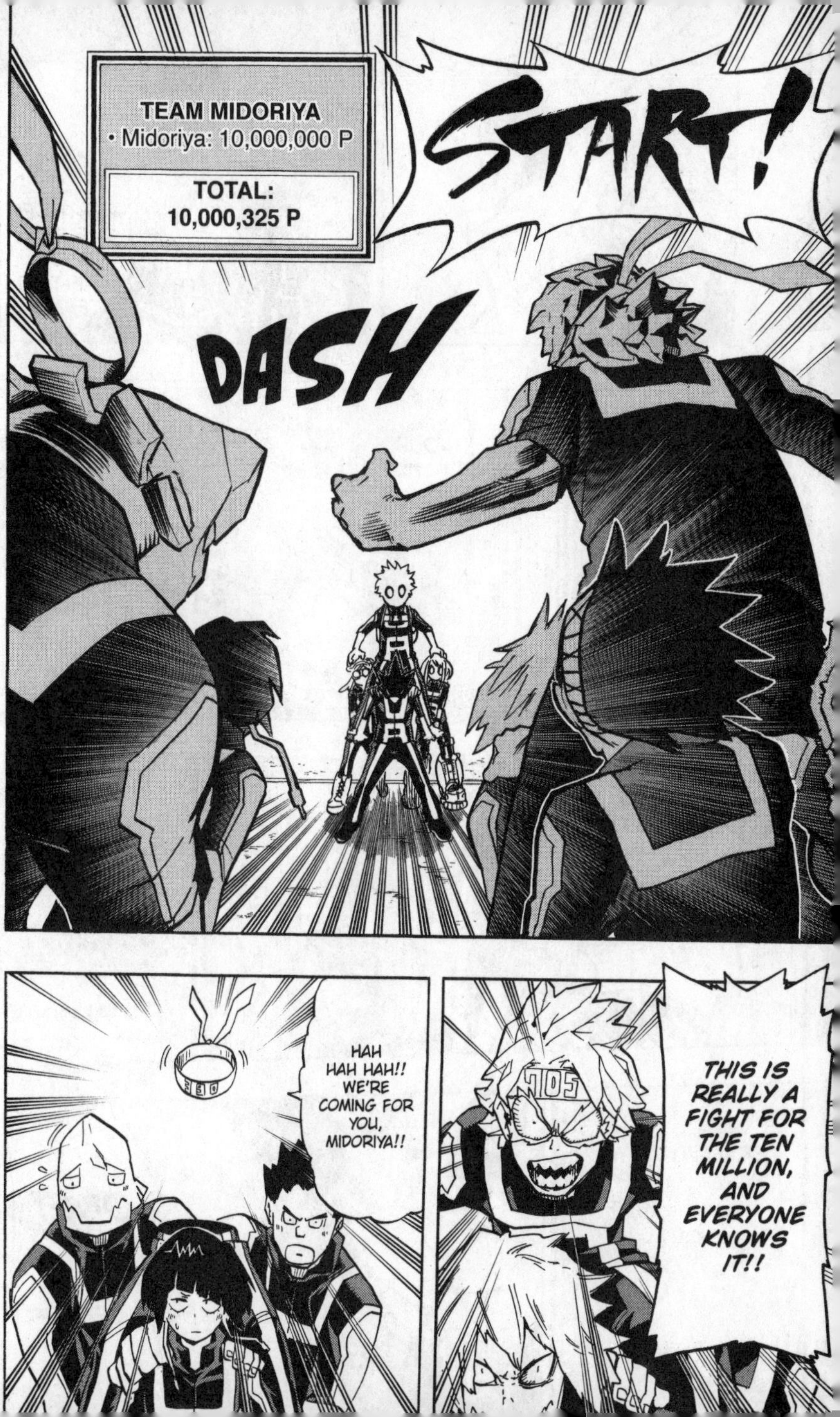
START!
TEAM MIDORIYA
• Midoriya: 10,000,000 P
TOTAL: 10,000,325 P
DASH
THIS IS REALLY A FIGHT FOR THE TEN MILLION, AND EVERYONE KNOWS IT!!
HAH HAH HAH!! WE'RE COMING FOR YOU, MIDORIYA!!

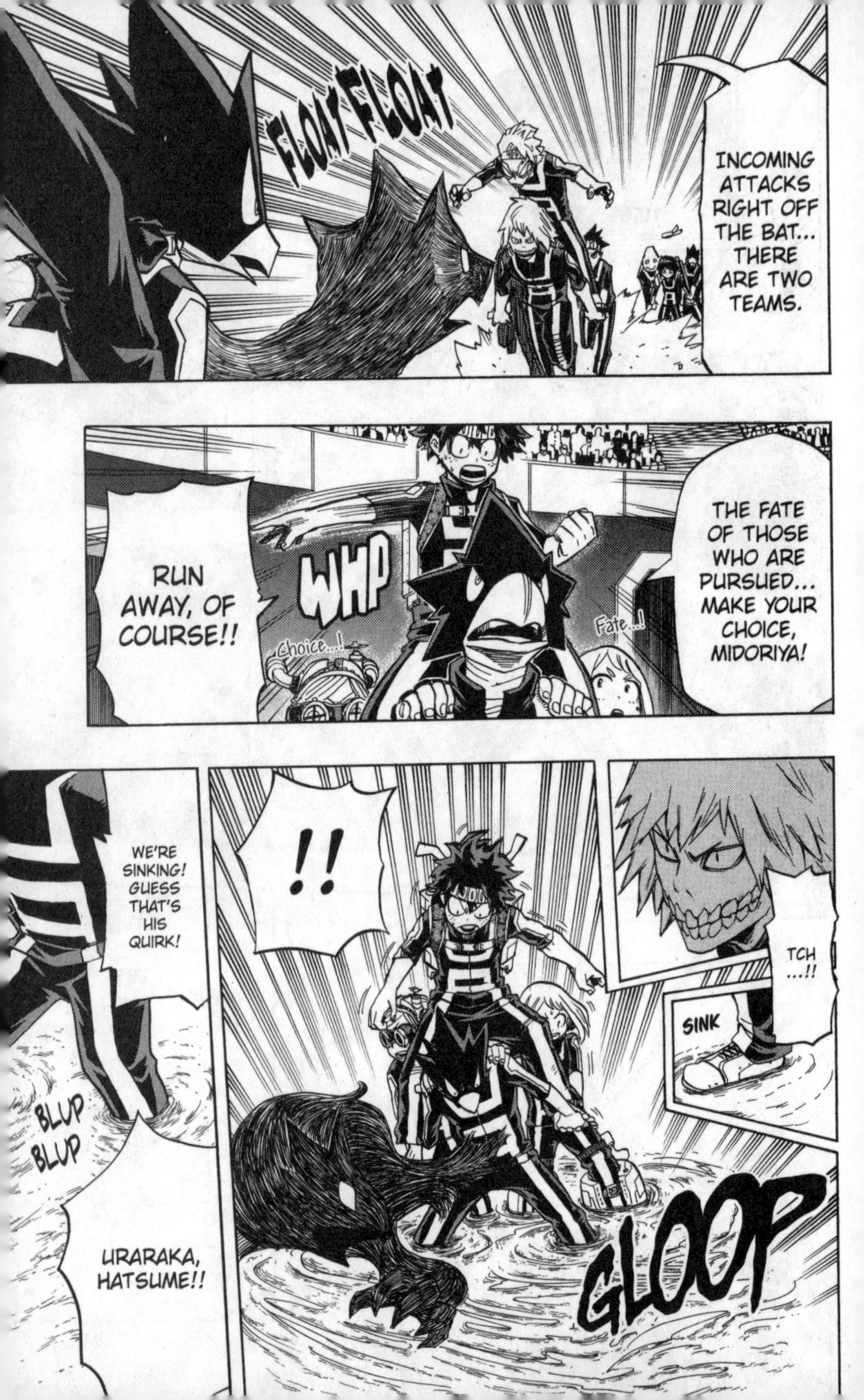
INCOMING ATTACKS RIGHT OFF THE BAT... THERE ARE TWO TEAMS.
FLOAT FLOAT
THE FATE OF THOSE WHO ARE PURSUED... MAKE YOUR CHOICE, MIDORIYA!
Fate...!
WHP
Choice...!
RUN AWAY, OF COURSE!!
TCH ...!!
SINK
!!
GLOOP
WE'RE SINKING! GUESS THAT'S HIS QUIRK!
BLUP BLUP
URARAKA, HATSUME!!

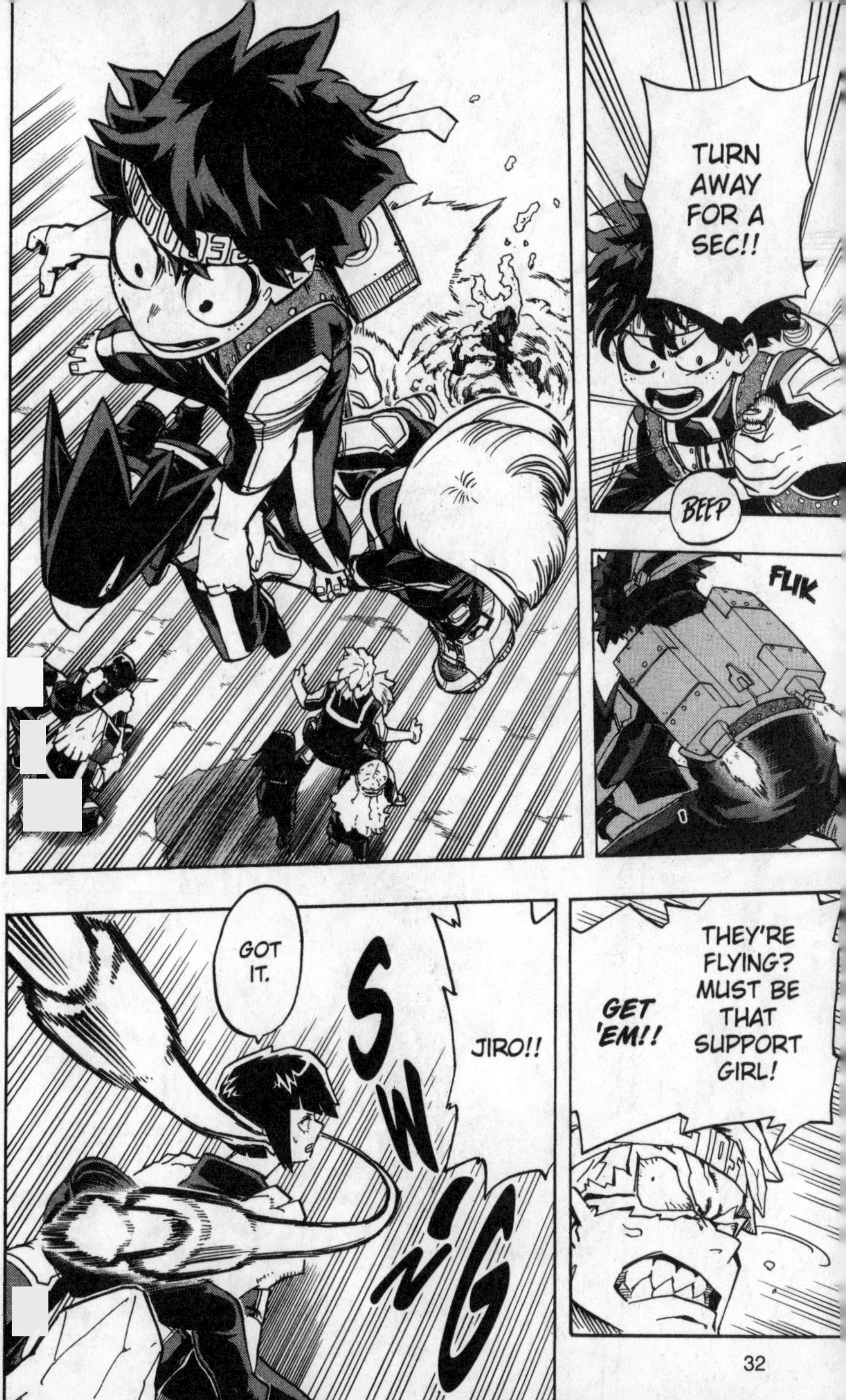
TURN AWAY FOR A SEC!!
BEEP
FLIK
THEY'RE FLYING? MUST BE THAT SUPPORT GIRL!
GET 'EM!!
JIRO!!
GOT IT.
SWING

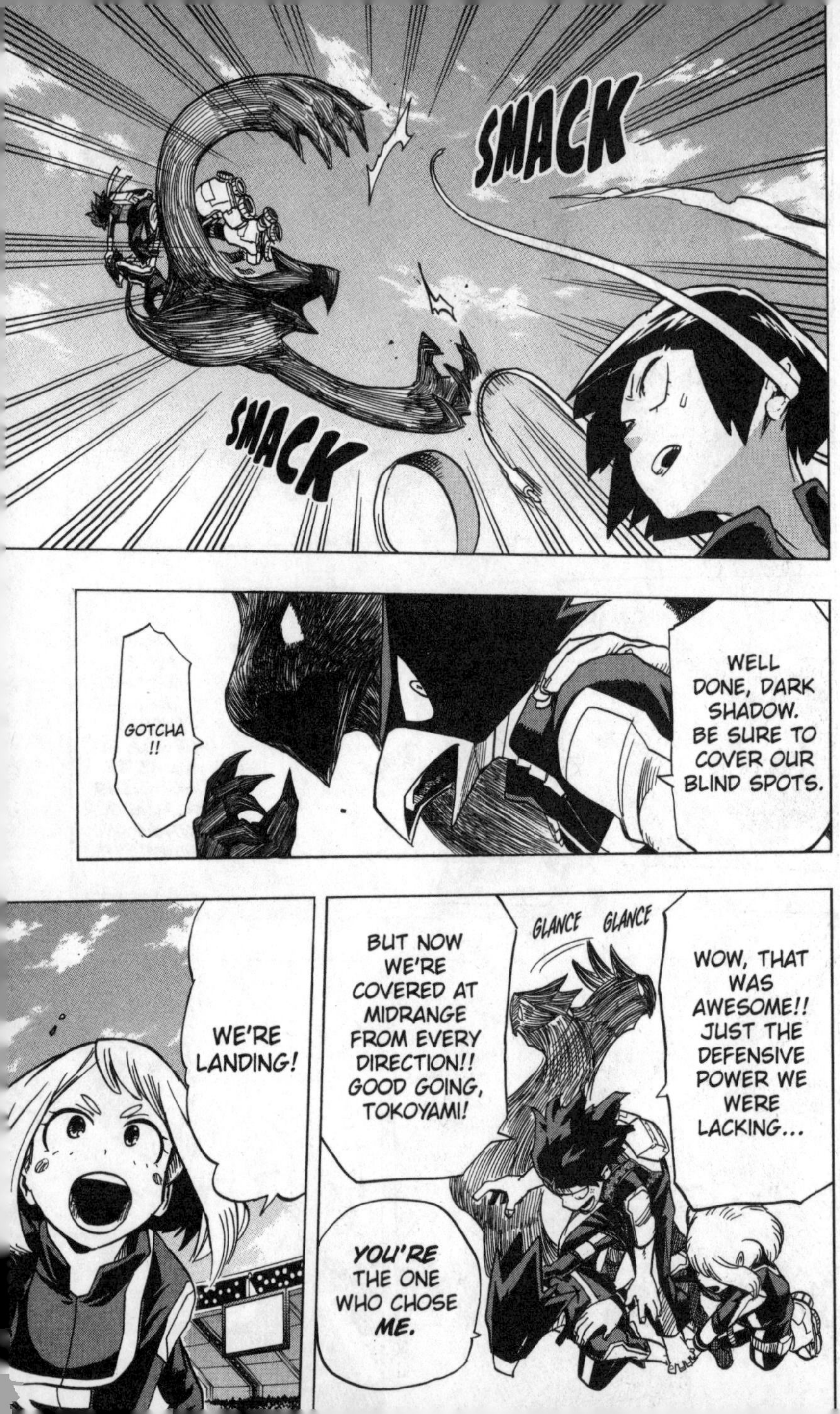
SMACK
SMACK
WELL DONE, DARK SHADOW. BE SURE TO COVER OUR BLIND SPOTS.
GOTCHA !!
GLANCE GLANCE
WOW, THAT WAS AWESOME!! JUST THE DEFENSIVE POWER WE WERE LACKING...
BUT NOW WE'RE COVERED AT MIDRANGE FROM EVERY DIRECTION!! GOOD GOING, TOKOYAMI!
YOU'RE THE ONE WHO CHOSE *ME.*
WE'RE LANDING!

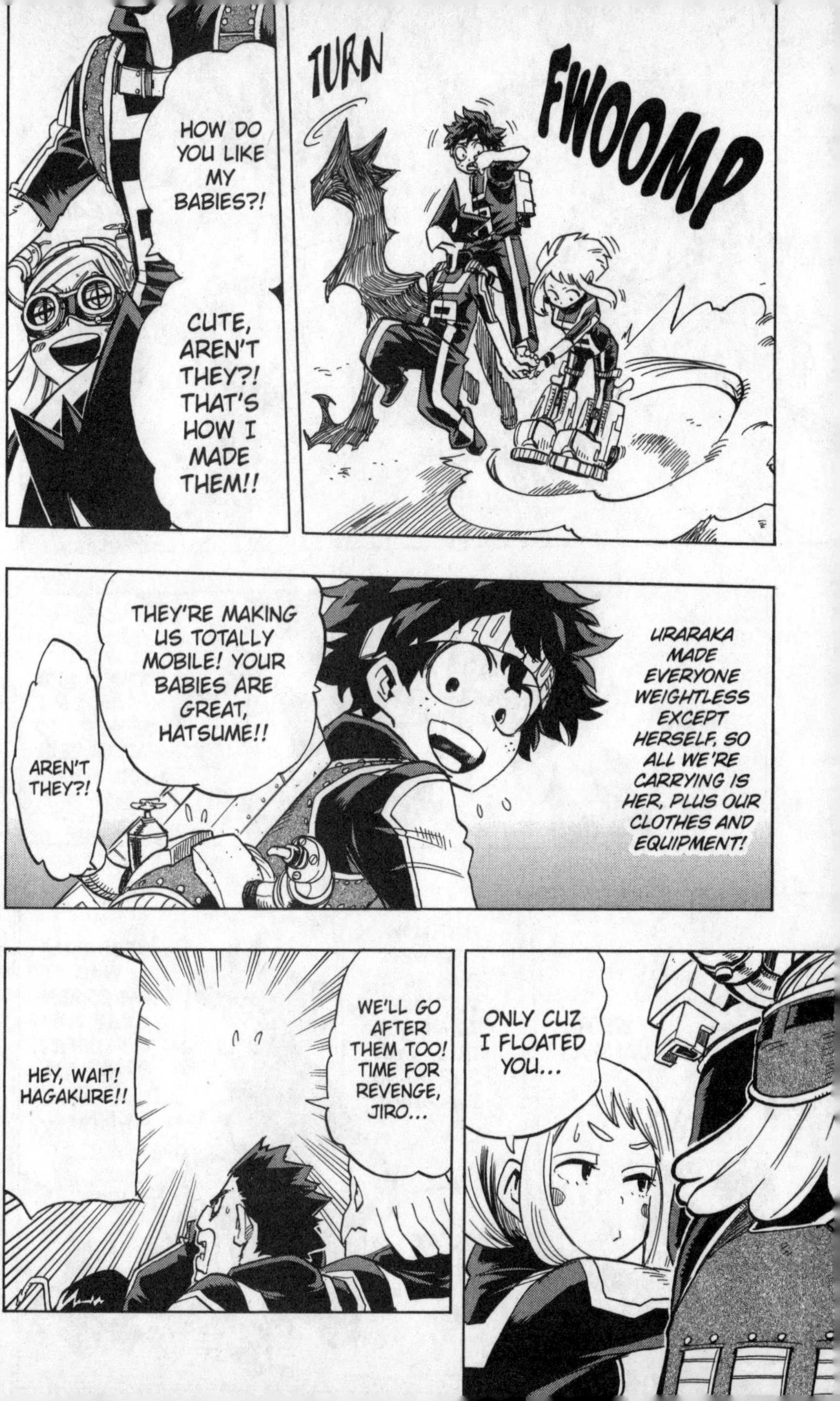
TURN
FWOOMP
HOW DO YOU LIKE MY BABIES?!
CUTE, AREN'T THEY?! THAT'S HOW I MADE THEM!!
URARAKA MADE EVERYONE WEIGHTLESS EXCEPT HERSELF, SO ALL WE'RE CARRYING IS HER, PLUS OUR CLOTHES AND EQUIPMENT!
THEY'RE MAKING US TOTALLY MOBILE! YOUR BABIES ARE GREAT, HATSUME!!
AREN'T THEY?!
ONLY CUZ I FLOATED YOU...
WE'LL GO AFTER THEM TOO! TIME FOR REVENGE, JIRO...
HEY, WAIT! HAGAKURE!!

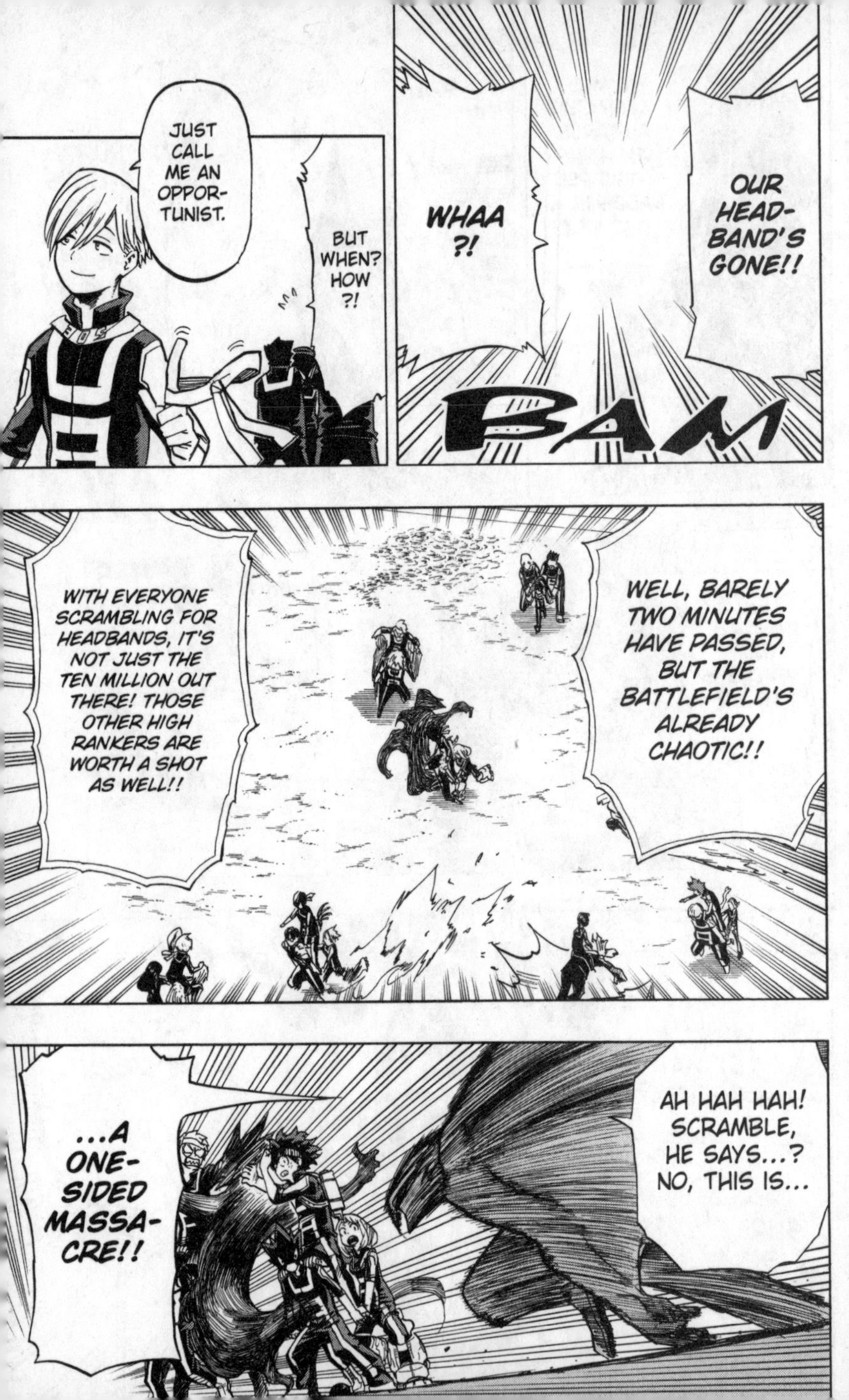
OUR HEAD-BAND'S GONE!!
WHAA?!
BAM
BUT WHEN? HOW?!
JUST CALL ME AN OPPOR-TUNIST.
WELL, BARELY TWO MINUTES HAVE PASSED, BUT THE BATTLEFIELD'S ALREADY CHAOTIC!!
WITH EVERYONE SCRAMBLING FOR HEADBANDS, IT'S NOT JUST THE TEN MILLION OUT THERE! THOSE OTHER HIGH RANKERS ARE WORTH A SHOT AS WELL!!
AH HAH HAH! SCRAMBLE, HE SAYS...? NO, THIS IS...
...A ONE-SIDED MASSA-CRE!!

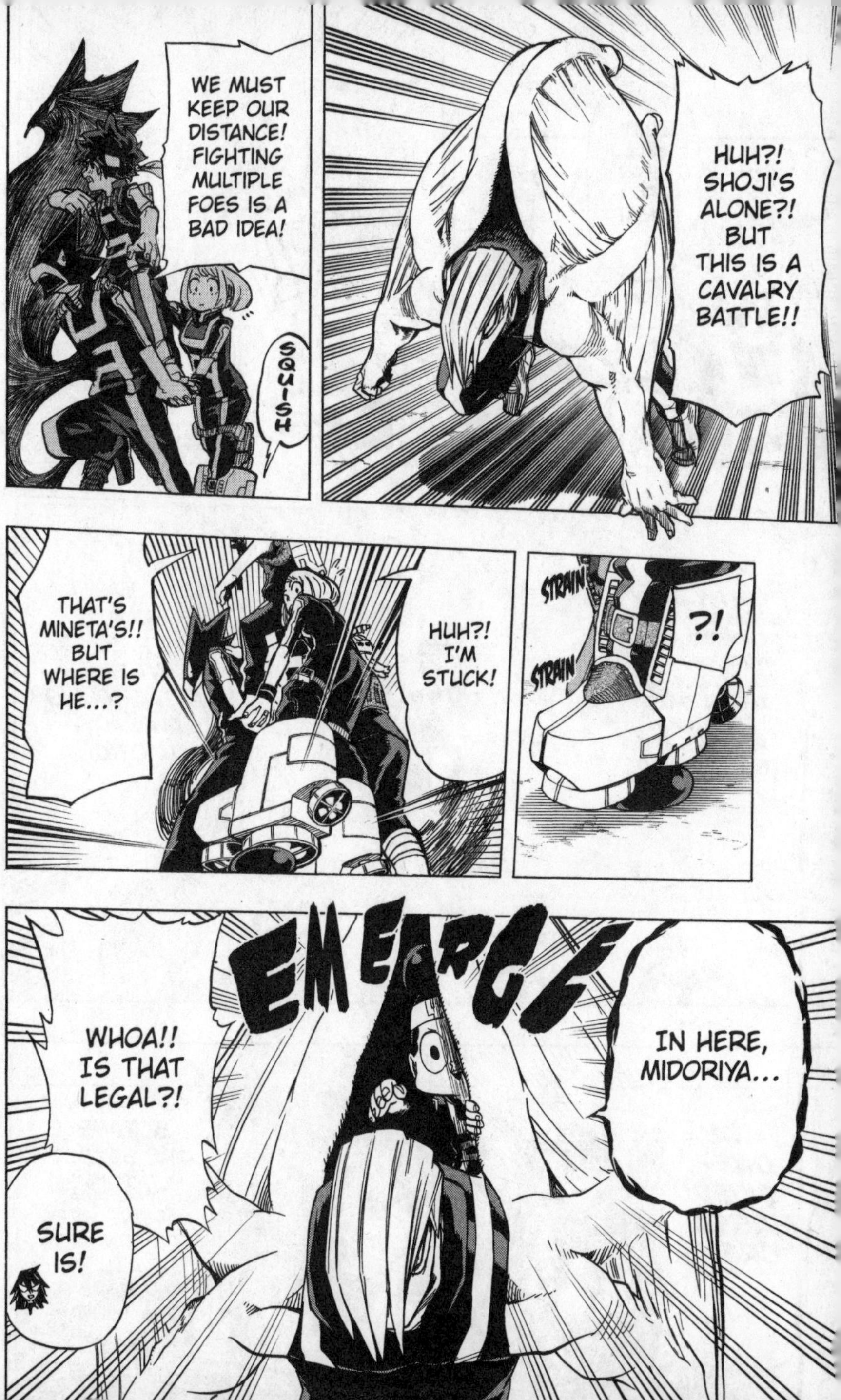
HUH?! SHOJI'S ALONE?! BUT THIS IS A CAVALRY BATTLE!!
WE MUST KEEP OUR DISTANCE! FIGHTING MULTIPLE FOES IS A BAD IDEA!
SQUISH
STRAIN
STRAIN
?!
HUH?! I'M STUCK!
THAT'S MINETA'S!! BUT WHERE IS HE...?
EMERGE
IN HERE, MIDORIYA...
WHOA!! IS THAT LEGAL?!
SURE IS!

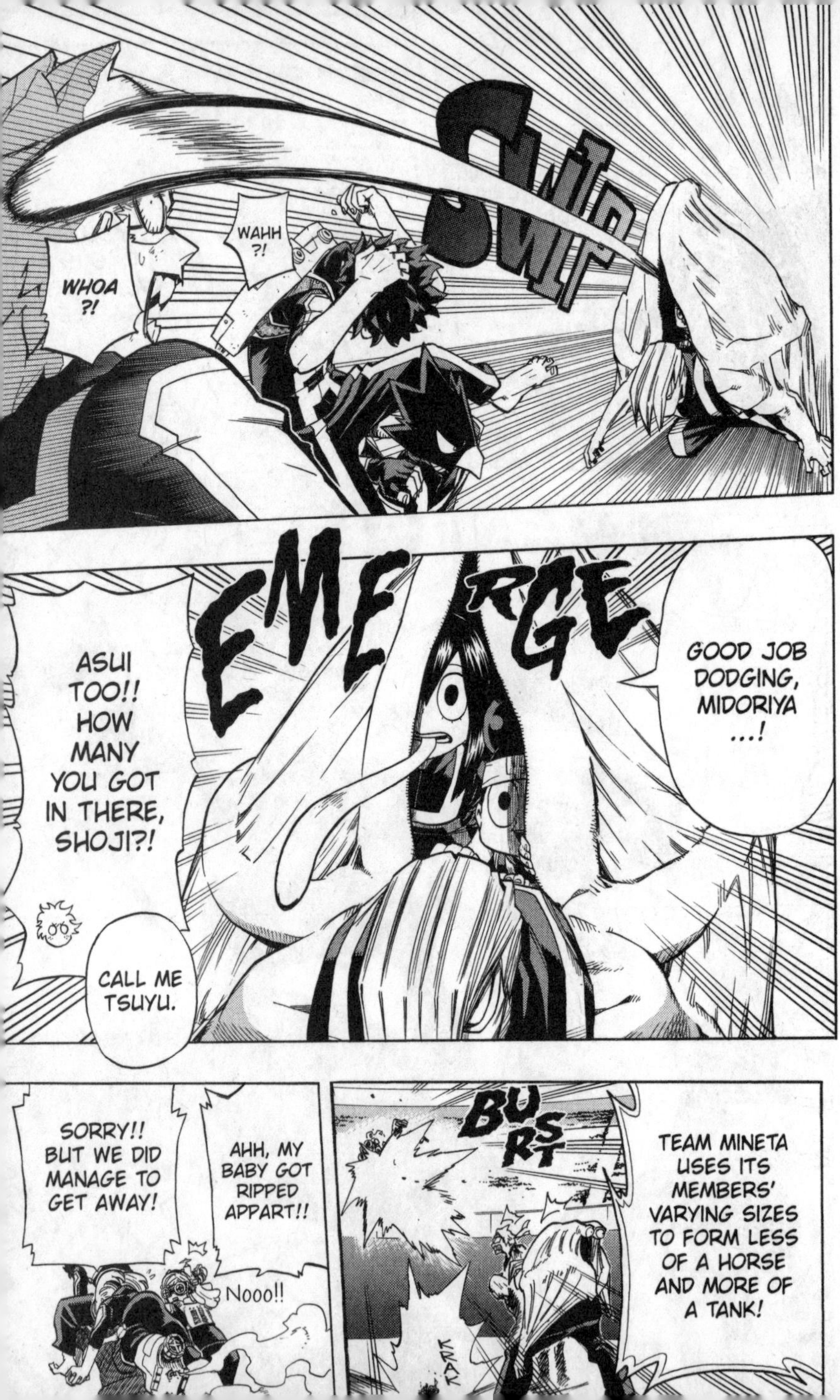
SWIP
WAHH ?!
WHOA ?!
EMERGE
GOOD JOB DODGING, MIDORIYA ...!
ASUI TOO!! HOW MANY YOU GOT IN THERE, SHOJI?!
CALL ME TSUYU.
BURST
TEAM MINETA USES ITS MEMBERS' VARYING SIZES TO FORM LESS OF A HORSE AND MORE OF A TANK!
KRAK
AHH, MY BABY GOT RIPPED APPART!!
SORRY!! BUT WE DID MANAGE TO GET AWAY!
Nooo!!

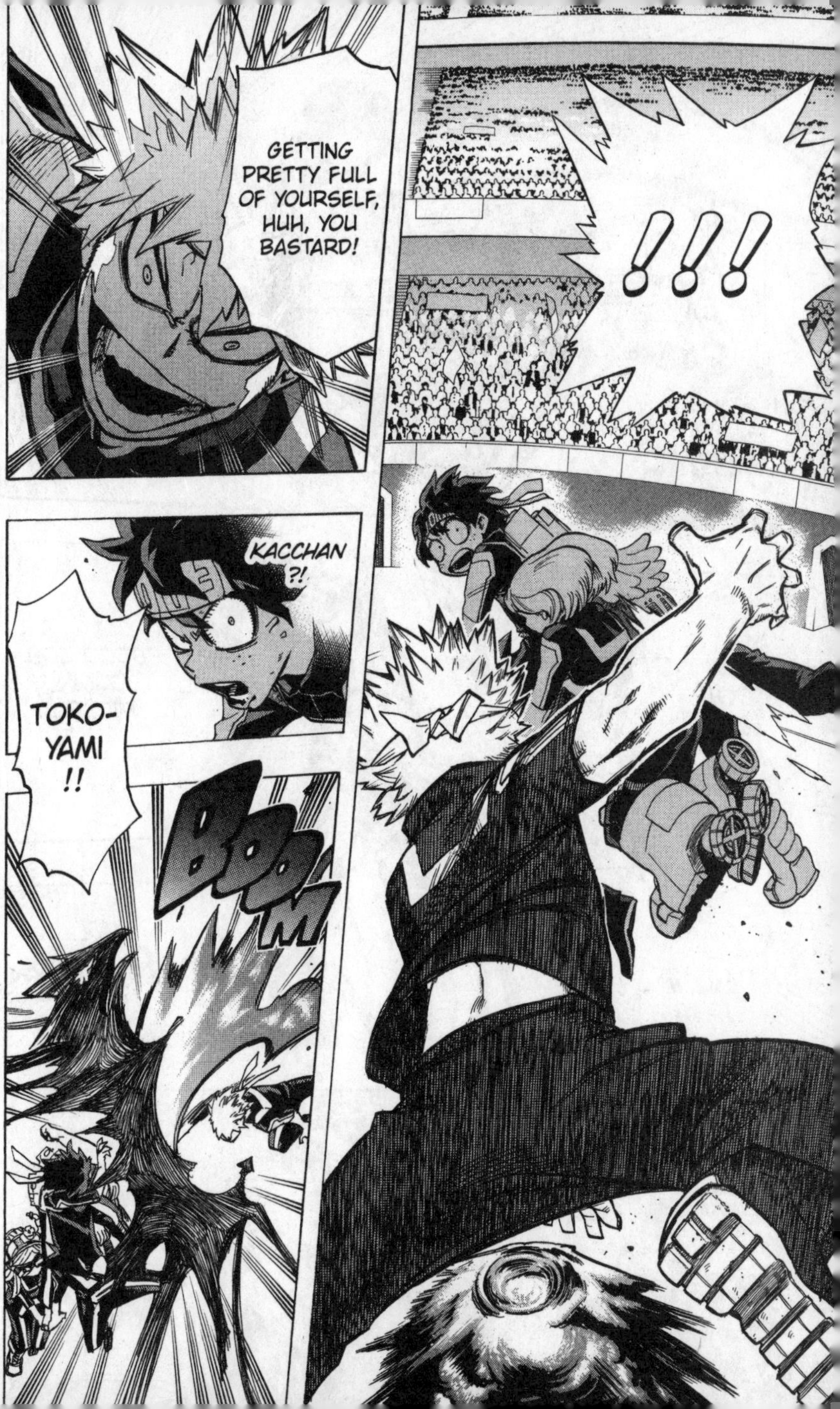
!!!
GETTING PRETTY FULL OF YOURSELF, HUH, YOU BASTARD!
KACCHAN?!
TOKO-YAMI!!
BOOM

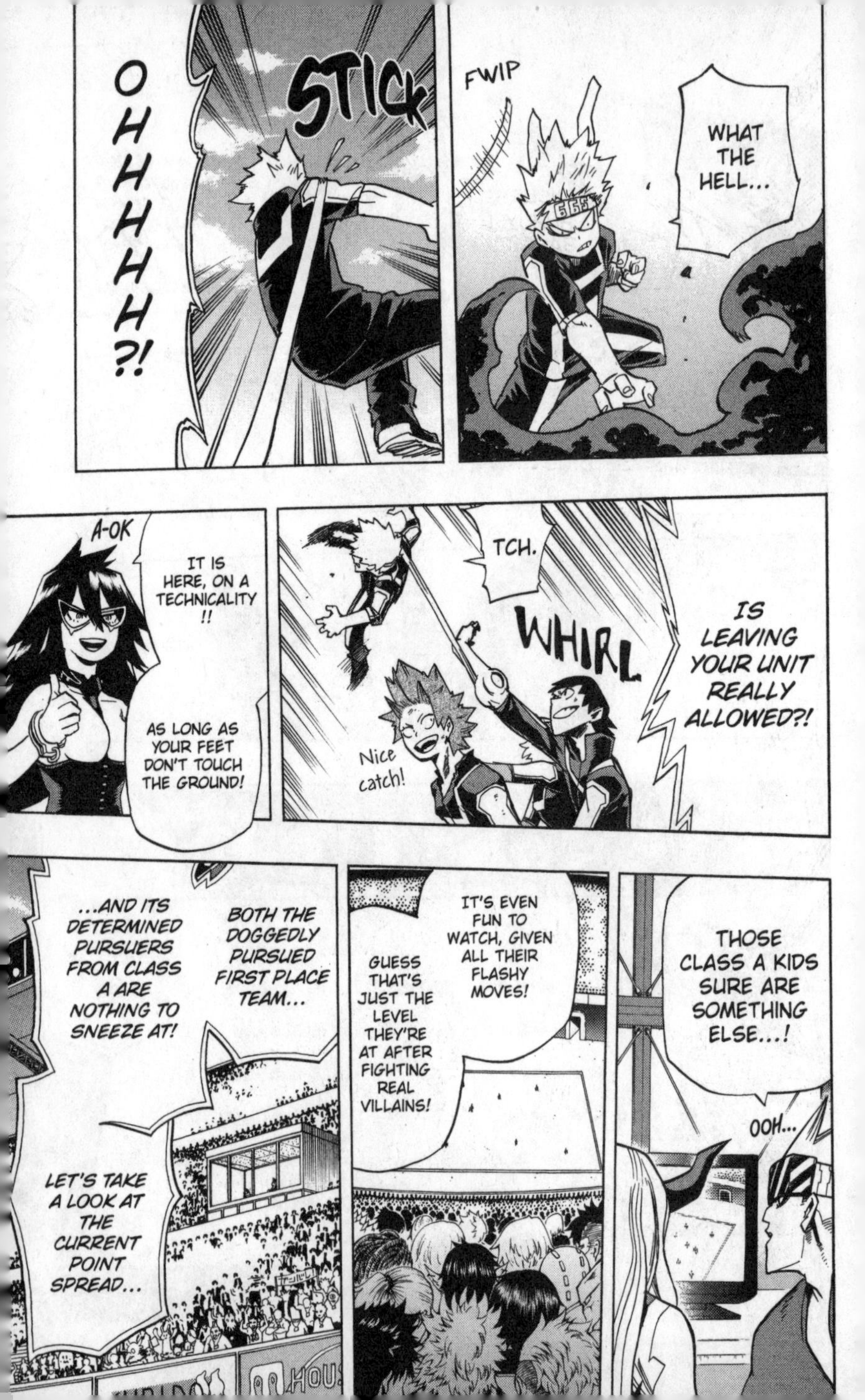
FWIP
WHAT THE HELL...
STICK
OHHHHHH?!
IS LEAVING YOUR UNIT REALLY ALLOWED?!
TCH.
WHIRL
Nice catch!
A-OK
IT IS HERE, ON A TECHNICALITY!!
AS LONG AS YOUR FEET DON'T TOUCH THE GROUND!
THOSE CLASS A KIDS SURE ARE SOMETHING ELSE...!
OOH...
IT'S EVEN FUN TO WATCH, GIVEN ALL THEIR FLASHY MOVES!
GUESS THAT'S JUST THE LEVEL THEY'RE AT AFTER FIGHTING REAL VILLAINS!
BOTH THE DOGGEDLY PURSUED FIRST PLACE TEAM...
...AND ITS DETERMINED PURSUERS FROM CLASS A ARE NOTHING TO SNEEZE AT!
LET'S TAKE A LOOK AT THE CURRENT POINT SPREAD...

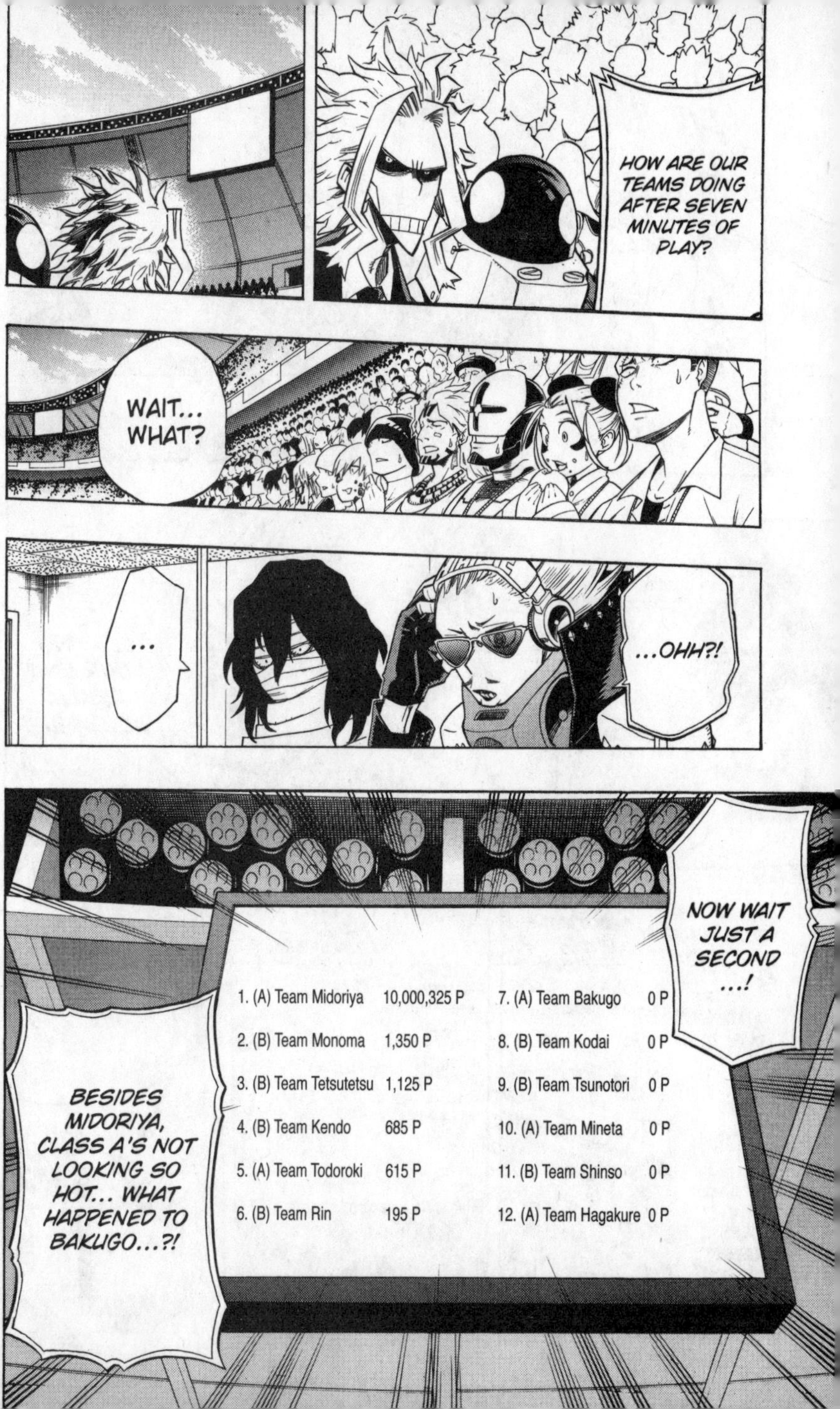
HOW ARE OUR TEAMS DOING AFTER SEVEN MINUTES OF PLAY?
WAIT... WHAT?
...OHH?!
...
NOW WAIT JUST A SECOND ...!
1. (A) Team Midoriya 10,000,325 P
2. (B) Team Monoma 1,350 P
3. (B) Team Tetsutetsu 1,125 P
4. (B) Team Kendo 685 P
5. (A) Team Todoroki 615 P
6. (B) Team Rin 195 P
7. (A) Team Bakugo 0 P
8. (B) Team Kodai 0 P
9. (B) Team Tsunotori 0 P
10. (A) Team Mineta 0 P
11. (B) Team Shinso 0 P
12. (A) Team Hagakure 0 P
BESIDES MIDORIYA, CLASS A'S NOT LOOKING SO HOT... WHAT HAPPENED TO BAKUGO...?!

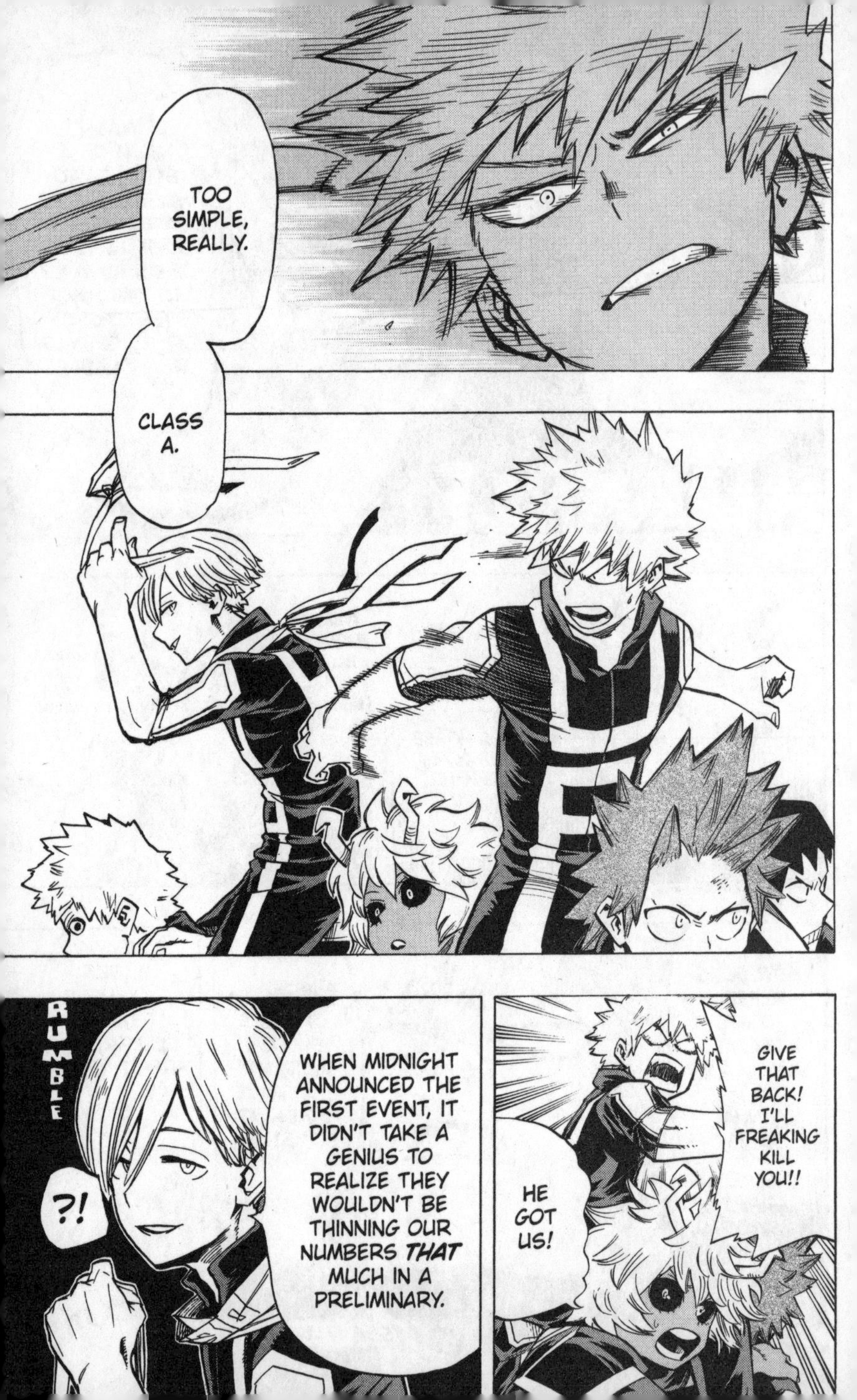
TOO SIMPLE, REALLY.
CLASS A.
GIVE THAT BACK! I'LL FREAKING KILL YOU!!
HE GOT US!
RUMBLE
?!
WHEN MIDNIGHT ANNOUNCED THE FIRST EVENT, IT DIDN'T TAKE A GENIUS TO REALIZE THEY WOULDN'T BE THINNING OUR NUMBERS *THAT* MUCH IN A PRELIMINARY.

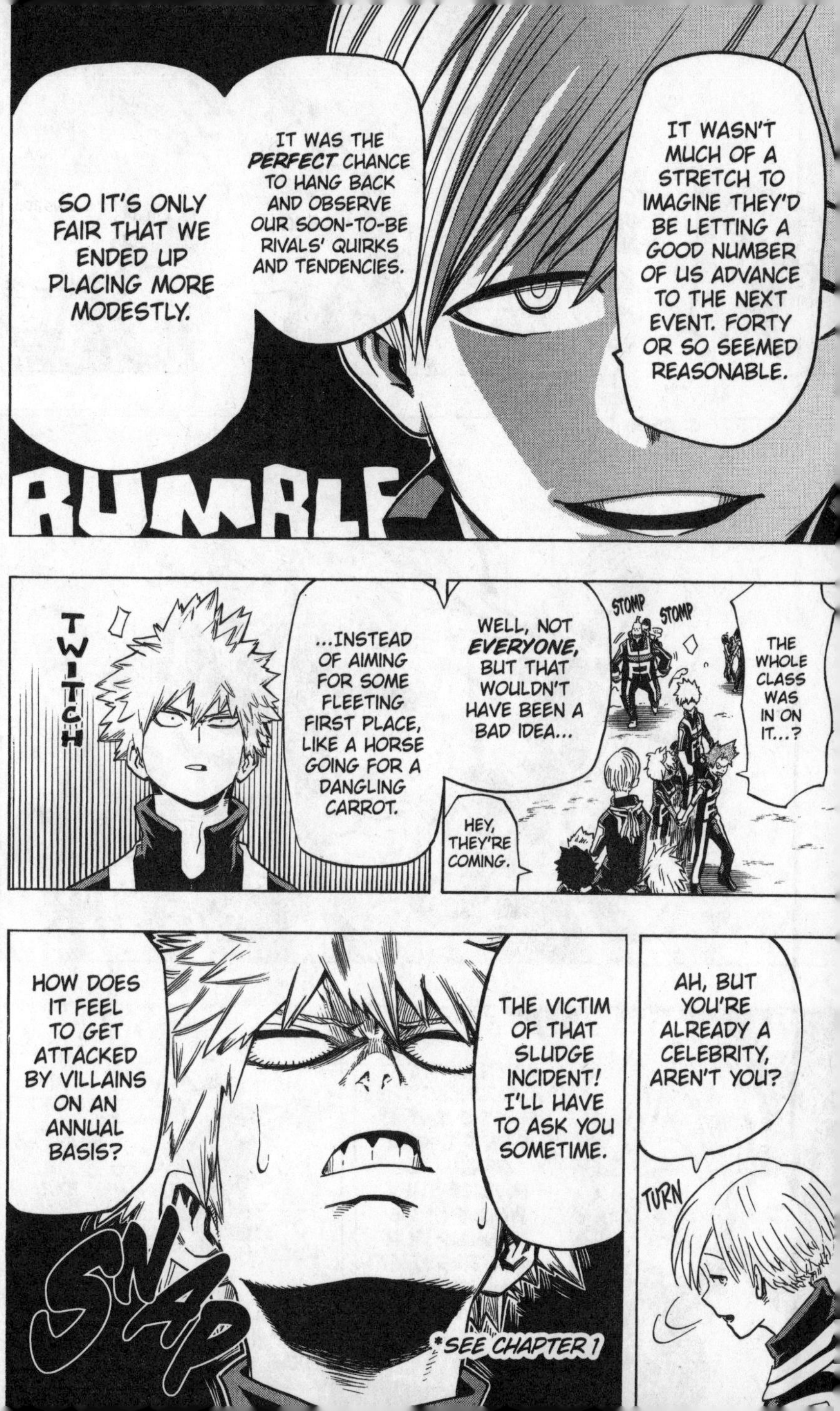
IT WASN'T MUCH OF A STRETCH TO IMAGINE THEY'D BE LETTING A GOOD NUMBER OF US ADVANCE TO THE NEXT EVENT. FORTY OR SO SEEMED REASONABLE.
IT WAS THE *PERFECT* CHANCE TO HANG BACK AND OBSERVE OUR SOON-TO-BE RIVALS' QUIRKS AND TENDENCIES.
SO IT'S ONLY FAIR THAT WE ENDED UP PLACING MORE MODESTLY.
RUMBLE
STOMP
STOMP
THE WHOLE CLASS WAS IN ON IT...?
WELL, NOT *EVERYONE,* BUT THAT WOULDN'T HAVE BEEN A BAD IDEA...
...INSTEAD OF AIMING FOR SOME FLEETING FIRST PLACE, LIKE A HORSE GOING FOR A DANGLING CARROT.
HEY, THEY'RE COMING.
TWITCH
AH, BUT YOU'RE ALREADY A CELEBRITY, AREN'T YOU?
TURN
THE VICTIM OF THAT SLUDGE INCIDENT! I'LL HAVE TO ASK YOU SOMETIME.
HOW DOES IT FEEL TO GET ATTACKED BY VILLAINS ON AN ANNUAL BASIS?
SNAP
*SEE CHAPTER 1

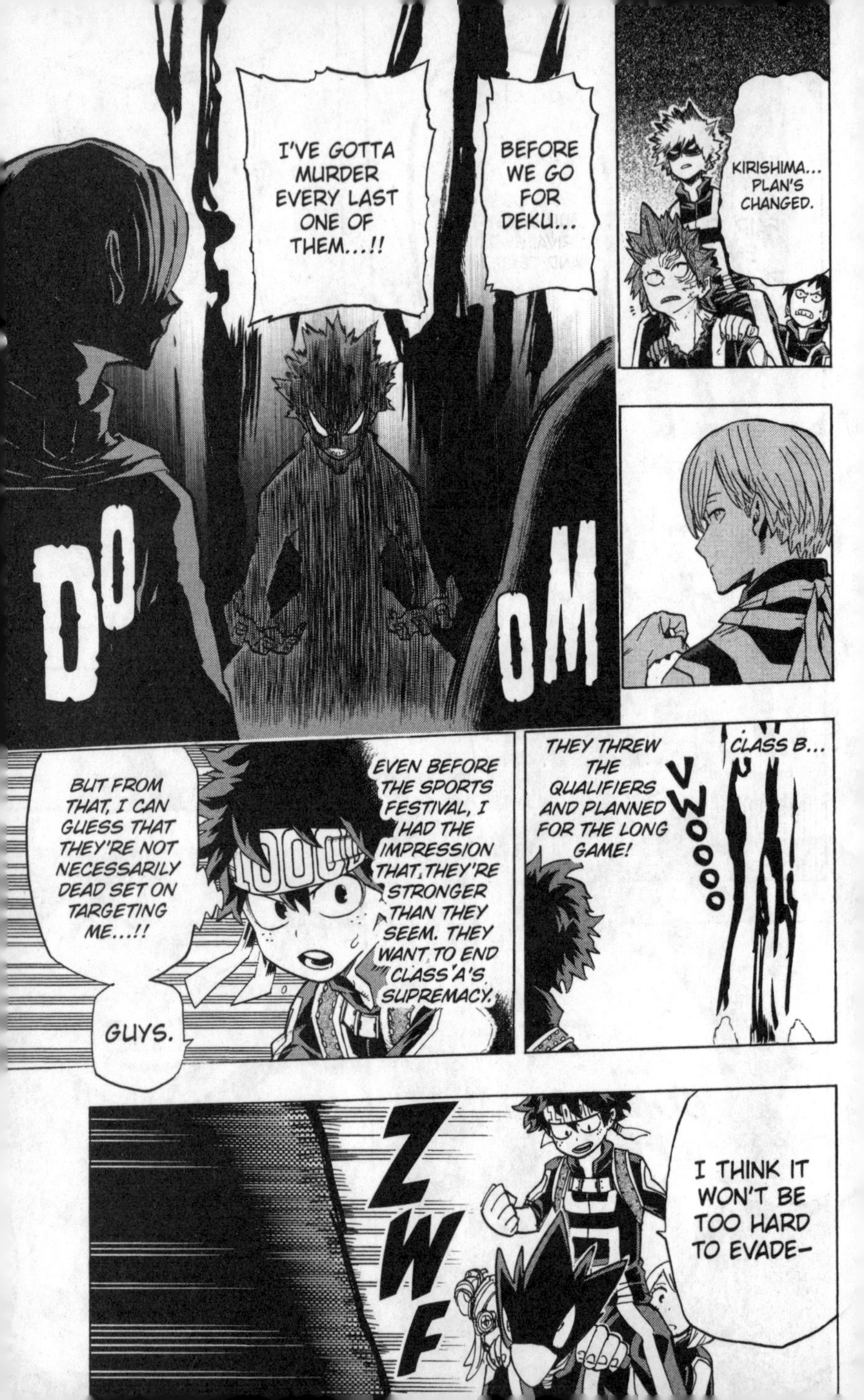
KIRISHIMA... PLAN'S CHANGED.
BEFORE WE GO FOR DEKU...
I'VE GOTTA MURDER EVERY LAST ONE OF THEM...!!
DOOM
CLASS B...
VWOOOO
THEY THREW THE QUALIFIERS AND PLANNED FOR THE LONG GAME!
EVEN BEFORE THE SPORTS FESTIVAL, I HAD THE IMPRESSION THAT THEY'RE STRONGER THAN THEY SEEM. THEY WANT TO END CLASS A'S SUPREMACY.
BUT FROM THAT, I CAN GUESS THAT THEY'RE NOT NECESSARILY DEAD SET ON TARGETING ME...!!
GUYS.
I THINK IT WON'T BE TOO HARD TO EVADE—
ZWF

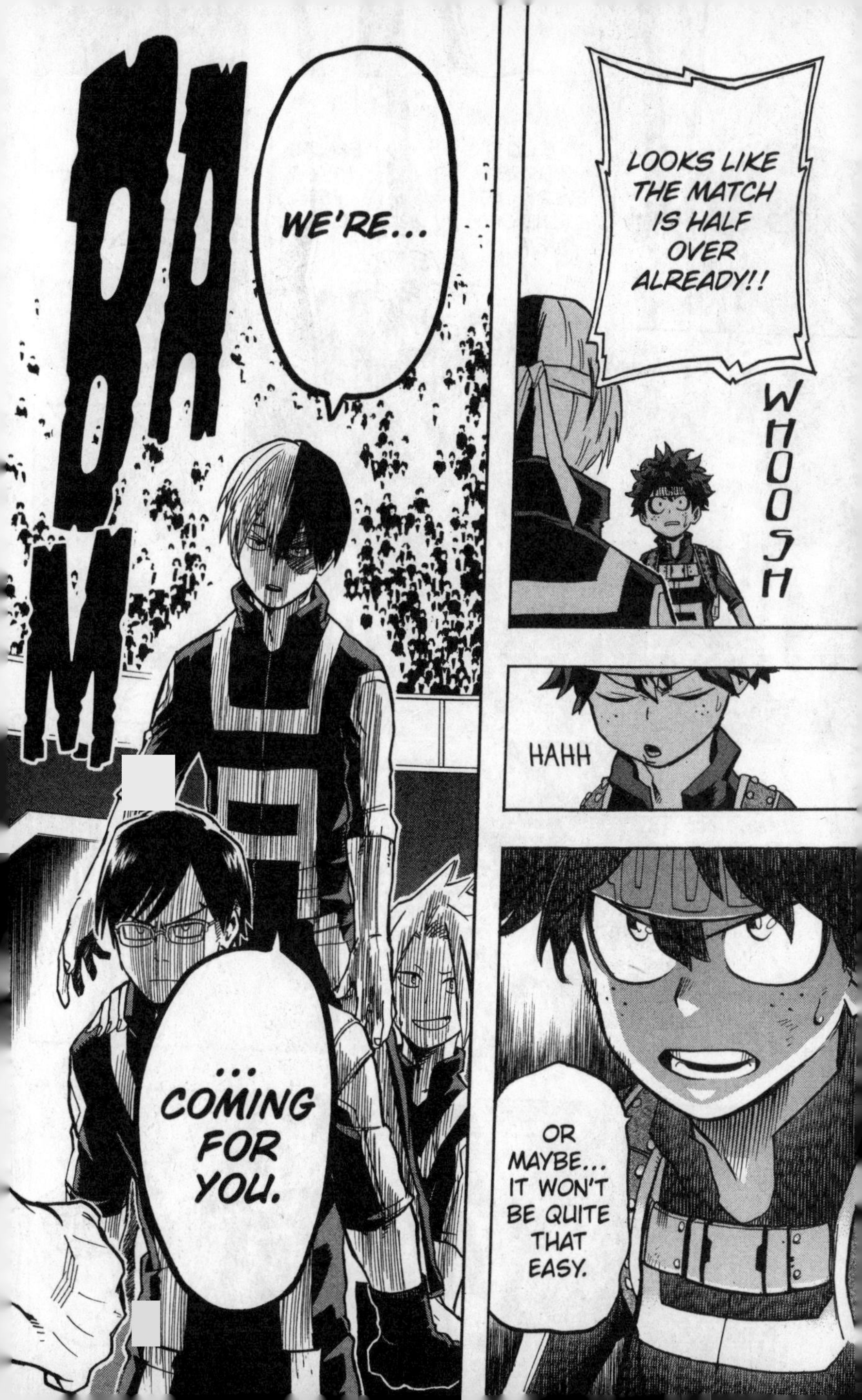
LOOKS LIKE THE MATCH IS HALF OVER ALREADY!!
WHOOSH
HAHH
OR MAYBE... IT WON'T BE QUITE THAT EASY.
WE'RE...
BAM
... COMING FOR YOU.

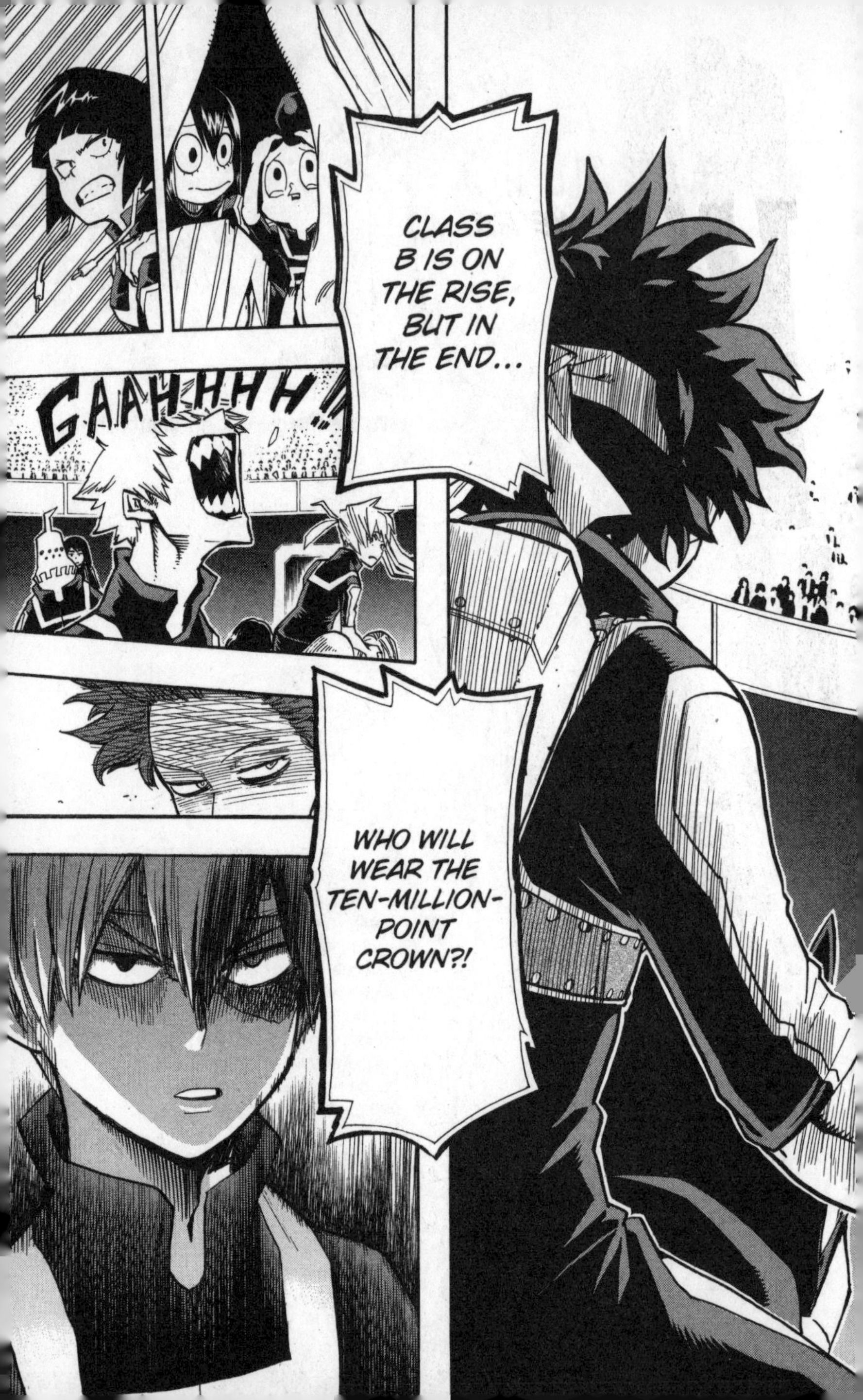
CLASS B IS ON THE RISE, BUT IN THE END...
GAAHHHH!!
WHO WILL WEAR THE TEN-MILLION-POINT CROWN?!

R-RATED HERO: MIDNIGHT (31)
[REAL NAME: NEMURI KAYAMA]

HOUSE CLOTHES

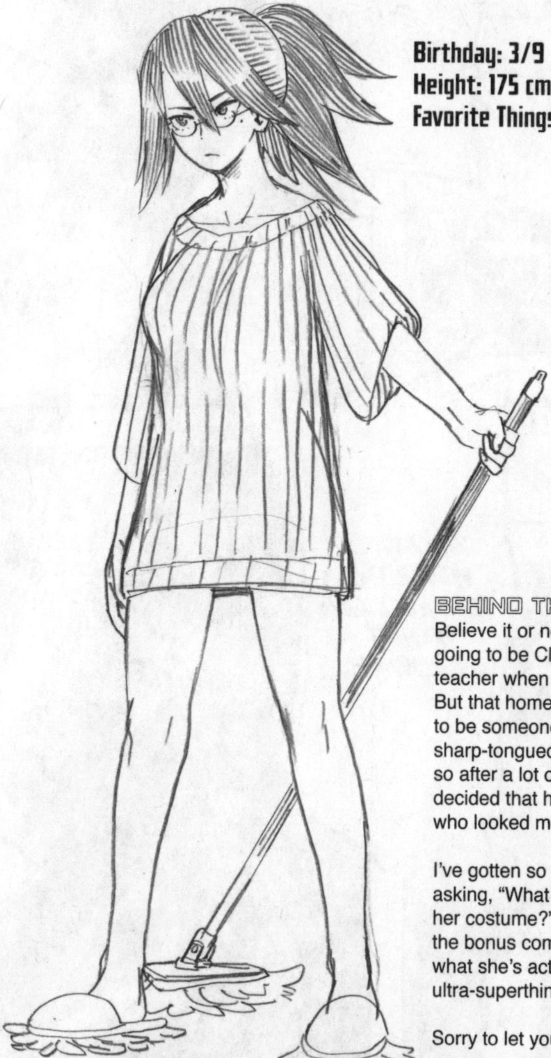

Birthday: 3/9
Height: 175 cm
Favorite Things: Vibrant youth, thrills

BEHIND THE SCENES

Believe it or not, she was actually going to be Class A's homeroom teacher when I first created her. But that homeroom teacher had to be someone willing to get sharp-tongued with the kids, so after a lot of consideration, I decided that had to be someone who looked more like Aizawa.

I've gotten so many letters asking, "What the heck's up with her costume?" As I explained in the bonus comic in *Jump NEXT!!*, what she's actually wearing is just ultra-superthin tights.

Sorry to let you down!

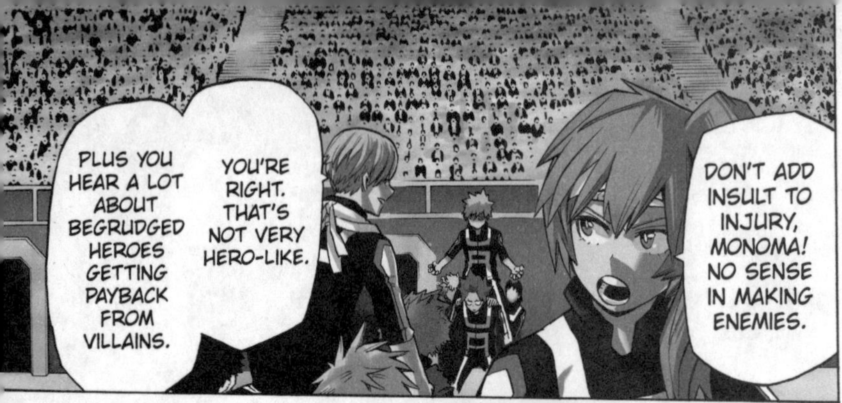
DON'T ADD INSULT TO INJURY, MONOMA! NO SENSE IN MAKING ENEMIES.
YOU'RE RIGHT. THAT'S NOT VERY HERO-LIKE.
PLUS YOU HEAR A LOT ABOUT BEGRUDGED HEROES GETTING PAYBACK FROM VILLAINS.

NO. 29 - UNAWARE

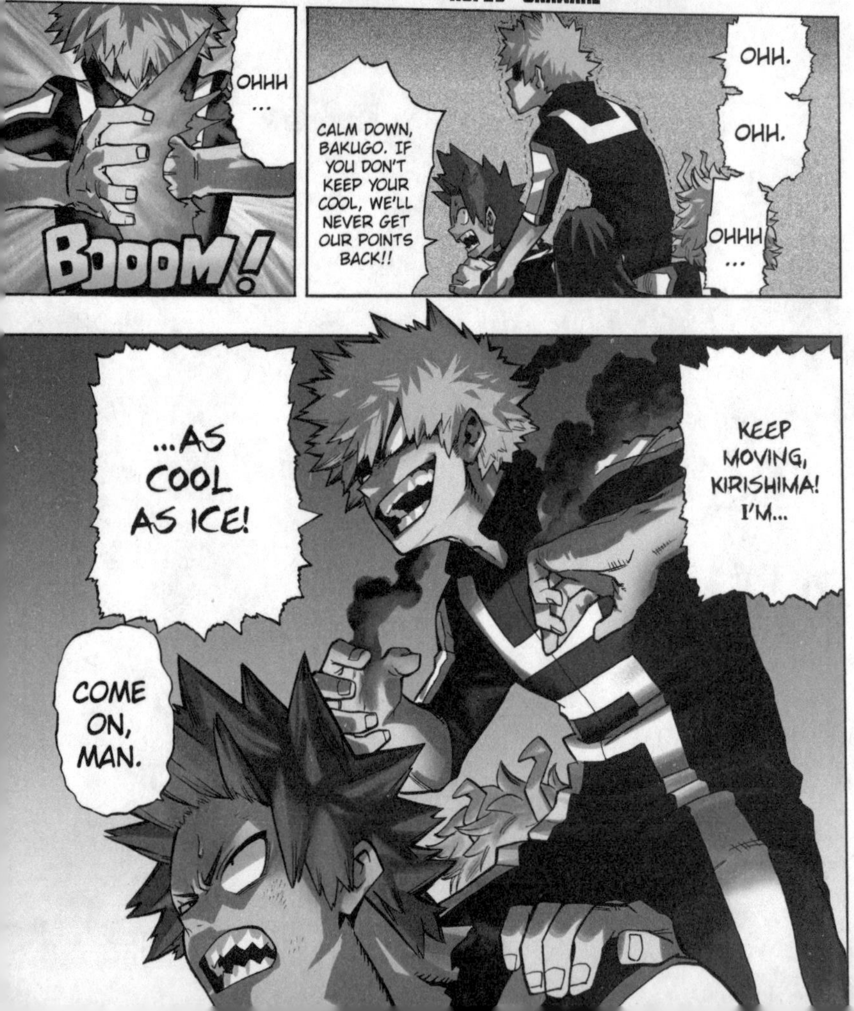
OHH.
OHH.
OHHH...
CALM DOWN, BAKUGO. IF YOU DON'T KEEP YOUR COOL, WE'LL NEVER GET OUR POINTS BACK!!
OHHH...
BOOOM!
KEEP MOVING, KIRISHIMA! I'M...
...AS COOL AS ICE!
COME ON, MAN.

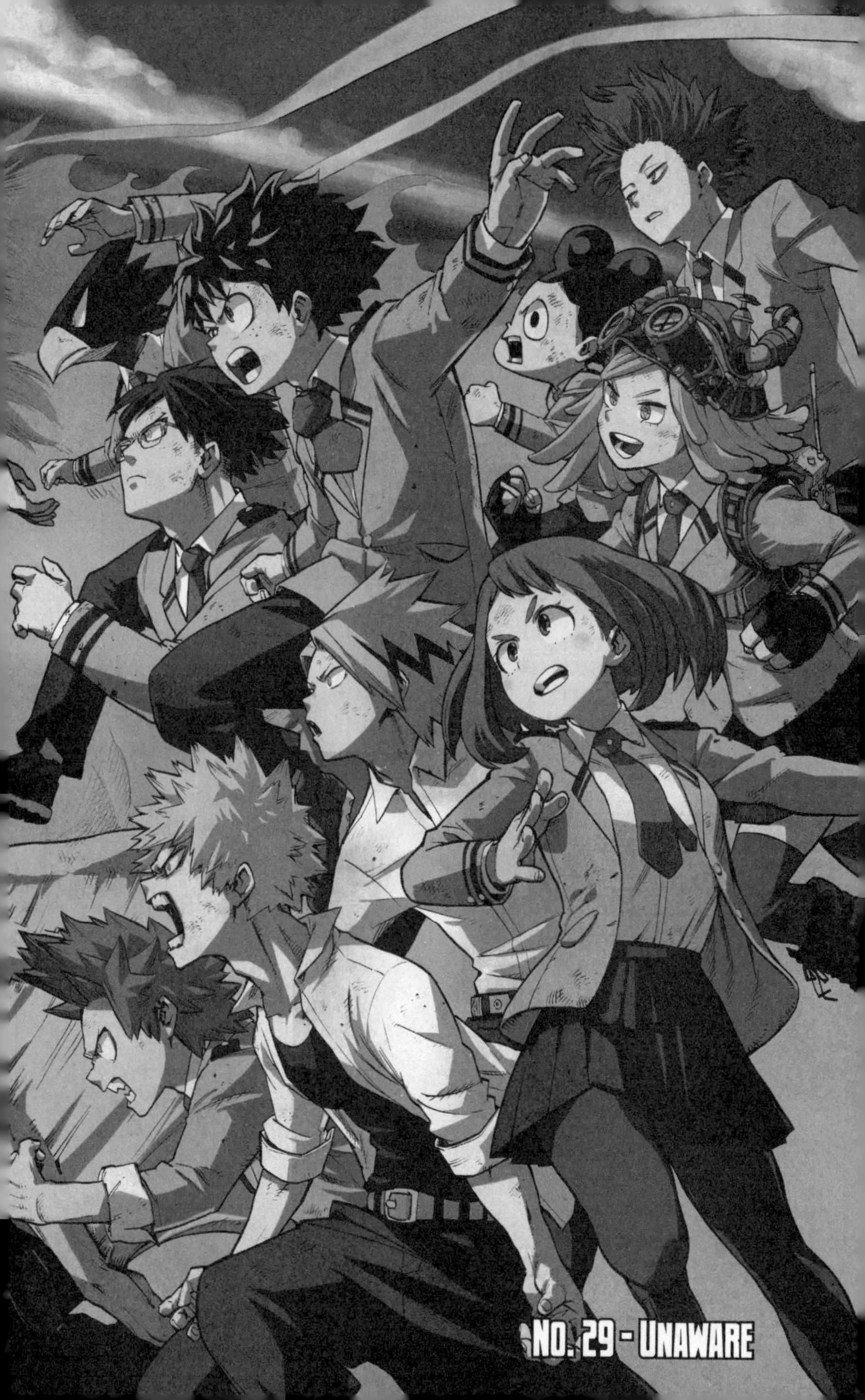
NO. 29 - UNAWARE

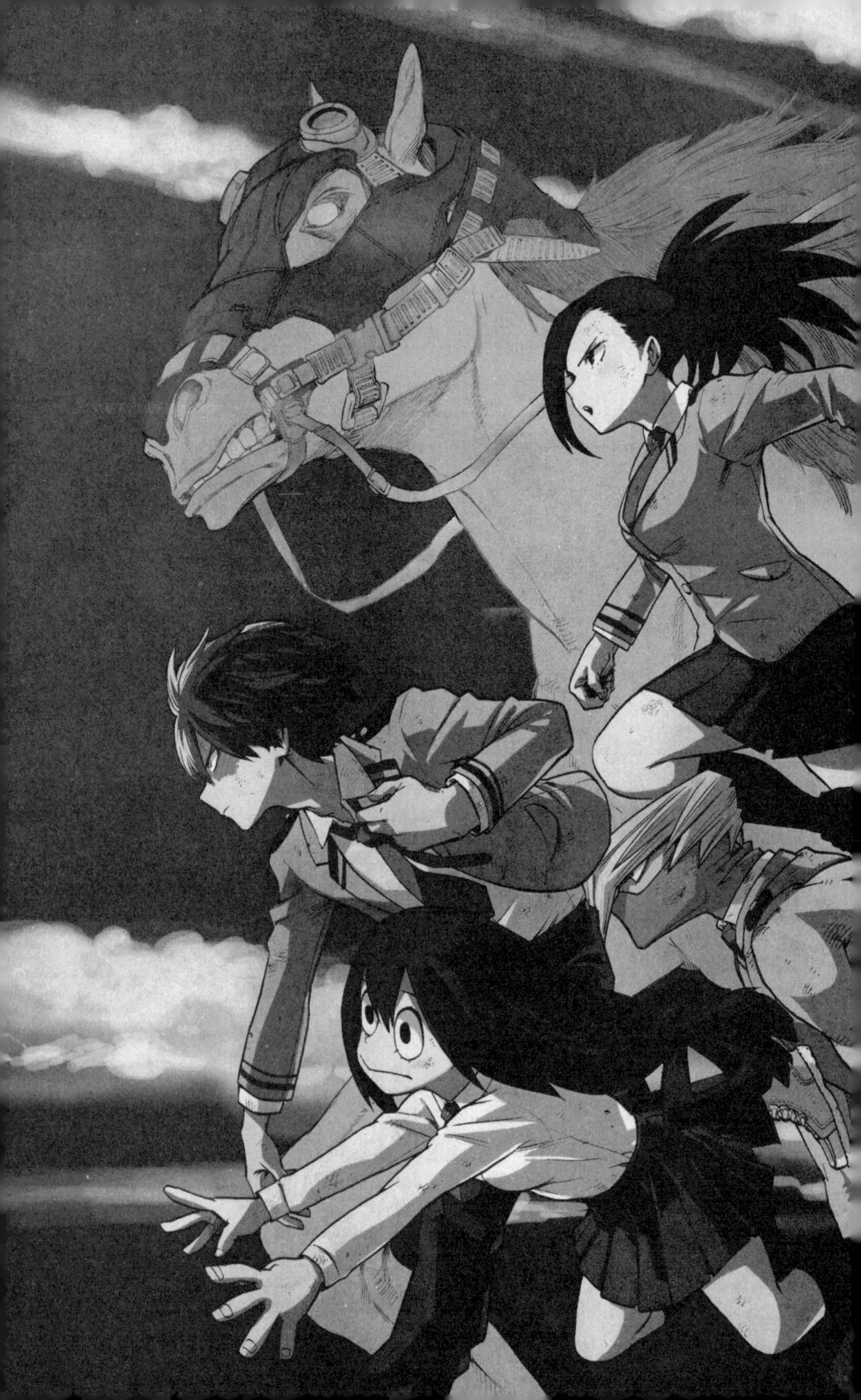

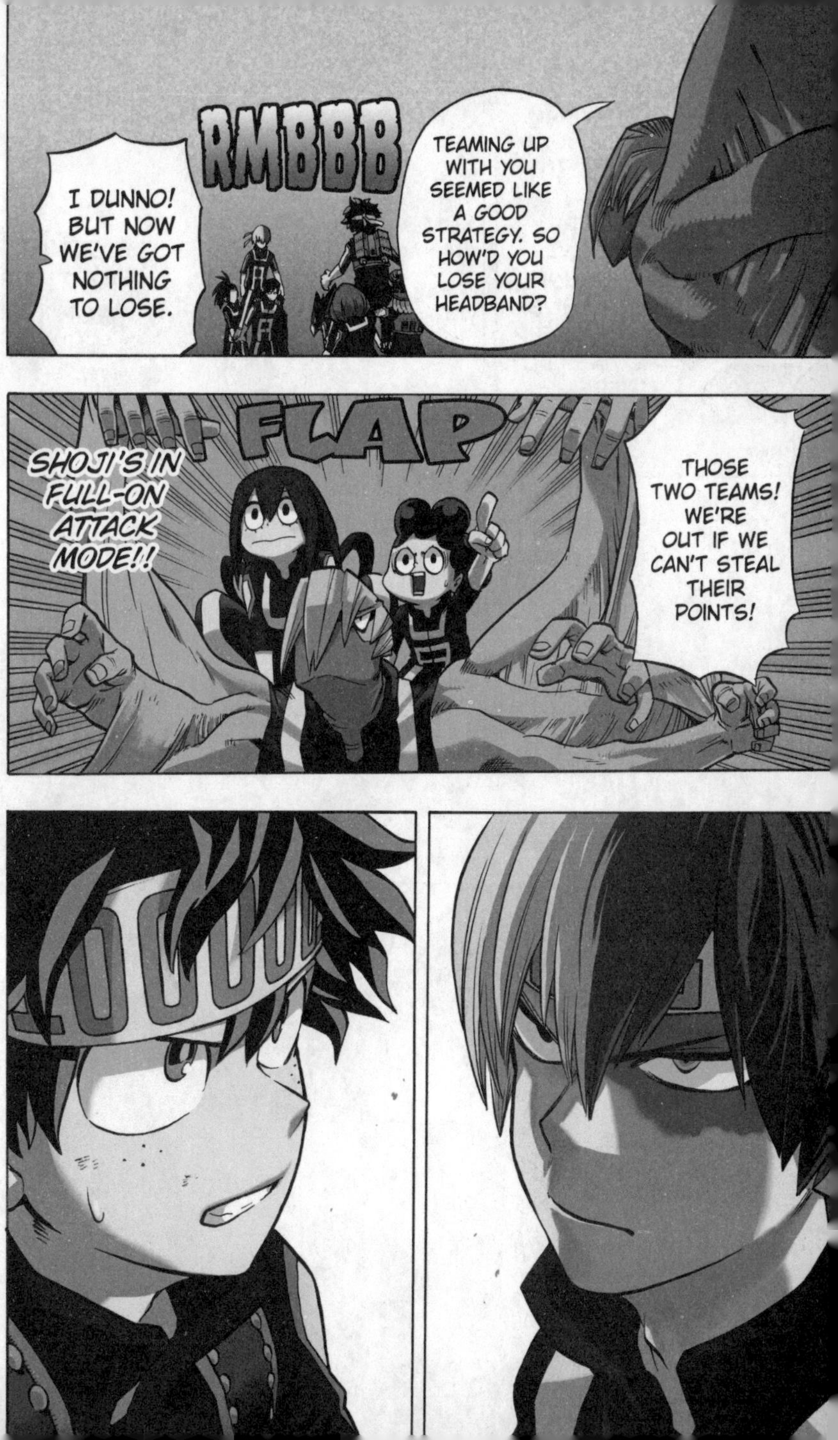
TEAMING UP WITH YOU SEEMED LIKE A GOOD STRATEGY. SO HOW'D YOU LOSE YOUR HEADBAND?
RMBBB
I DUNNO! BUT NOW WE'VE GOT NOTHING TO LOSE.
THOSE TWO TEAMS! WE'RE OUT IF WE CAN'T STEAL THEIR POINTS!
FLAP
SHOJI'S IN FULL-ON ATTACK MODE!!

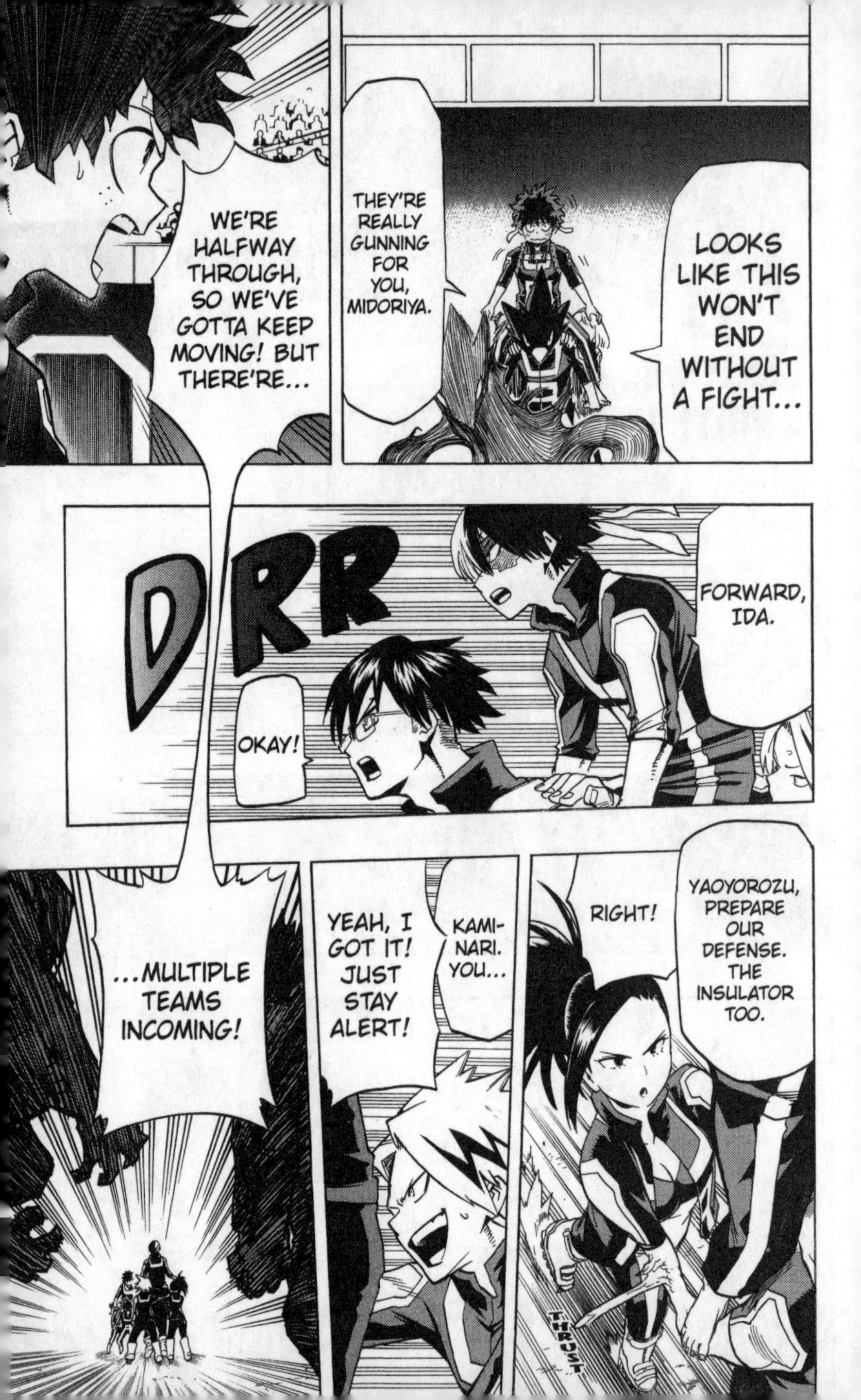
LOOKS LIKE THIS WON'T END WITHOUT A FIGHT...
THEY'RE REALLY GUNNING FOR YOU, MIDORIYA.
WE'RE HALFWAY THROUGH, SO WE'VE GOTTA KEEP MOVING! BUT THERE'RE...
FORWARD, IDA.
DRR
OKAY!
YAOYOROZU, PREPARE OUR DEFENSE. THE INSULATOR TOO.
RIGHT!
THRUST
KAMI-NARI. YOU...
YEAH, I GOT IT! JUST STAY ALERT!
...MULTIPLE TEAMS INCOMING!

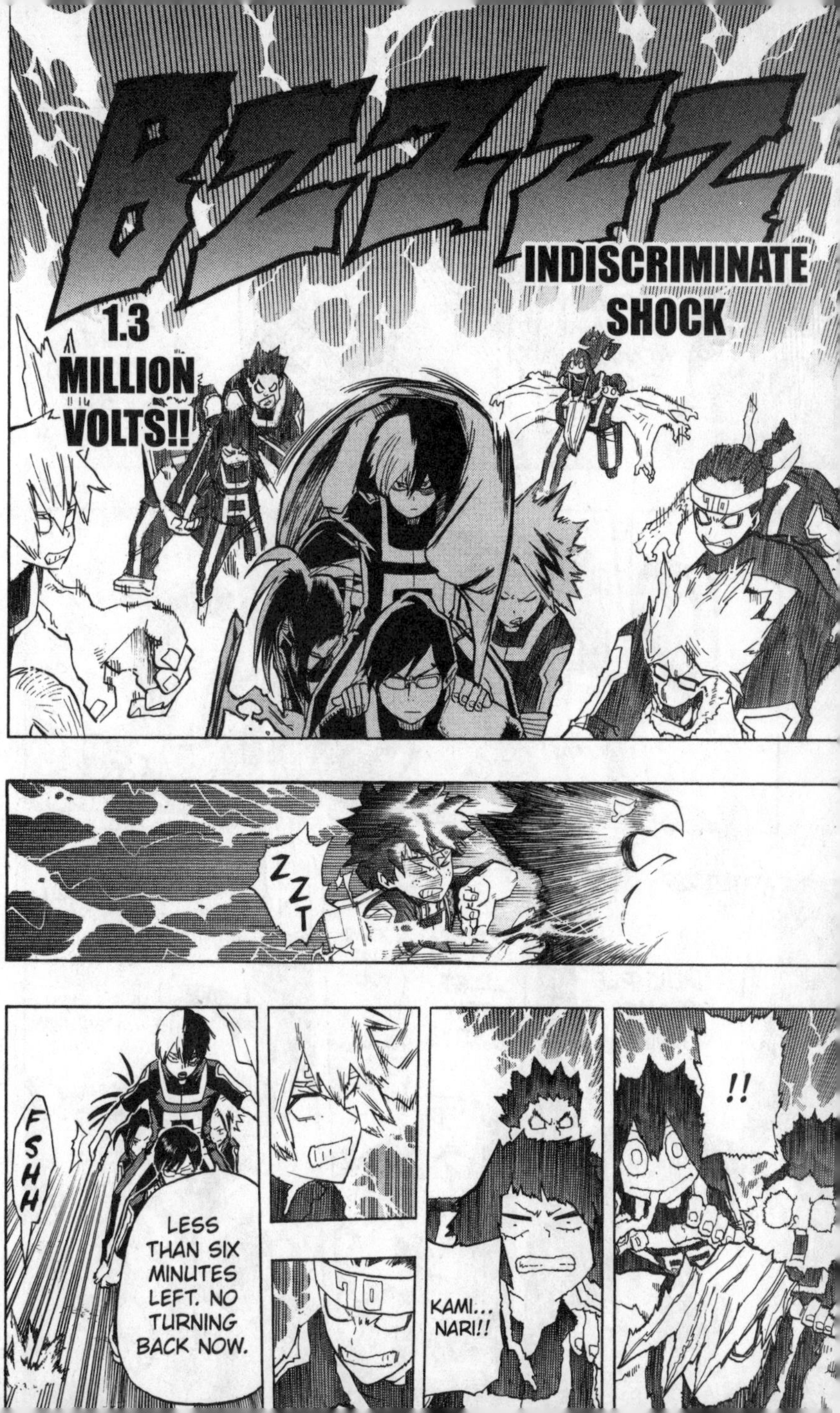
INDISCRIMINATE SHOCK
1.3 MILLION VOLTS!!
ZZZT
!!
KAMI... NARI!!
FSHH
LESS THAN SIX MINUTES LEFT. NO TURNING BACK NOW.

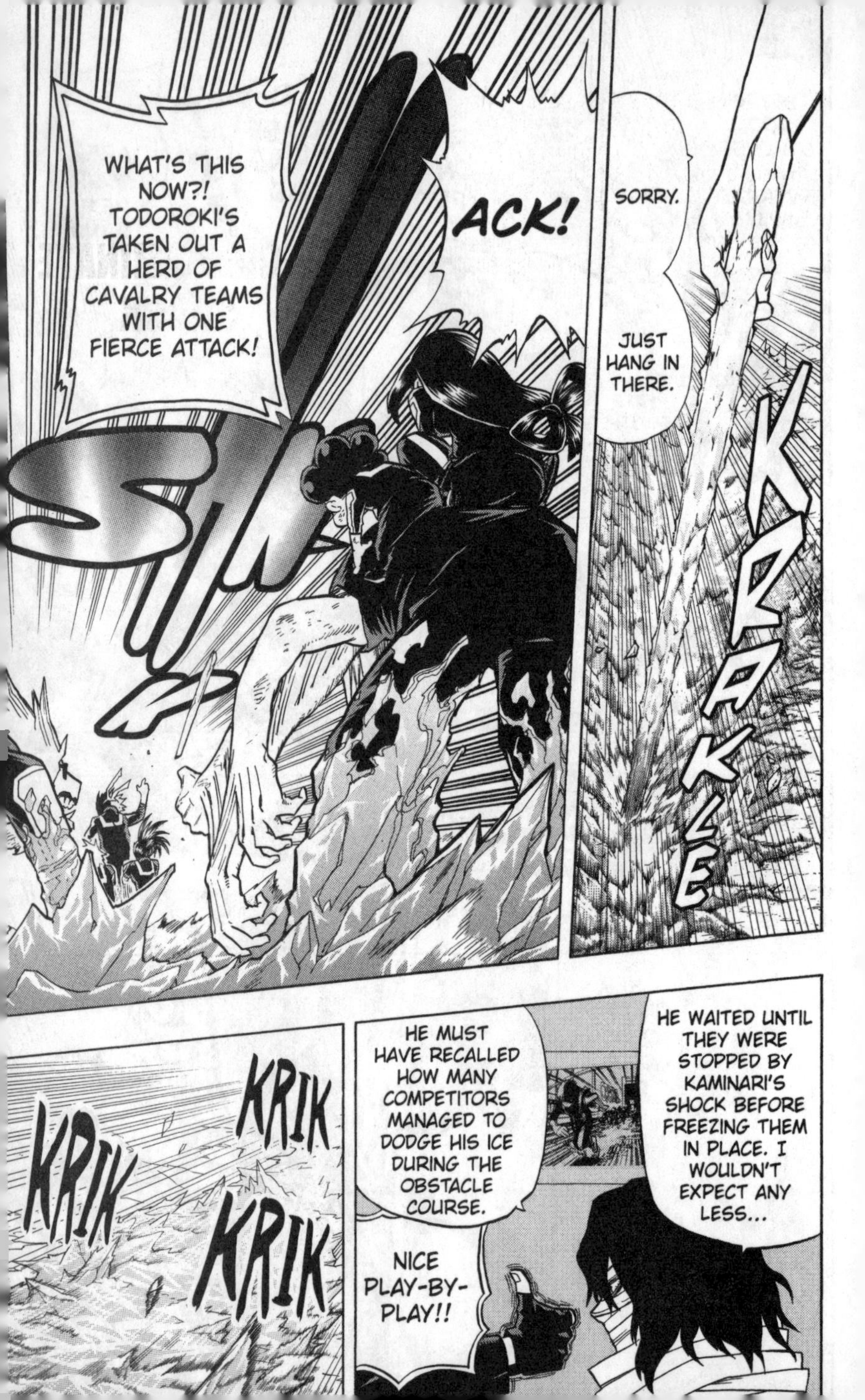
SORRY.
JUST HANG IN THERE.
KRAKKLE
ACK!
WHAT'S THIS NOW?! TODOROKI'S TAKEN OUT A HERD OF CAVALRY TEAMS WITH ONE FIERCE ATTACK!
HE WAITED UNTIL THEY WERE STOPPED BY KAMINARI'S SHOCK BEFORE FREEZING THEM IN PLACE. I WOULDN'T EXPECT ANY LESS...
HE MUST HAVE RECALLED HOW MANY COMPETITORS MANAGED TO DODGE HIS ICE DURING THE OBSTACLE COURSE.
NICE PLAY-BY-PLAY!!
KRIK
KRIK
KRIK

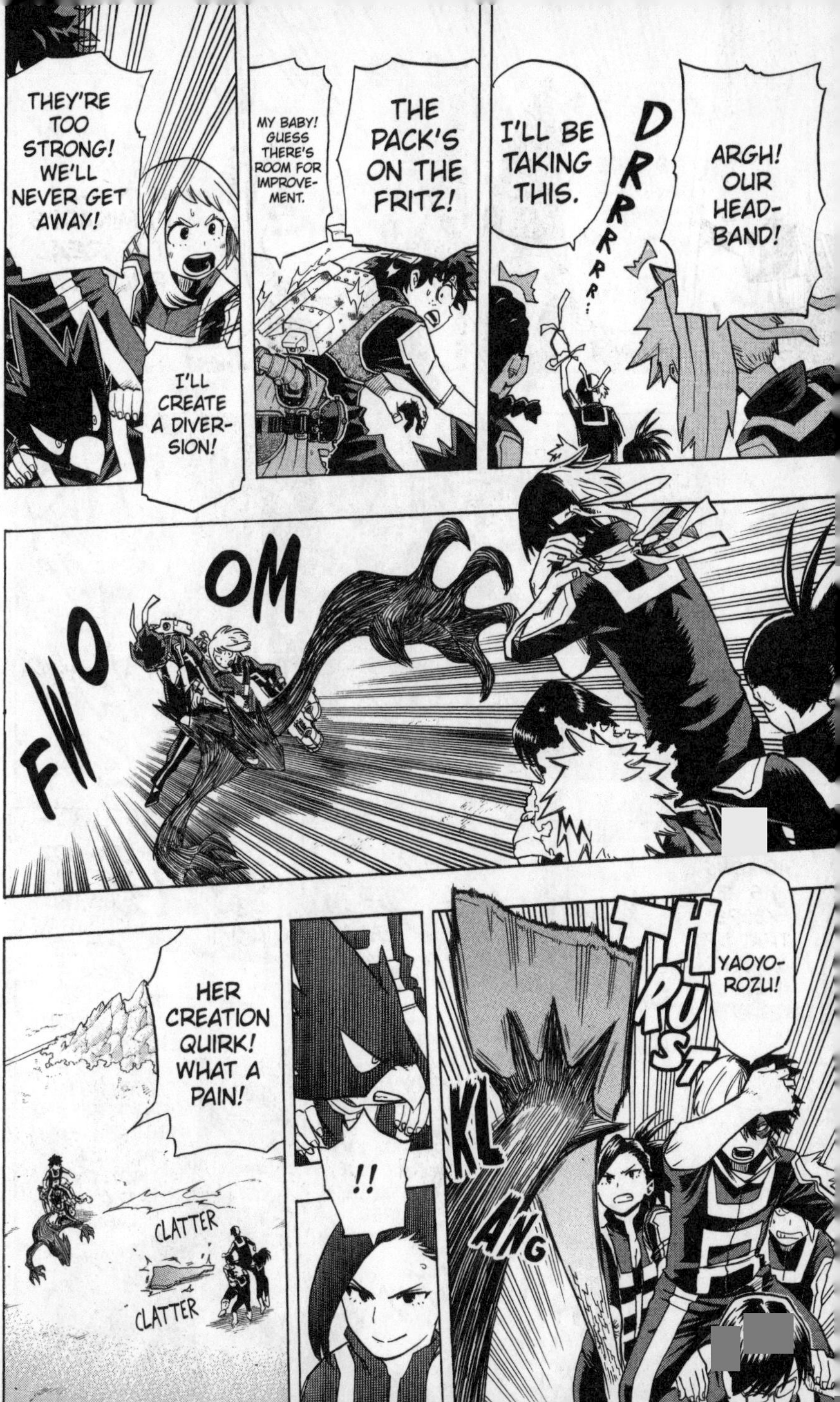
ARGH! OUR HEAD-BAND!
DRRRRRR...
I'LL BE TAKING THIS.
THE PACK'S ON THE FRITZ!
MY BABY! GUESS THERE'S ROOM FOR IMPROVE-MENT.
THEY'RE TOO STRONG! WE'LL NEVER GET AWAY!
I'LL CREATE A DIVER-SION!
FWOOM
YAOYO-ROZU!
THRUST
KLANG
!!
HER CREATION QUIRK! WHAT A PAIN!
CLATTER
CLATTER

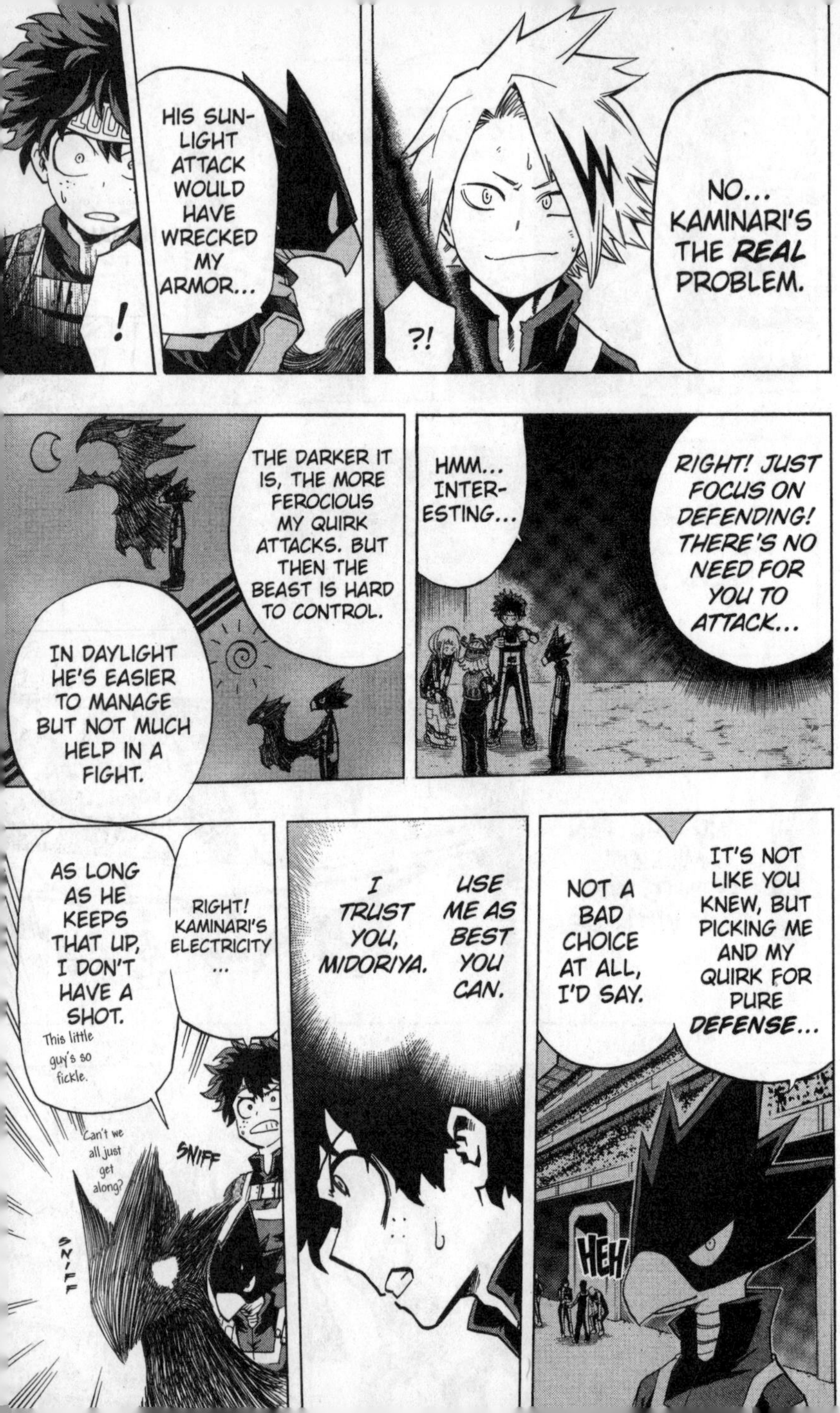
NO... KAMINARI'S THE REAL PROBLEM.
?!
HIS SUNLIGHT ATTACK WOULD HAVE WRECKED MY ARMOR...
!
RIGHT! JUST FOCUS ON DEFENDING! THERE'S NO NEED FOR YOU TO ATTACK...
HMM... INTERESTING...
THE DARKER IT IS, THE MORE FEROCIOUS MY QUIRK ATTACKS. BUT THEN THE BEAST IS HARD TO CONTROL.
IN DAYLIGHT HE'S EASIER TO MANAGE BUT NOT MUCH HELP IN A FIGHT.
IT'S NOT LIKE YOU KNEW, BUT PICKING ME AND MY QUIRK FOR PURE DEFENSE...
NOT A BAD CHOICE AT ALL, I'D SAY.
HEH
USE ME AS BEST YOU CAN.
I TRUST YOU, MIDORIYA.
RIGHT! KAMINARI'S ELECTRICITY...
AS LONG AS HE KEEPS THAT UP, I DON'T HAVE A SHOT.
This little guy's so fickle.
SNIFF
Can't we all just get along?
SNIFF

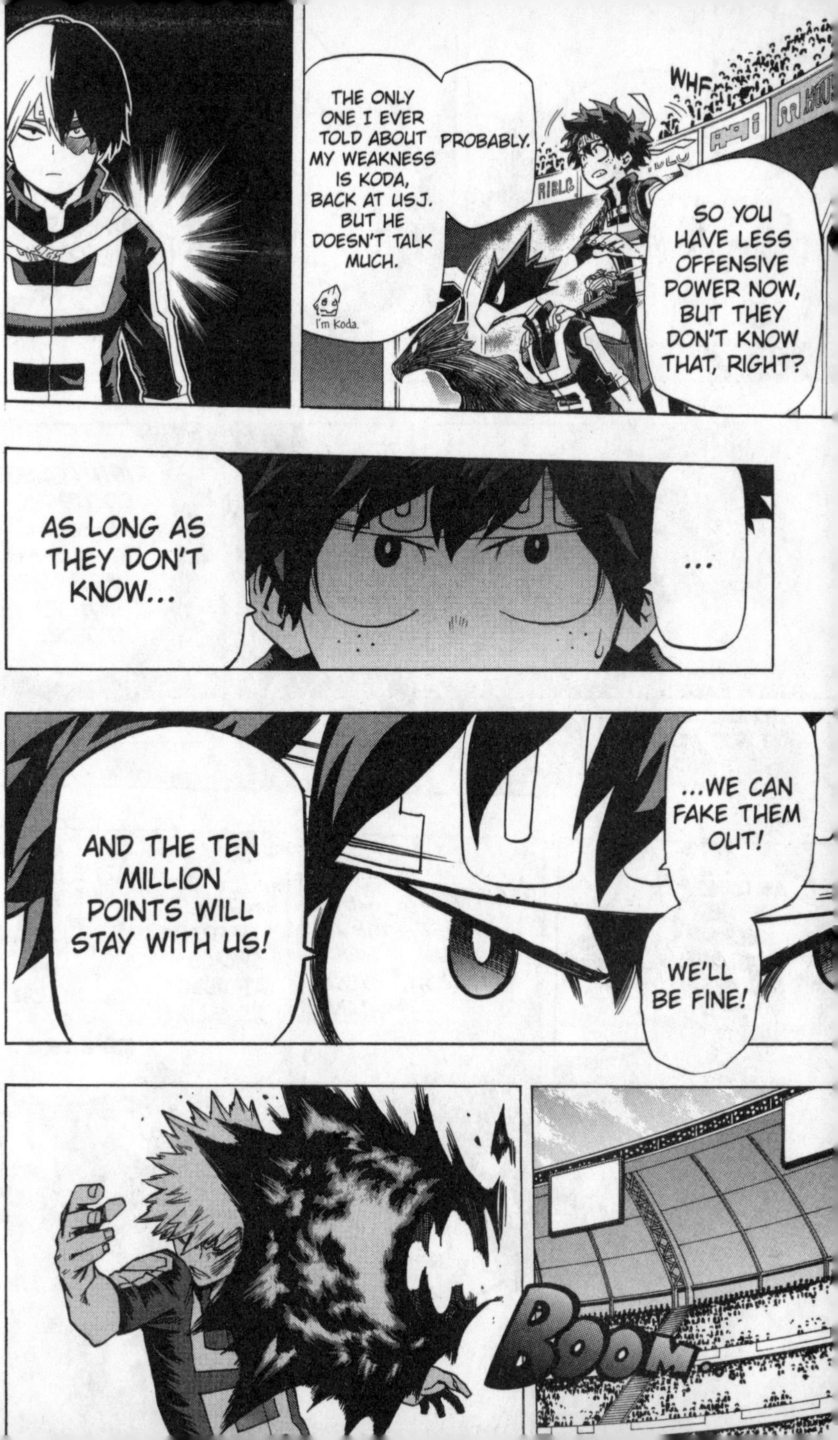
WHF
SO YOU HAVE LESS OFFENSIVE POWER NOW, BUT THEY DON'T KNOW THAT, RIGHT?
PROBABLY.
THE ONLY ONE I EVER TOLD ABOUT MY WEAKNESS IS KODA, BACK AT USJ. BUT HE DOESN'T TALK MUCH.
I'm Koda.
...
AS LONG AS THEY DON'T KNOW...
...WE CAN FAKE THEM OUT!
WE'LL BE FINE!
AND THE TEN MILLION POINTS WILL STAY WITH US!
BOOM

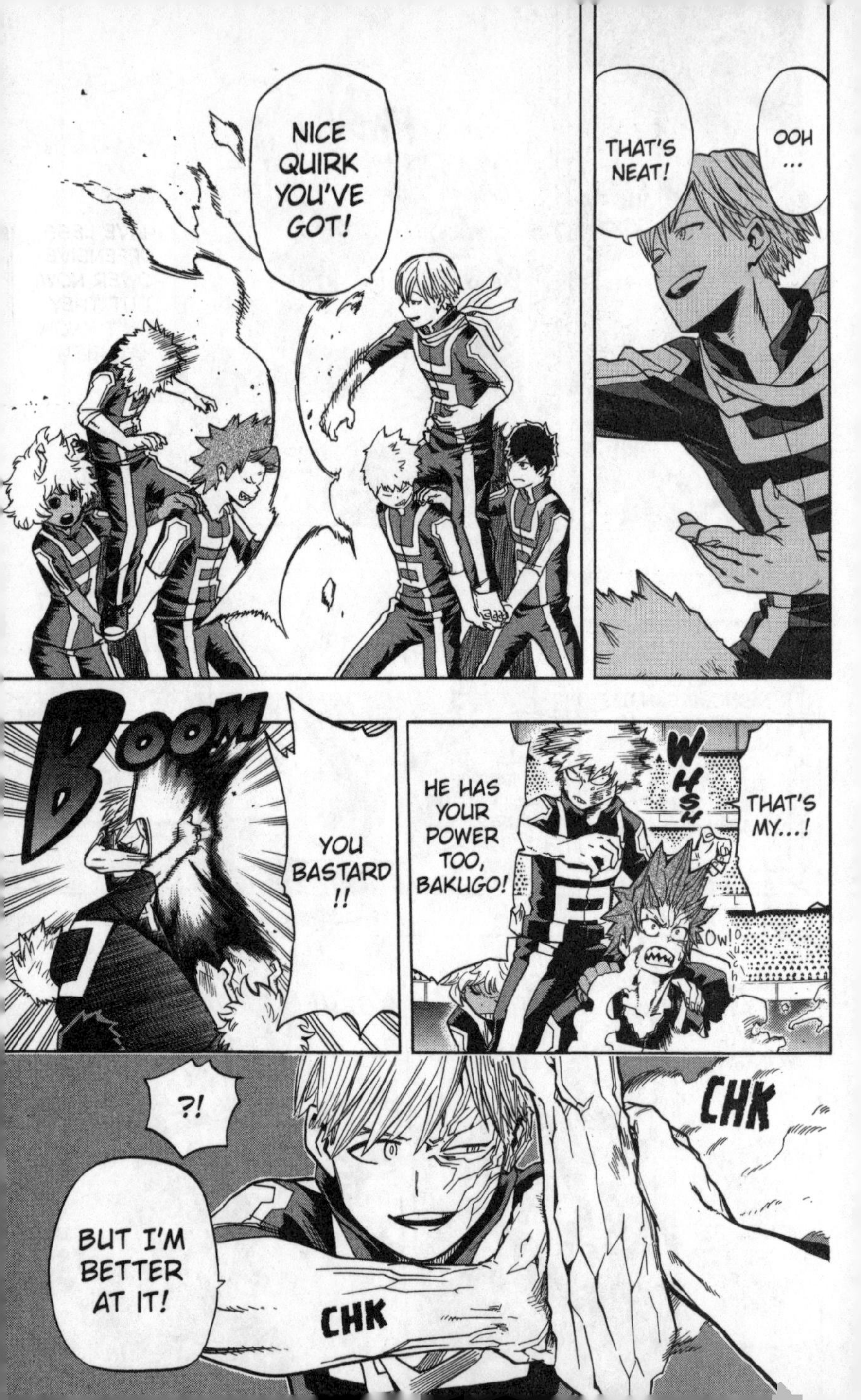
OOH ...
THAT'S NEAT!
NICE QUIRK YOU'VE GOT!
THAT'S MY...!
WHSH
HE HAS YOUR POWER TOO, BAKUGO!
OW! ouch!
YOU BASTARD!!
BOOM
CHK
?!
BUT I'M BETTER AT IT!
CHK

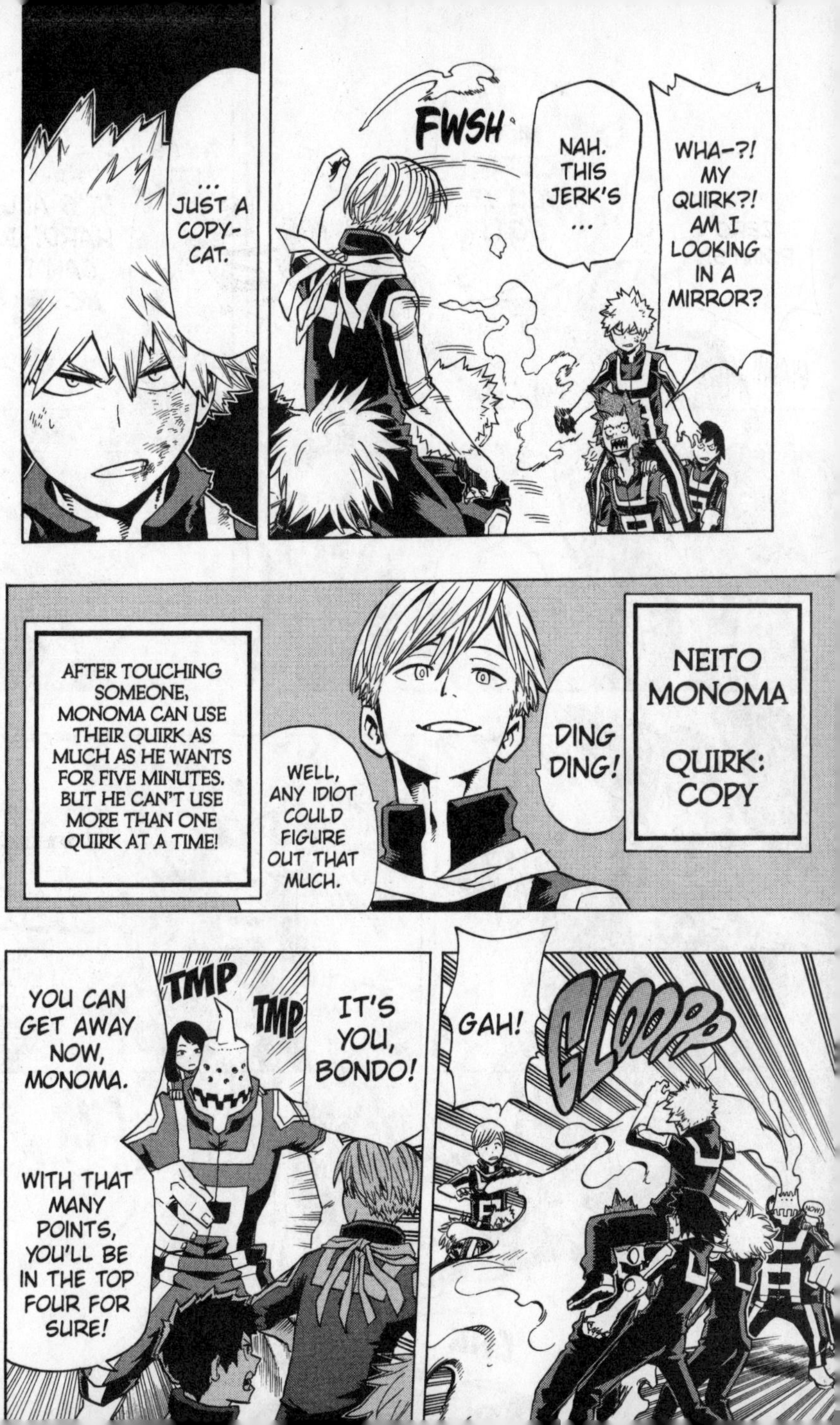

WHA-?! MY QUIRK?! AM I LOOKING IN A MIRROR?
FWSH
NAH. THIS JERK'S ...
... JUST A COPY-CAT.
NEITO MONOMA
QUIRK: COPY
DING DING!
WELL, ANY IDIOT COULD FIGURE OUT THAT MUCH.
AFTER TOUCHING SOMEONE, MONOMA CAN USE THEIR QUIRK AS MUCH AS HE WANTS FOR FIVE MINUTES. BUT HE CAN'T USE MORE THAN ONE QUIRK AT A TIME!
GLOOP
GAH!
IT'S YOU, BONDO!
TMP
TMP
YOU CAN GET AWAY NOW, MONOMA.
WITH THAT MANY POINTS, YOU'LL BE IN THE TOP FOUR FOR SURE!

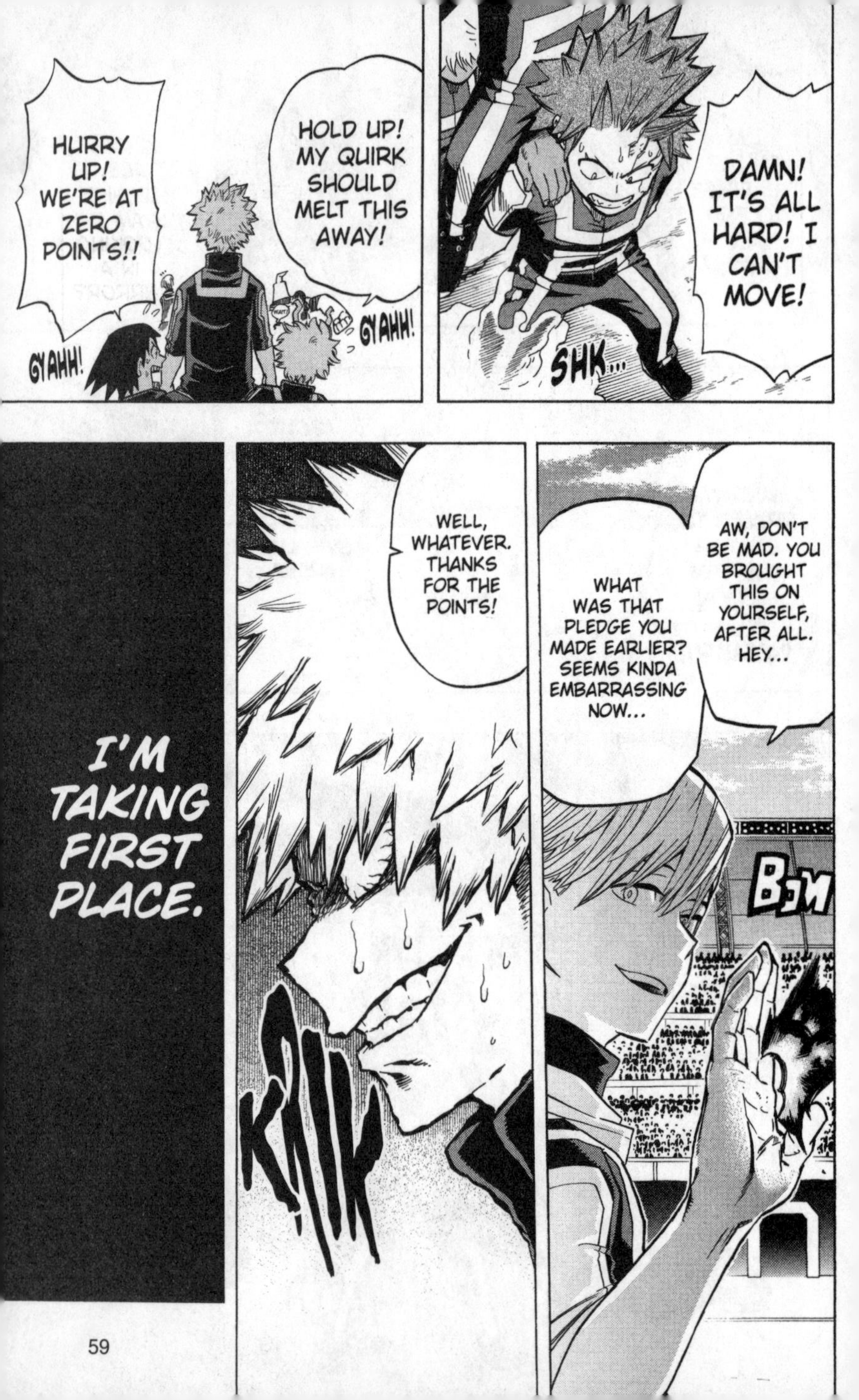
DAMN! IT'S ALL HARD! I CAN'T MOVE!
SHK...
HOLD UP! MY QUIRK SHOULD MELT THIS AWAY!
HURRY UP! WE'RE AT ZERO POINTS!!
GYAHH!
GYAHH!
AW, DON'T BE MAD. YOU BROUGHT THIS ON YOURSELF, AFTER ALL. HEY...
WHAT WAS THAT PLEDGE YOU MADE EARLIER? SEEMS KINDA EMBARRASSING NOW...
WELL, WHATEVER. THANKS FOR THE POINTS!
KRIK
I'M TAKING FIRST PLACE.

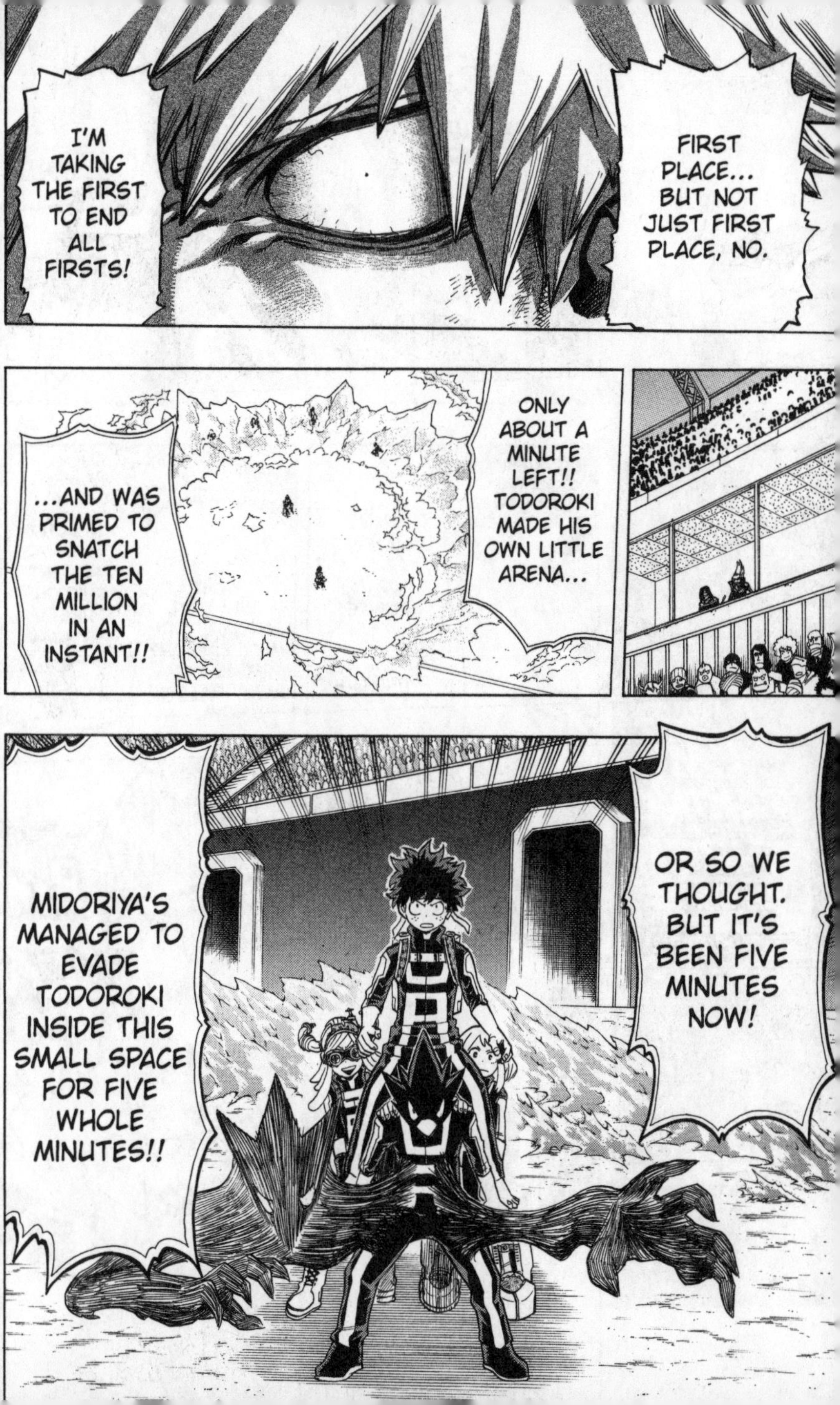
FIRST PLACE... BUT NOT JUST FIRST PLACE, NO.
I'M TAKING THE FIRST TO END ALL FIRSTS!
ONLY ABOUT A MINUTE LEFT!! TODOROKI MADE HIS OWN LITTLE ARENA...
...AND WAS PRIMED TO SNATCH THE TEN MILLION IN AN INSTANT!!
OR SO WE THOUGHT. BUT IT'S BEEN FIVE MINUTES NOW!
MIDORIYA'S MANAGED TO EVADE TODOROKI INSIDE THIS SMALL SPACE FOR FIVE WHOLE MINUTES!!

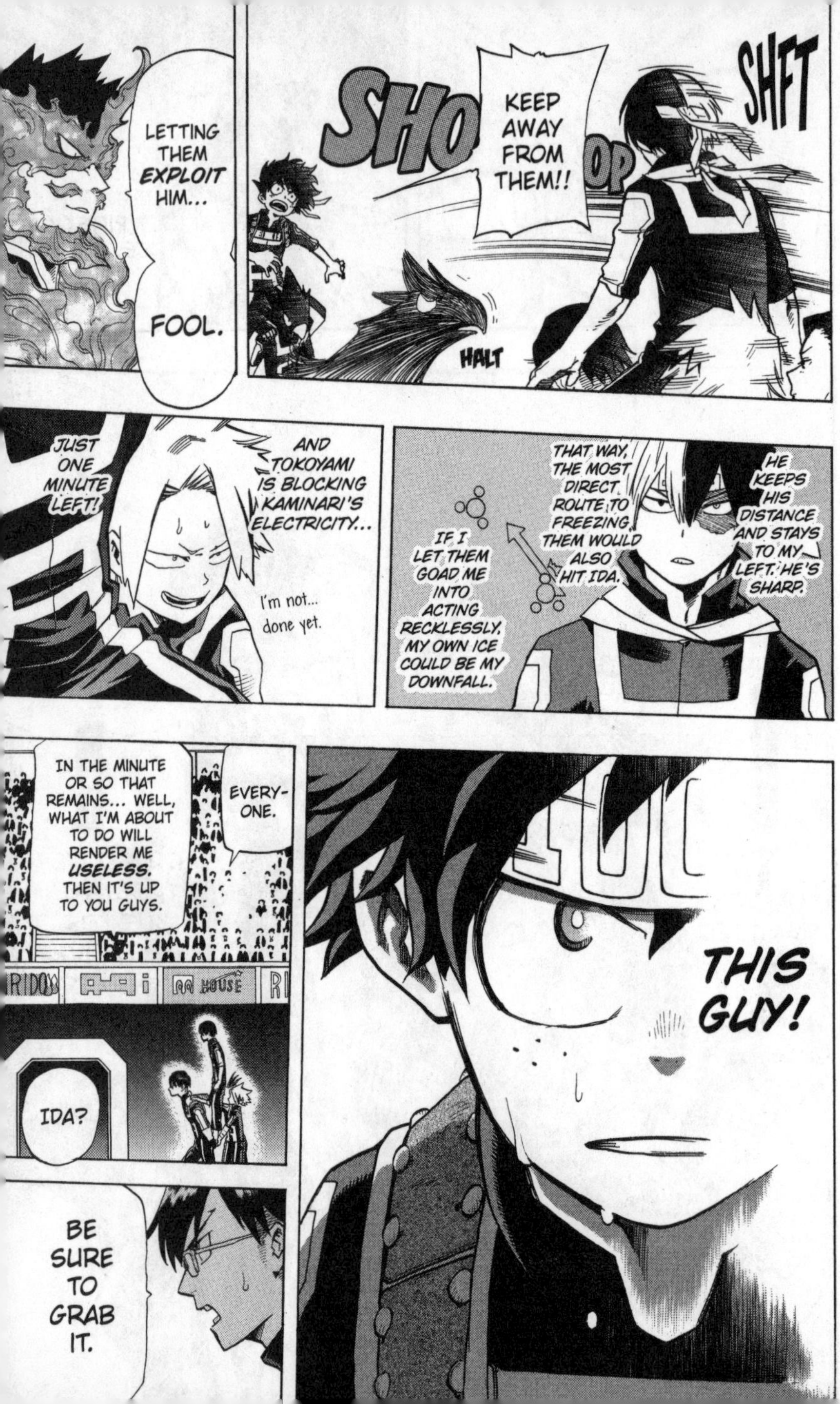

SHFT
SHOOOP
KEEP AWAY FROM THEM!!
HALT
LETTING THEM EXPLOIT HIM...
FOOL.
HE KEEPS HIS DISTANCE AND STAYS TO MY LEFT. HE'S SHARP.
THAT WAY, THE MOST DIRECT ROUTE TO FREEZING THEM WOULD ALSO HIT IDA.
IF I LET THEM GOAD ME INTO ACTING RECKLESSLY, MY OWN ICE COULD BE MY DOWNFALL.
AND TOKOYAMI IS BLOCKING KAMINARI'S ELECTRICITY...
JUST ONE MINUTE LEFT!
I'm not... done yet.
THIS GUY!
EVERY-ONE.
IN THE MINUTE OR SO THAT REMAINS... WELL, WHAT I'M ABOUT TO DO WILL RENDER ME USELESS. THEN IT'S UP TO YOU GUYS.
IDA?
BE SURE TO GRAB IT.

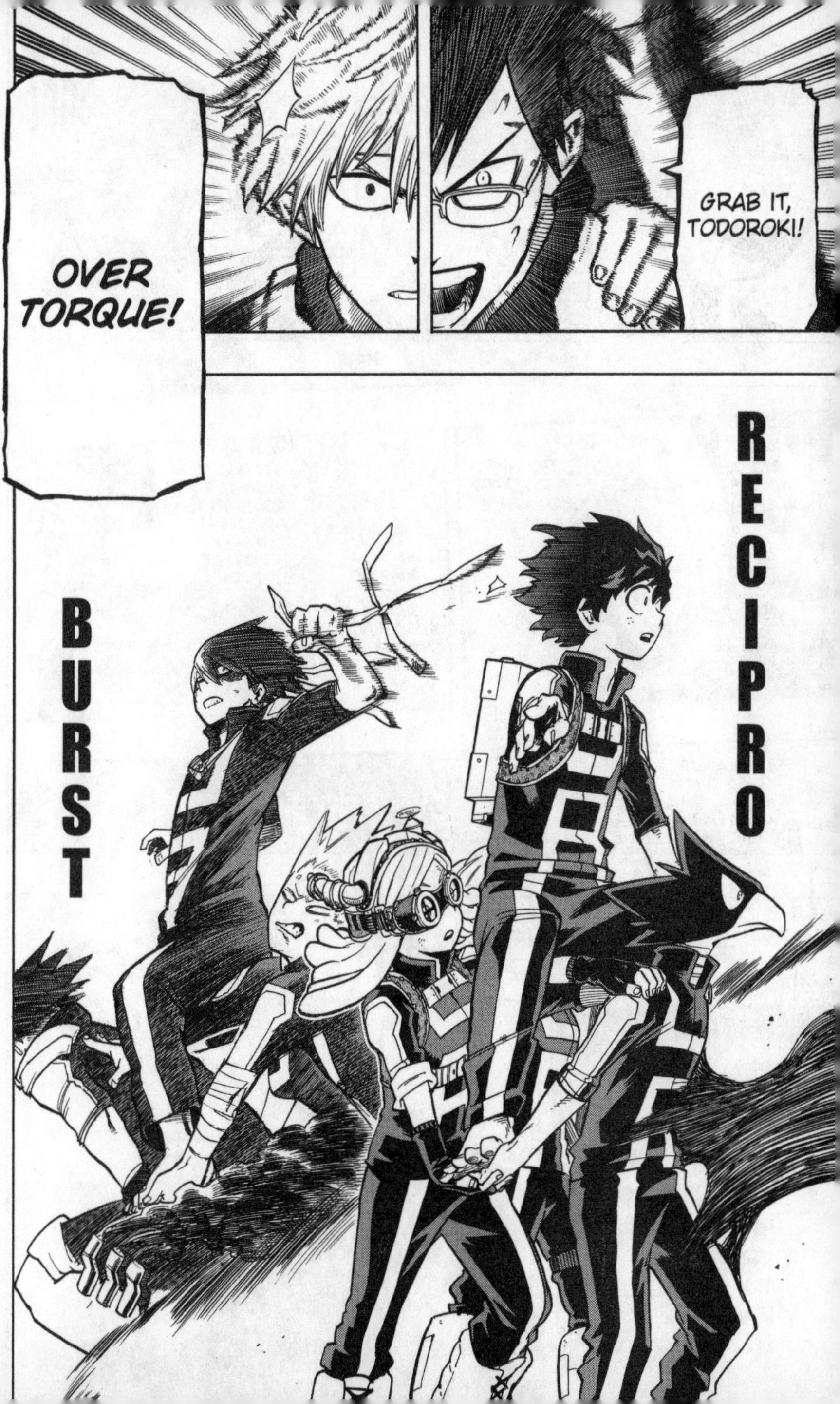
GRAB IT, TODOROKI!
OVER TORQUE!
RECIPRO
BURST

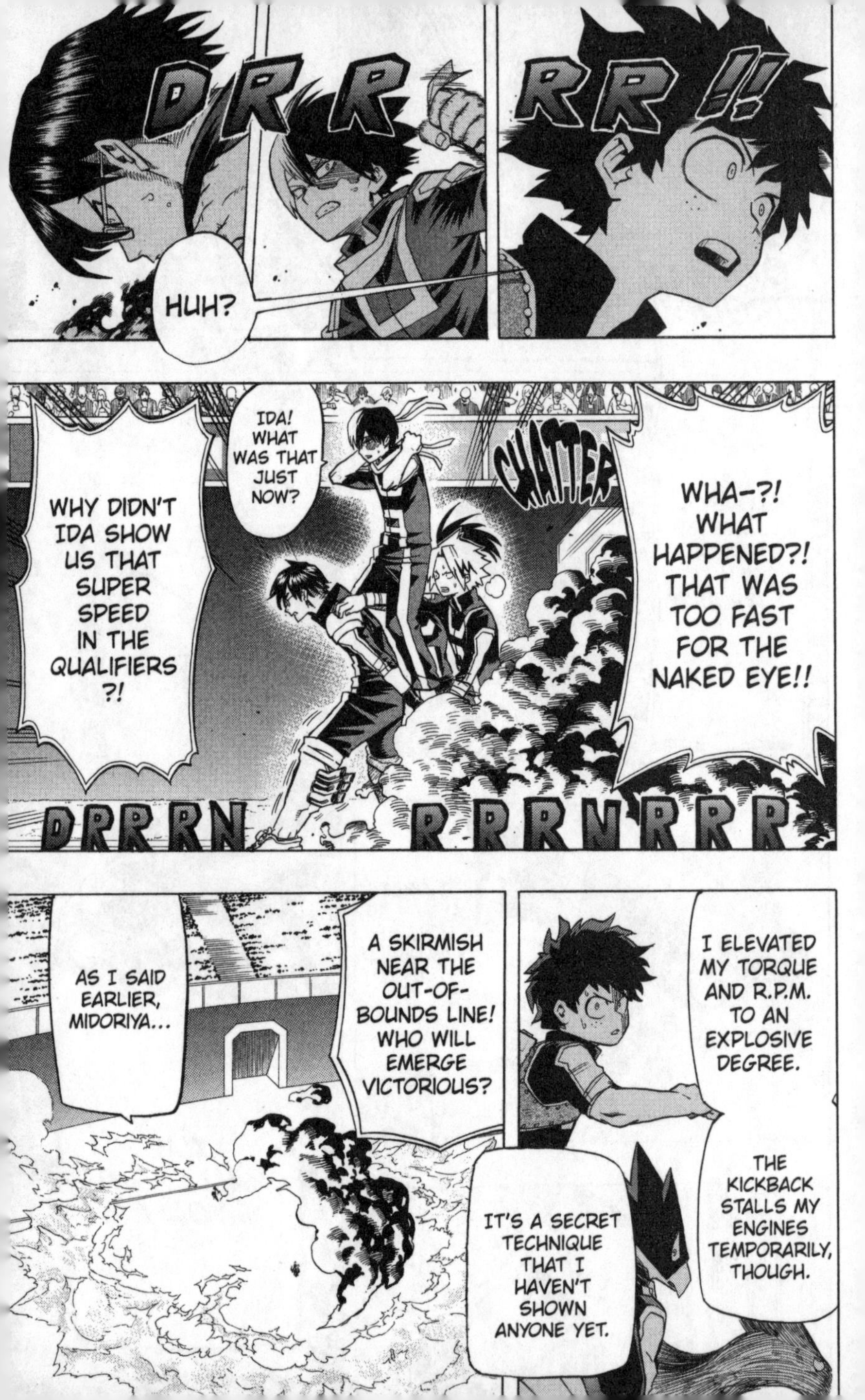

DRRRR!!
HUH?
WHA-?! WHAT HAPPENED?! THAT WAS TOO FAST FOR THE NAKED EYE!!
CHATTER
IDA! WHAT WAS THAT JUST NOW?
WHY DIDN'T IDA SHOW US THAT SUPER SPEED IN THE QUALIFIERS?!
DRRRN RRRNRRR
I ELEVATED MY TORQUE AND R.P.M. TO AN EXPLOSIVE DEGREE.
THE KICKBACK STALLS MY ENGINES TEMPORARILY, THOUGH.
IT'S A SECRET TECHNIQUE THAT I HAVEN'T SHOWN ANYONE YET.
A SKIRMISH NEAR THE OUT-OF-BOUNDS LINE! WHO WILL EMERGE VICTORIOUS?
AS I SAID EARLIER, MIDORIYA...

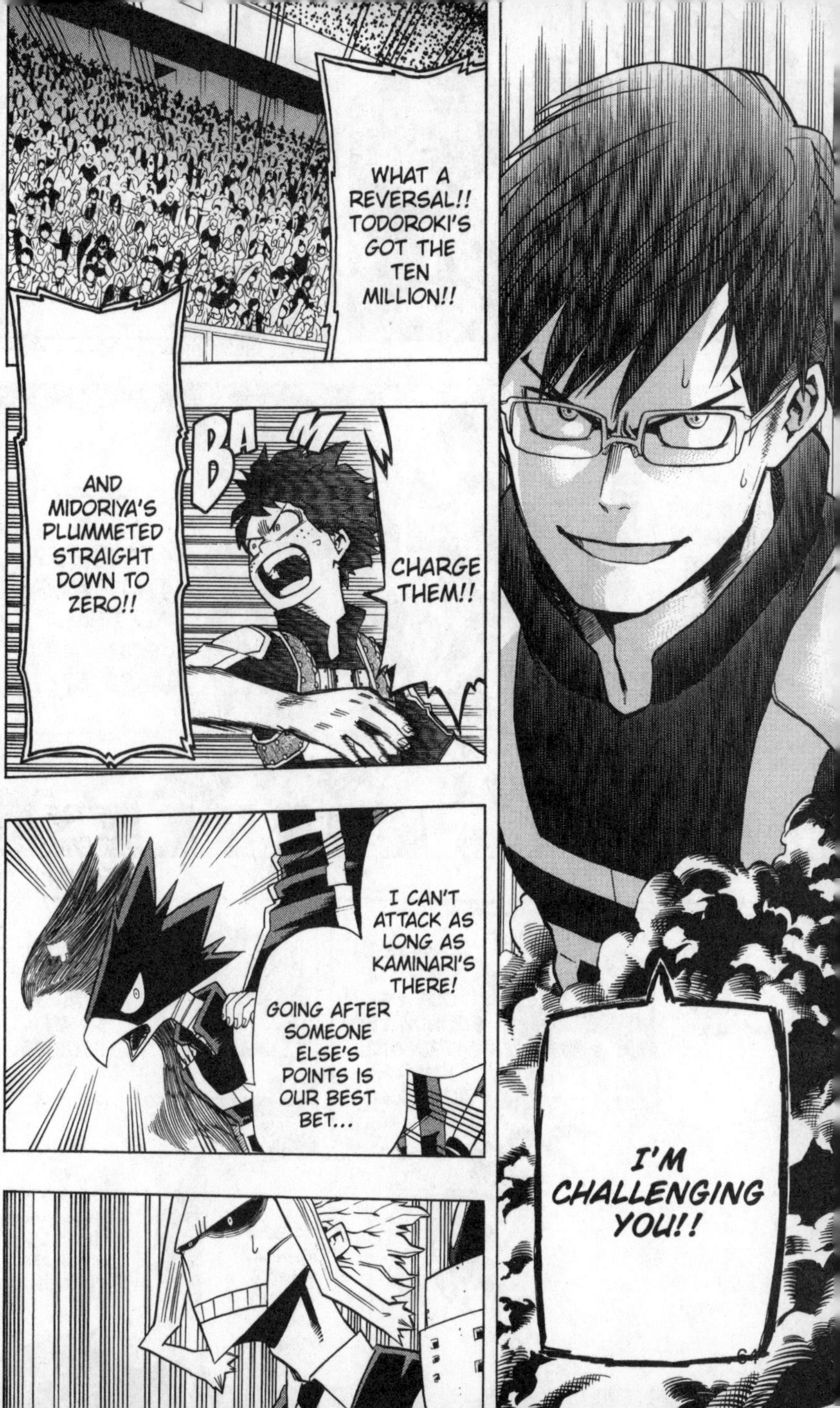
I'M CHALLENGING YOU!!
WHAT A REVERSAL!! TODOROKI'S GOT THE TEN MILLION!!
AND MIDORIYA'S PLUMMETED STRAIGHT DOWN TO ZERO!!
BAM
CHARGE THEM!!
I CAN'T ATTACK AS LONG AS KAMINARI'S THERE!
GOING AFTER SOMEONE ELSE'S POINTS IS OUR BEST BET...

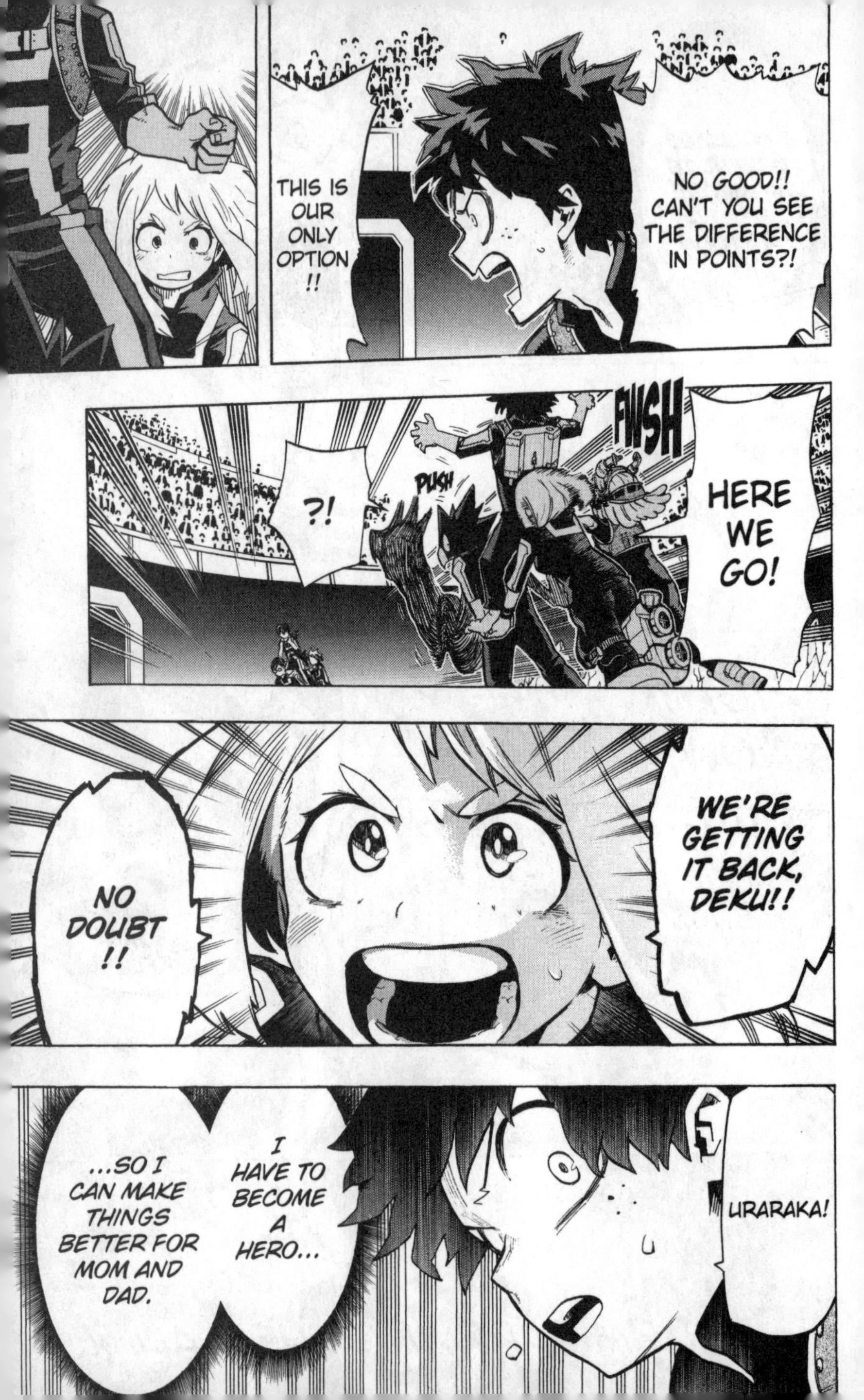
NO GOOD!! CAN'T YOU SEE THE DIFFERENCE IN POINTS?!
THIS IS OUR ONLY OPTION !!
FWSH
HERE WE GO!
PUSH
?!
WE'RE GETTING IT BACK, DEKU!!
NO DOUBT !!
URARAKA!
I HAVE TO BECOME A HERO...
...SO I CAN MAKE THINGS BETTER FOR MOM AND DAD.

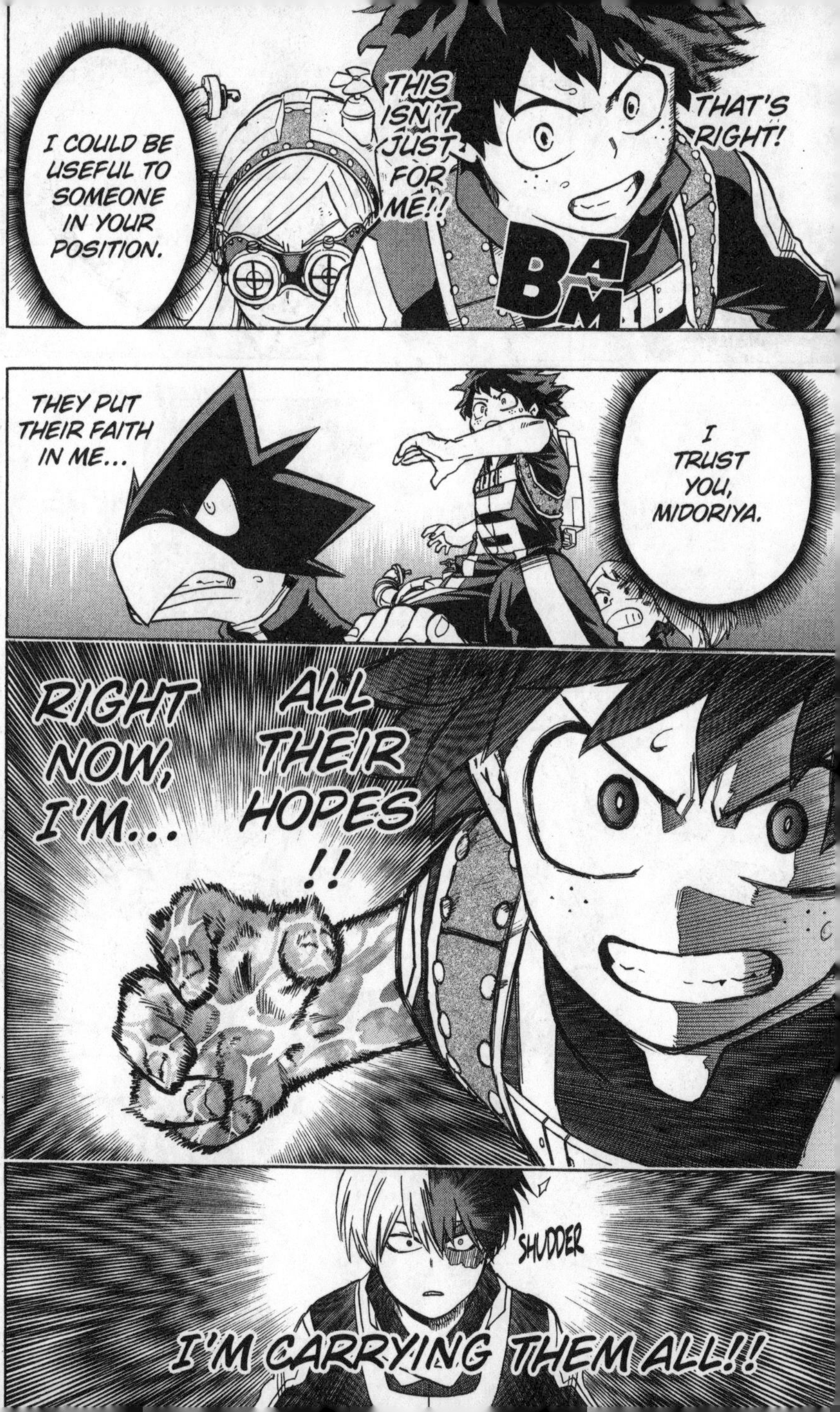
THAT'S RIGHT!
THIS ISN'T JUST FOR ME!!
BAM
I COULD BE USEFUL TO SOMEONE IN YOUR POSITION.
I TRUST YOU, MIDORIYA.
THEY PUT THEIR FAITH IN ME...
ALL THEIR HOPES!!
RIGHT NOW, I'M...
SHUDDER
I'M CARRYING THEM ALL!!

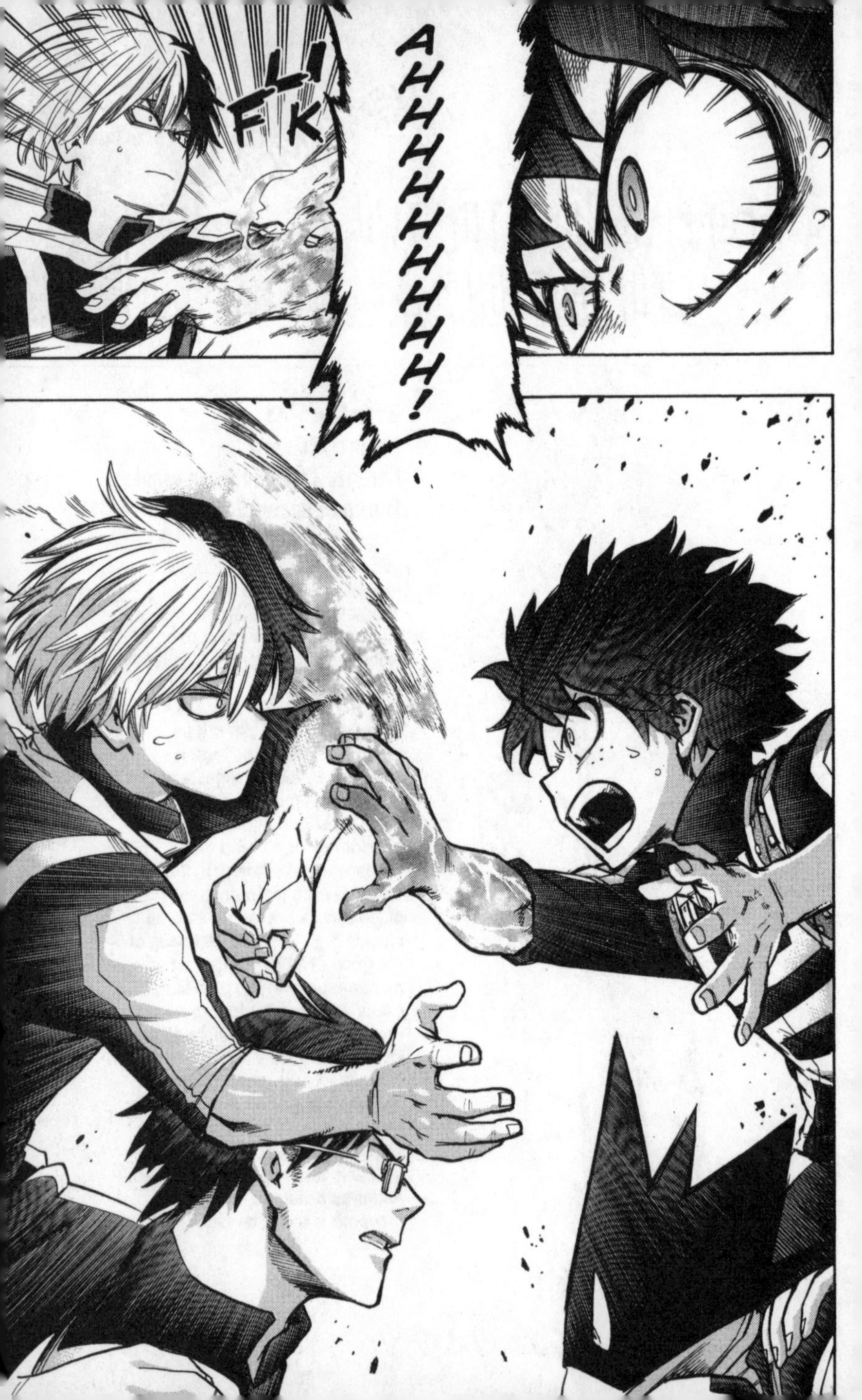
FLIK
AHHHHHHHHHH!

NEITO MONOMA (15)

POPPING OPEN THE TWO TOP BUTTONS

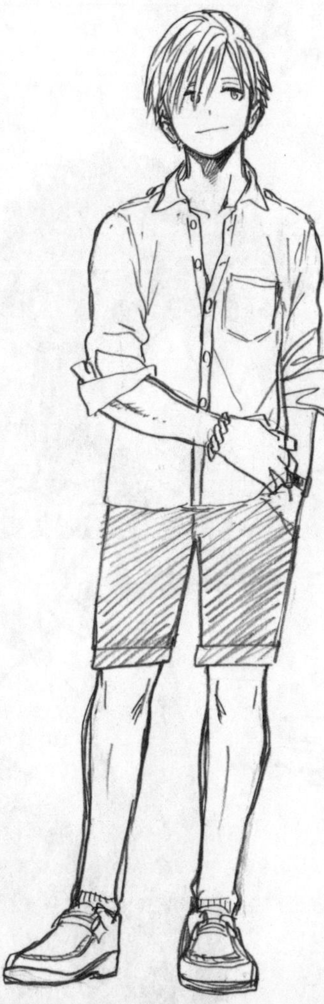

Birthday: 5/13
Height: 170 cm
Favorite Things: French cooking, Franco-Belgian comics

BEHIND THE SCENES

I usually don't base my characters on real-life people, but this guy alone is an exception. Not sure why anyone would really care, though.

He's super unlikable, but as the unofficial spokesperson for Class B, the spotlight is on him for the time being. He's not class president, though. Those classmates of his who didn't agree with his strategy in the obstacle race (to intentionally place somewhat low) ended up placing highly. He was thinking of the good of all of Class B when he came up with the plan to rip Class A off their high horses, and that's mostly because all he knew about Class A came from Tetsutetsu's report and Katsuki's opening statement. So I guess he's not really a bad guy, but I somehow went and made him unlikable anyway. What a waste. As far as Katsuki's concerned, Monoma is a war criminal.

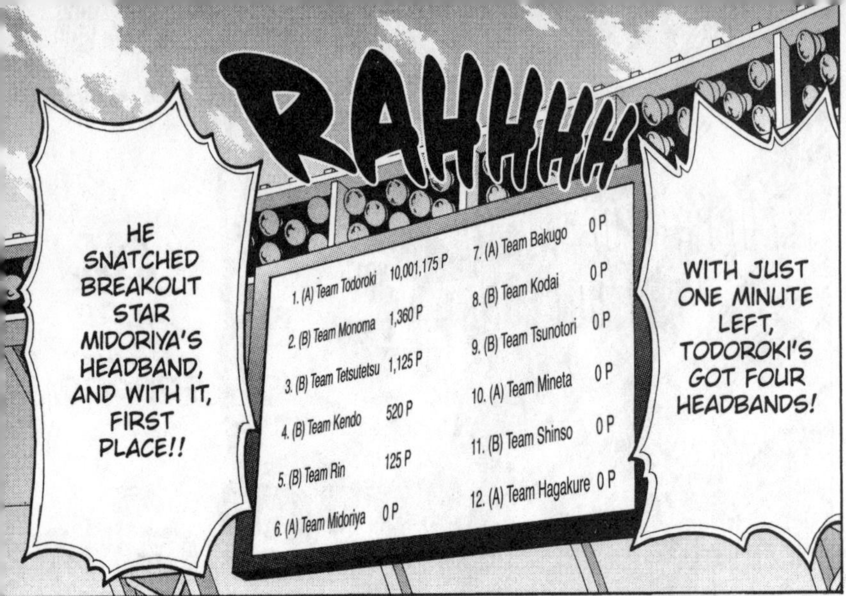
RAHHHH
WITH JUST ONE MINUTE LEFT, TODOROKI'S GOT FOUR HEADBANDS!
1. (A) Team Todoroki 10,001,175 P
2. (B) Team Monoma 1,360 P
3. (B) Team Tetsutetsu 1,125 P
4. (B) Team Kendo 520 P
5. (B) Team Rin 125 P
6. (A) Team Midoriya 0 P
7. (A) Team Bakugo 0 P
8. (B) Team Kodai 0 P
9. (B) Team Tsunotori 0 P
10. (A) Team Mineta 0 P
11. (B) Team Shinso 0 P
12. (A) Team Hagakure 0 P
HE SNATCHED BREAKOUT STAR MIDORIYA'S HEADBAND, AND WITH IT, FIRST PLACE!!

NO.30 - CAVALRY-MATCH FINALE

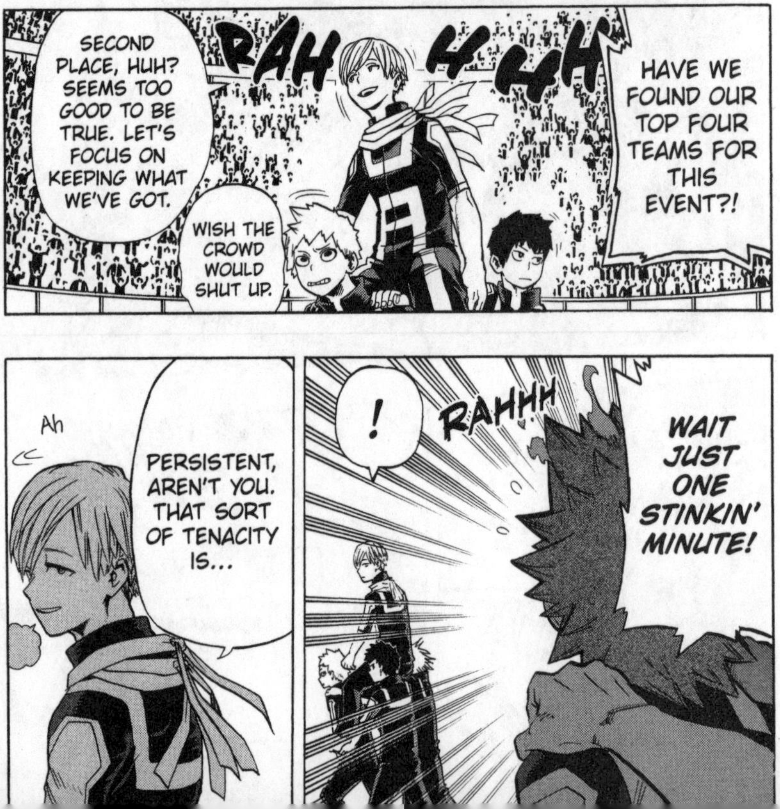
HAVE WE FOUND OUR TOP FOUR TEAMS FOR THIS EVENT?!
RAH HHH
SECOND PLACE, HUH? SEEMS TOO GOOD TO BE TRUE. LET'S FOCUS ON KEEPING WHAT WE'VE GOT.
WISH THE CROWD WOULD SHUT UP.
WAIT JUST ONE STINKIN' MINUTE!
RAHHH
!
Ah
PERSISTENT, AREN'T YOU. THAT SORT OF TENACITY IS...

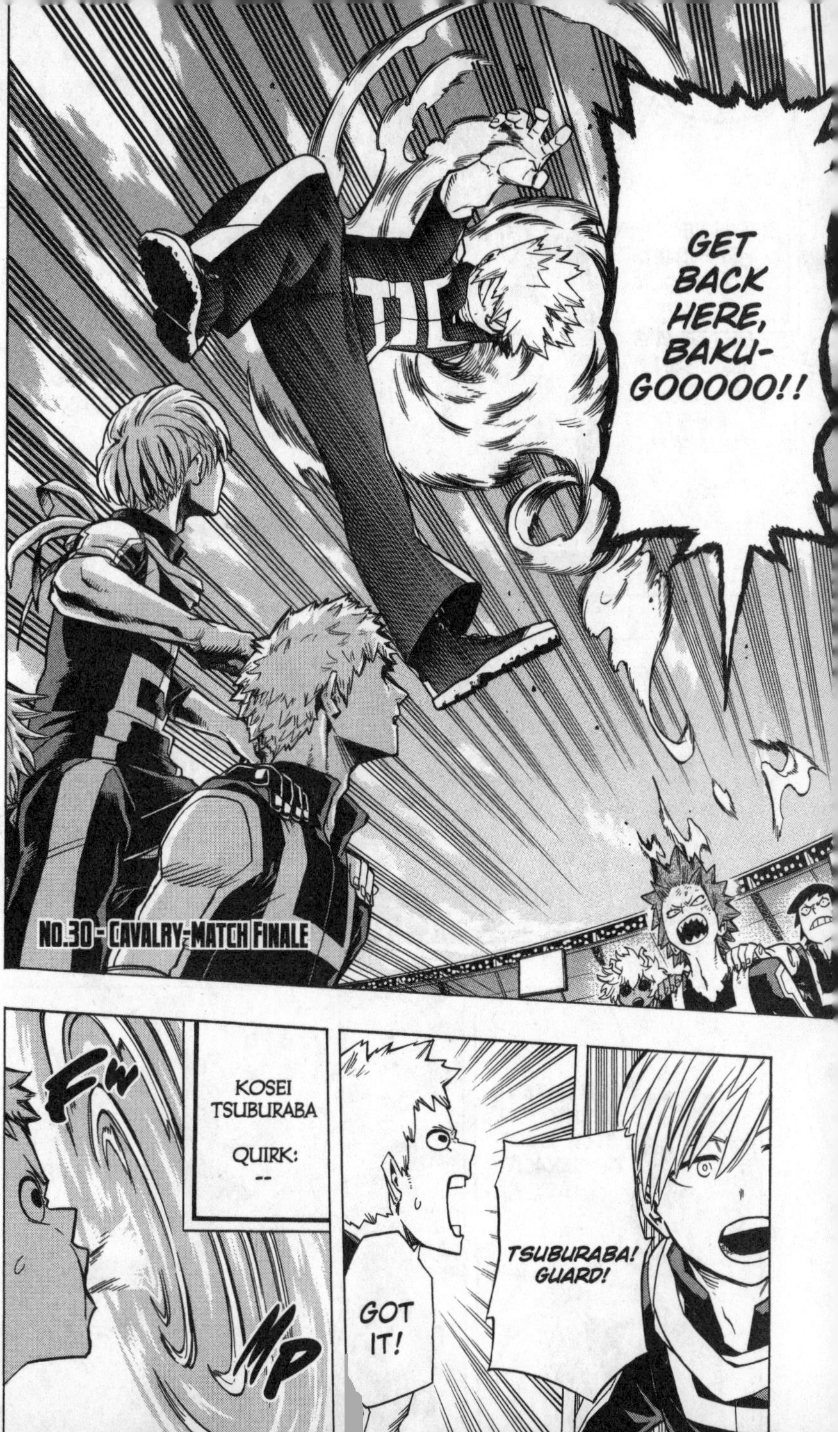
GET BACK HERE, BAKU-GOOOOO!!
No.30 - Cavalry-Match Finale
TSUBURABA! GUARD!
GOT IT!
KOSEI TSUBURABA
QUIRK:
--
FW
MP

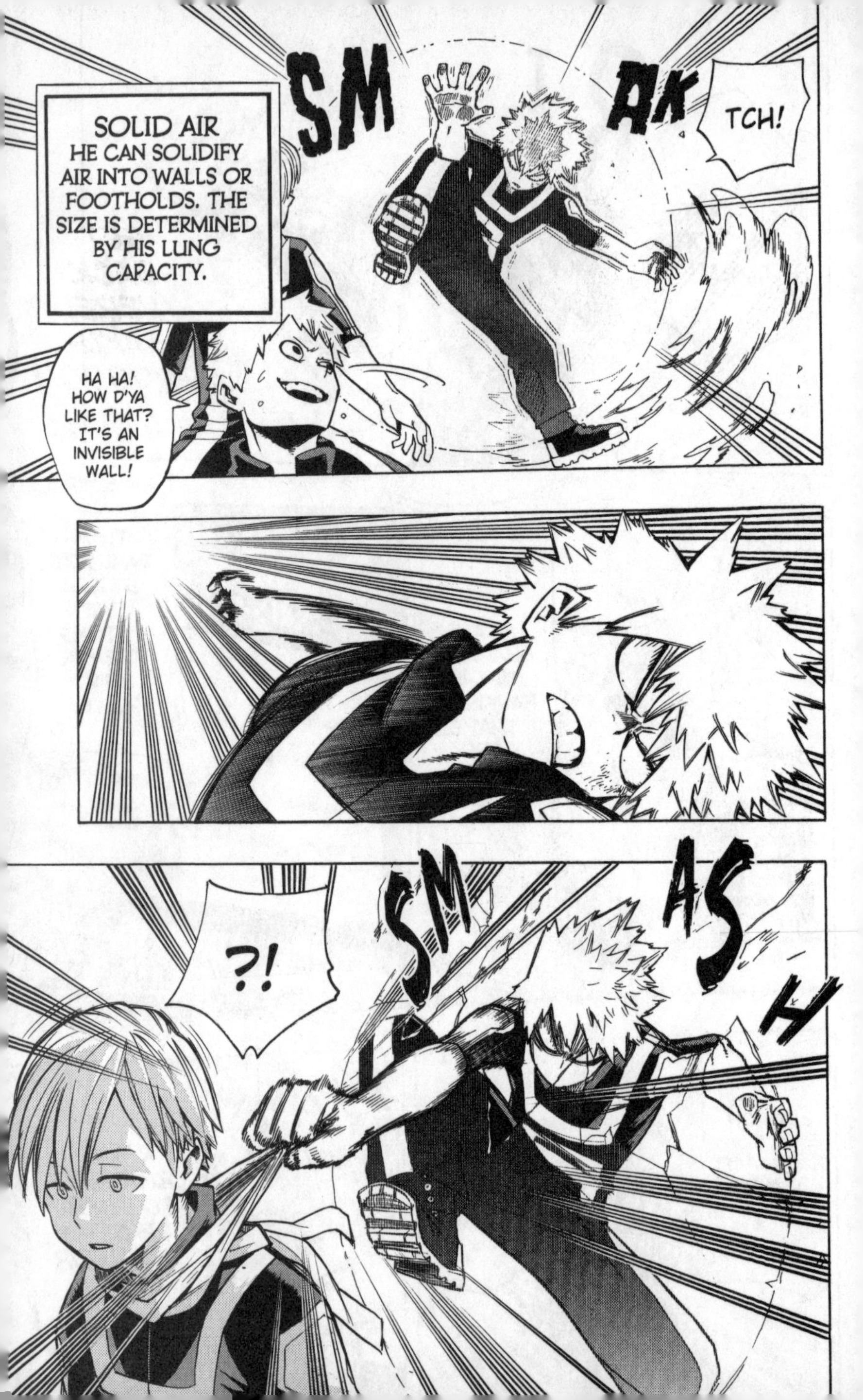
TCH!
SM AK
SOLID AIR
HE CAN SOLIDIFY AIR INTO WALLS OR FOOTHOLDS. THE SIZE IS DETERMINED BY HIS LUNG CAPACITY.
HA HA! HOW D'YA LIKE THAT? IT'S AN INVISIBLE WALL!
SM AS H
?!

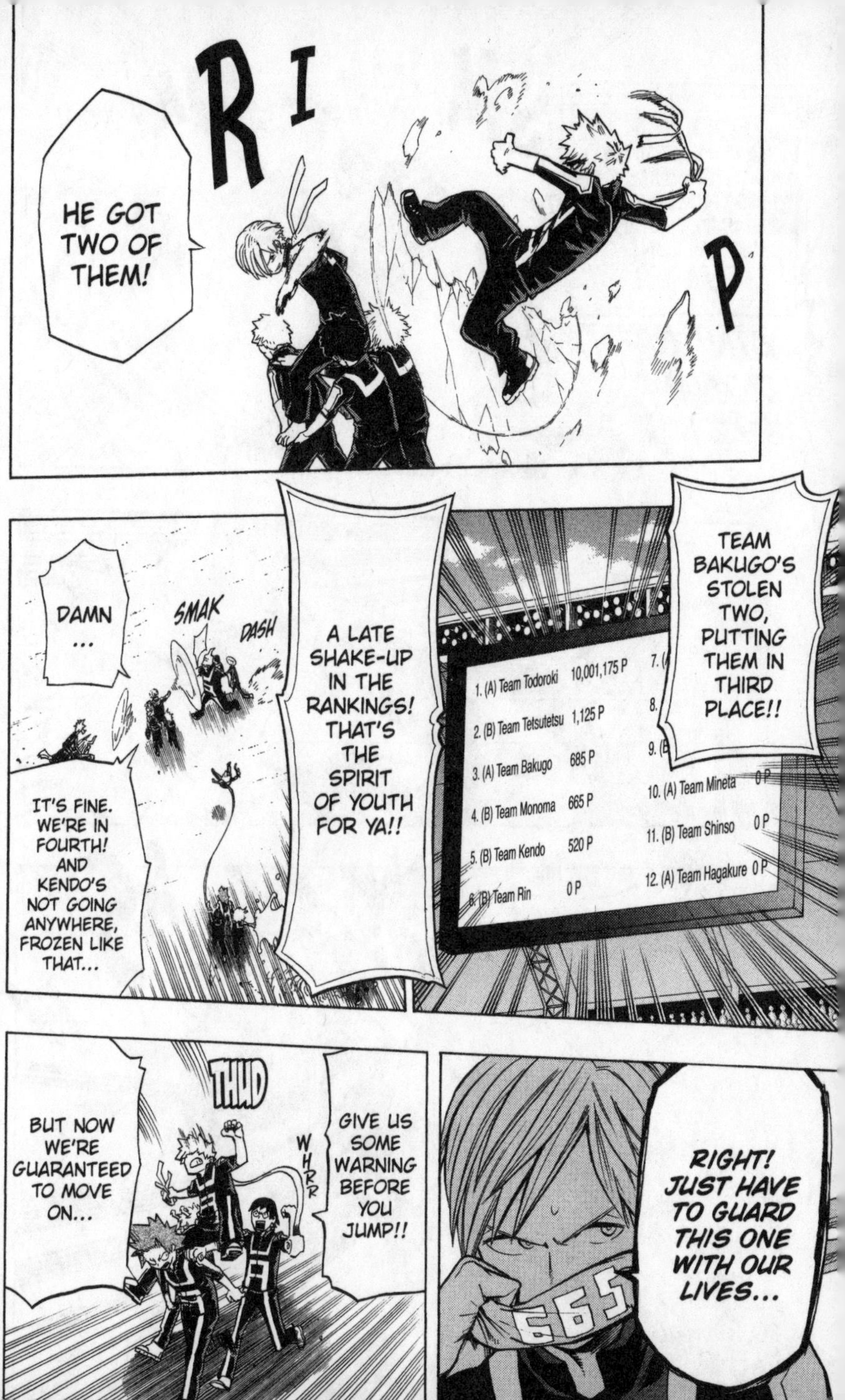
R
I
HE GOT TWO OF THEM!
P
TEAM BAKUGO'S STOLEN TWO, PUTTING THEM IN THIRD PLACE!!
A LATE SHAKE-UP IN THE RANKINGS! THAT'S THE SPIRIT OF YOUTH FOR YA!!
1. (A) Team Todoroki 10,001,175 P
2. (B) Team Tetsutetsu 1,125 P
3. (A) Team Bakugo 685 P
4. (B) Team Monoma 665 P
5. (B) Team Kendo 520 P
6. (B) Team Rin 0 P
10. (A) Team Mineta 0 P
11. (B) Team Shinso 0 P
12. (A) Team Hagakure 0 P
DAMN...
SMAK
DASH
IT'S FINE. WE'RE IN FOURTH! AND KENDO'S NOT GOING ANYWHERE, FROZEN LIKE THAT...
RIGHT! JUST HAVE TO GUARD THIS ONE WITH OUR LIVES...
665
THUD
GIVE US SOME WARNING BEFORE YOU JUMP!!
WHRR
BUT NOW WE'RE GUARANTEED TO MOVE ON...

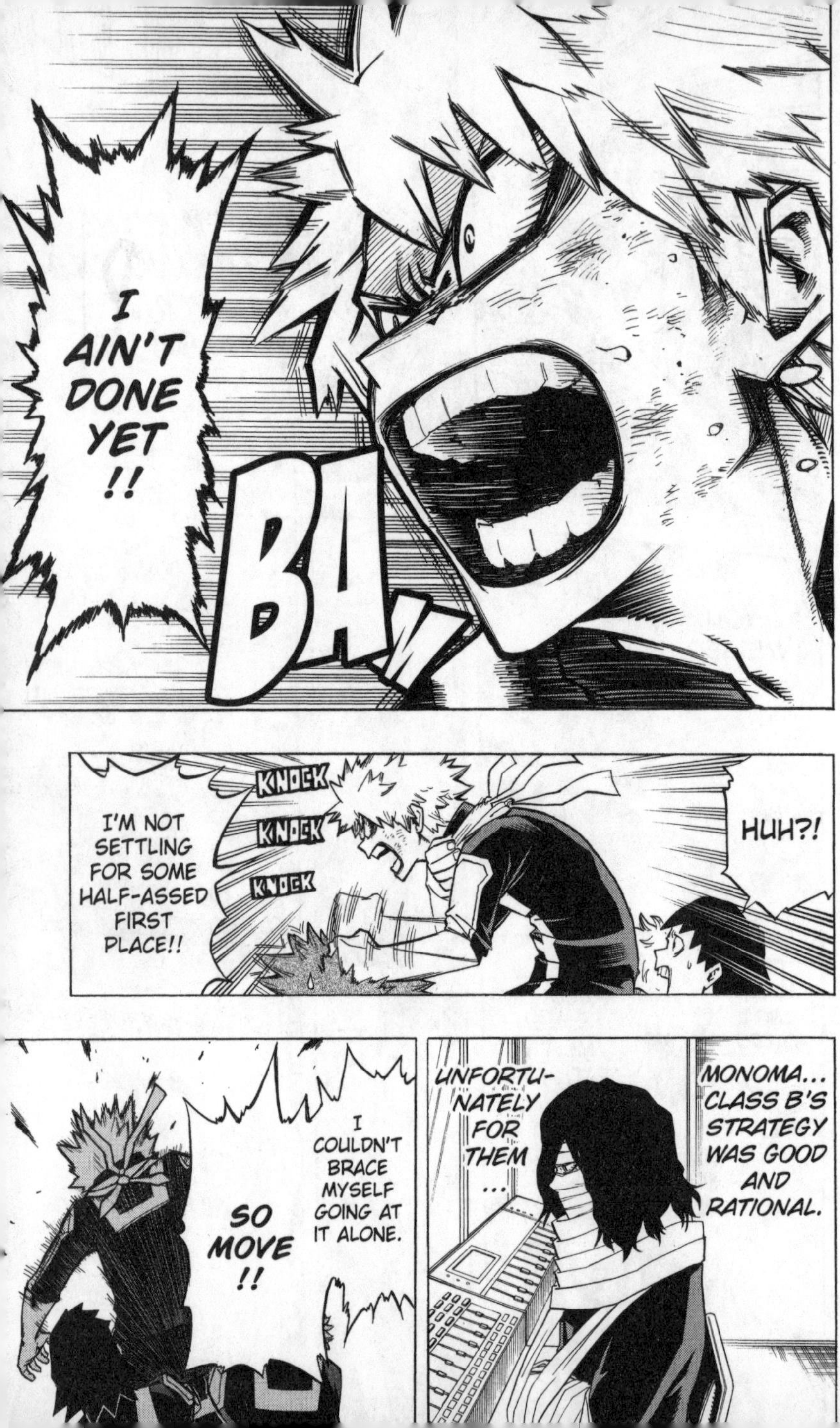
I AIN'T DONE YET!!
BAM
HUH?!
KNOCK
KNOCK
KNOCK
I'M NOT SETTLING FOR SOME HALF-ASSED FIRST PLACE!!
MONOMA... CLASS B'S STRATEGY WAS GOOD AND RATIONAL.
UNFORTUNATELY FOR THEM...
I COULDN'T BRACE MYSELF GOING AT IT ALONE.
SO MOVE!!

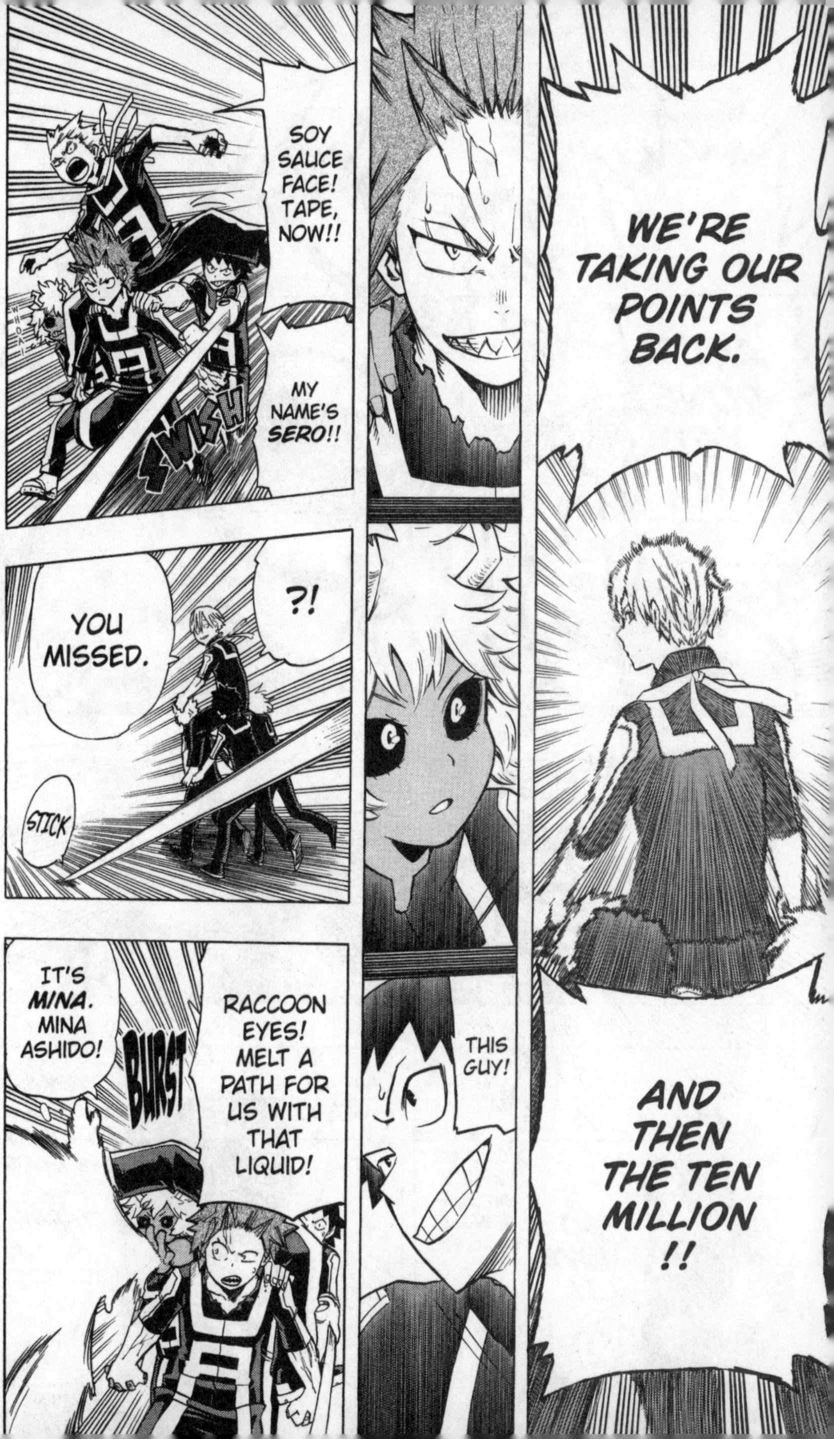
WE'RE TAKING OUR POINTS BACK.
AND THEN THE TEN MILLION!!
SOY SAUCE FACE! TAPE, NOW!!
WHOA!
MY NAME'S SERO!!
SWISH
?!
YOU MISSED.
STICK
THIS GUY!
RACCOON EYES! MELT A PATH FOR US WITH THAT LIQUID!
BURST
IT'S MINA. MINA ASHIDO!

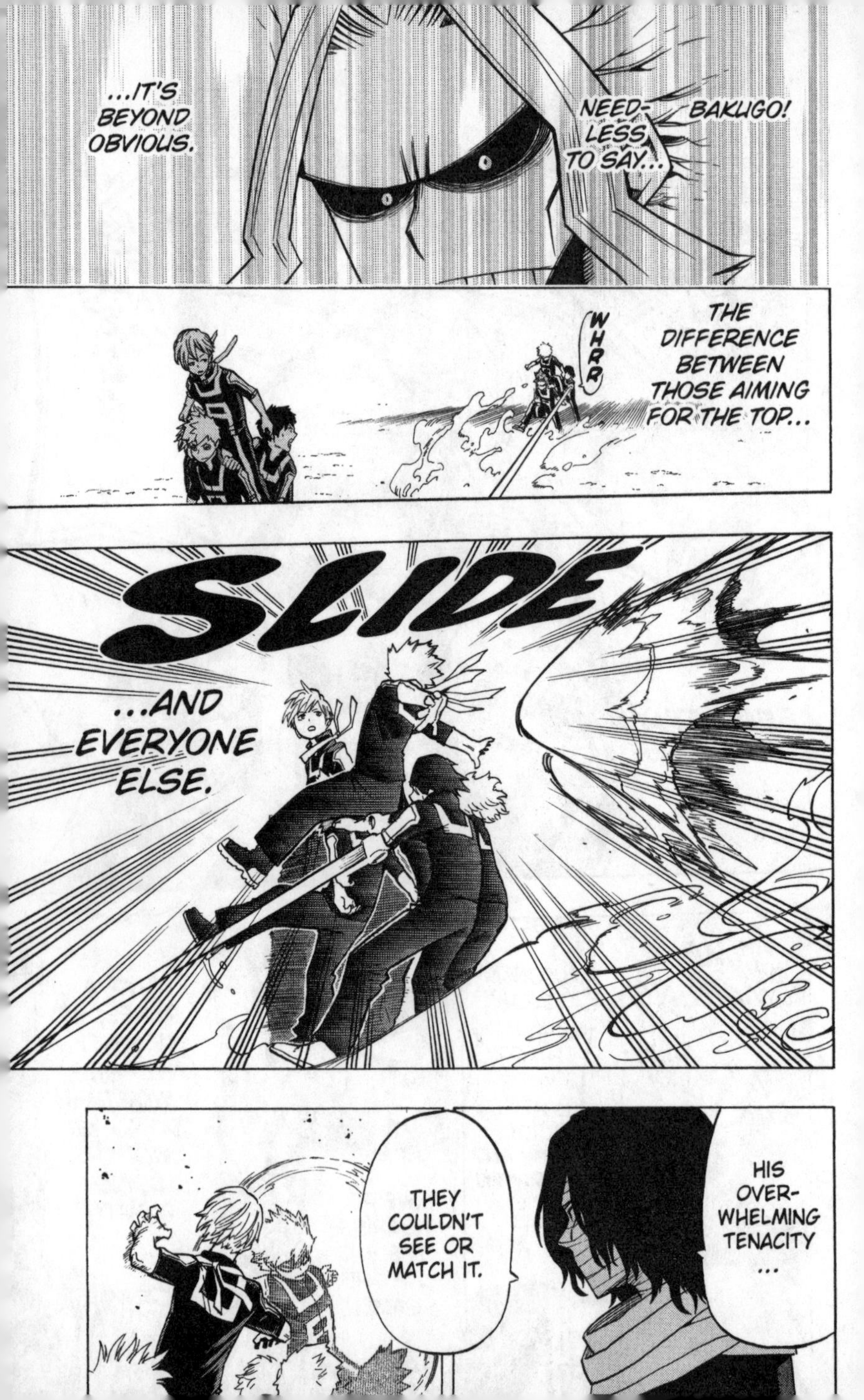
BAKUGO!
NEED-LESS TO SAY...
...IT'S BEYOND OBVIOUS.
THE DIFFERENCE BETWEEN THOSE AIMING FOR THE TOP...
WHRR
SLIDE
...AND EVERYONE ELSE.
HIS OVER-WHELMING TENACITY ...
THEY COULDN'T SEE OR MATCH IT.

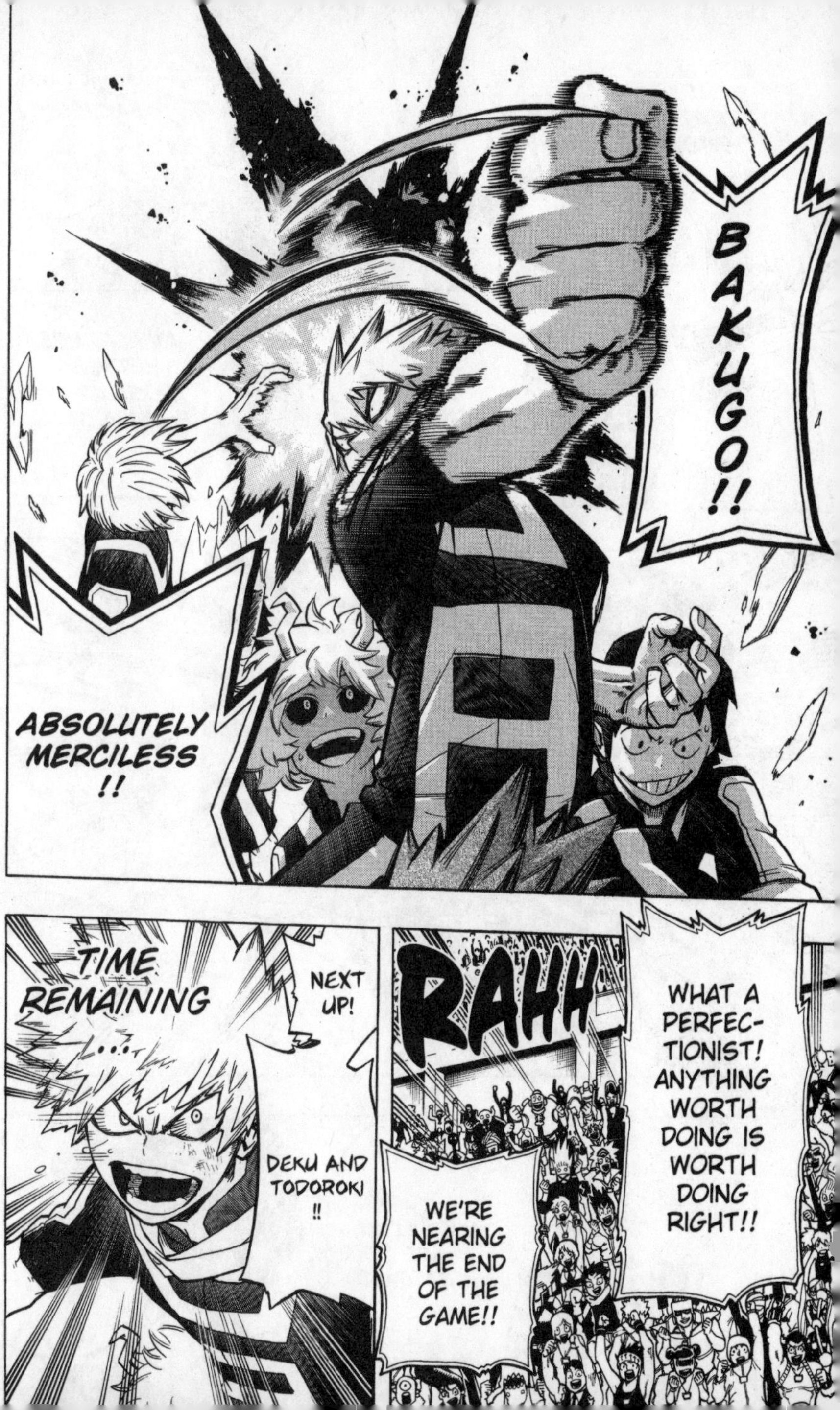
BAKUGO!!
ABSOLUTELY MERCILESS!!
WHAT A PERFECTIONIST! ANYTHING WORTH DOING IS WORTH DOING RIGHT!!
RAHH
WE'RE NEARING THE END OF THE GAME!!
NEXT UP!
TIME REMAINING
...
DEKU AND TODOROKI!!

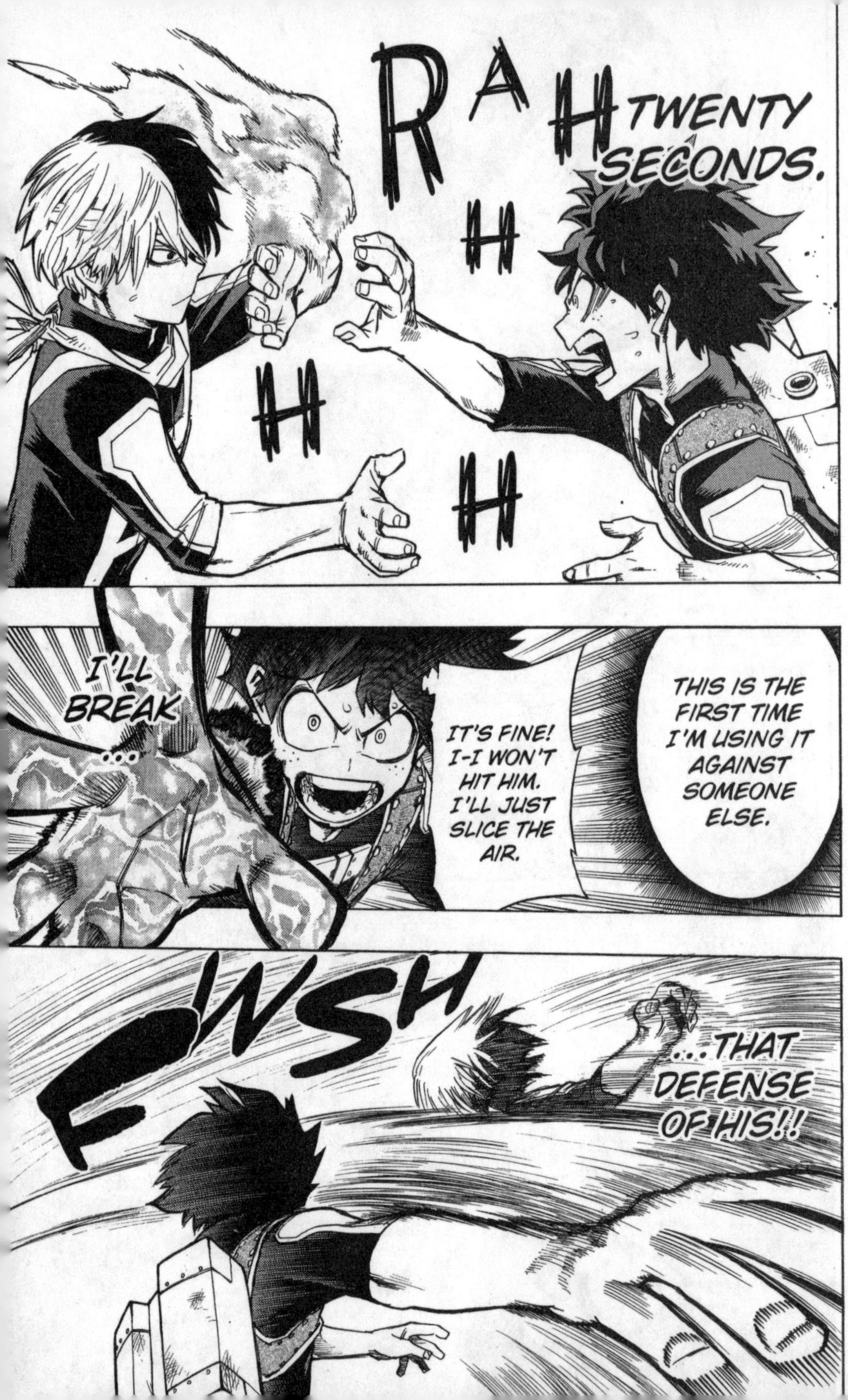
TWENTY SECONDS.
RAHHHH
THIS IS THE FIRST TIME I'M USING IT AGAINST SOMEONE ELSE.
IT'S FINE! I-I WON'T HIT HIM. I'LL JUST SLICE THE AIR.
I'LL BREAK...
...THAT DEFENSE OF HIS!!
FWSH

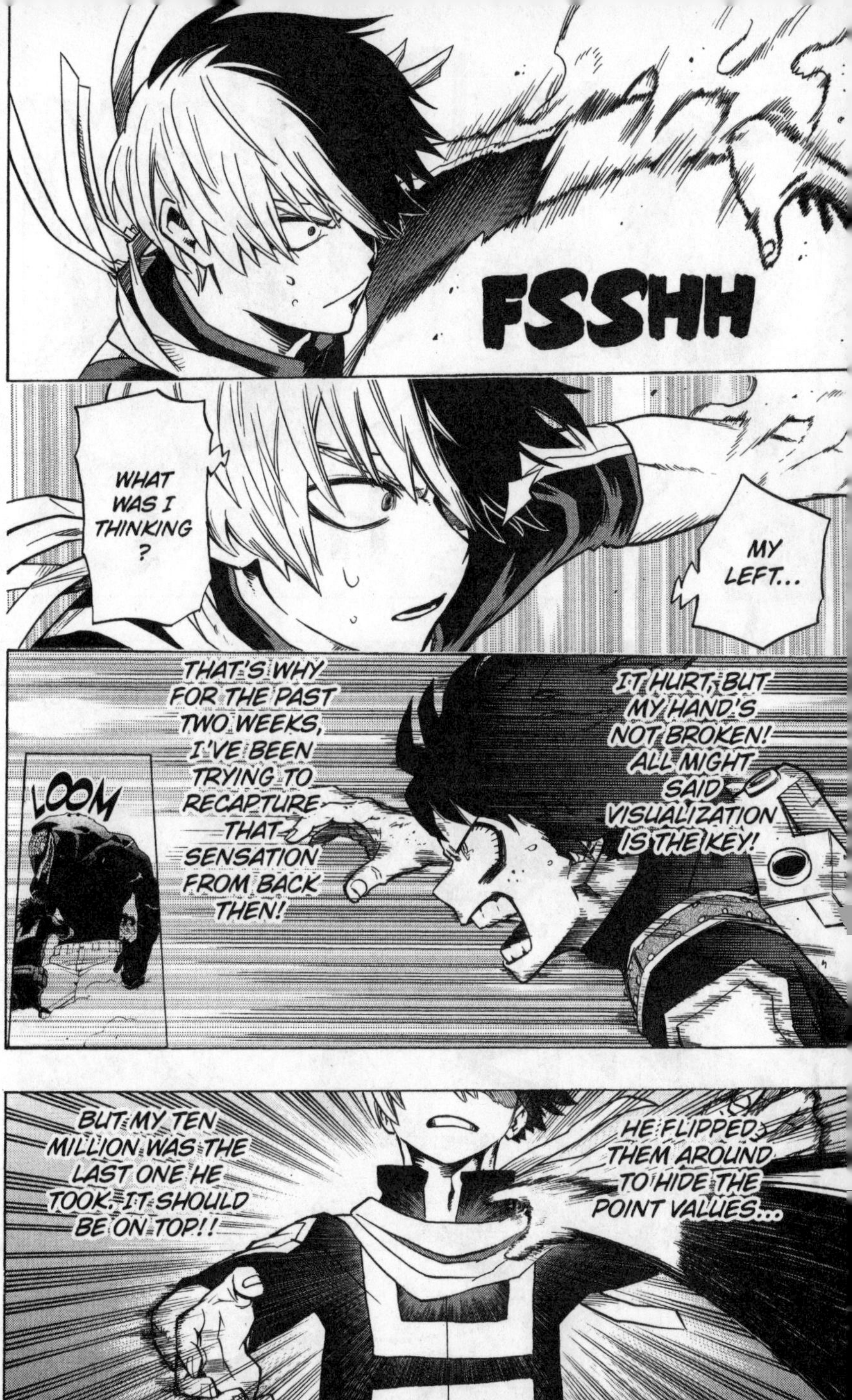
FSSHH
MY LEFT...
WHAT WAS I THINKING?
IT HURT, BUT MY HAND'S NOT BROKEN! ALL MIGHT SAID VISUALIZATION IS THE KEY!
THAT'S WHY FOR THE PAST TWO WEEKS, I'VE BEEN TRYING TO RECAPTURE THAT SENSATION FROM BACK THEN!
LOOM
HE FLIPPED THEM AROUND TO HIDE THE POINT VALUES...
BUT MY TEN MILLION WAS THE LAST ONE HE TOOK. IT SHOULD BE ON TOP!!

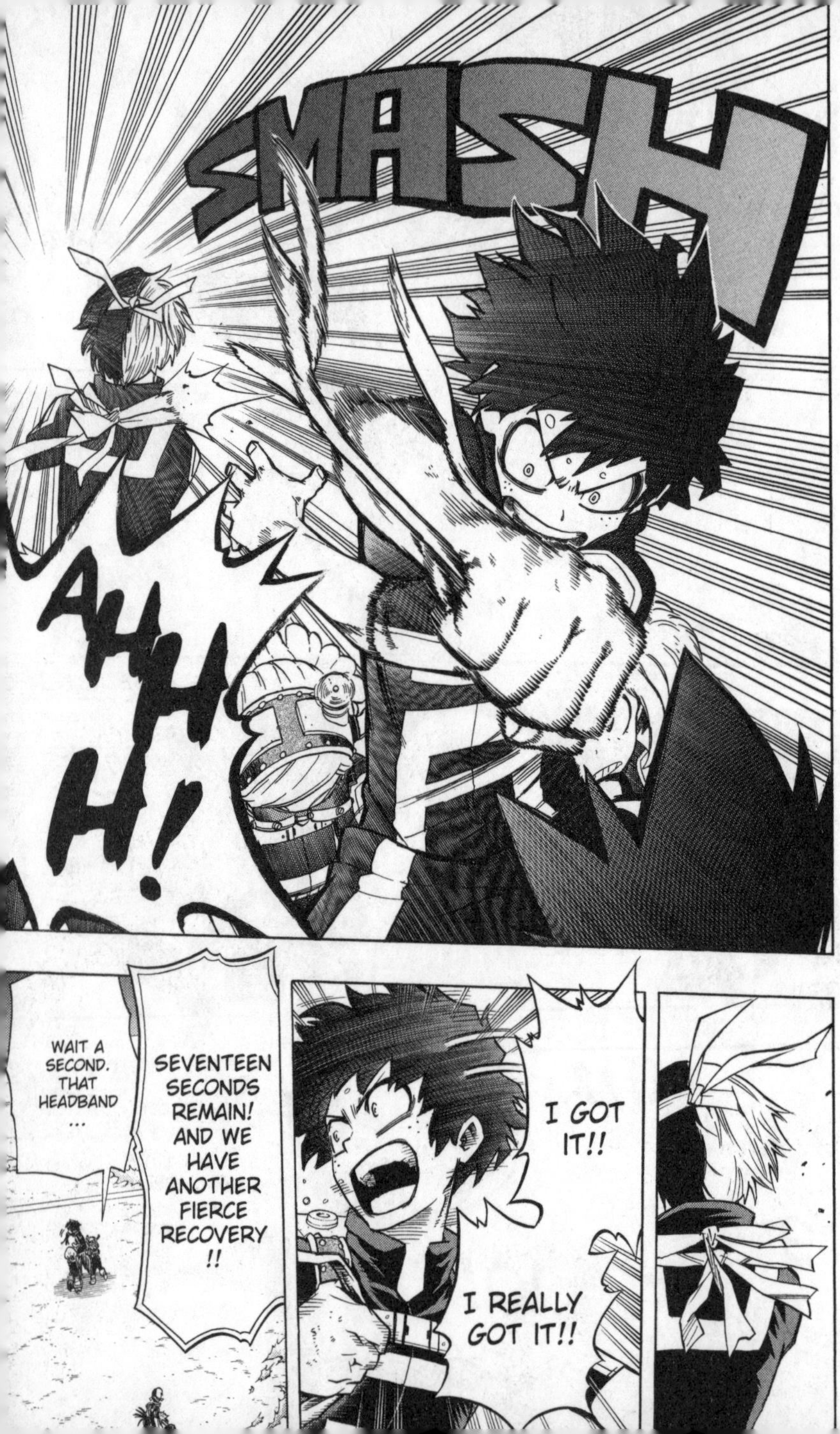
SMASH
AHHHH!
I GOT IT!!
I REALLY GOT IT!!
SEVENTEEN SECONDS REMAIN! AND WE HAVE ANOTHER FIERCE RECOVERY!!
WAIT A SECOND. THAT HEADBAND...

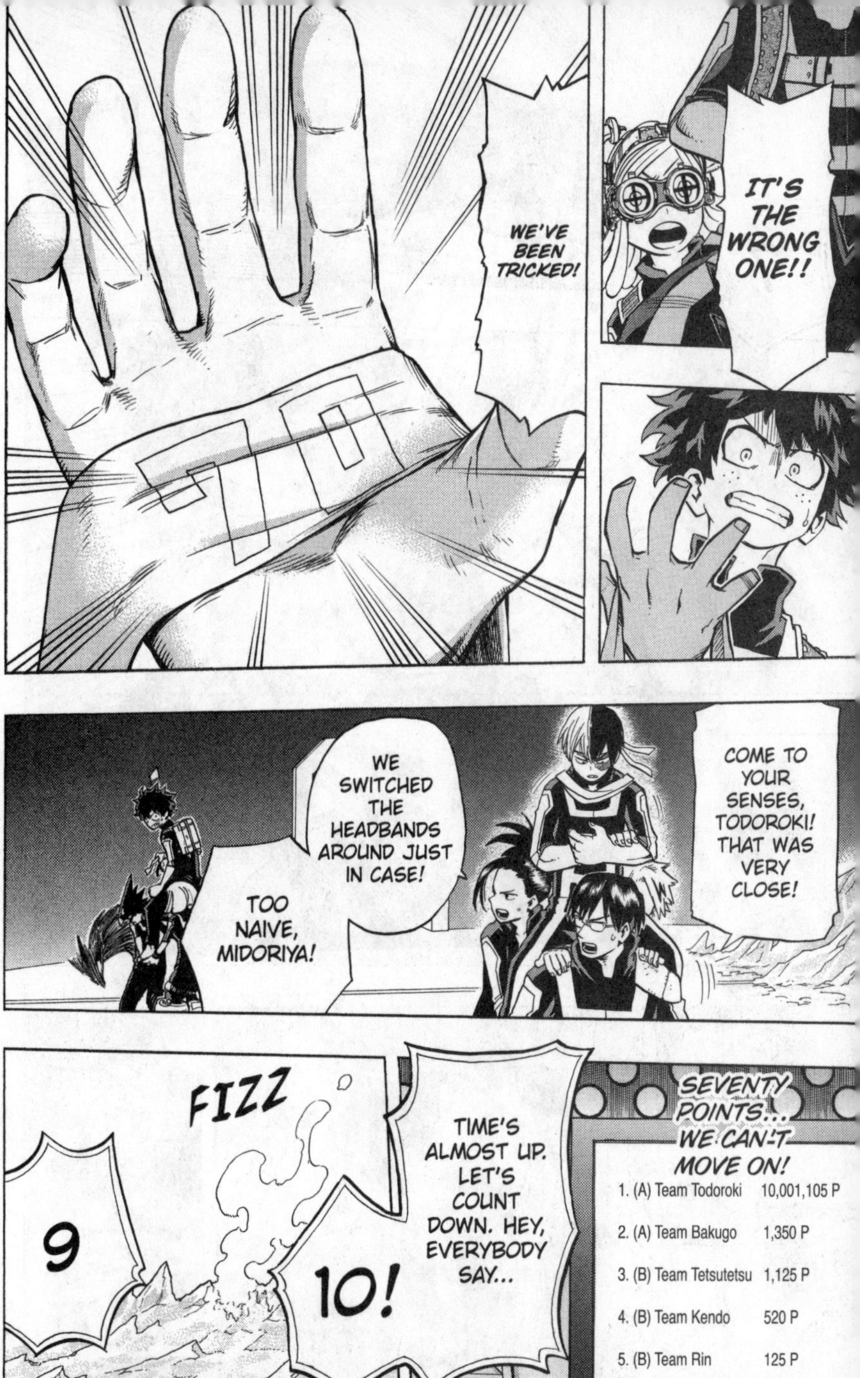
IT'S THE WRONG ONE!!
WE'VE BEEN TRICKED!
COME TO YOUR SENSES, TODOROKI! THAT WAS VERY CLOSE!
WE SWITCHED THE HEADBANDS AROUND JUST IN CASE!
TOO NAIVE, MIDORIYA!
SEVENTY POINTS... WE CAN'T MOVE ON!
1. (A) Team Todoroki 10,001,105 P
2. (A) Team Bakugo 1,350 P
3. (B) Team Tetsutetsu 1,125 P
4. (B) Team Kendo 520 P
5. (B) Team Rin 125 P
6. (A) Team Midoriya 70 P
TIME'S ALMOST UP. LET'S COUNT DOWN. HEY, EVERYBODY SAY...
10!
FIZZ
9

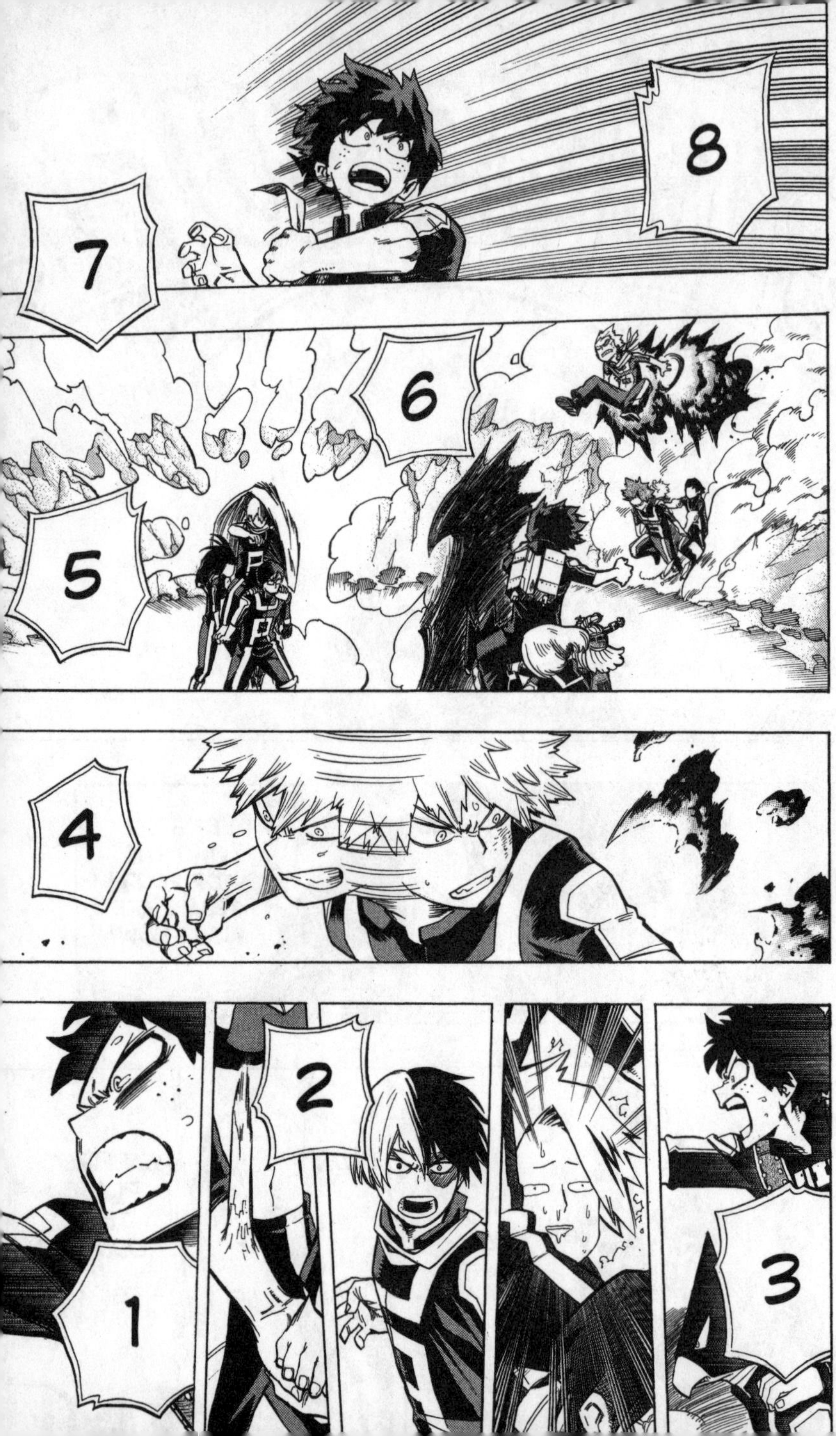
1
2
3
4
5
6
7
8

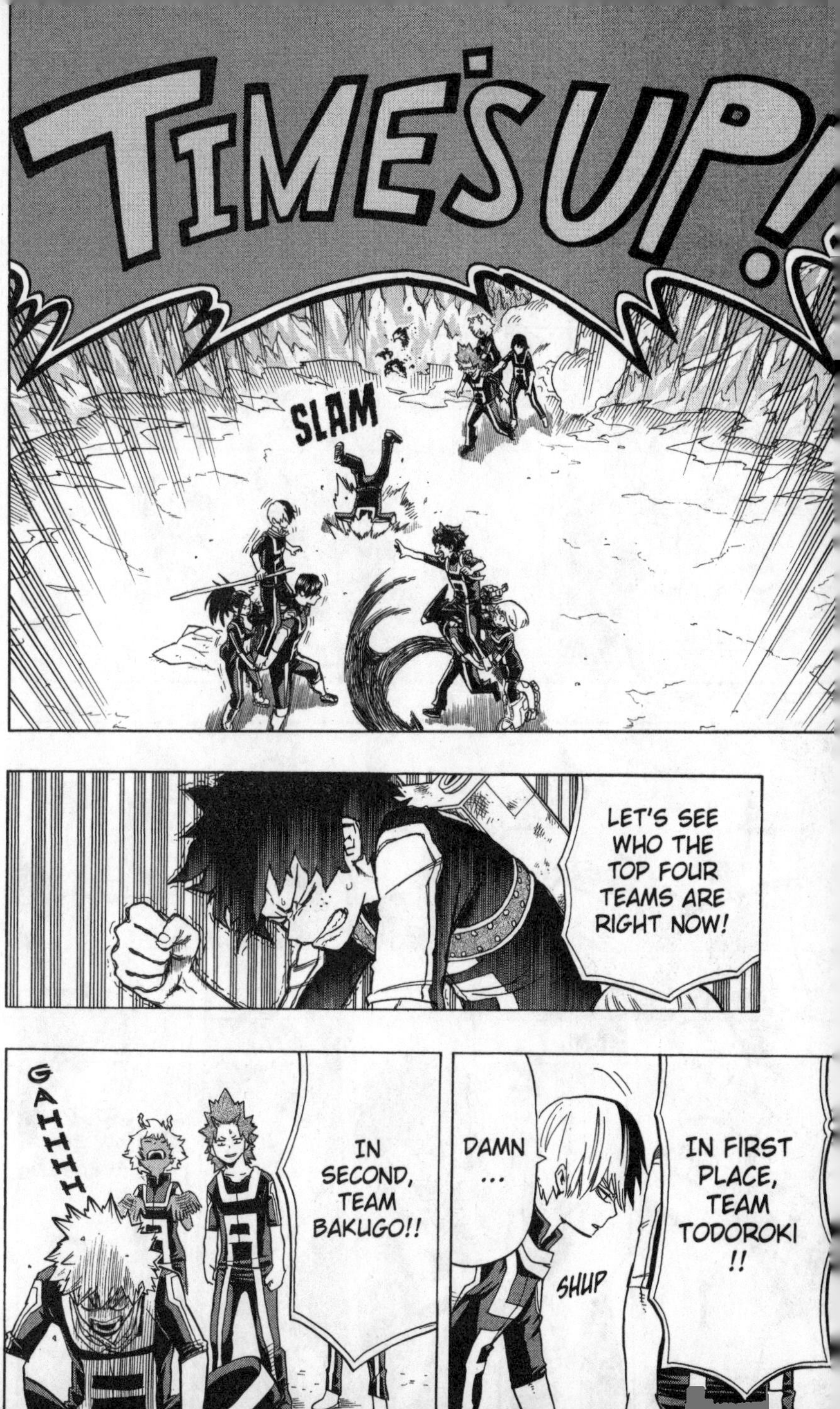
TIME'S UP!!
SLAM
LET'S SEE WHO THE TOP FOUR TEAMS ARE RIGHT NOW!
IN FIRST PLACE, TEAM TODOROKI!!
DAMN...
SHUP
IN SECOND, TEAM BAKUGO!!
GAHHHH

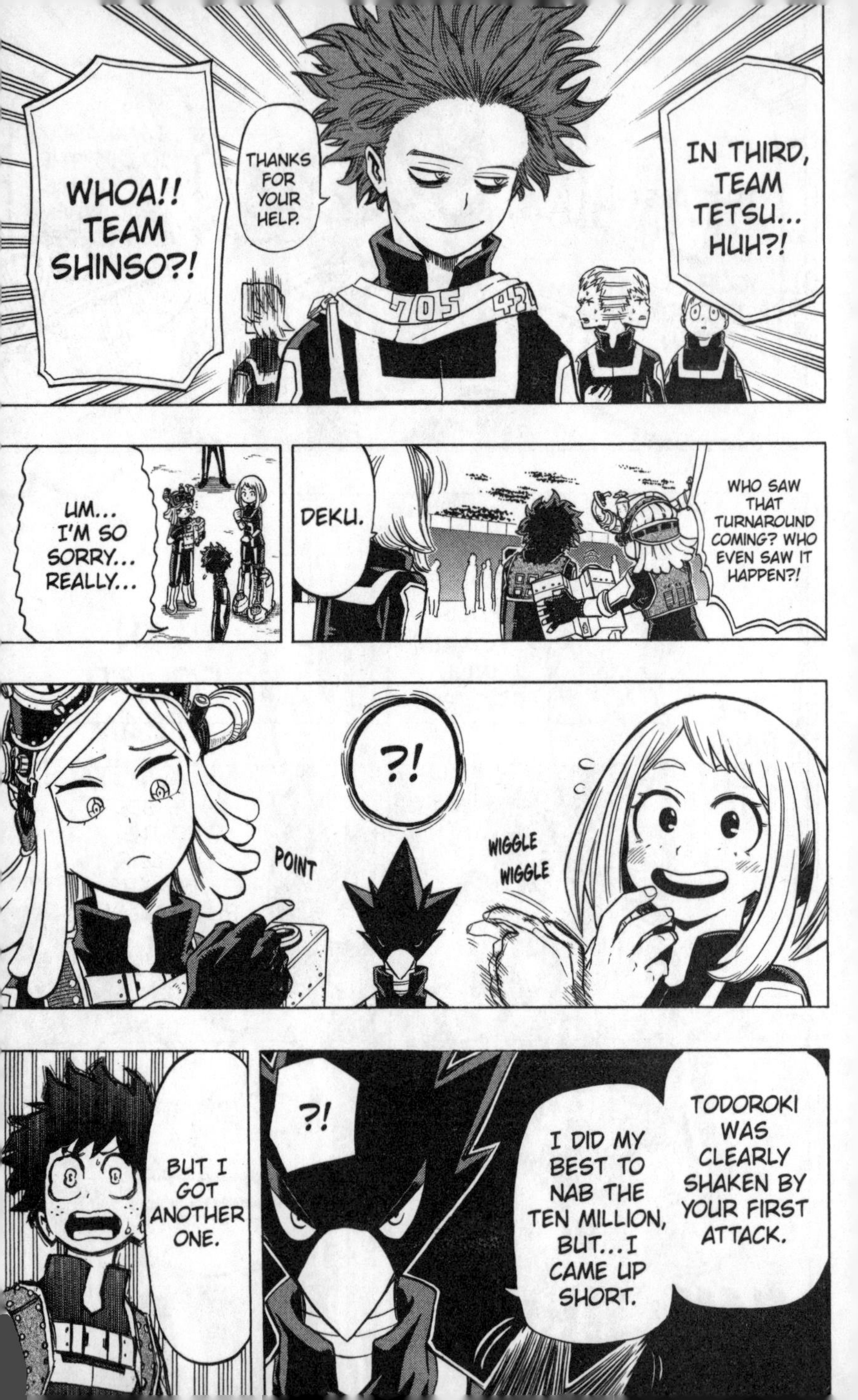

IN THIRD, TEAM TETSU... HUH?!
THANKS FOR YOUR HELP.
WHOA!! TEAM SHINSO?!
WHO SAW THAT TURNAROUND COMING? WHO EVEN SAW IT HAPPEN?!
DEKU.
UM... I'M SO SORRY... REALLY...
WIGGLE WIGGLE
?!
POINT
TODOROKI WAS CLEARLY SHAKEN BY YOUR FIRST ATTACK.
I DID MY BEST TO NAB THE TEN MILLION, BUT...I CAME UP SHORT.
?!
BUT I GOT ANOTHER ONE.

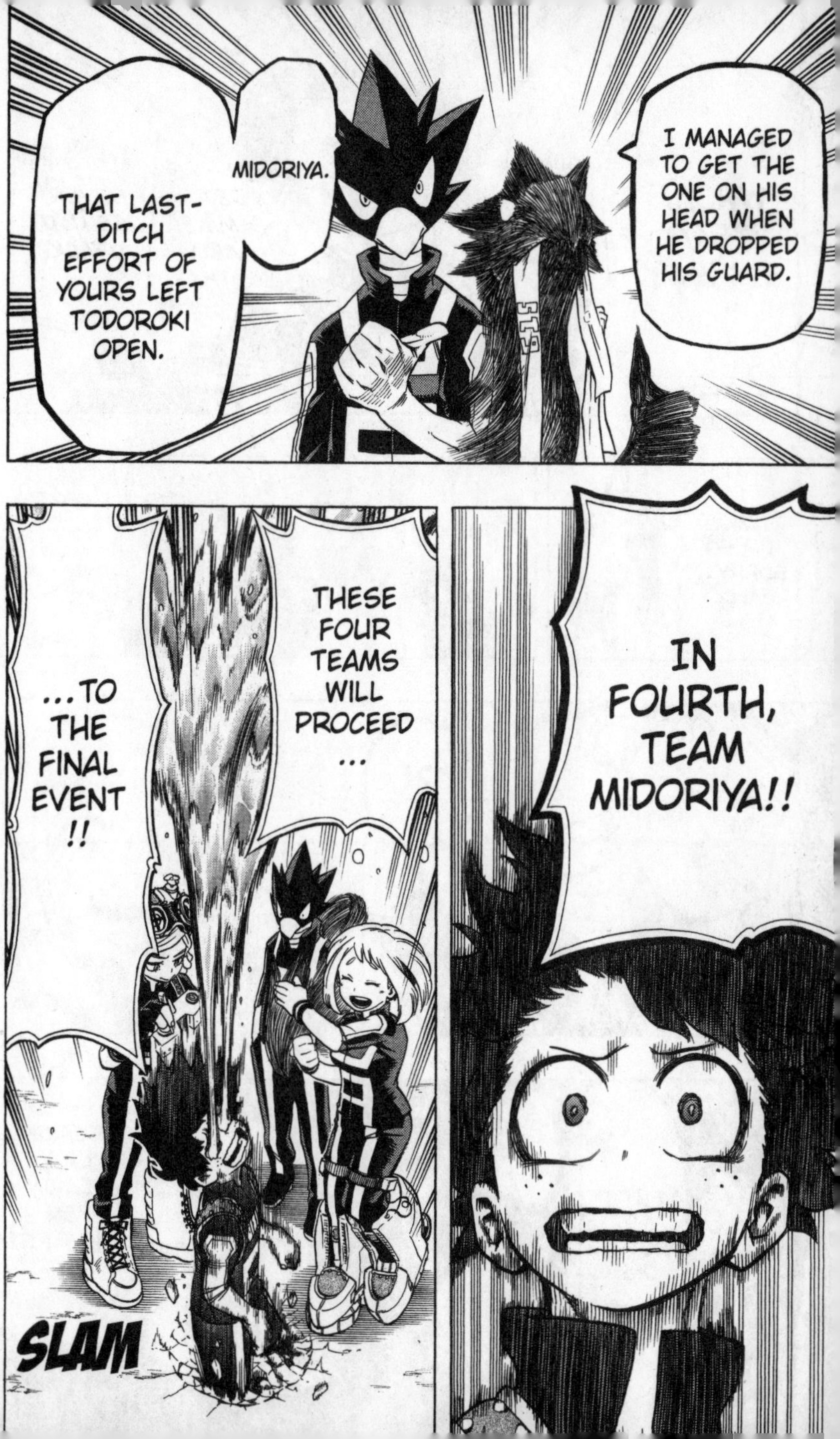
MIDORIYA.
THAT LAST-DITCH EFFORT OF YOURS LEFT TODOROKI OPEN.
I MANAGED TO GET THE ONE ON HIS HEAD WHEN HE DROPPED HIS GUARD.
IN FOURTH, TEAM MIDORIYA!!
THESE FOUR TEAMS WILL PROCEED...
...TO THE FINAL EVENT!!
SLAM

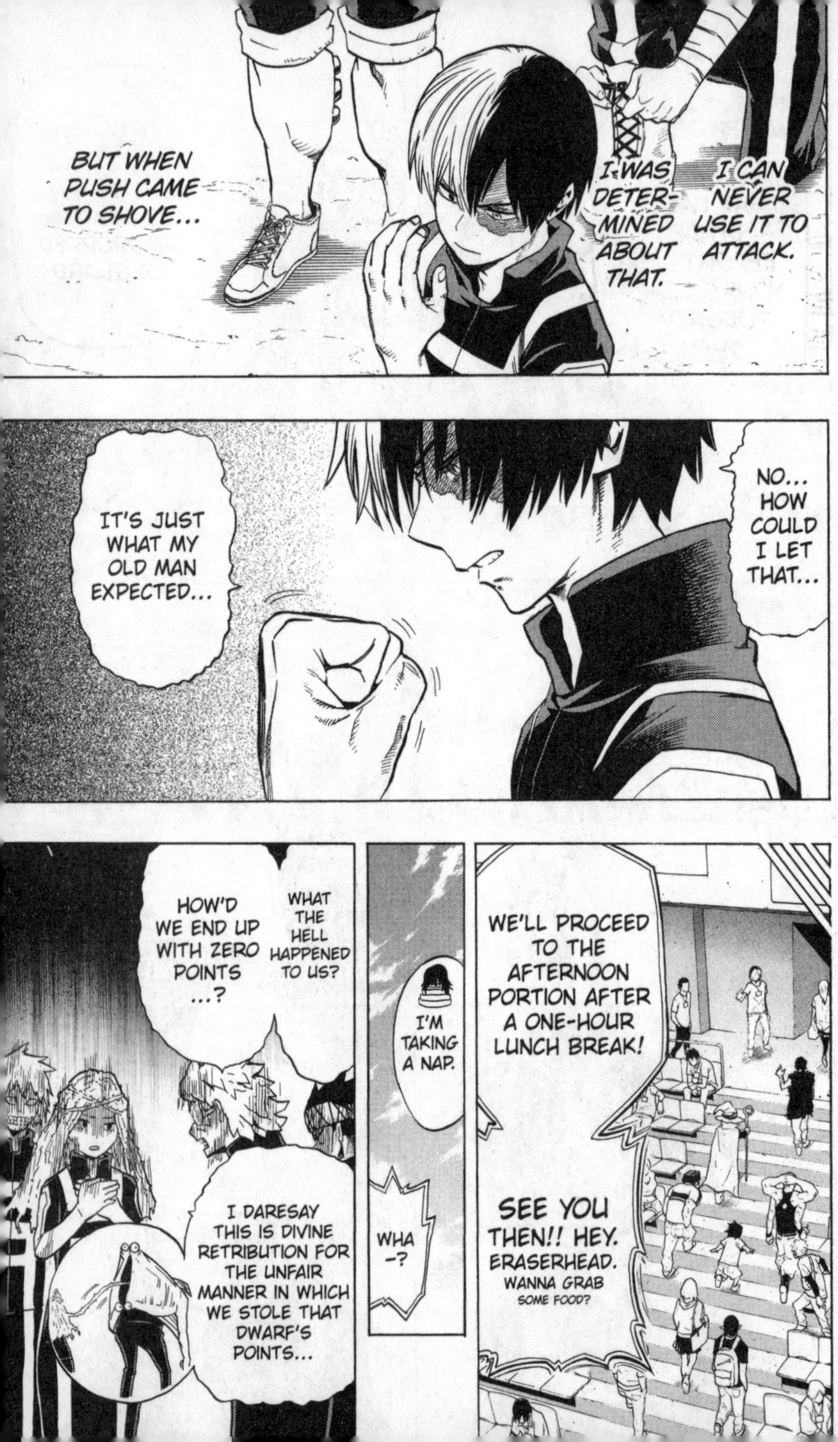
I CAN NEVER USE IT TO ATTACK.
I WAS DETERMINED ABOUT THAT.
BUT WHEN PUSH CAME TO SHOVE...
NO... HOW COULD I LET THAT...
IT'S JUST WHAT MY OLD MAN EXPECTED...
WE'LL PROCEED TO THE AFTERNOON PORTION AFTER A ONE-HOUR LUNCH BREAK!
SEE YOU THEN!! HEY. ERASERHEAD. WANNA GRAB SOME FOOD?
I'M TAKING A NAP.
WHA —?
WHAT THE HELL HAPPENED TO US?
HOW'D WE END UP WITH ZERO POINTS ...?
I DARESAY THIS IS DIVINE RETRIBUTION FOR THE UNFAIR MANNER IN WHICH WE STOLE THAT DWARF'S POINTS...

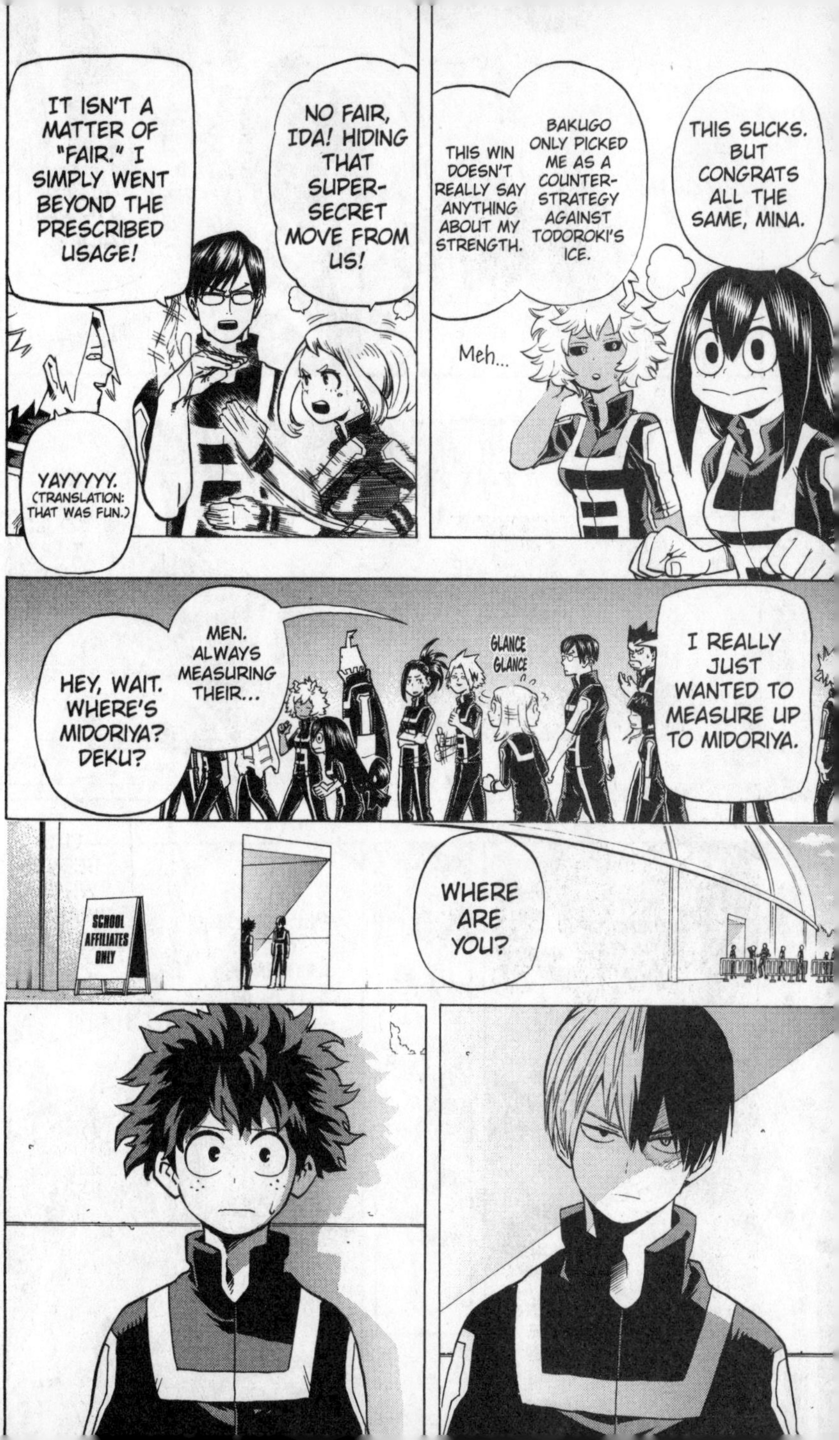
THIS SUCKS. BUT CONGRATS ALL THE SAME, MINA.
BAKUGO ONLY PICKED ME AS A COUNTER-STRATEGY AGAINST TODOROKI'S ICE.
THIS WIN DOESN'T REALLY SAY ANYTHING ABOUT MY STRENGTH.
Meh...
NO FAIR, IDA! HIDING THAT SUPER-SECRET MOVE FROM US!
IT ISN'T A MATTER OF "FAIR." I SIMPLY WENT BEYOND THE PRESCRIBED USAGE!
YAYYYYY. (TRANSLATION: THAT WAS FUN.)
I REALLY JUST WANTED TO MEASURE UP TO MIDORIYA.
GLANCE GLANCE
MEN. ALWAYS MEASURING THEIR...
HEY, WAIT. WHERE'S MIDORIYA? DEKU?
WHERE ARE YOU?
SCHOOL AFFILIATES ONLY

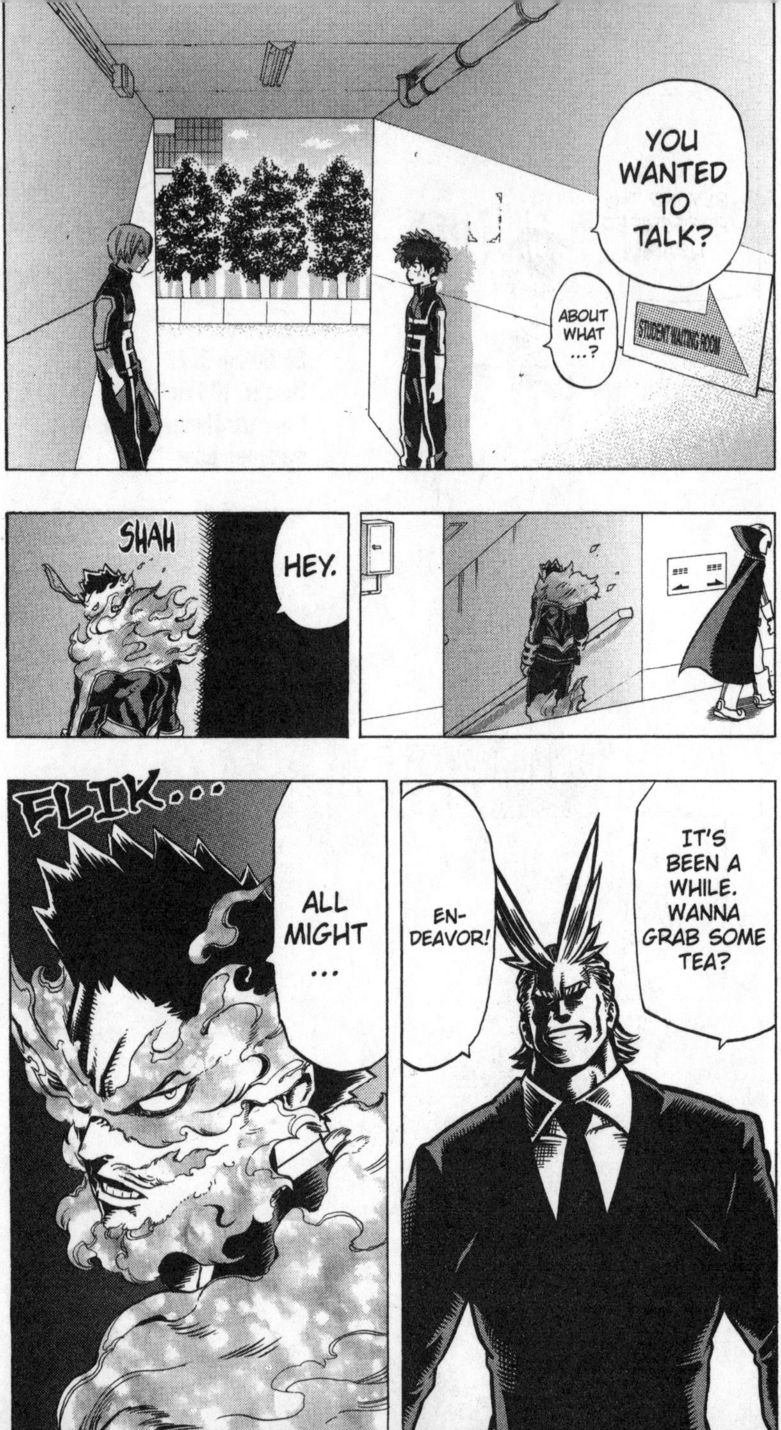
YOU WANTED TO TALK?
STUDENT WAITING ROOM
ABOUT WHAT ...?
SHAH
HEY.
IT'S BEEN A WHILE. WANNA GRAB SOME TEA?
EN-DEAVOR!
FLIK...
ALL MIGHT ...

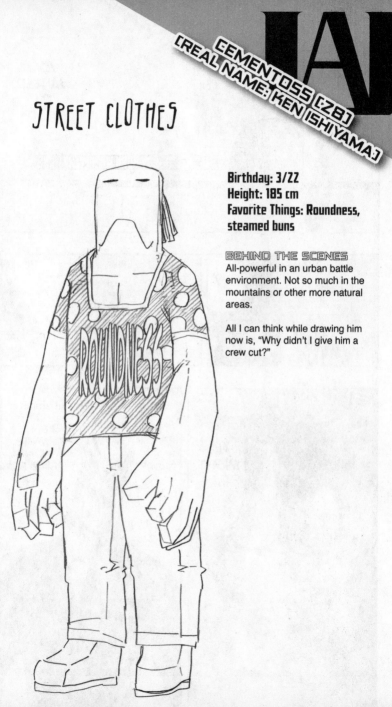

CEMENTOSS (28)
(REAL NAME: KEN ISHIYAMA)

STREET CLOTHES

ROUNDNESS

Birthday: 3/22
Height: 185 cm
Favorite Things: Roundness, steamed buns

BEHIND THE SCENES

All-powerful in an urban battle environment. Not so much in the mountains or other more natural areas.

All I can think while drawing him now is, "Why didn't I give him a crew cut?"

No. 31 - The Boy Born with Everything

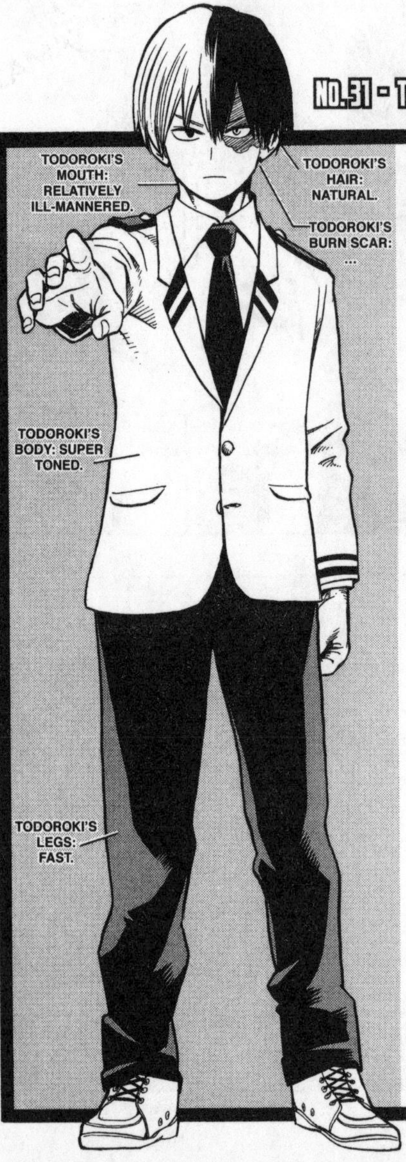
TODOROKI'S MOUTH: RELATIVELY ILL-MANNERED.
TODOROKI'S HAIR: NATURAL.
TODOROKI'S BURN SCAR: ...
TODOROKI'S BODY: SUPER TONED.
TODOROKI'S LEGS: FAST.

U.A. FILE.05

CLASS No.15 SHOTO TODOROKI

Quirk: Half-Cold, Half-Hot

He can freeze anything that touches the right half of his body! And his left half erupts with a blazing inferno!

He can give himself frostbite if he keeps freezing things for too long, so he has to use the heat on his left side to regulate his own body temperature. If he uses his left side for too long, well… what in tarnation would happen?!

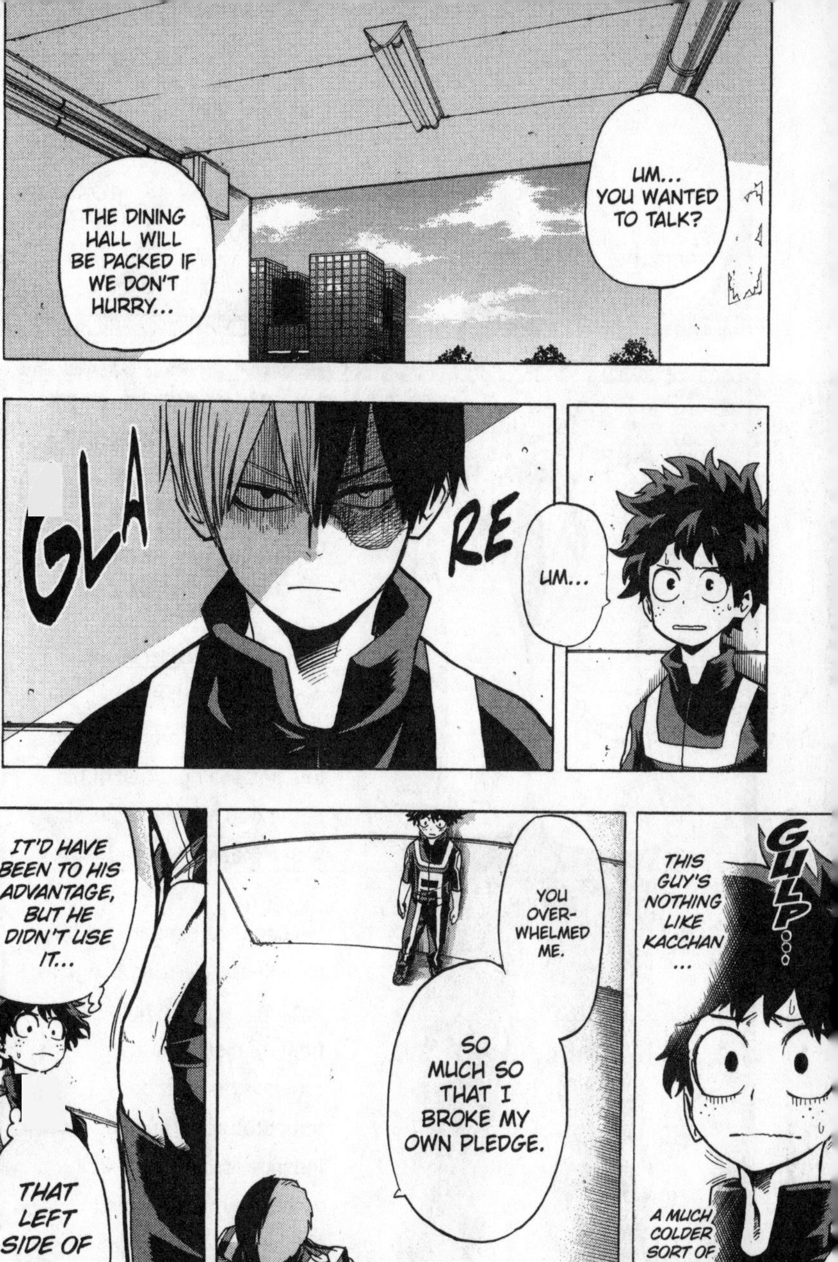
UM... YOU WANTED TO TALK?
THE DINING HALL WILL BE PACKED IF WE DON'T HURRY...
UM...
GLARE
GULP
THIS GUY'S NOTHING LIKE KACCHAN...
A MUCH COLDER SORT OF INTIMIDATION...
YOU OVER-WHELMED ME.
SO MUCH SO THAT I BROKE MY OWN PLEDGE.
IT'D HAVE BEEN TO HIS ADVANTAGE, BUT HE DIDN'T USE IT...
THAT LEFT SIDE OF HIS...

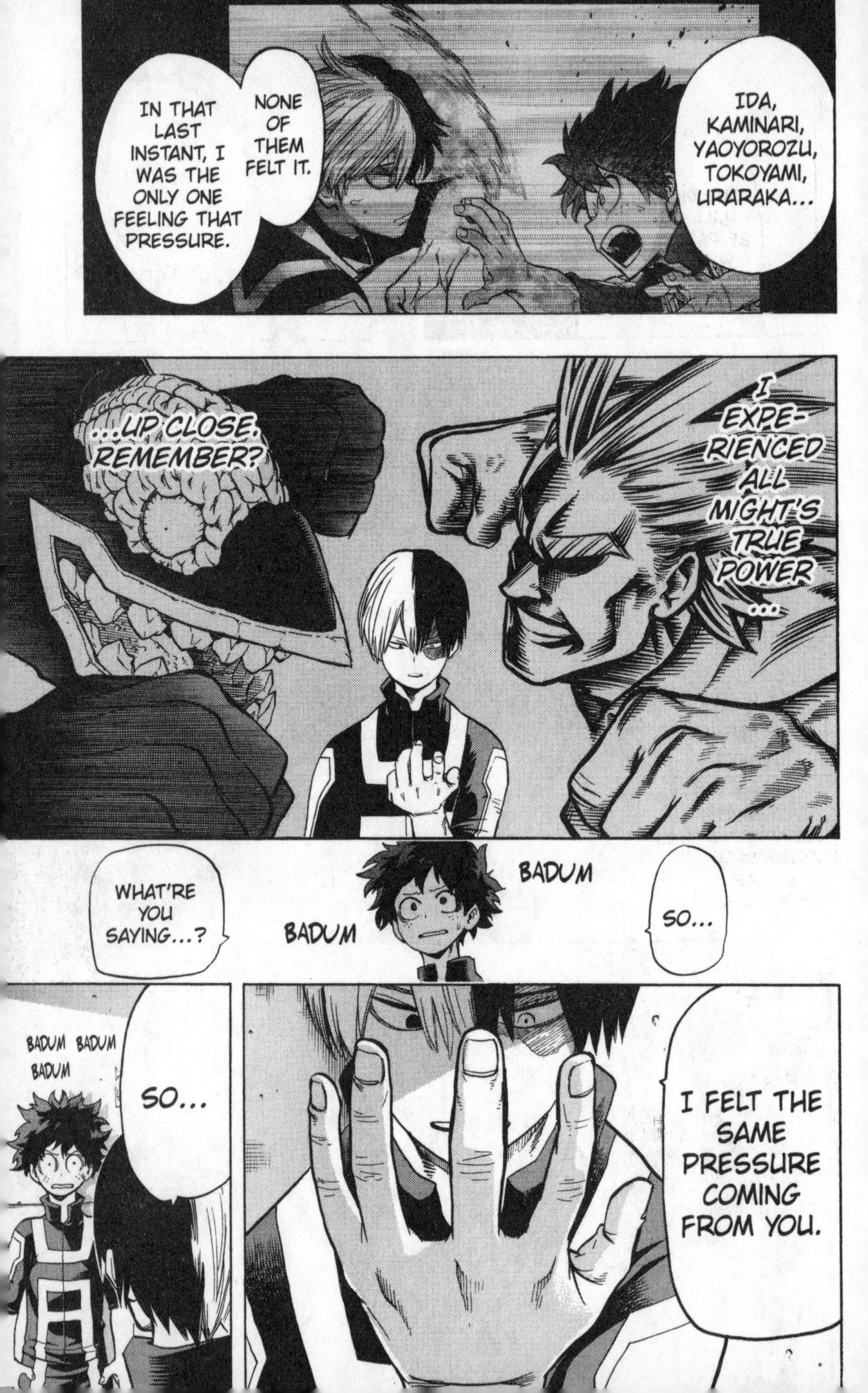
IDA, KAMINARI, YAOYOROZU, TOKOYAMI, URARAKA...
NONE OF THEM FELT IT.
IN THAT LAST INSTANT, I WAS THE ONLY ONE FEELING THAT PRESSURE.
I EXPE-RIENCED ALL MIGHT'S TRUE POWER...
...UP CLOSE. REMEMBER?
SO...
BADUM
BADUM
WHAT'RE YOU SAYING...?
I FELT THE SAME PRESSURE COMING FROM YOU.
SO...
BADUM BADUM BADUM

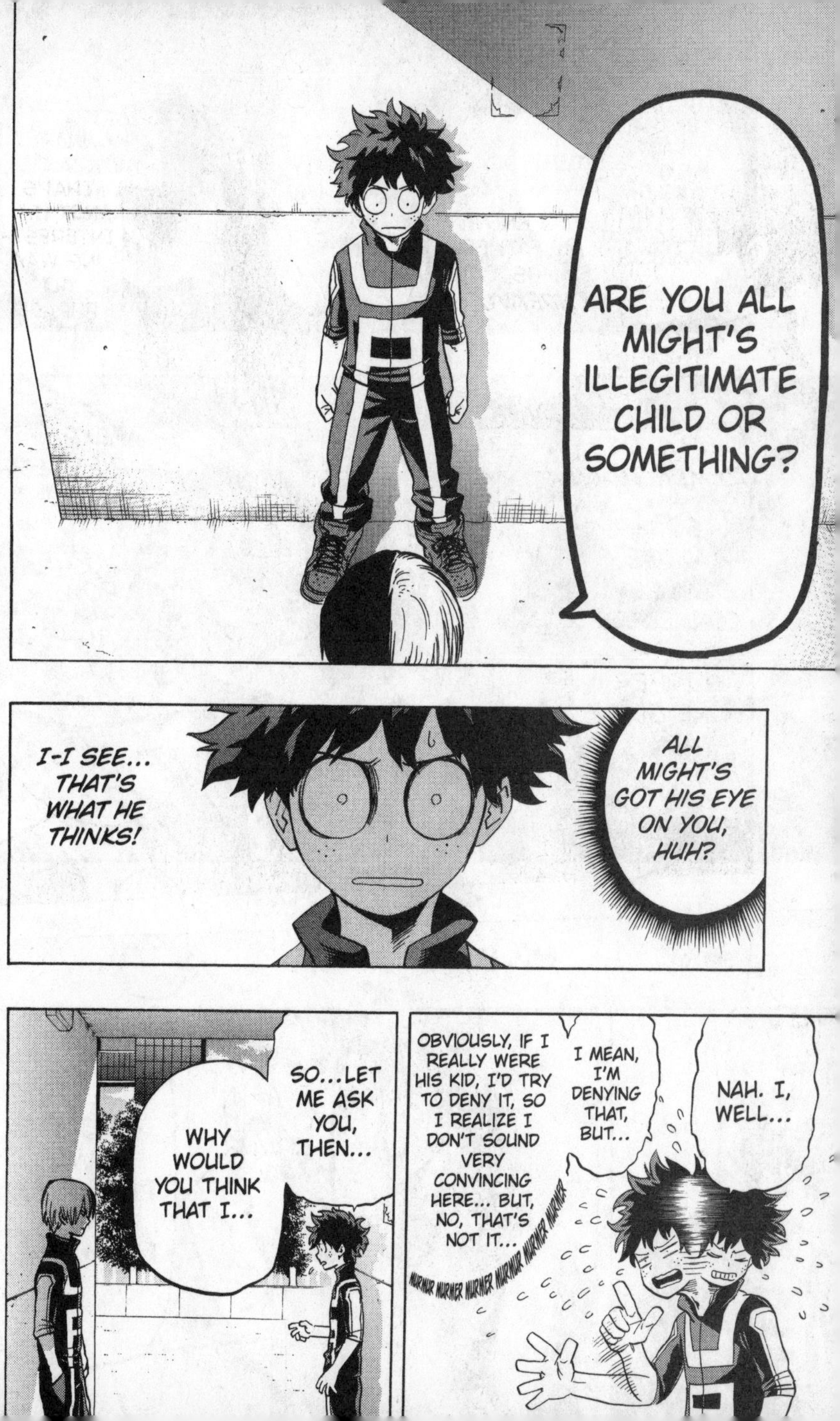
ARE YOU ALL MIGHT'S ILLEGITIMATE CHILD OR SOMETHING?
ALL MIGHT'S GOT HIS EYE ON YOU, HUH?
I-I SEE... THAT'S WHAT HE THINKS!
NAH. I, WELL...
I MEAN, I'M DENYING THAT, BUT...
OBVIOUSLY, IF I REALLY WERE HIS KID, I'D TRY TO DENY IT, SO I REALIZE I DON'T SOUND VERY CONVINCING HERE... BUT, NO, THAT'S NOT IT...
MURMUR MURMUR MURMUR MURMUR MURMUR MURMUR
SO...LET ME ASK YOU, THEN...
WHY WOULD YOU THINK THAT I...

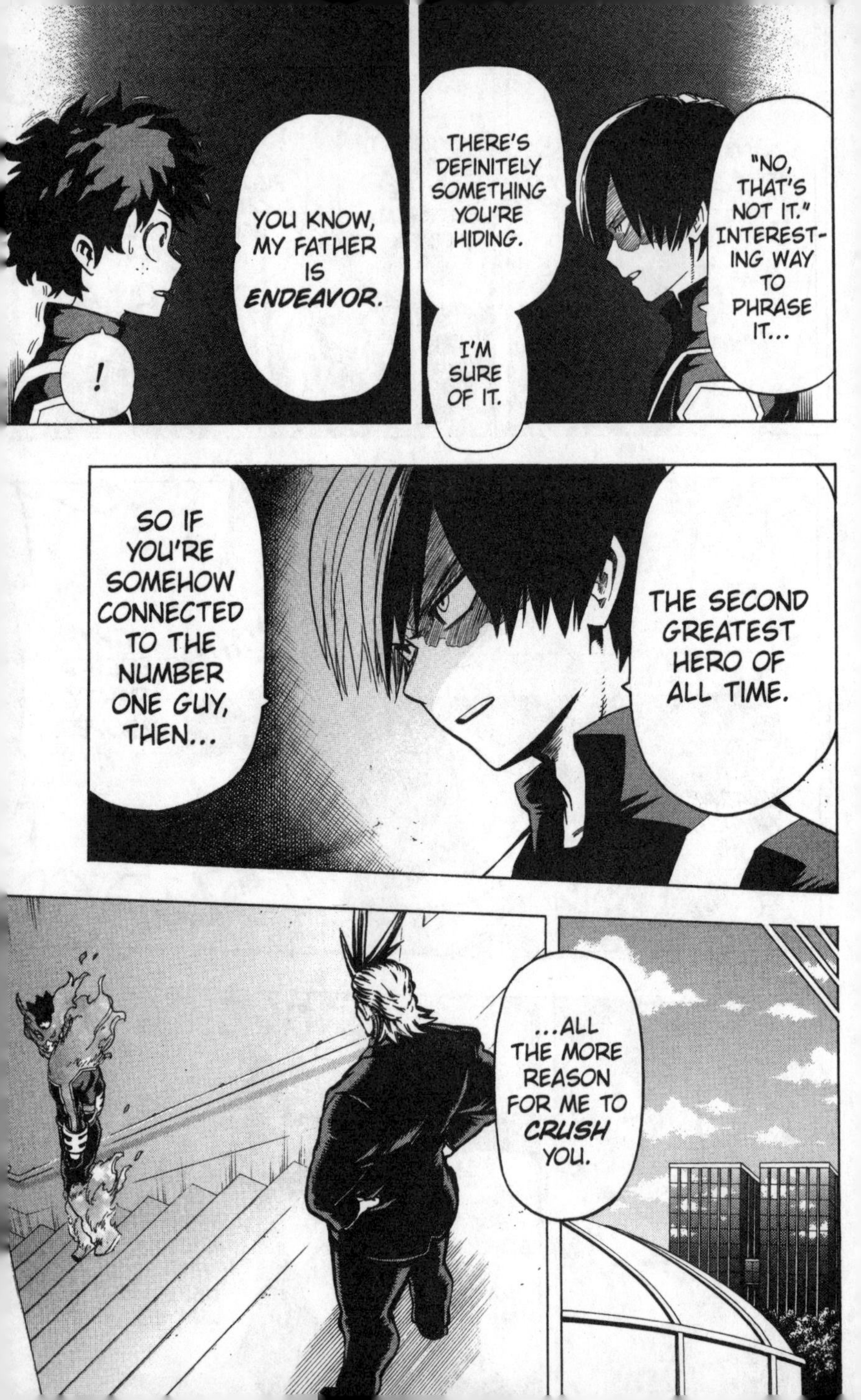
"NO, THAT'S NOT IT." INTERESTING WAY TO PHRASE IT...
THERE'S DEFINITELY SOMETHING YOU'RE HIDING.
I'M SURE OF IT.
YOU KNOW, MY FATHER IS ENDEAVOR.
!
THE SECOND GREATEST HERO OF ALL TIME.
SO IF YOU'RE SOMEHOW CONNECTED TO THE NUMBER ONE GUY, THEN...
...ALL THE MORE REASON FOR ME TO CRUSH YOU.

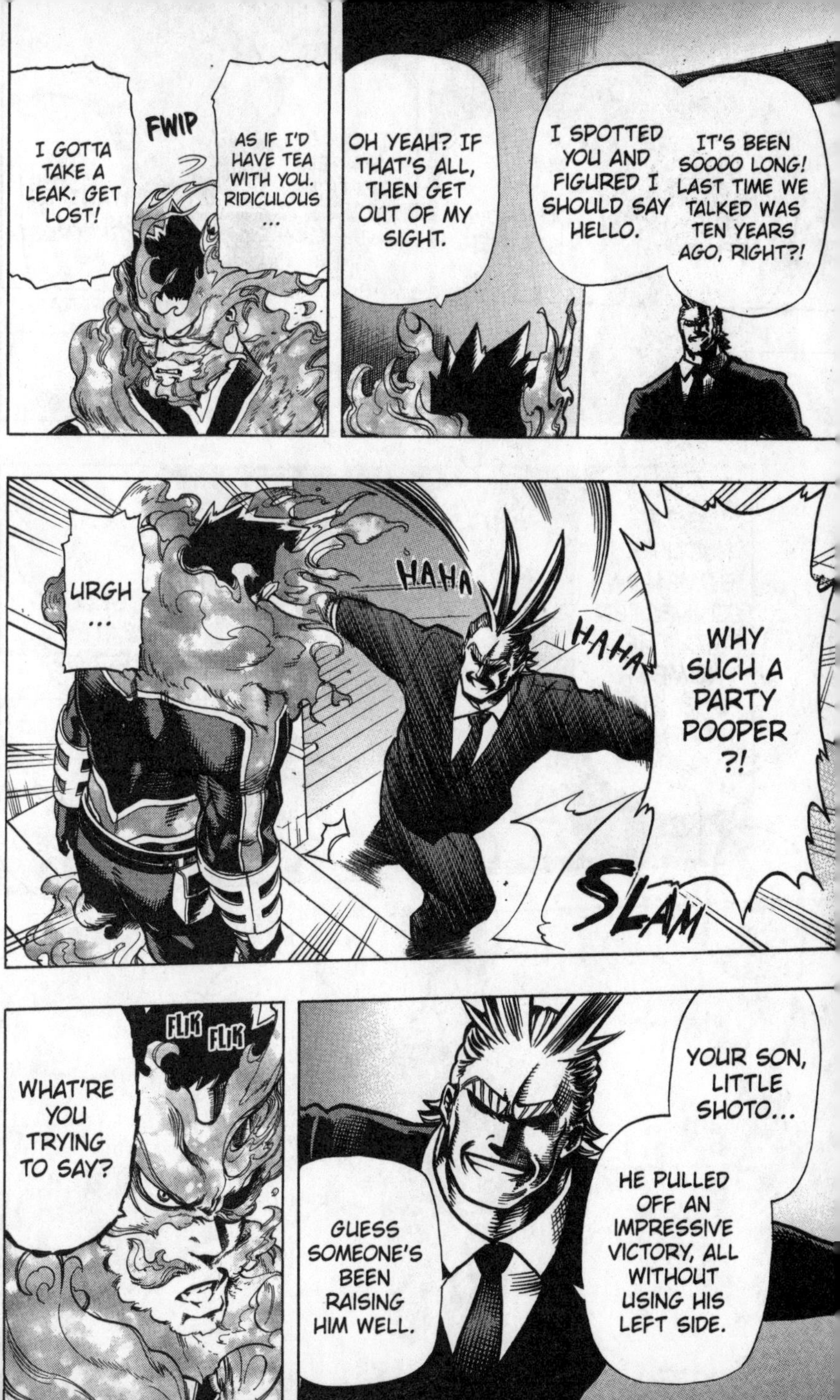
IT'S BEEN SOOOO LONG! LAST TIME WE TALKED WAS TEN YEARS AGO, RIGHT?!
I SPOTTED YOU AND FIGURED I SHOULD SAY HELLO.
OH YEAH? IF THAT'S ALL, THEN GET OUT OF MY SIGHT.
AS IF I'D HAVE TEA WITH YOU. RIDICULOUS ...
FWIP
I GOTTA TAKE A LEAK. GET LOST!
WHY SUCH A PARTY POOPER ?!
SLAM
HAHA
HAHA
URGH ...
YOUR SON, LITTLE SHOTO...
HE PULLED OFF AN IMPRESSIVE VICTORY, ALL WITHOUT USING HIS LEFT SIDE.
GUESS SOMEONE'S BEEN RAISING HIM WELL.
FLIK FLIK
WHAT'RE YOU TRYING TO SAY?

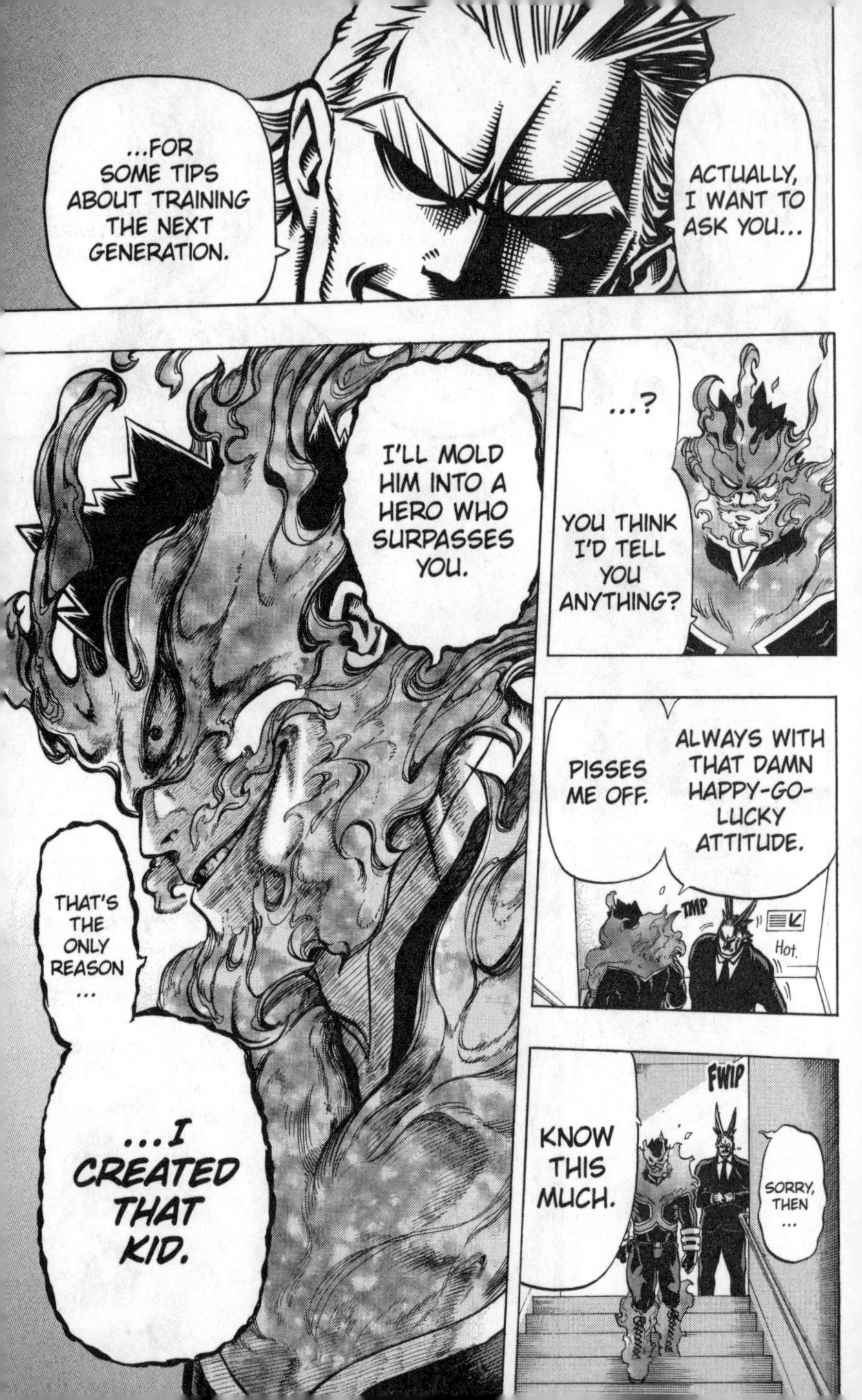
ACTUALLY, I WANT TO ASK YOU...
...FOR SOME TIPS ABOUT TRAINING THE NEXT GENERATION.
...?
YOU THINK I'D TELL YOU ANYTHING?
ALWAYS WITH THAT DAMN HAPPY-GO-LUCKY ATTITUDE.
PISSES ME OFF.
TMP
Hot.
FWIP
SORRY, THEN...
KNOW THIS MUCH.
I'LL MOLD HIM INTO A HERO WHO SURPASSES YOU.
THAT'S THE ONLY REASON...
...I CREATED THAT KID.

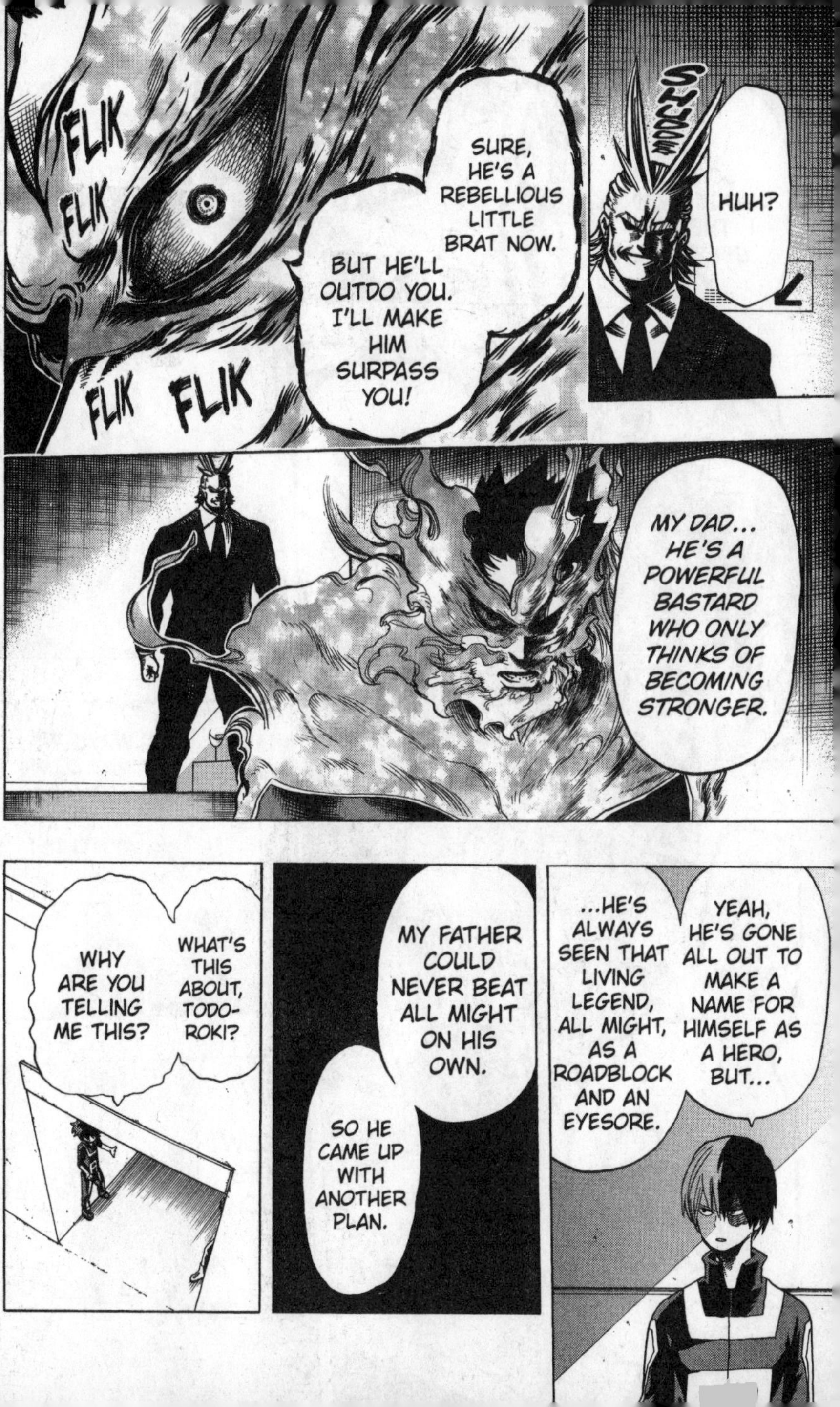
SHUDDER
HUH?
SURE, HE'S A REBELLIOUS LITTLE BRAT NOW.
BUT HE'LL OUTDO YOU. I'LL MAKE HIM SURPASS YOU!
FLIK
FLIK
FLIK
FLIK
MY DAD... HE'S A POWERFUL BASTARD WHO ONLY THINKS OF BECOMING STRONGER.
YEAH, HE'S GONE ALL OUT TO MAKE A NAME FOR HIMSELF AS A HERO, BUT...
...HE'S ALWAYS SEEN THAT LIVING LEGEND, ALL MIGHT, AS A ROADBLOCK AND AN EYESORE.
MY FATHER COULD NEVER BEAT ALL MIGHT ON HIS OWN.
SO HE CAME UP WITH ANOTHER PLAN.
WHAT'S THIS ABOUT, TODO-ROKI?
WHY ARE YOU TELLING ME THIS?

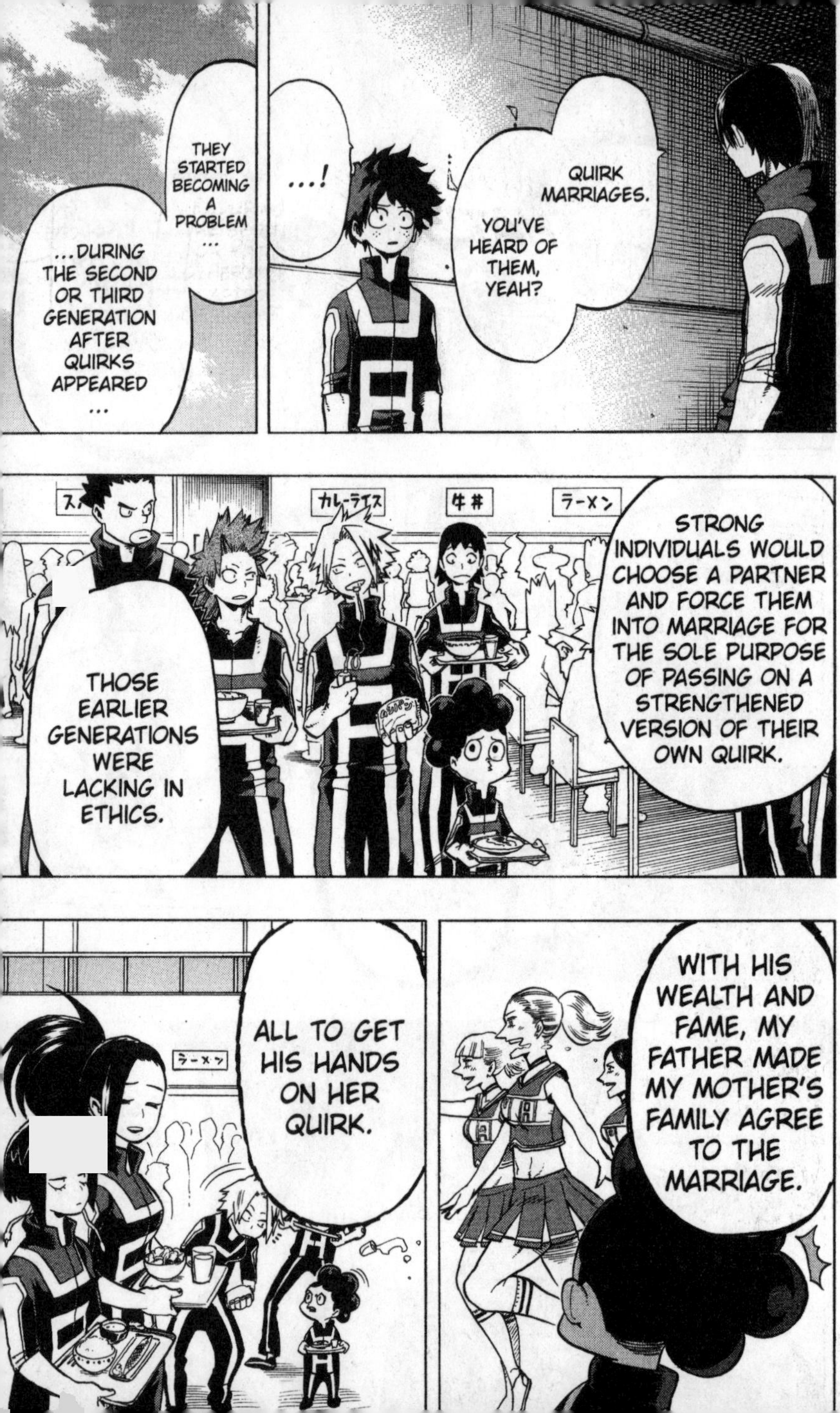
QUIRK MARRIAGES.
YOU'VE HEARD OF THEM, YEAH?
...!
THEY STARTED BECOMING A PROBLEM ...
...DURING THE SECOND OR THIRD GENERATION AFTER QUIRKS APPEARED ...
ラーメン
牛丼
カレーライス
STRONG INDIVIDUALS WOULD CHOOSE A PARTNER AND FORCE THEM INTO MARRIAGE FOR THE SOLE PURPOSE OF PASSING ON A STRENGTHENED VERSION OF THEIR OWN QUIRK.
THOSE EARLIER GENERATIONS WERE LACKING IN ETHICS.
WITH HIS WEALTH AND FAME, MY FATHER MADE MY MOTHER'S FAMILY AGREE TO THE MARRIAGE.
ALL TO GET HIS HANDS ON HER QUIRK.
ラーメン

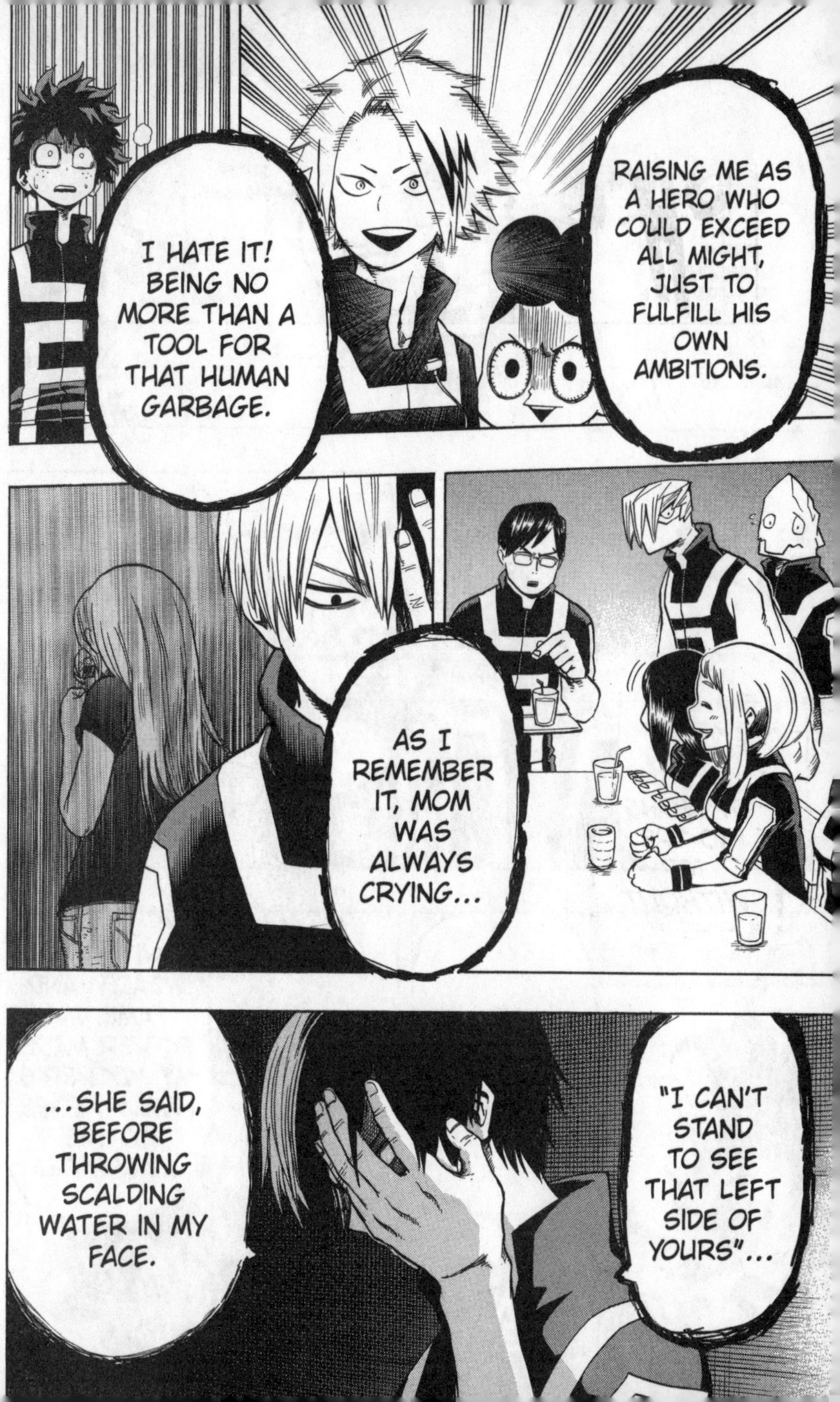
RAISING ME AS A HERO WHO COULD EXCEED ALL MIGHT, JUST TO FULFILL HIS OWN AMBITIONS.
I HATE IT! BEING NO MORE THAN A TOOL FOR THAT HUMAN GARBAGE.
AS I REMEMBER IT, MOM WAS ALWAYS CRYING...
"I CAN'T STAND TO SEE THAT LEFT SIDE OF YOURS"...
...SHE SAID, BEFORE THROWING SCALDING WATER IN MY FACE.

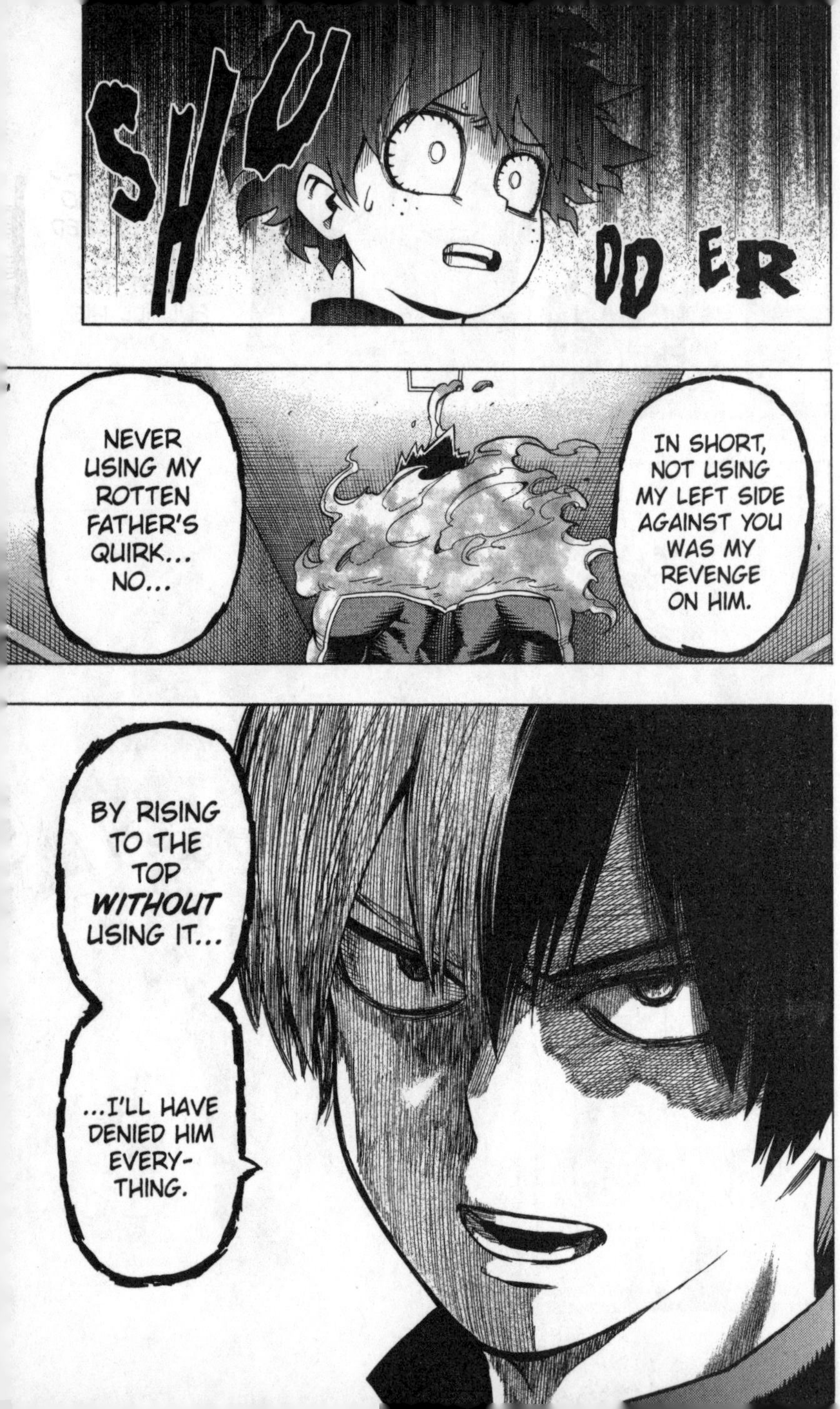
SHUDDER
IN SHORT, NOT USING MY LEFT SIDE AGAINST YOU WAS MY REVENGE ON HIM.
NEVER USING MY ROTTEN FATHER'S QUIRK... NO...
BY RISING TO THE TOP *WITHOUT* USING IT...
...I'LL HAVE DENIED HIM EVERY-THING.

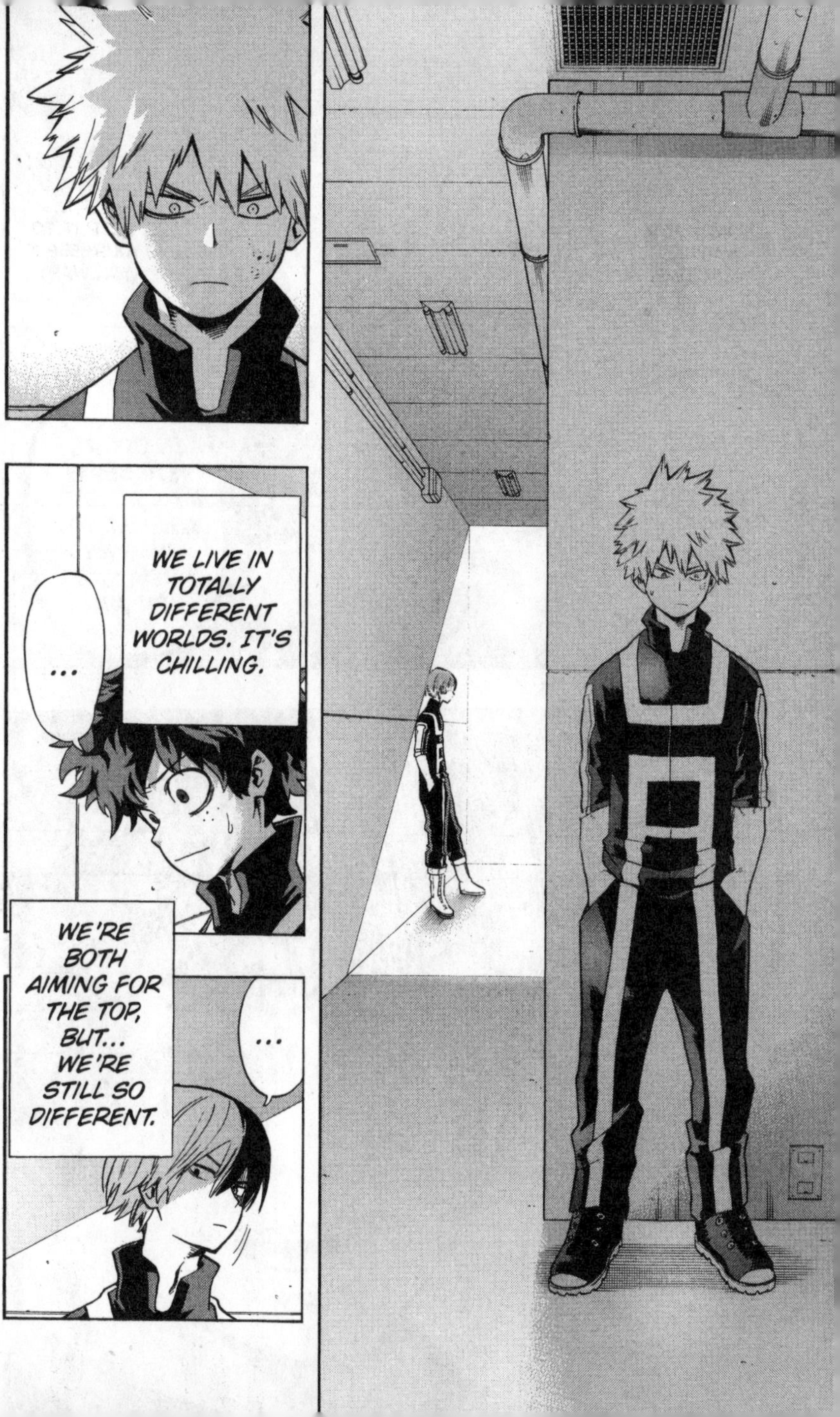
WE LIVE IN TOTALLY DIFFERENT WORLDS. IT'S CHILLING.
...
WE'RE BOTH AIMING FOR THE TOP, BUT... WE'RE STILL SO DIFFERENT.
...

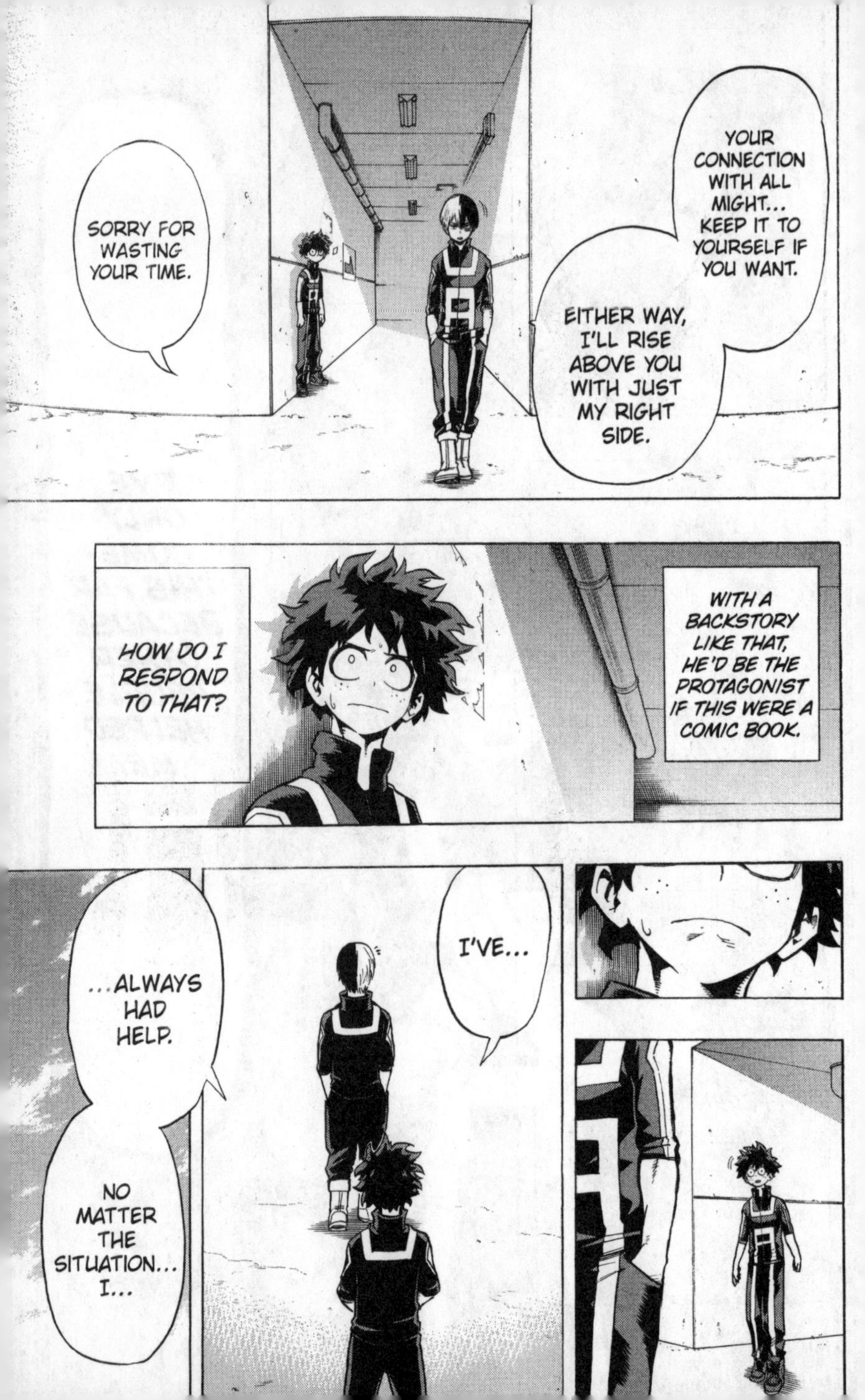
YOUR CONNECTION WITH ALL MIGHT... KEEP IT TO YOURSELF IF YOU WANT.
EITHER WAY, I'LL RISE ABOVE YOU WITH JUST MY RIGHT SIDE.
SORRY FOR WASTING YOUR TIME.
WITH A BACKSTORY LIKE THAT, HE'D BE THE PROTAGONIST IF THIS WERE A COMIC BOOK.
HOW DO I RESPOND TO THAT?
I'VE...
...ALWAYS HAD HELP.
NO MATTER THE SITUATION... I...

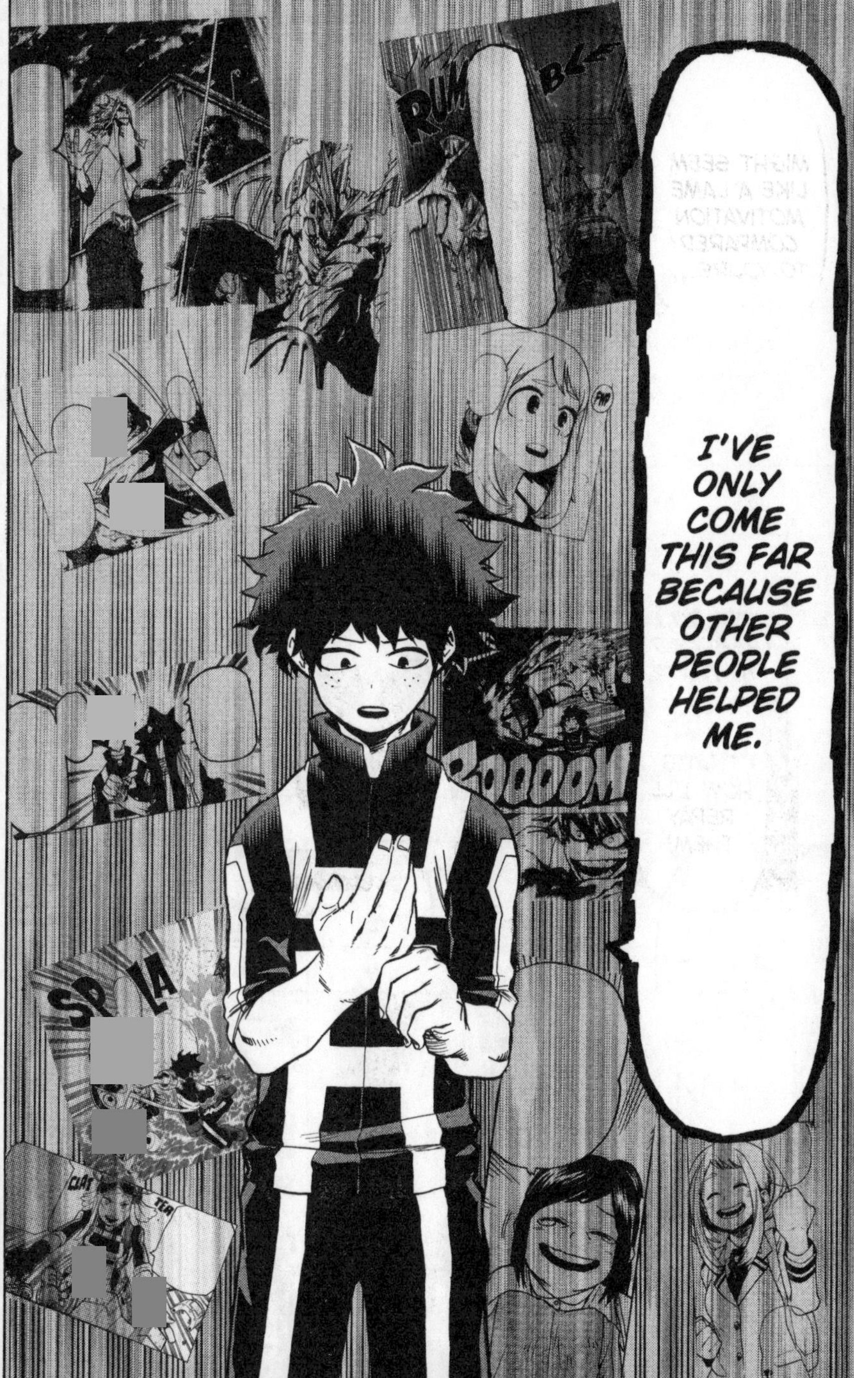
I'VE ONLY COME THIS FAR BECAUSE OTHER PEOPLE HELPED ME.
RUM
BOOOOM
SP LA

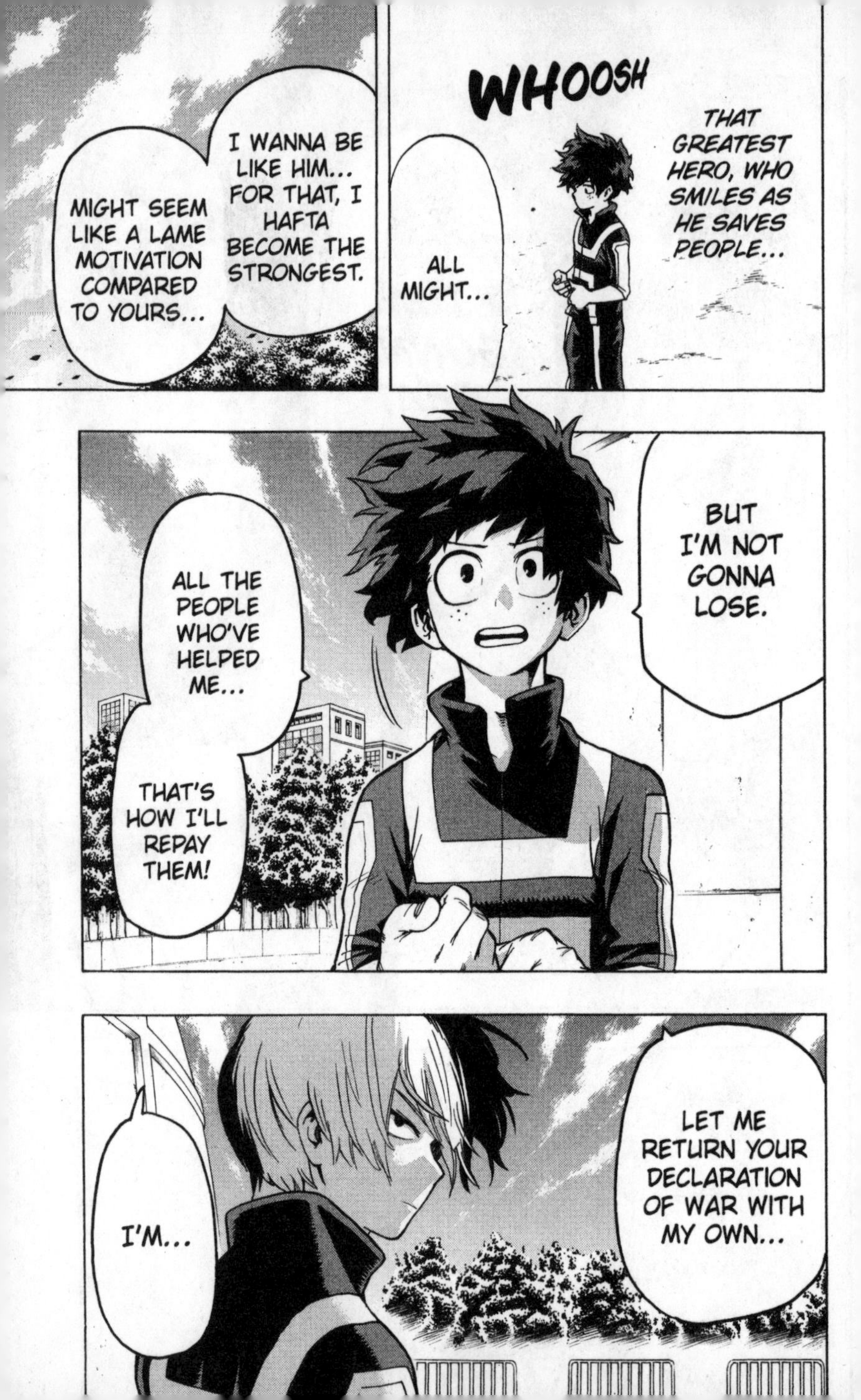
WHOOSH
THAT GREATEST HERO, WHO SMILES AS HE SAVES PEOPLE...
ALL MIGHT...
I WANNA BE LIKE HIM... FOR THAT, I HAFTA BECOME THE STRONGEST.
MIGHT SEEM LIKE A LAME MOTIVATION COMPARED TO YOURS...
BUT I'M NOT GONNA LOSE.
ALL THE PEOPLE WHO'VE HELPED ME...
THAT'S HOW I'LL REPAY THEM!
LET ME RETURN YOUR DECLARATION OF WAR WITH MY OWN...
I'M...

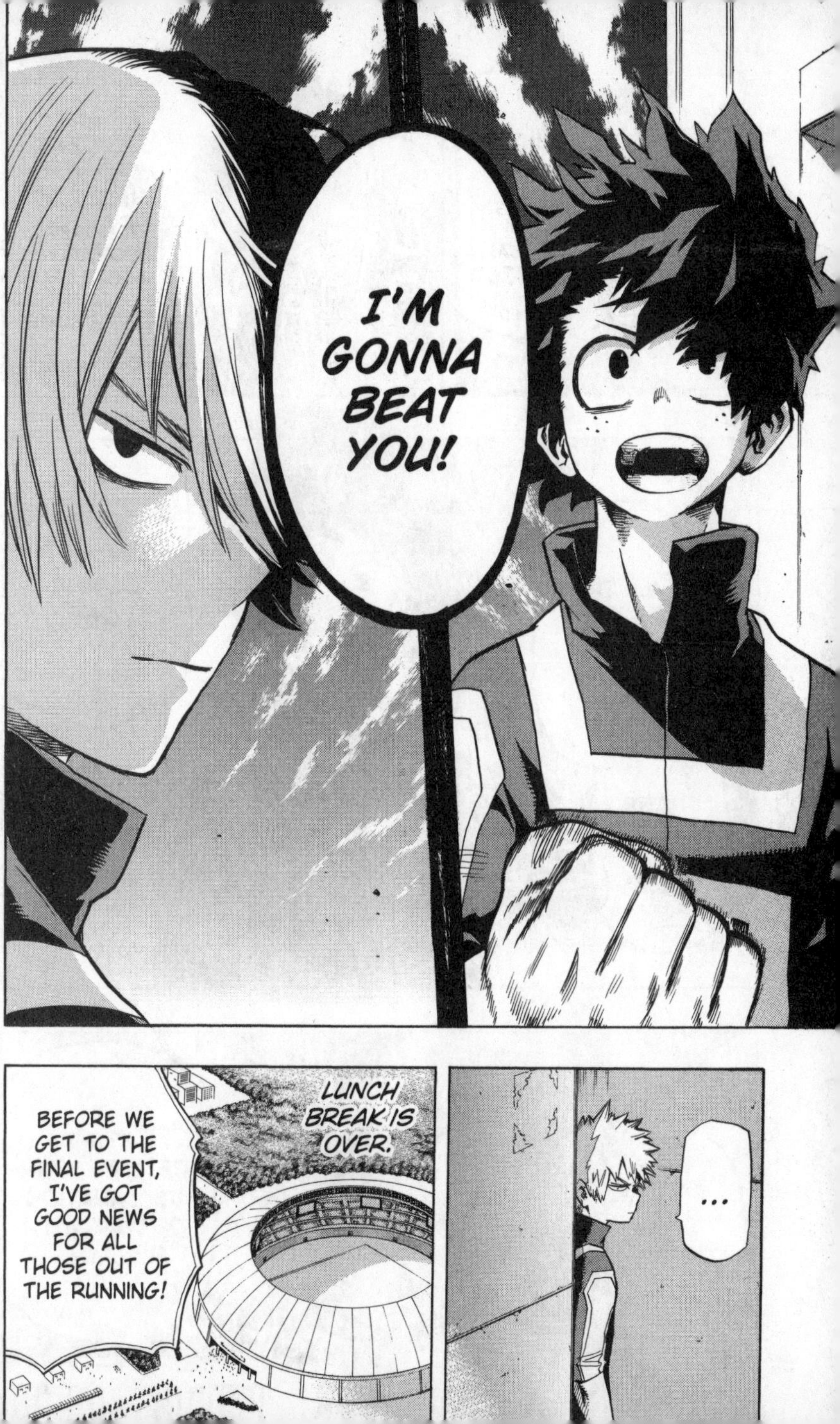
I'M GONNA BEAT YOU!
...
LUNCH BREAK IS OVER.
BEFORE WE GET TO THE FINAL EVENT, I'VE GOT GOOD NEWS FOR ALL THOSE OUT OF THE RUNNING!

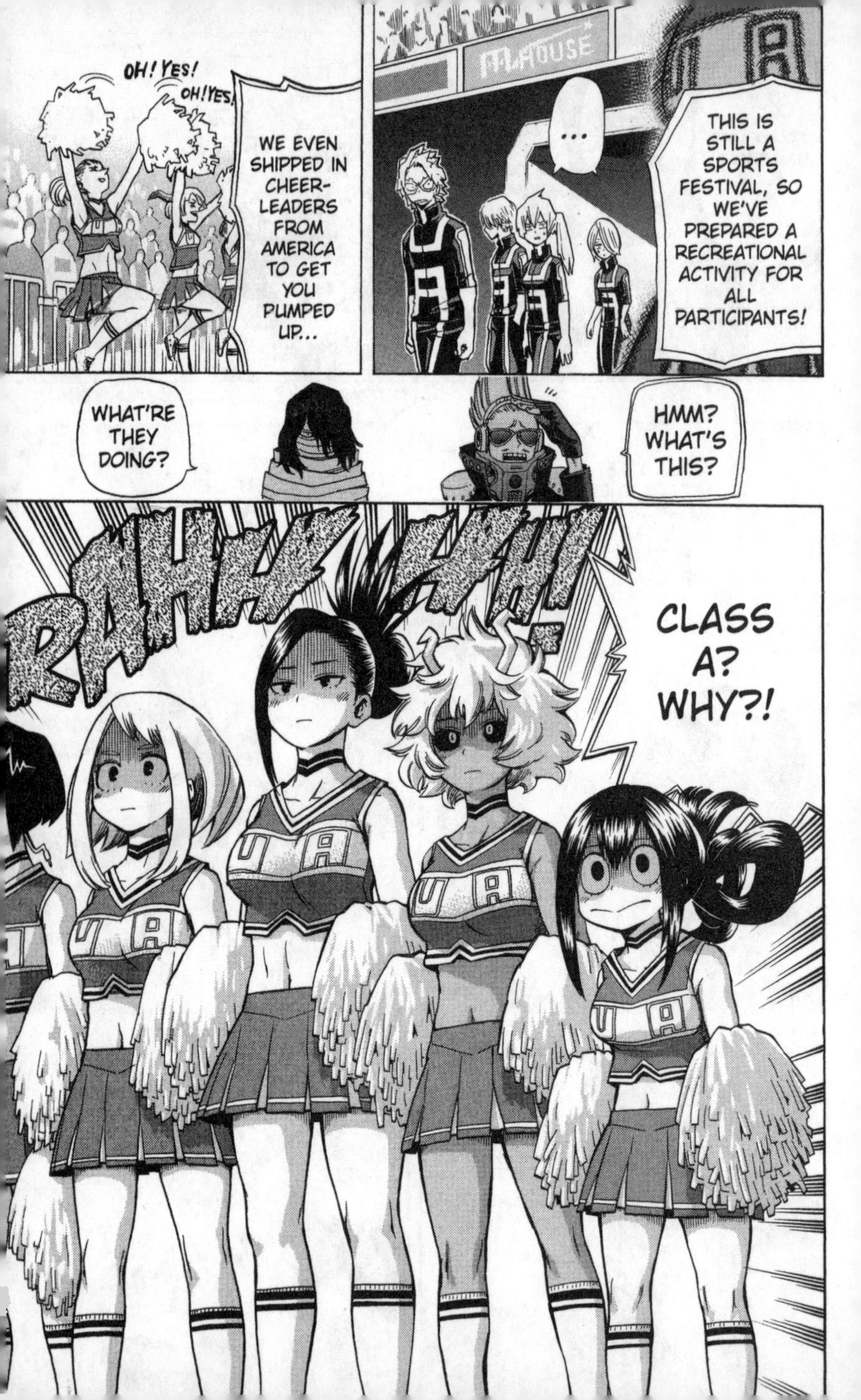
...
THIS IS STILL A SPORTS FESTIVAL, SO WE'VE PREPARED A RECREATIONAL ACTIVITY FOR ALL PARTICIPANTS!
WE EVEN SHIPPED IN CHEER-LEADERS FROM AMERICA TO GET YOU PUMPED UP...
OH! YES!
OH! YES!
HMM? WHAT'S THIS?
WHAT'RE THEY DOING?
CLASS A? WHY?!

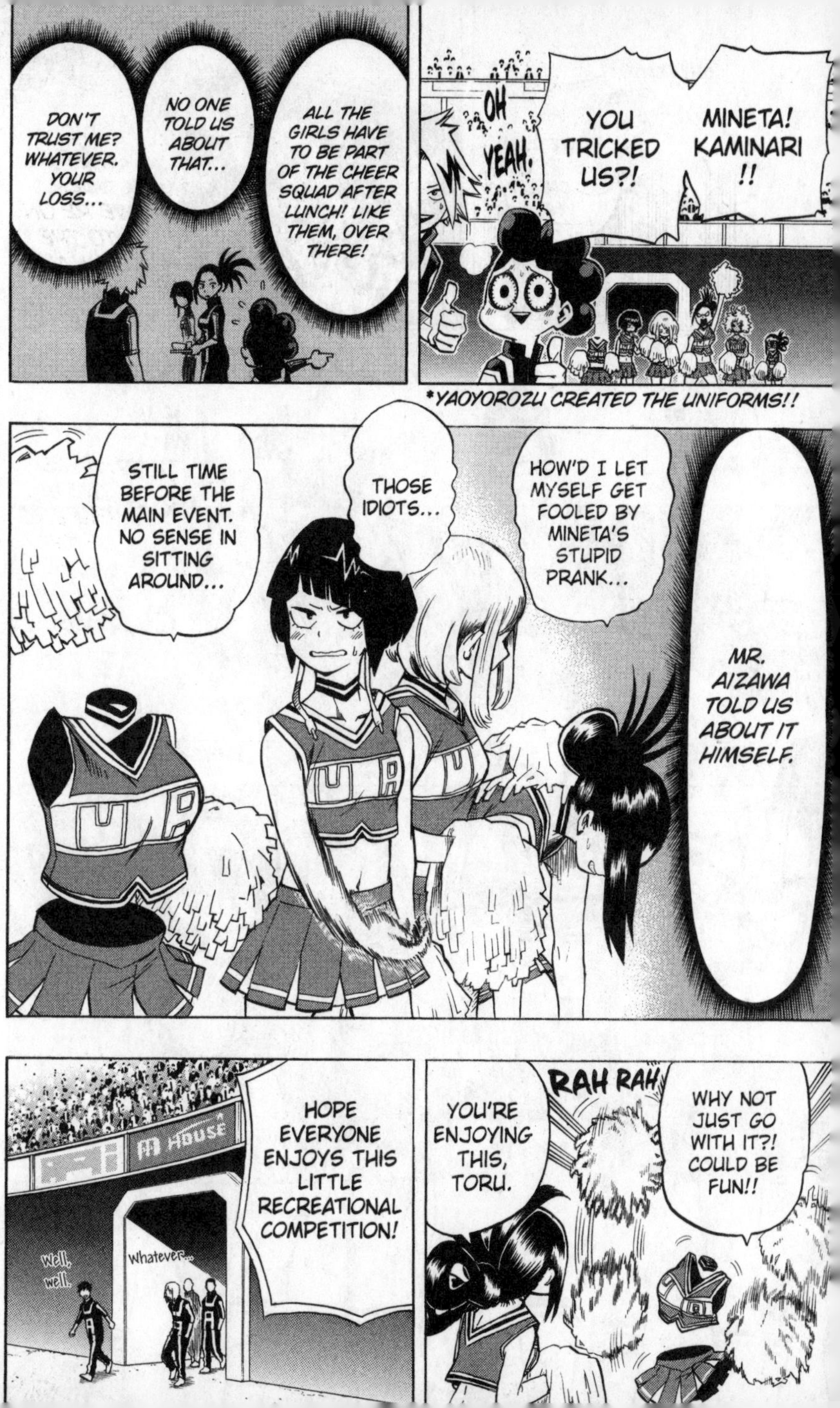
MINETA! KAMINARI!!
YOU TRICKED US?!
OH YEAH.
ALL THE GIRLS HAVE TO BE PART OF THE CHEER SQUAD AFTER LUNCH! LIKE THEM, OVER THERE!
NO ONE TOLD US ABOUT THAT...
DON'T TRUST ME? WHATEVER. YOUR LOSS...
*YAOYOROZU CREATED THE UNIFORMS!!
MR. AIZAWA TOLD US ABOUT IT HIMSELF.
HOW'D I LET MYSELF GET FOOLED BY MINETA'S STUPID PRANK...
THOSE IDIOTS...
STILL TIME BEFORE THE MAIN EVENT. NO SENSE IN SITTING AROUND...
WHY NOT JUST GO WITH IT?! COULD BE FUN!!
RAH RAH
YOU'RE ENJOYING THIS, TORU.
HOPE EVERYONE ENJOYS THIS LITTLE RECREATIONAL COMPETITION!
HOUSE
Whatever...
Well, well.

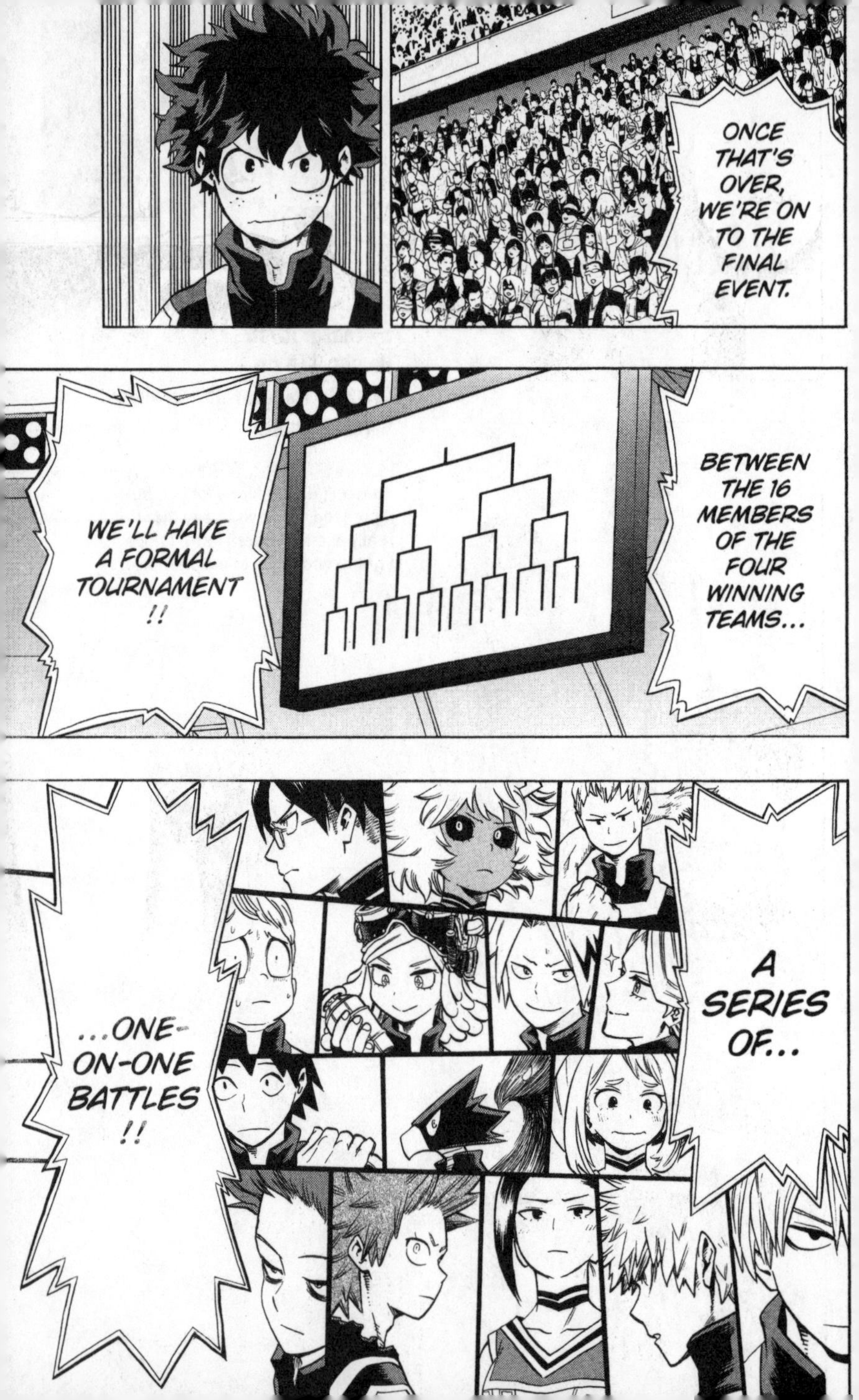
ONCE THAT'S OVER, WE'RE ON TO THE FINAL EVENT.
BETWEEN THE 16 MEMBERS OF THE FOUR WINNING TEAMS...
WE'LL HAVE A FORMAL TOURNAMENT!!
A SERIES OF...
...ONE-ON-ONE BATTLES!!

TETSUTETSU TETSUTETSU (15)

STREET CLOTHES

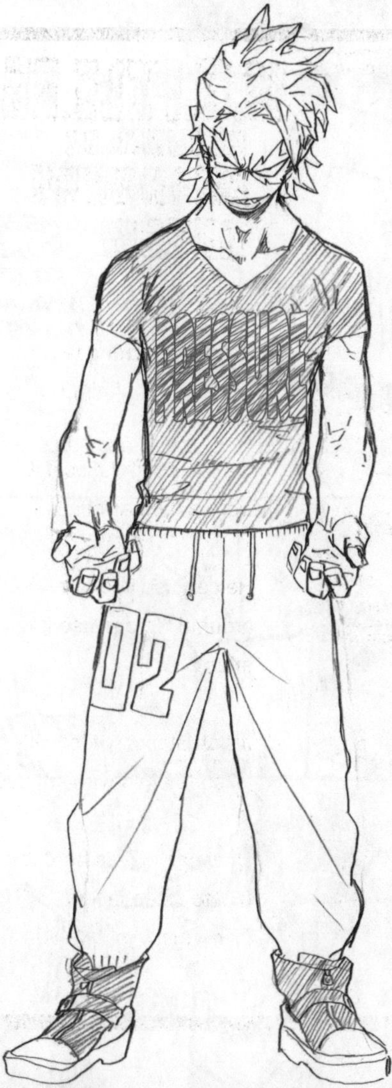
PRESSURE
02

Birthday: 10/16
Height: 174 cm
Favorite Things: Fighting video games, spinach

BEHIND THE SCENES

I haven't drawn him a lot yet, but if pressed, I'd have to say that I really like his overall form. I hope I get to show him in action more.

No.32 - Smile, Prince of Nonsense Land!

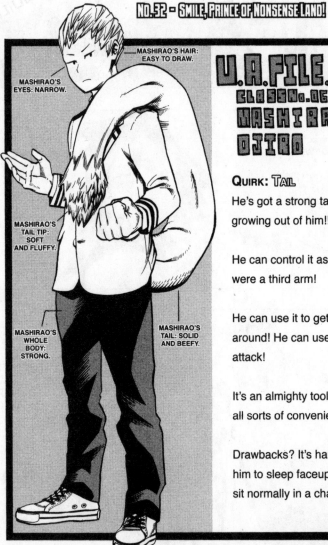

MASHIRAO'S HAIR: EASY TO DRAW.
MASHIRAO'S EYES: NARROW.
MASHIRAO'S TAIL TIP: SOFT AND FLUFFY.
MASHIRAO'S WHOLE BODY: STRONG.
MASHIRAO'S TAIL: SOLID AND BEEFY.

U.A. FILE.06

CLASS No.06 MASHIRAO OJIRO

Quirk: Tail

He's got a strong tail growing out of him!!

He can control it as if it were a third arm!

He can use it to get around! He can use it to attack!

It's an almighty tool with all sorts of convenient uses!

Drawbacks? It's hard for him to sleep faceup or sit normally in a chair!

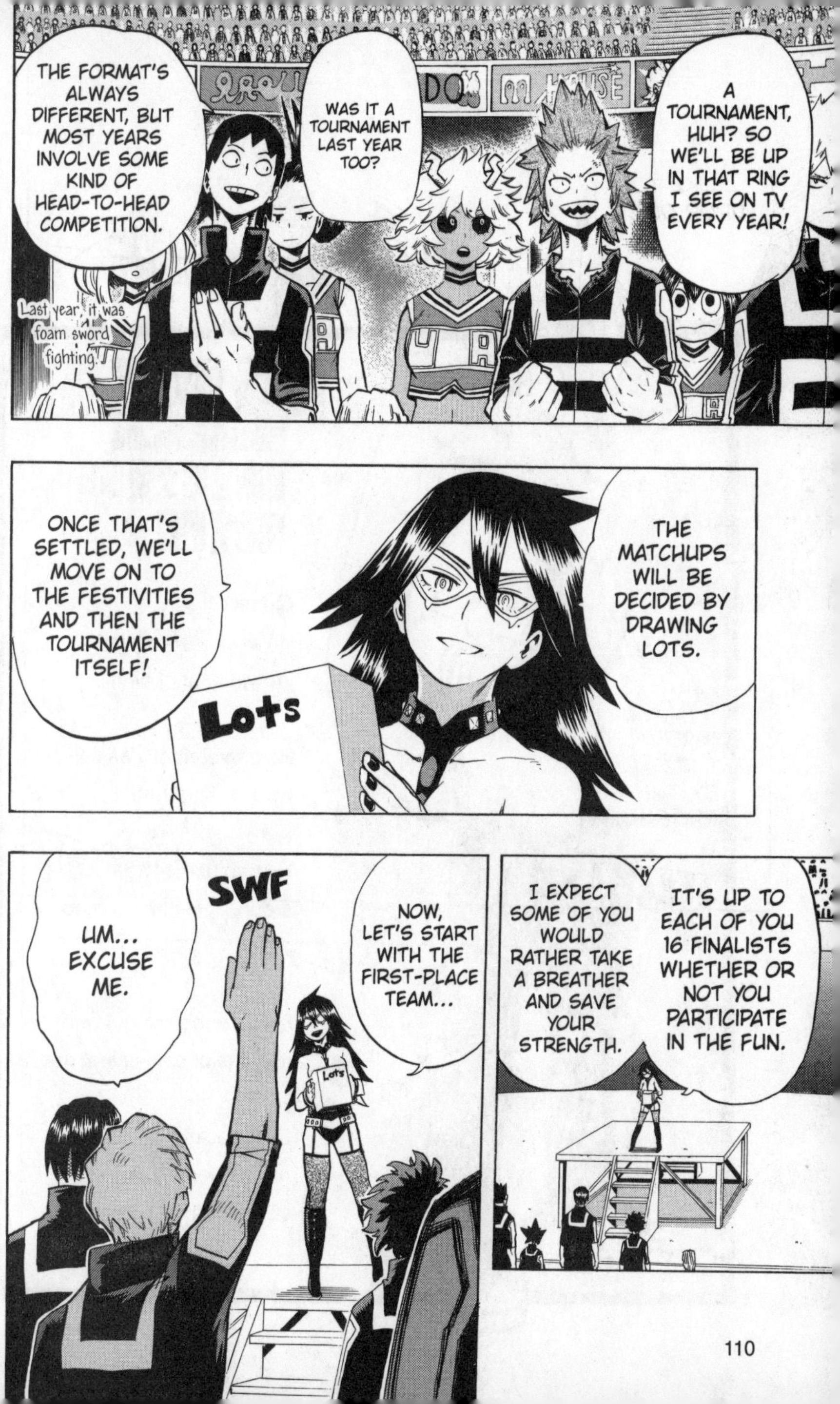
A TOURNAMENT, HUH? SO WE'LL BE UP IN THAT RING I SEE ON TV EVERY YEAR!
WAS IT A TOURNAMENT LAST YEAR TOO?
THE FORMAT'S ALWAYS DIFFERENT, BUT MOST YEARS INVOLVE SOME KIND OF HEAD-TO-HEAD COMPETITION.
Last year, it was foam sword fighting!
THE MATCHUPS WILL BE DECIDED BY DRAWING LOTS.
ONCE THAT'S SETTLED, WE'LL MOVE ON TO THE FESTIVITIES AND THEN THE TOURNAMENT ITSELF!
Lots
IT'S UP TO EACH OF YOU 16 FINALISTS WHETHER OR NOT YOU PARTICIPATE IN THE FUN.
I EXPECT SOME OF YOU WOULD RATHER TAKE A BREATHER AND SAVE YOUR STRENGTH.
NOW, LET'S START WITH THE FIRST-PLACE TEAM...
Lots
SWF
UM... EXCUSE ME.

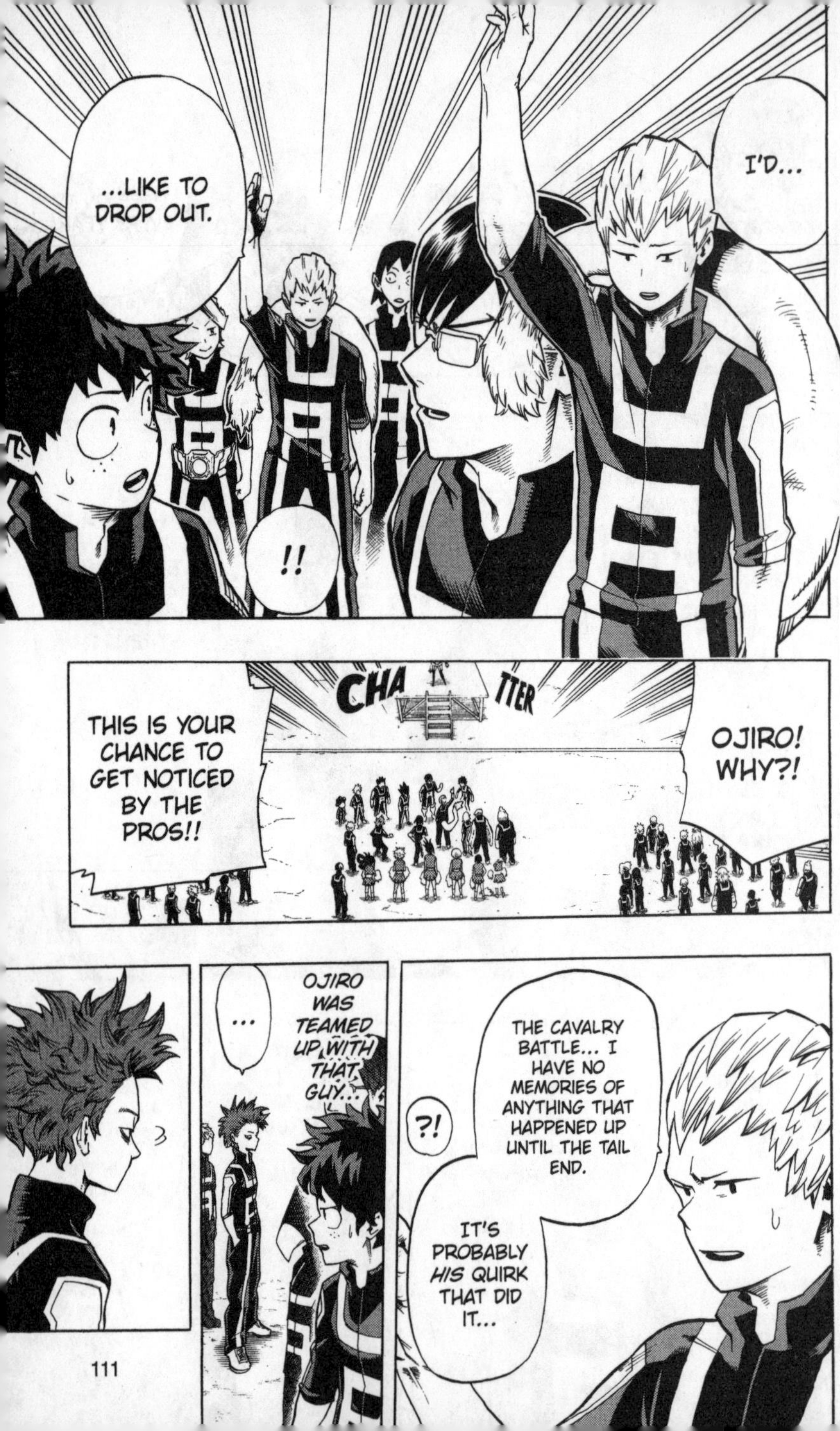
I'D...
...LIKE TO DROP OUT.
!!
OJIRO! WHY?!
CHATTER
THIS IS YOUR CHANCE TO GET NOTICED BY THE PROS!!
THE CAVALRY BATTLE... I HAVE NO MEMORIES OF ANYTHING THAT HAPPENED UP UNTIL THE TAIL END.
IT'S PROBABLY *HIS* QUIRK THAT DID IT...
?!
OJIRO WAS TEAMED UP WITH THAT GUY...
...

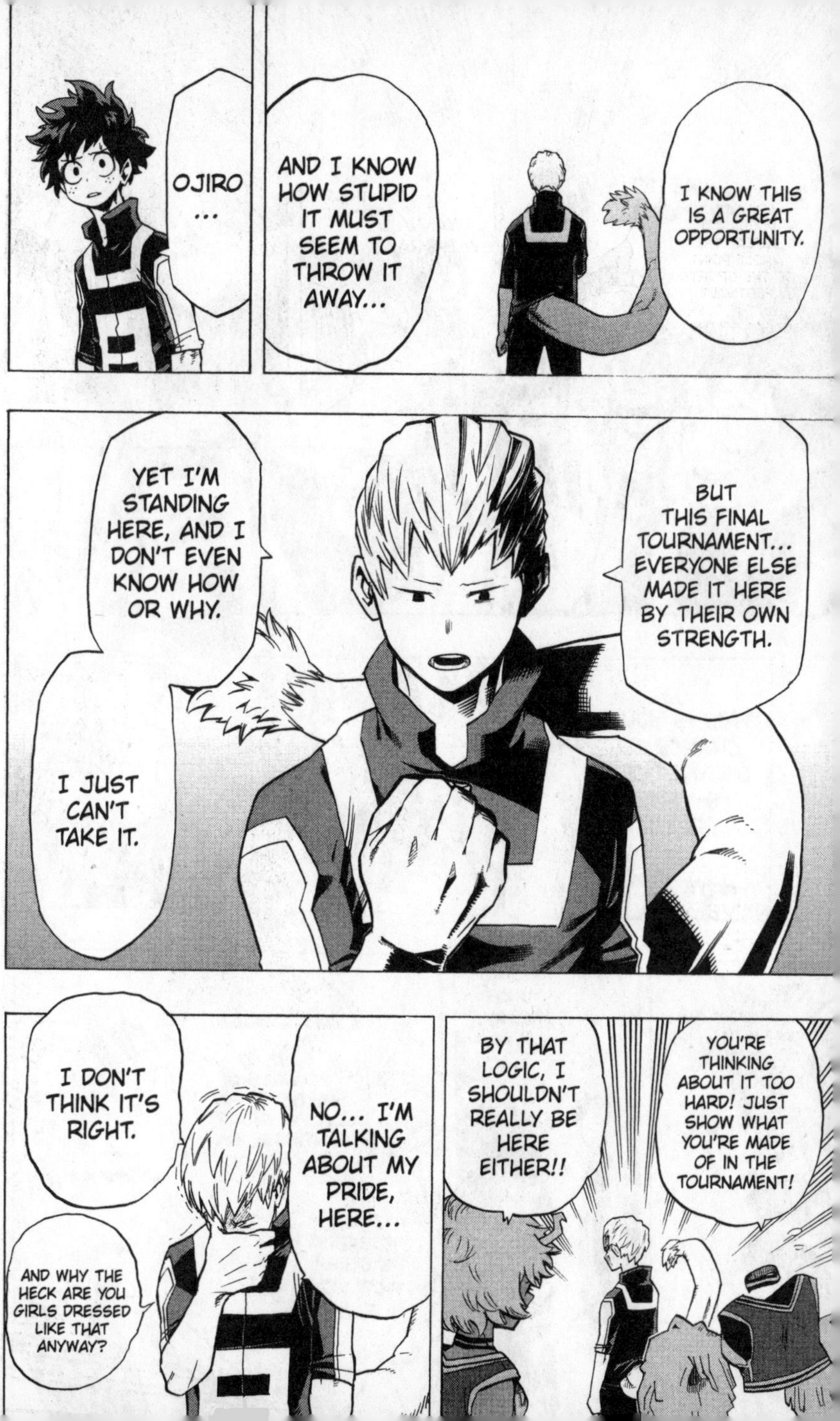
I KNOW THIS IS A GREAT OPPORTUNITY.
AND I KNOW HOW STUPID IT MUST SEEM TO THROW IT AWAY...
OJIRO ...
BUT THIS FINAL TOURNAMENT... EVERYONE ELSE MADE IT HERE BY THEIR OWN STRENGTH.
YET I'M STANDING HERE, AND I DON'T EVEN KNOW HOW OR WHY.
I JUST CAN'T TAKE IT.
YOU'RE THINKING ABOUT IT TOO HARD! JUST SHOW WHAT YOU'RE MADE OF IN THE TOURNAMENT!
BY THAT LOGIC, I SHOULDN'T REALLY BE HERE EITHER!!
NO... I'M TALKING ABOUT MY PRIDE, HERE...
I DON'T THINK IT'S RIGHT.
AND WHY THE HECK ARE YOU GIRLS DRESSED LIKE THAT ANYWAY?

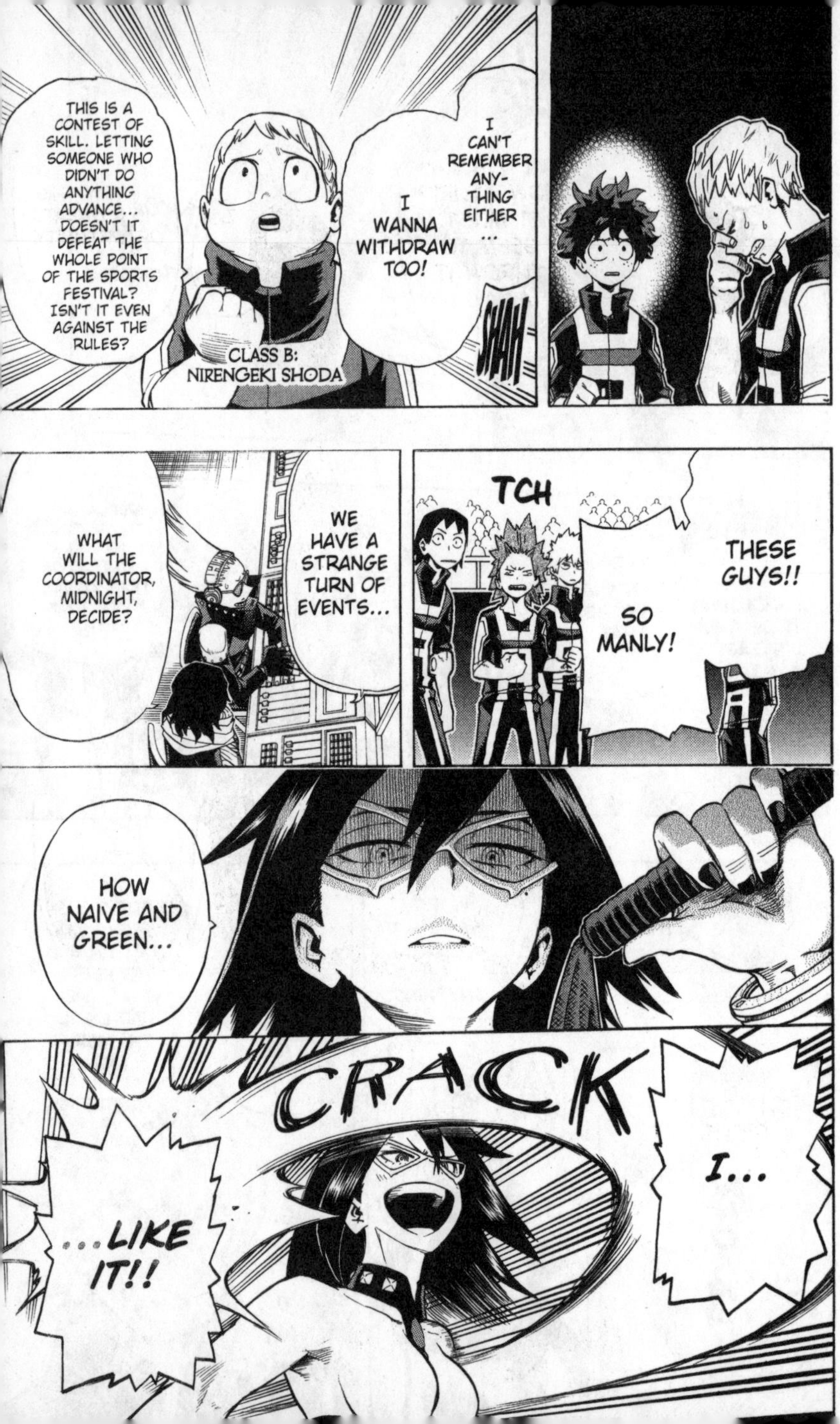

I CAN'T REMEMBER ANYTHING EITHER...
I WANNA WITHDRAW TOO!
SHAH
THIS IS A CONTEST OF SKILL. LETTING SOMEONE WHO DIDN'T DO ANYTHING ADVANCE... DOESN'T IT DEFEAT THE WHOLE POINT OF THE SPORTS FESTIVAL? ISN'T IT EVEN AGAINST THE RULES?
CLASS B: NIRENGEKI SHODA
THESE GUYS!!
SO MANLY!
TCH
WE HAVE A STRANGE TURN OF EVENTS...
WHAT WILL THE COORDINATOR, MIDNIGHT, DECIDE?
HOW NAIVE AND GREEN...
CRACK
I...
...LIKE IT!!

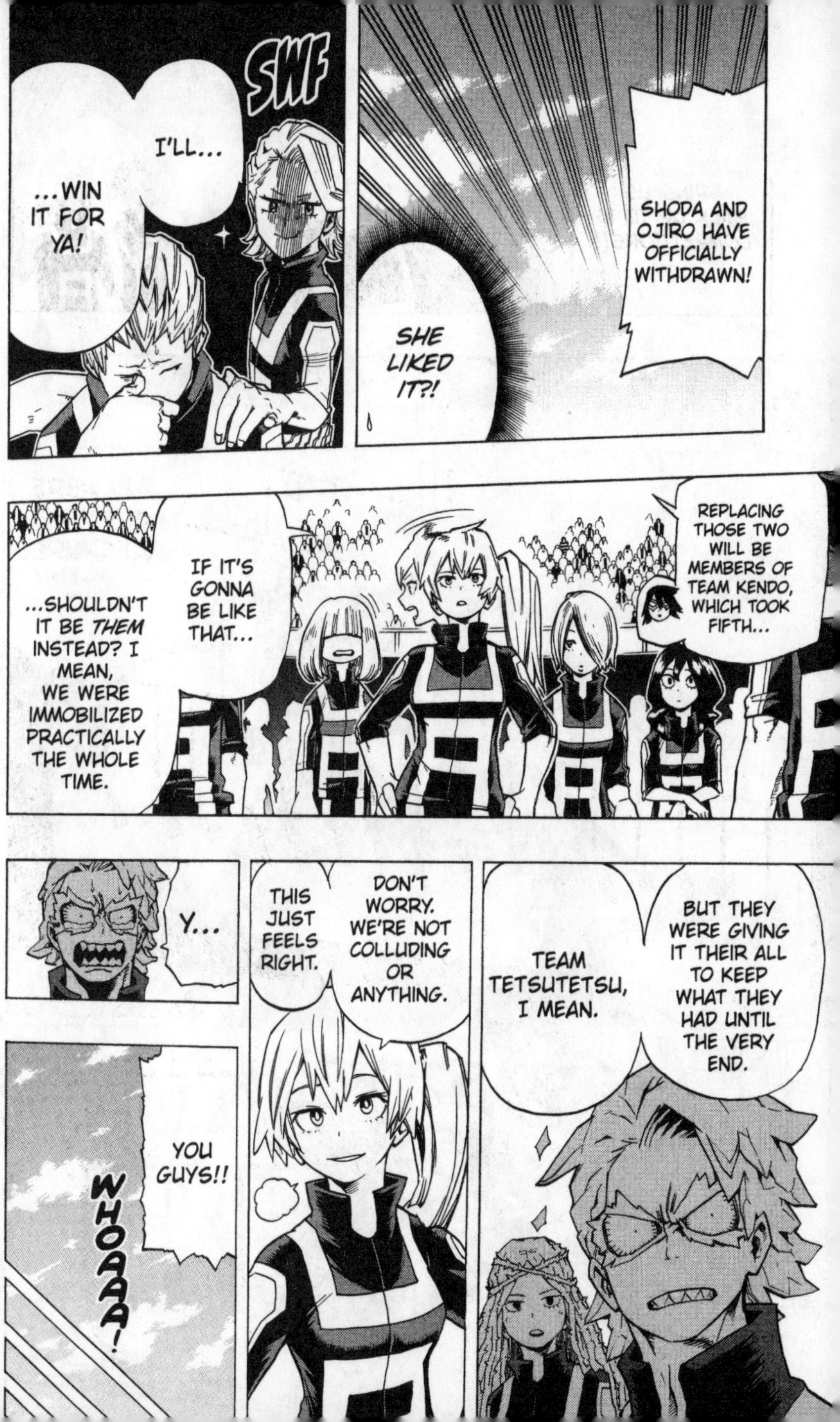
SHODA AND OJIRO HAVE OFFICIALLY WITHDRAWN!
SHE LIKED IT?!
SWF
I'LL...
...WIN IT FOR YA!
REPLACING THOSE TWO WILL BE MEMBERS OF TEAM KENDO, WHICH TOOK FIFTH...
IF IT'S GONNA BE LIKE THAT...
...SHOULDN'T IT BE *THEM* INSTEAD? I MEAN, WE WERE IMMOBILIZED PRACTICALLY THE WHOLE TIME.
BUT THEY WERE GIVING IT THEIR ALL TO KEEP WHAT THEY HAD UNTIL THE VERY END.
TEAM TETSUTETSU, I MEAN.
DON'T WORRY. WE'RE NOT COLLUDING OR ANYTHING.
THIS JUST FEELS RIGHT.
Y...
YOU GUYS!!
WHOAAA!

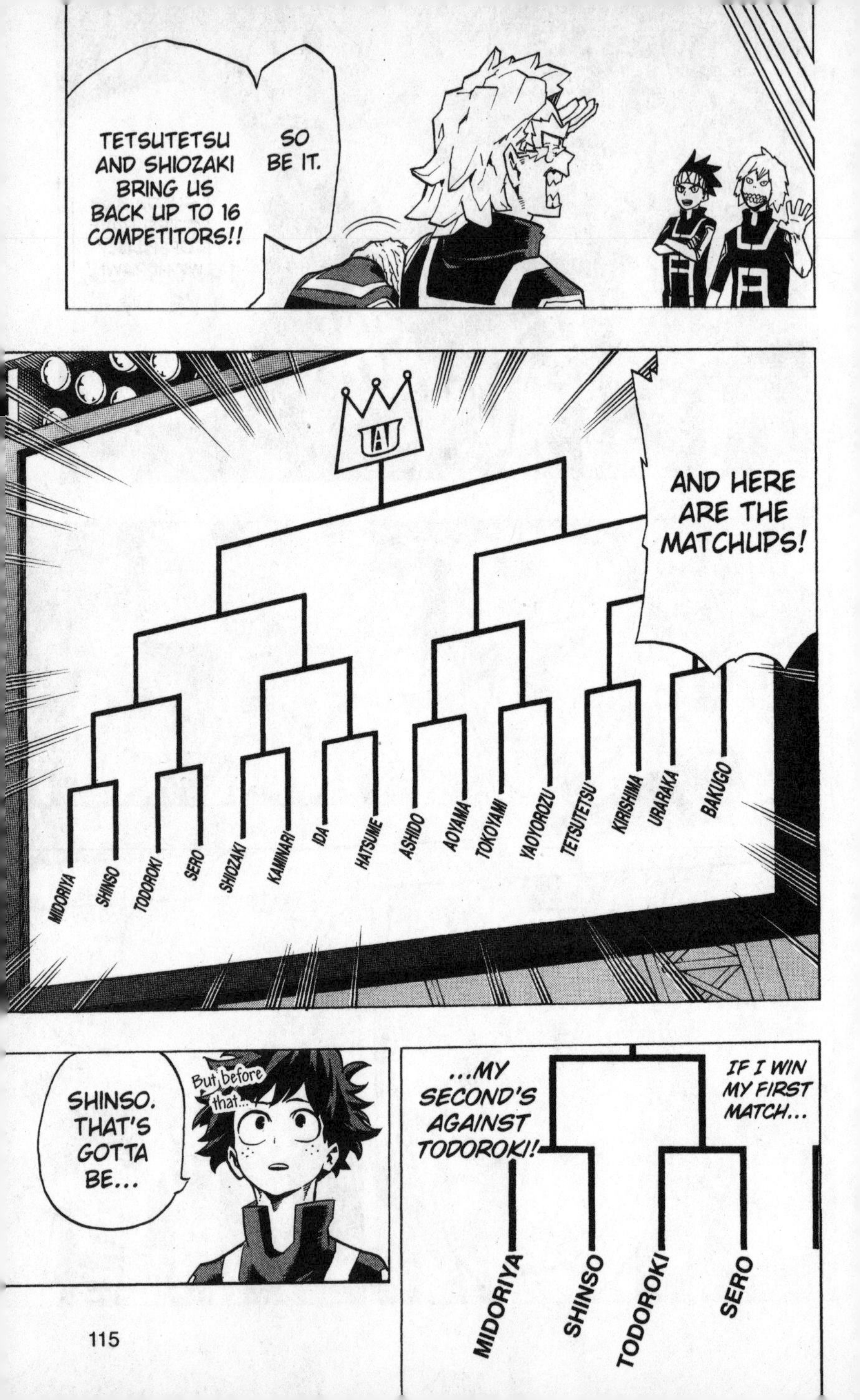
SO BE IT.
TETSUTETSU AND SHIOZAKI BRING US BACK UP TO 16 COMPETITORS!!
AND HERE ARE THE MATCHUPS!
MIDORIYA
SHINSO
TODOROKI
SERO
SHIOZAKI
KAMINARI
IDA
HATSUME
ASHIDO
AOYAMA
TOKOYAMI
YAOYOROZU
TETSUTETSU
KIRISHIMA
URARAKA
BAKUGO
IF I WIN MY FIRST MATCH...
...MY SECOND'S AGAINST TODOROKI!
MIDORIYA
SHINSO
TODOROKI
SERO
But before that...
SHINSO. THAT'S GOTTA BE...

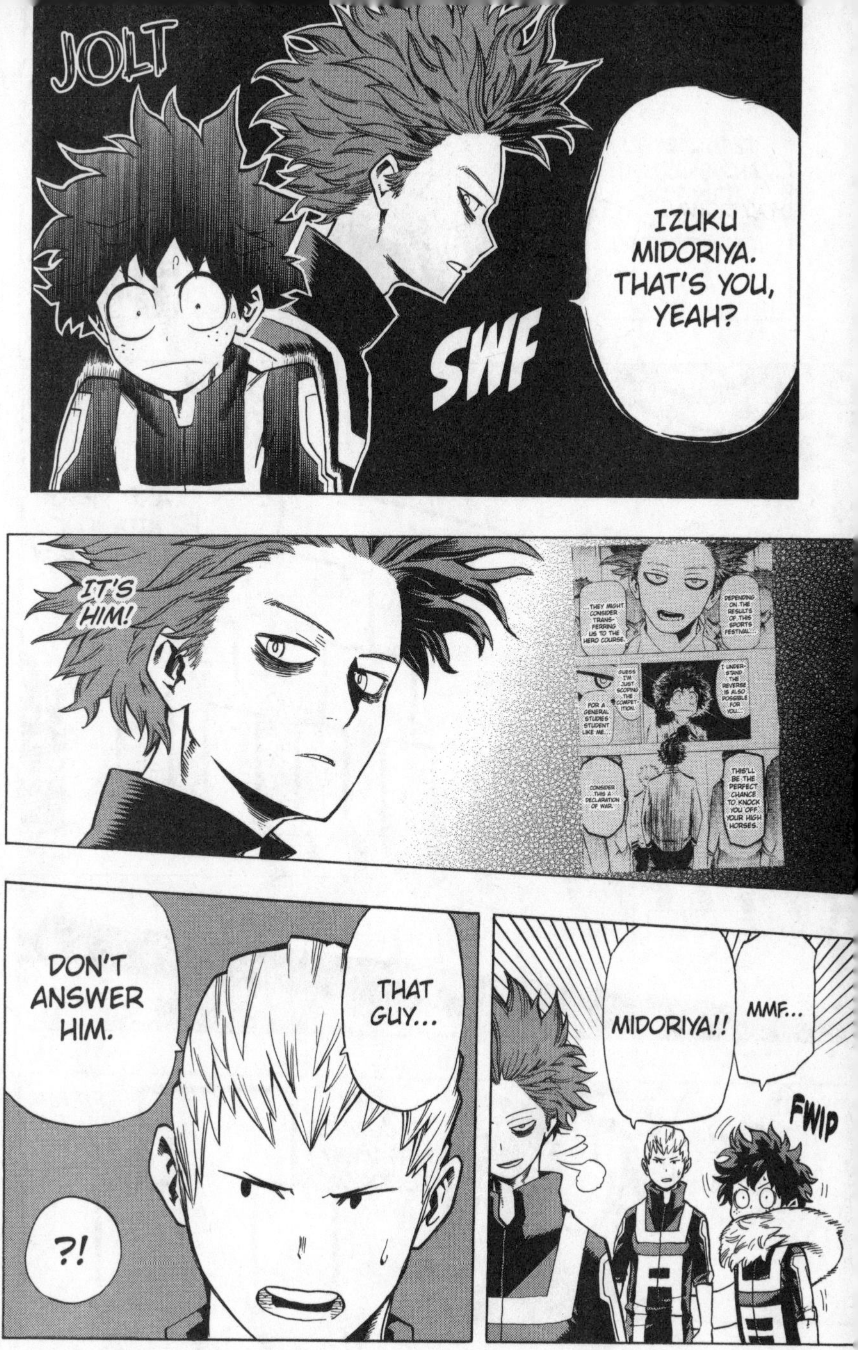
IZUKU MIDORIYA. THAT'S YOU, YEAH?
SWF
JOLT
DEPENDING ON THE RESULTS OF THIS SPORTS FESTIVAL...
THEY MIGHT CONSIDER TRANS-FERRING US TO THE HERO COURSE.
I UNDER-STAND THE REVERSE IS ALSO POSSIBLE FOR YOU...
GUESS I'M JUST SCOPING THE COMPET-ITION.
FOR A GENERAL STUDIES STUDENT LIKE ME...
THIS'LL BE THE PERFECT CHANCE TO KNOCK YOU OFF YOUR HIGH HORSES.
CONSIDER THIS A DECLARATION OF WAR.
IT'S HIM!
MMF...
MIDORIYA!!
FWIP
THAT GUY...
DON'T ANSWER HIM.
?!

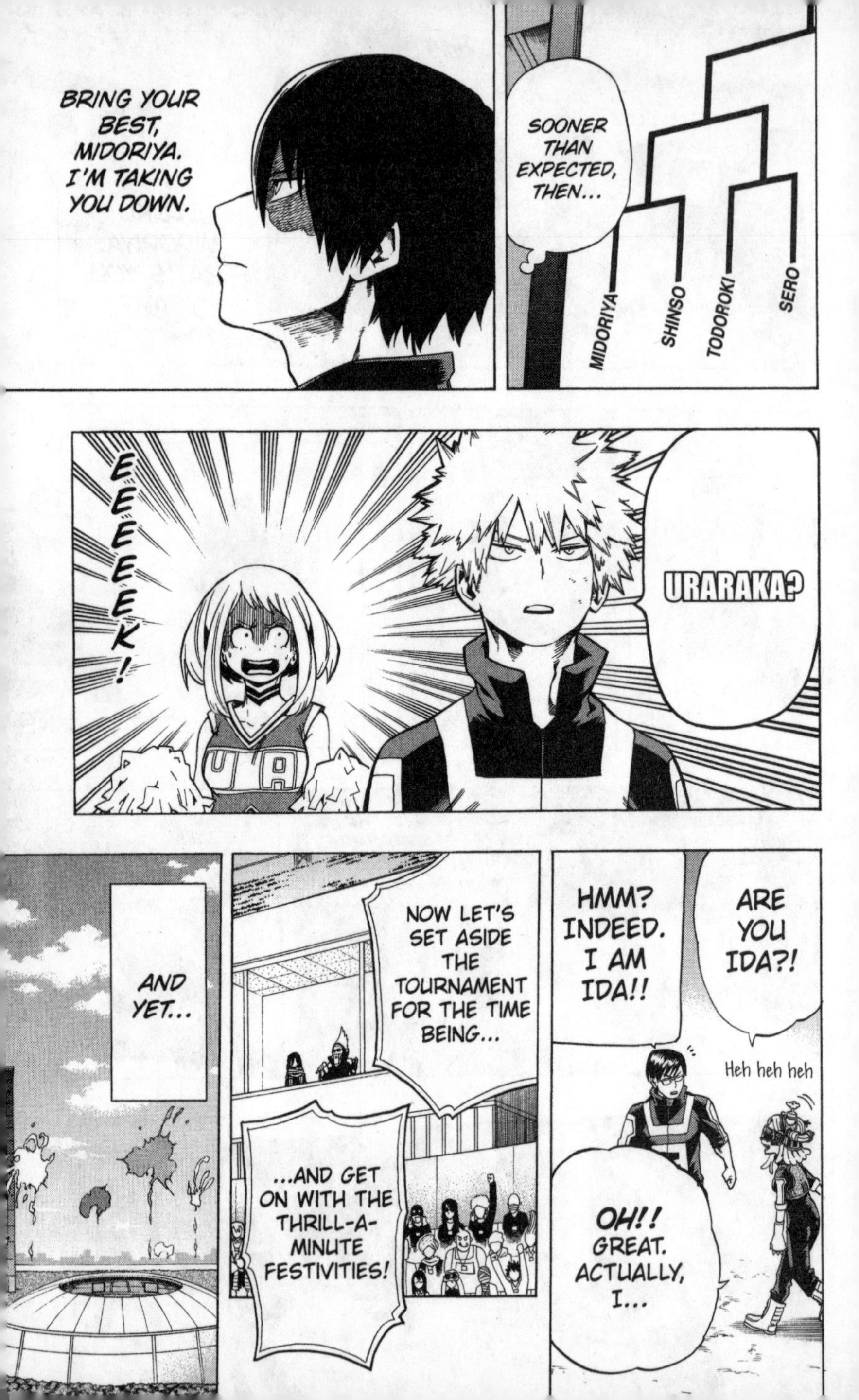
SOONER THAN EXPECTED, THEN...
MIDORIYA
SHINSO
TODOROKI
SERO
BRING YOUR BEST, MIDORIYA. I'M TAKING YOU DOWN.
URARAKA?
EEEEEK!
ARE YOU IDA?!
HMM? INDEED. I AM IDA!!
Heh heh heh
OH!! GREAT. ACTUALLY, I...
NOW LET'S SET ASIDE THE TOURNAMENT FOR THE TIME BEING...
...AND GET ON WITH THE THRILL-A-MINUTE FESTIVITIES!
AND YET...

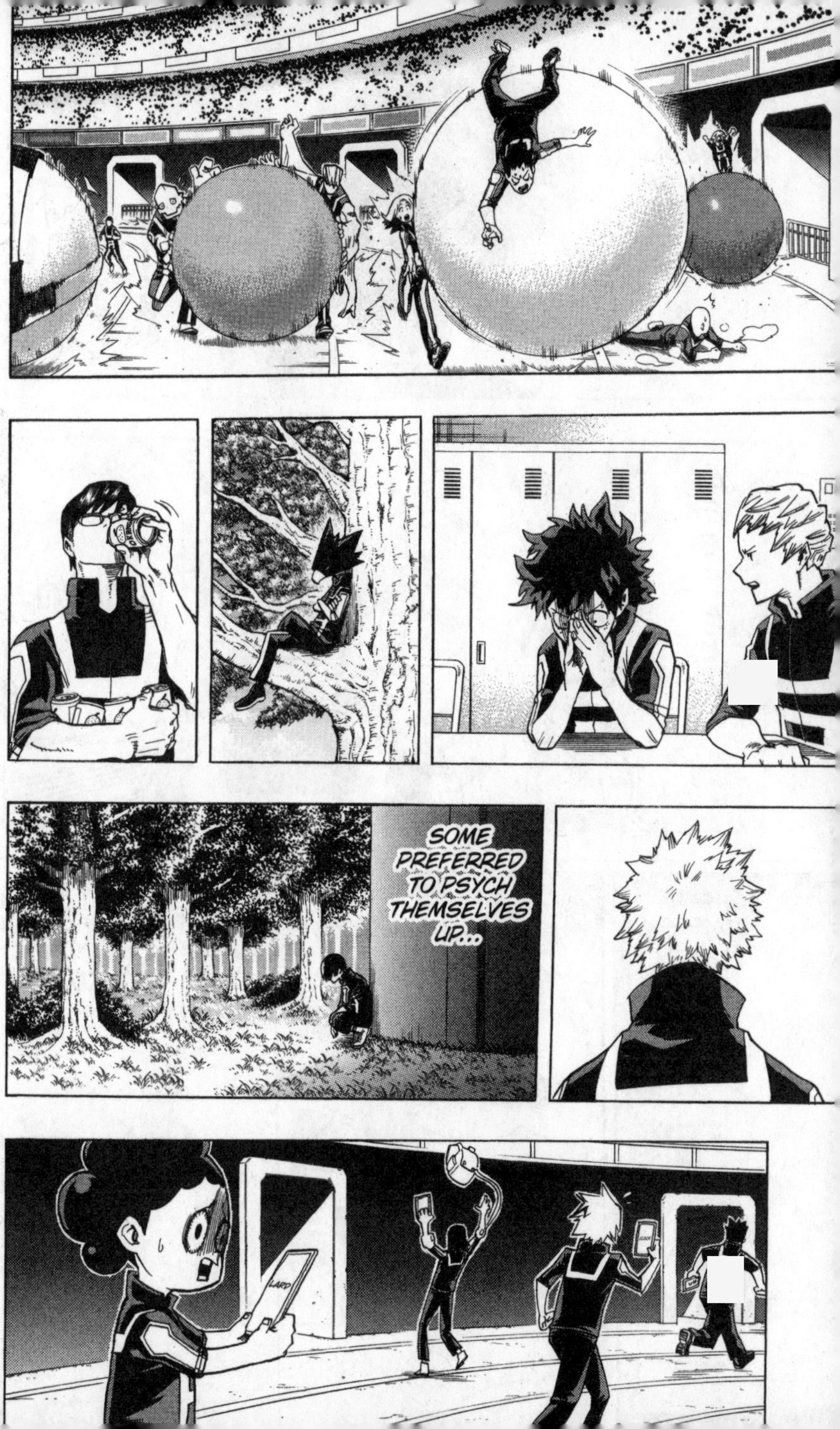
SOME PREFERRED TO PSYCH THEMSELVES UP...
LARD

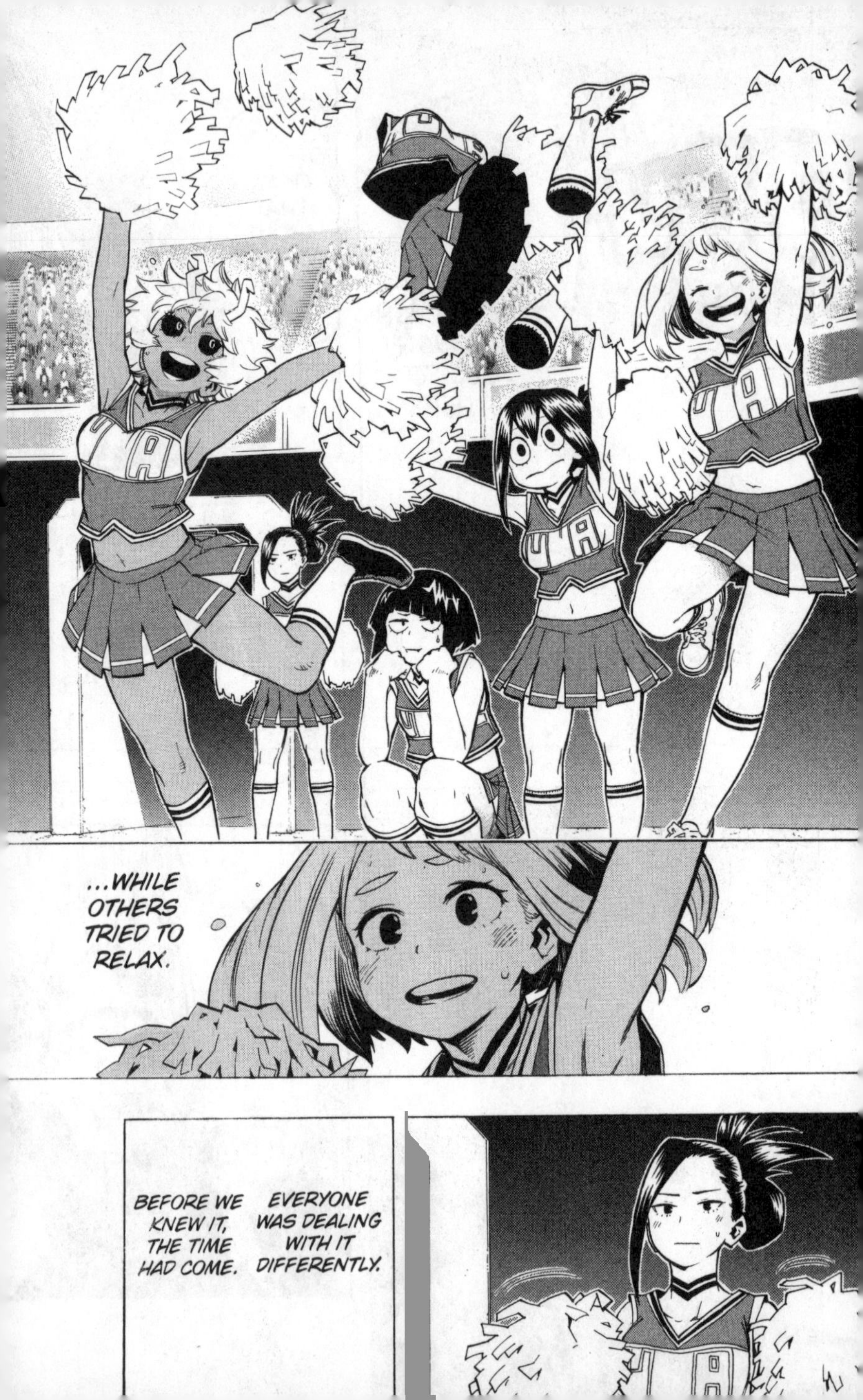
...WHILE OTHERS TRIED TO RELAX.
EVERYONE WAS DEALING WITH IT DIFFERENTLY.
BEFORE WE KNEW IT, THE TIME HAD COME.

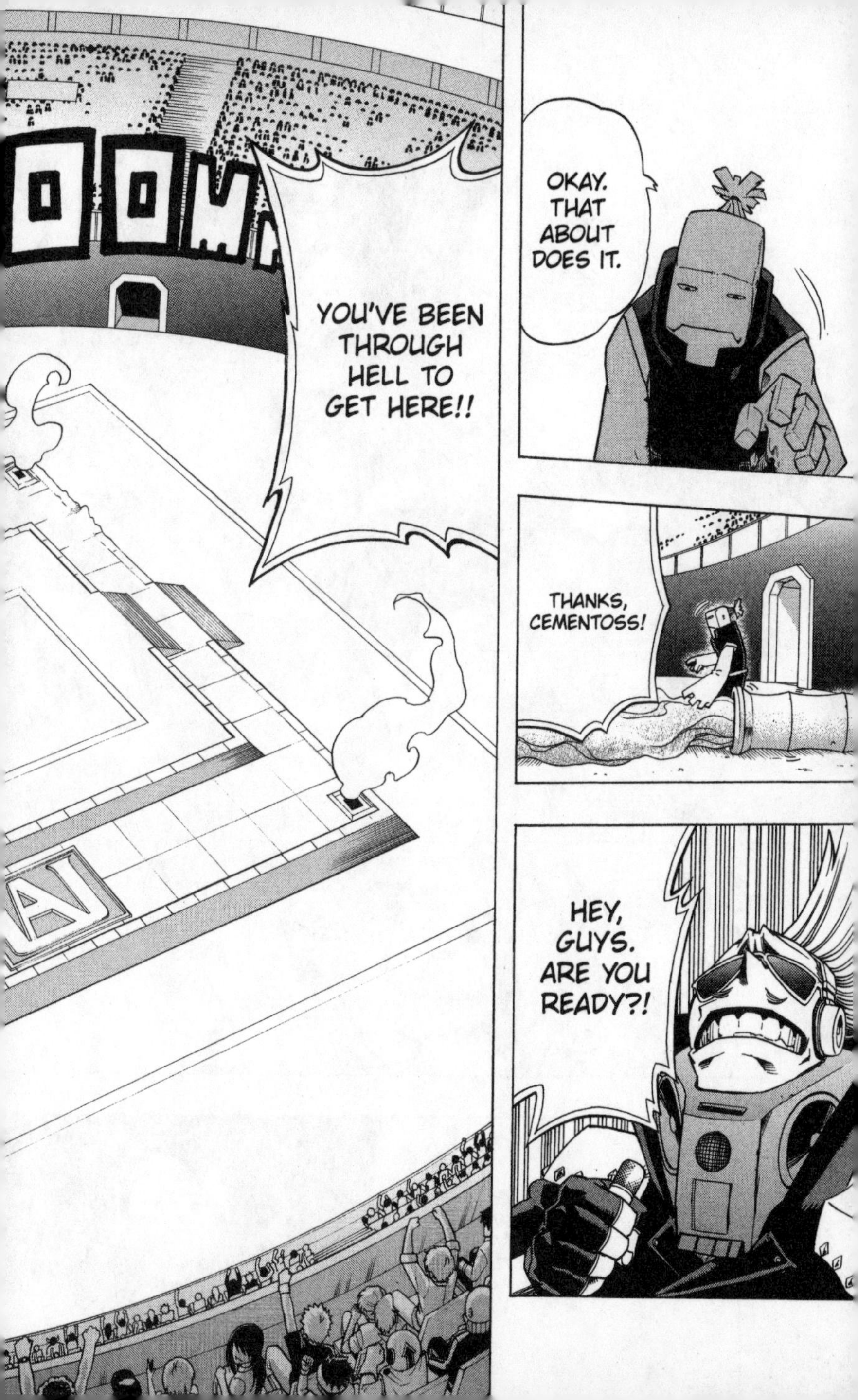
OKAY. THAT ABOUT DOES IT.
THANKS, CEMENTOSS!
HEY, GUYS. ARE YOU READY?!
YOU'VE BEEN THROUGH HELL TO GET HERE!!

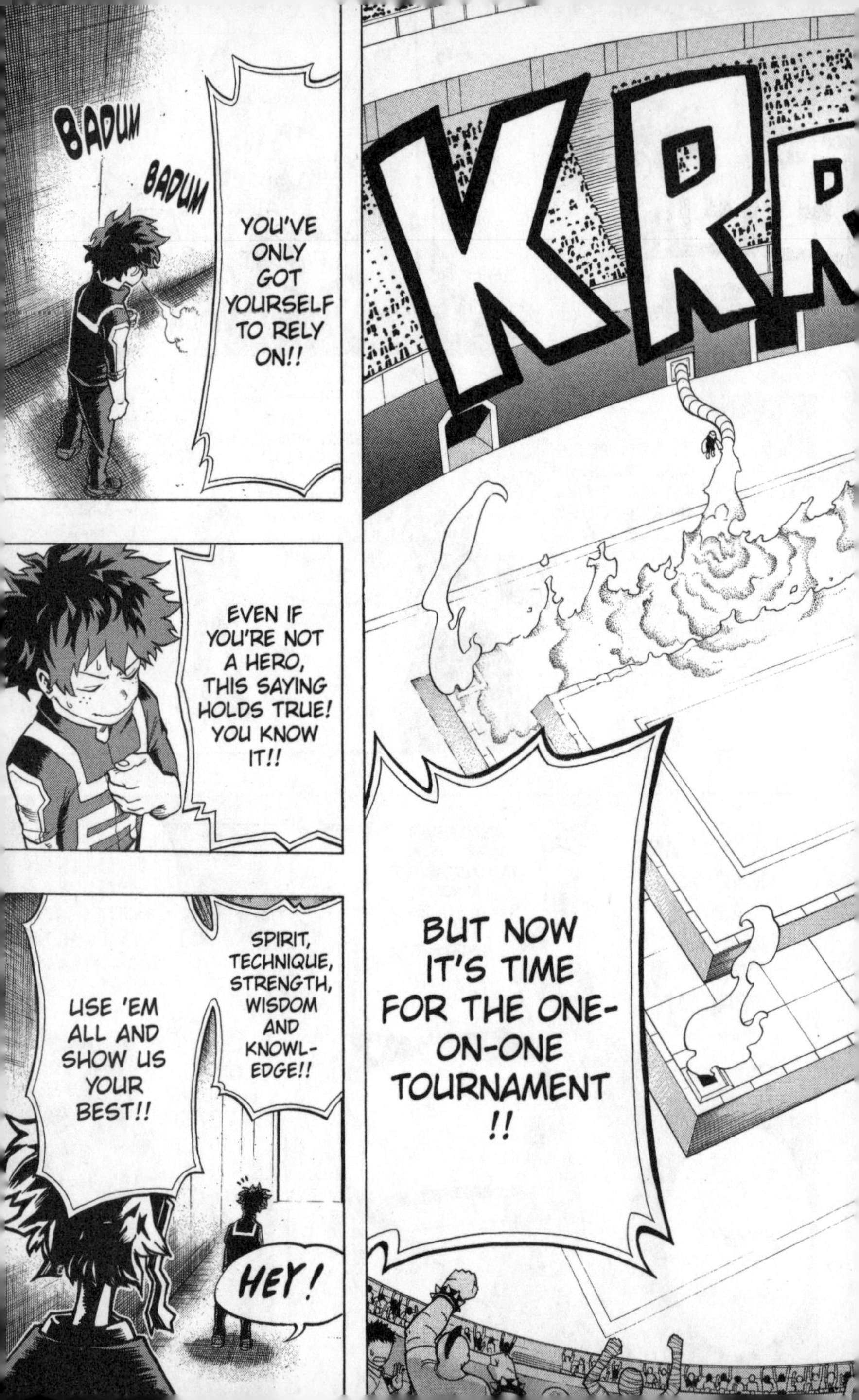
KRR
BUT NOW IT'S TIME FOR THE ONE-ON-ONE TOURNAMENT!!
BADUM
BADUM
YOU'VE ONLY GOT YOURSELF TO RELY ON!!
EVEN IF YOU'RE NOT A HERO, THIS SAYING HOLDS TRUE! YOU KNOW IT!!
SPIRIT, TECHNIQUE, STRENGTH, WISDOM AND KNOWL-EDGE!!
USE 'EM ALL AND SHOW US YOUR BEST!!
HEY!

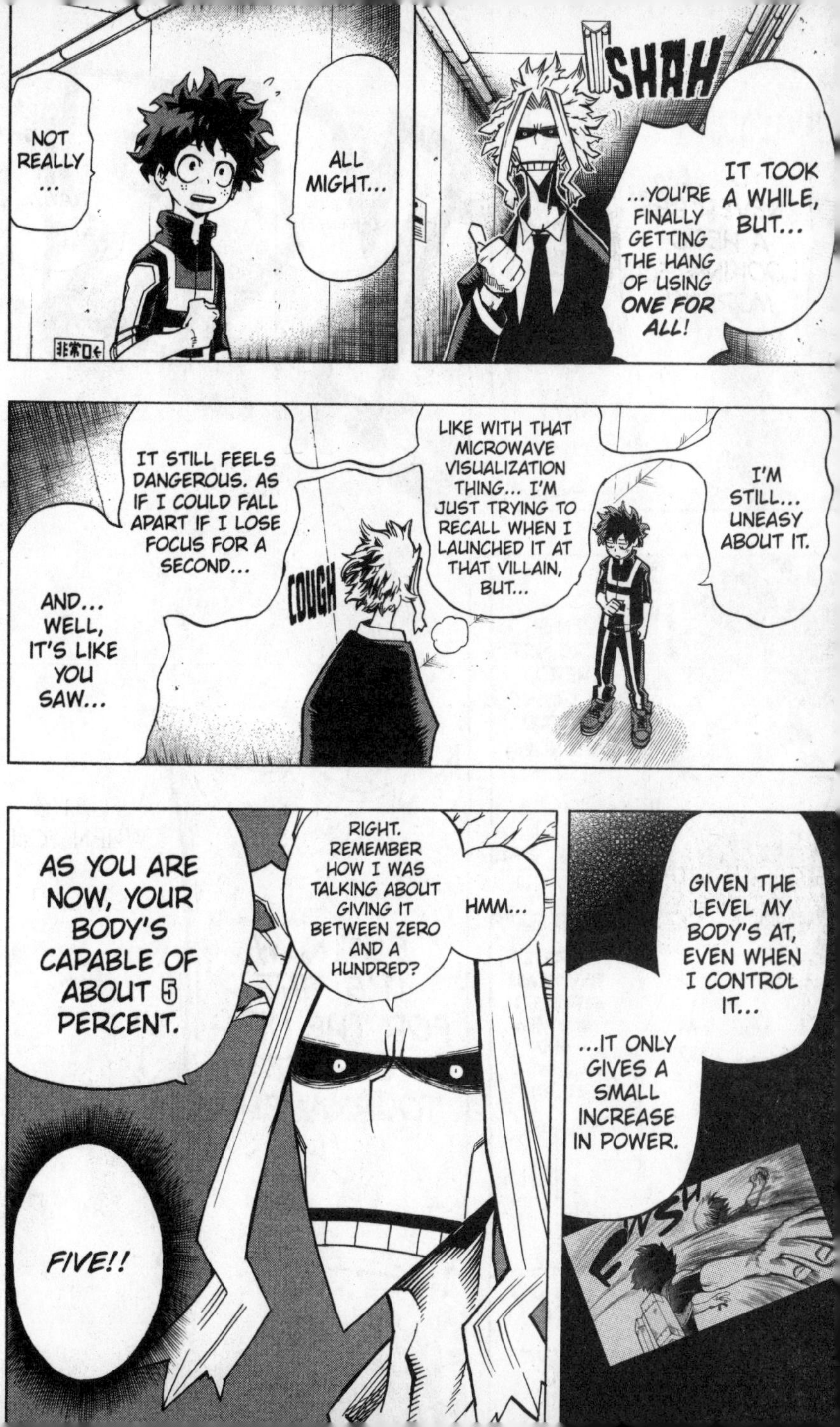
SHAH
IT TOOK A WHILE, BUT...
...YOU'RE FINALLY GETTING THE HANG OF USING ONE FOR ALL!
ALL MIGHT...
NOT REALLY...
非常口
I'M STILL... UNEASY ABOUT IT.
LIKE WITH THAT MICROWAVE VISUALIZATION THING... I'M JUST TRYING TO RECALL WHEN I LAUNCHED IT AT THAT VILLAIN, BUT...
COUGH
IT STILL FEELS DANGEROUS. AS IF I COULD FALL APART IF I LOSE FOCUS FOR A SECOND...
AND... WELL, IT'S LIKE YOU SAW...
GIVEN THE LEVEL MY BODY'S AT, EVEN WHEN I CONTROL IT...
...IT ONLY GIVES A SMALL INCREASE IN POWER.
FWSH
HMM...
RIGHT. REMEMBER HOW I WAS TALKING ABOUT GIVING IT BETWEEN ZERO AND A HUNDRED?
AS YOU ARE NOW, YOUR BODY'S CAPABLE OF ABOUT 5 PERCENT.
FIVE!!

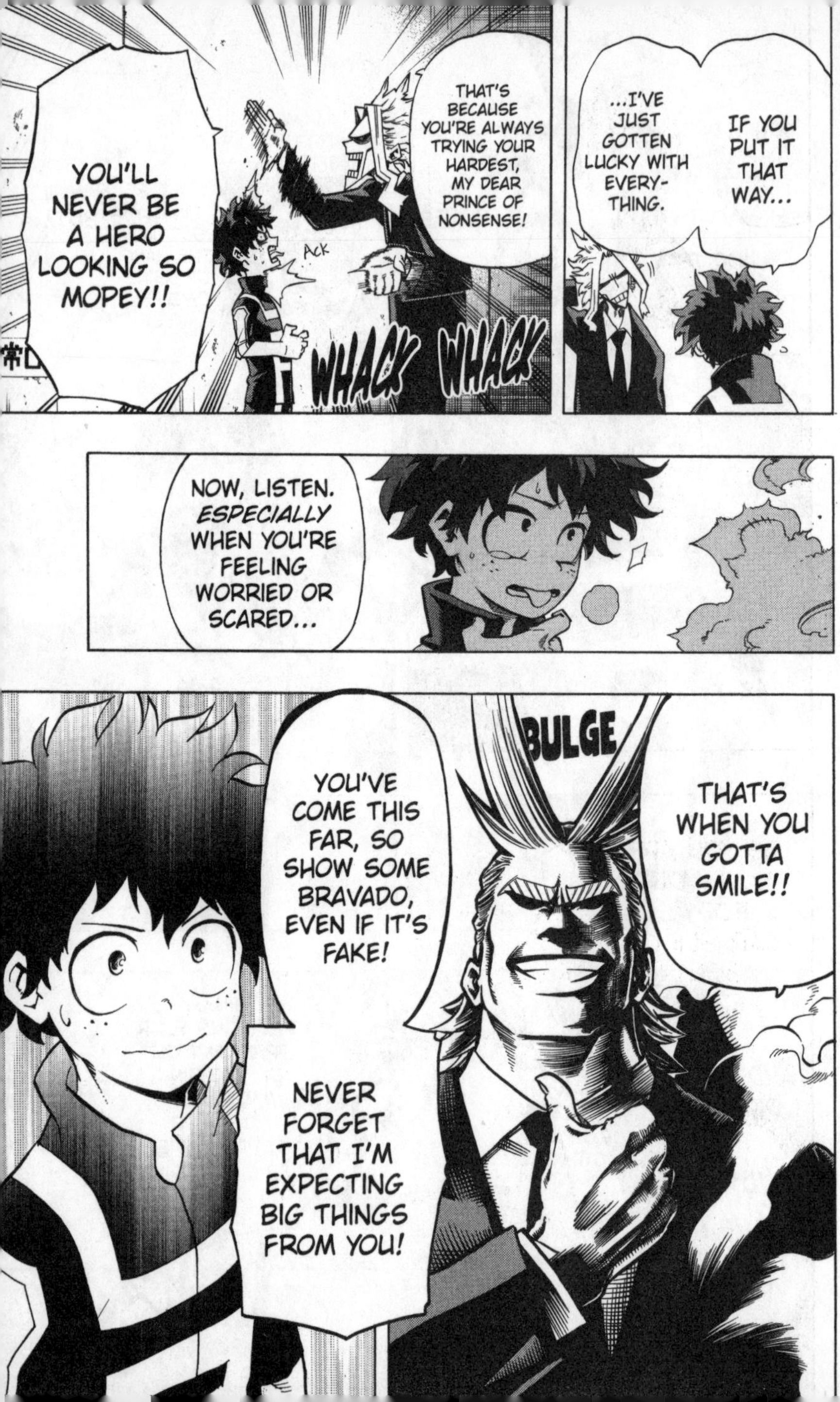

IF YOU PUT IT THAT WAY...
...I'VE JUST GOTTEN LUCKY WITH EVERY-THING.
THAT'S BECAUSE YOU'RE ALWAYS TRYING YOUR HARDEST, MY DEAR PRINCE OF NONSENSE!
WHACK WHACK
ACK
YOU'LL NEVER BE A HERO LOOKING SO MOPEY!!
NOW, LISTEN. *ESPECIALLY* WHEN YOU'RE FEELING WORRIED OR SCARED...
BULGE
THAT'S WHEN YOU GOTTA SMILE!!
YOU'VE COME THIS FAR, SO SHOW SOME BRAVADO, EVEN IF IT'S FAKE!
NEVER FORGET THAT I'M EXPECTING BIG THINGS FROM YOU!

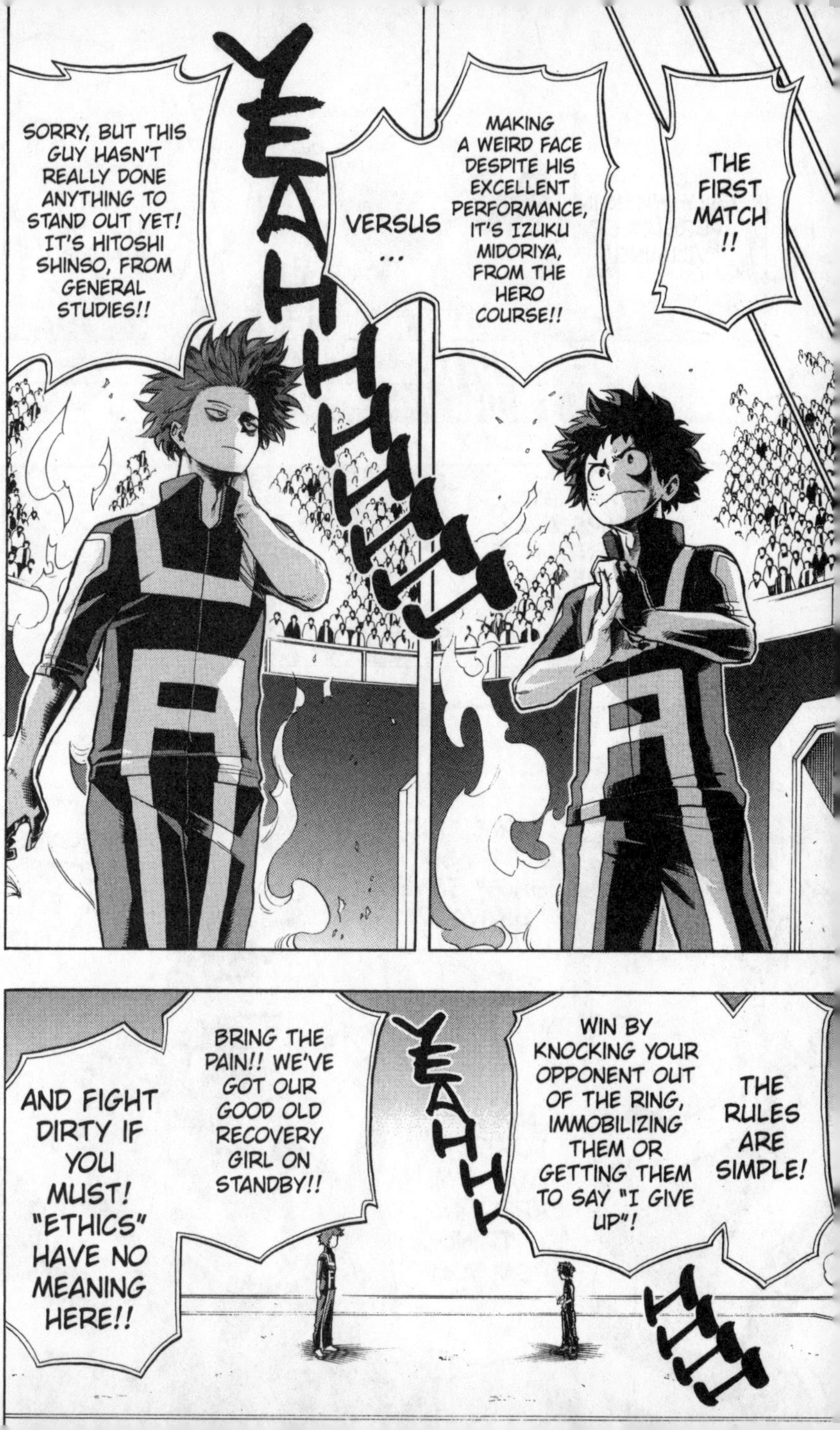
THE FIRST MATCH!!
MAKING A WEIRD FACE DESPITE HIS EXCELLENT PERFORMANCE, IT'S IZUKU MIDORIYA, FROM THE HERO COURSE!!
VERSUS...
SORRY, BUT THIS GUY HASN'T REALLY DONE ANYTHING TO STAND OUT YET! IT'S HITOSHI SHINSO, FROM GENERAL STUDIES!!
YEAHHHHH
THE RULES ARE SIMPLE!
WIN BY KNOCKING YOUR OPPONENT OUT OF THE RING, IMMOBILIZING THEM OR GETTING THEM TO SAY "I GIVE UP"!
YEAHHHHH
BRING THE PAIN!! WE'VE GOT OUR GOOD OLD RECOVERY GIRL ON STANDBY!!
AND FIGHT DIRTY IF YOU MUST! "ETHICS" HAVE NO MEANING HERE!!

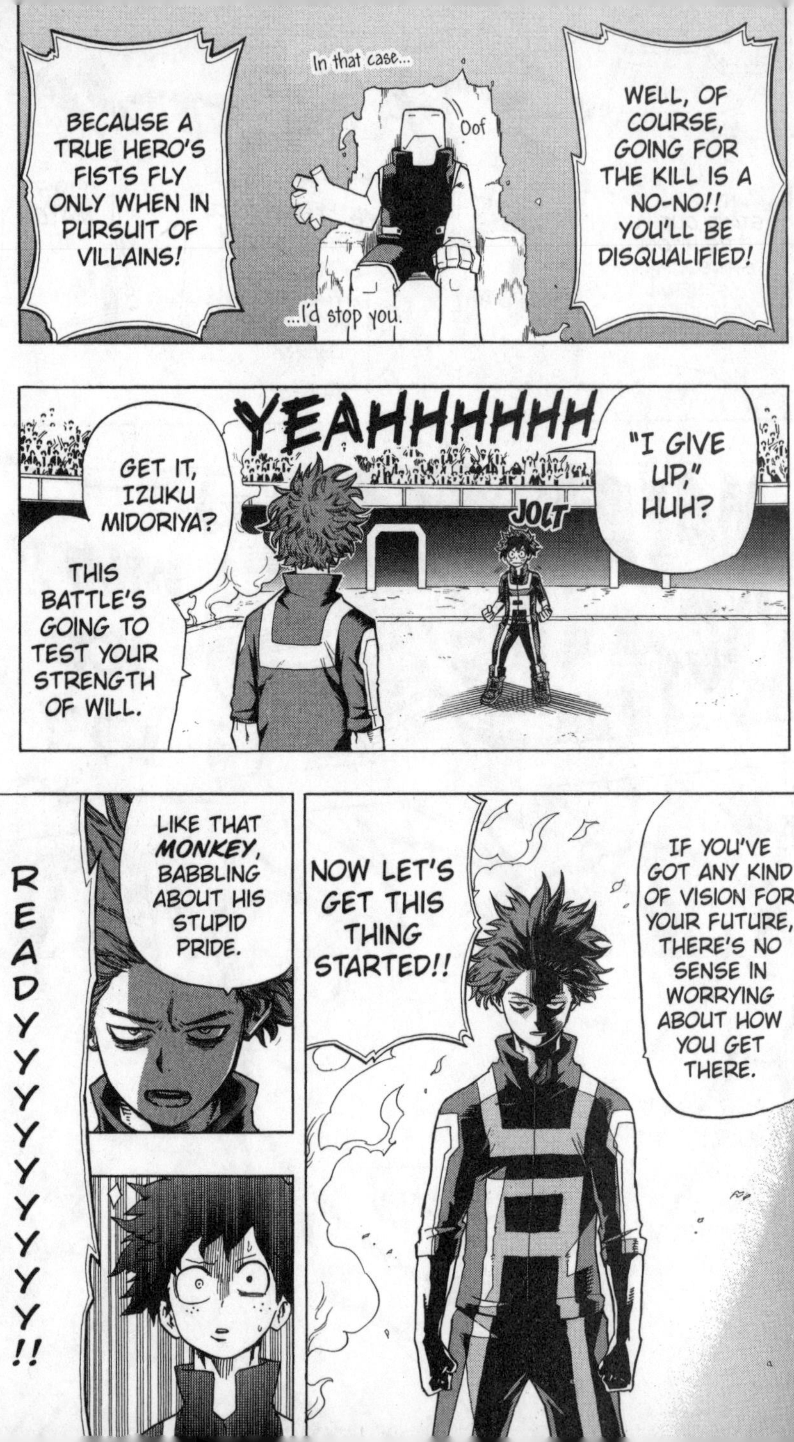
WELL, OF COURSE, GOING FOR THE KILL IS A NO-NO!! YOU'LL BE DISQUALIFIED!
In that case...
Oof
...I'd stop you.
BECAUSE A TRUE HERO'S FISTS FLY ONLY WHEN IN PURSUIT OF VILLAINS!
"I GIVE UP," HUH?
YEAHHHHHH
JOLT
GET IT, IZUKU MIDORIYA?
THIS BATTLE'S GOING TO TEST YOUR STRENGTH OF WILL.
IF YOU'VE GOT ANY KIND OF VISION FOR YOUR FUTURE, THERE'S NO SENSE IN WORRYING ABOUT HOW YOU GET THERE.
NOW LET'S GET THIS THING STARTED!!
LIKE THAT *MONKEY*, BABBLING ABOUT HIS STUPID PRIDE.
READYYYYYYYYY!!

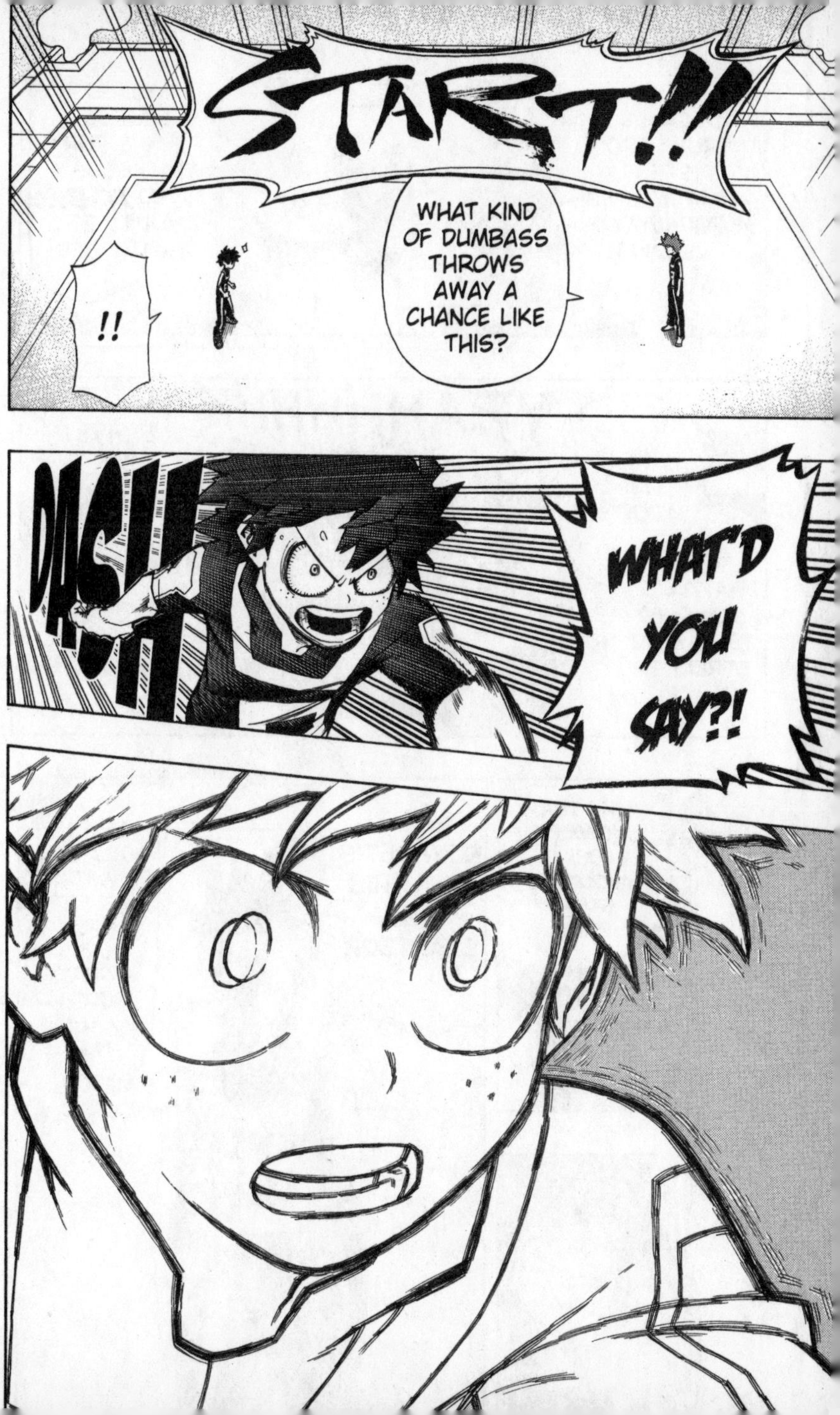
START!!
WHAT KIND OF DUMBASS THROWS AWAY A CHANCE LIKE THIS?
!!
WHAT'D YOU SAY?!
DASH

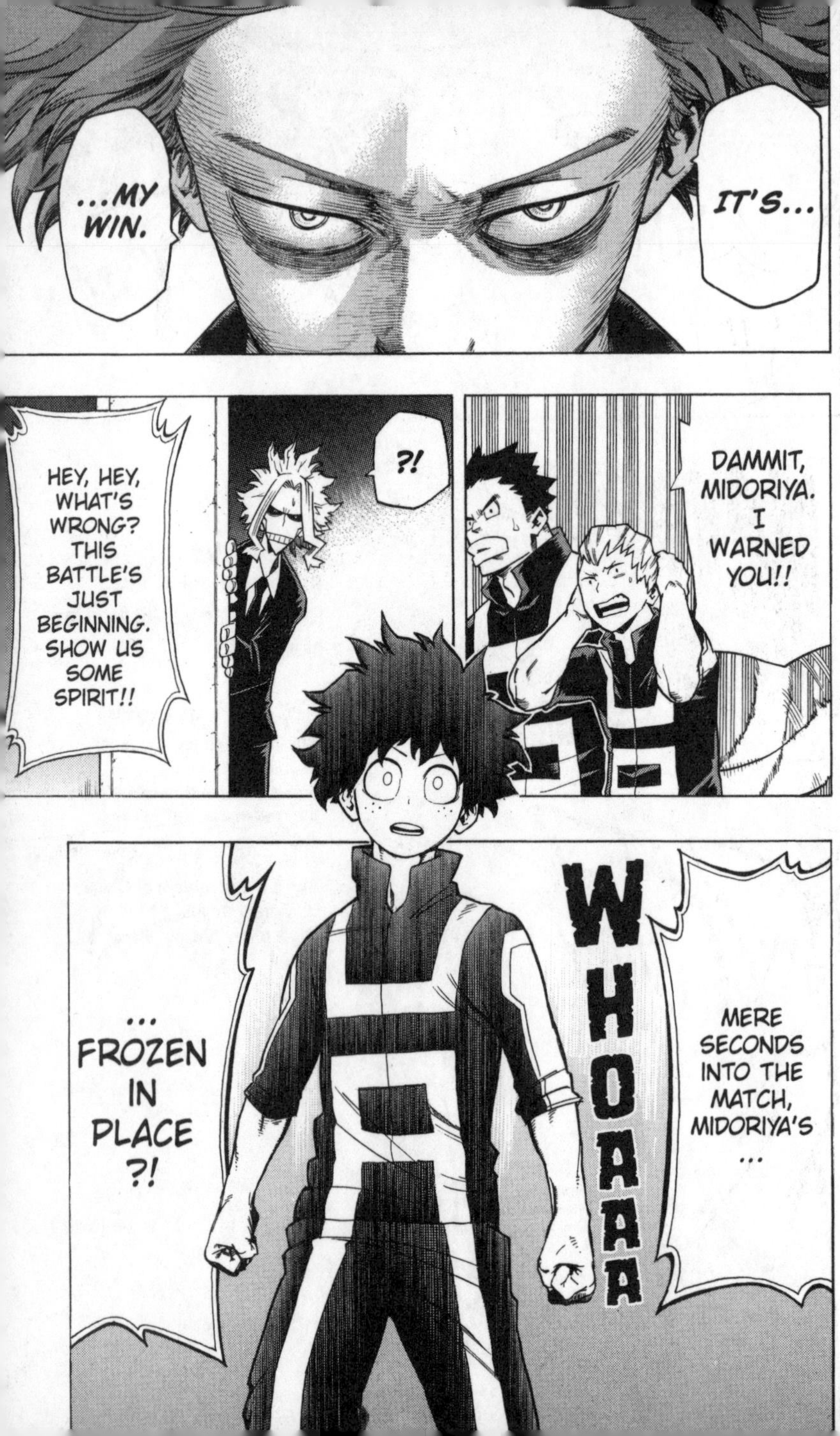
IT'S...
...MY WIN.
DAMMIT, MIDORIYA. I WARNED YOU!!
?!
HEY, HEY, WHAT'S WRONG? THIS BATTLE'S JUST BEGINNING. SHOW US SOME SPIRIT!!
MERE SECONDS INTO THE MATCH, MIDORIYA'S ...
WHOAAA
... FROZEN IN PLACE ?!

ITSUKA KENDO (15)

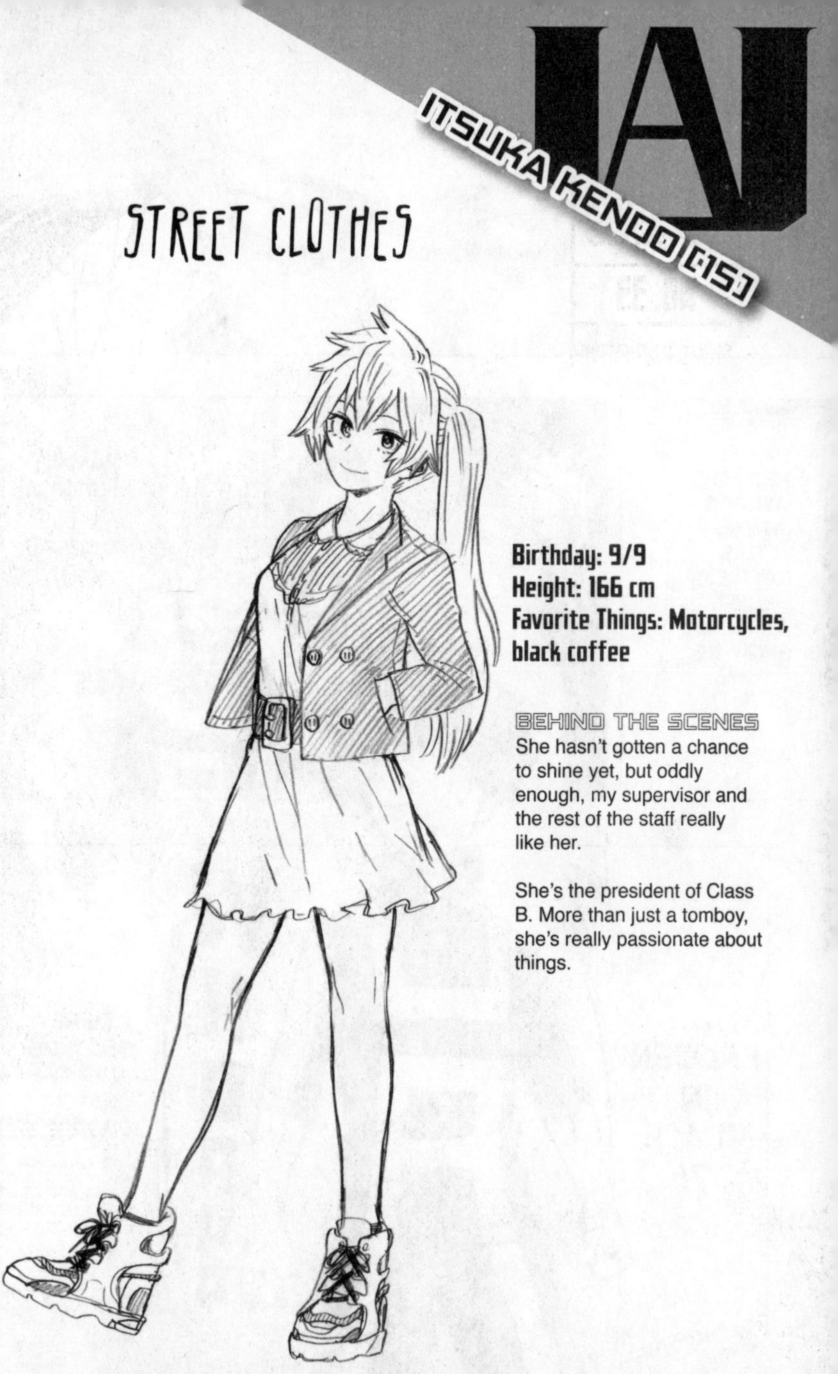
STREET CLOTHES

Birthday: 9/9
Height: 166 cm
Favorite Things: Motorcycles, black coffee

BEHIND THE SCENES

She hasn't gotten a chance to shine yet, but oddly enough, my supervisor and the rest of the staff really like her.

She's the president of Class B. More than just a tomboy, she's really passionate about things.

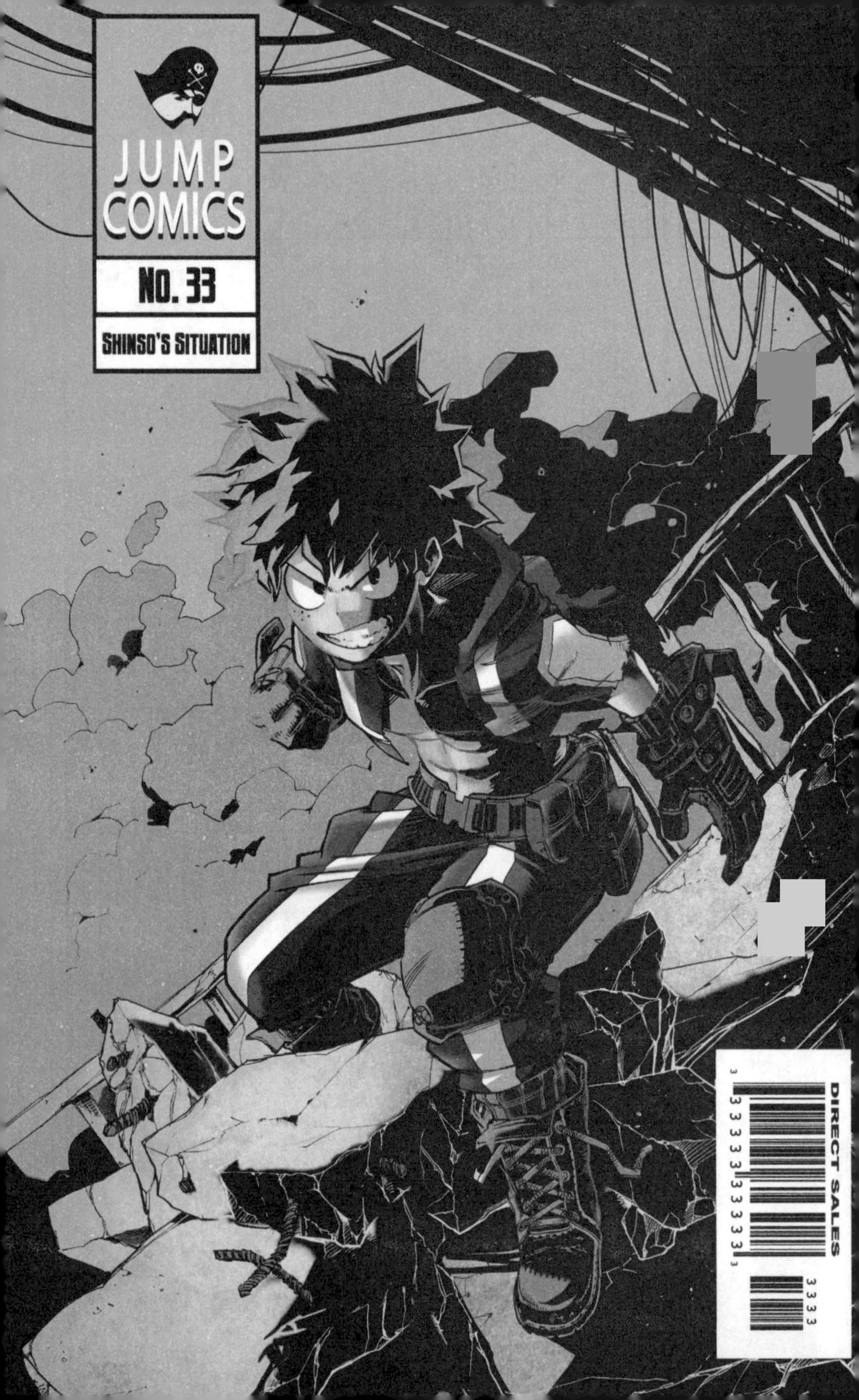
JUMP COMICS
NO. 33
SHINSO'S SITUATION
DIRECT SALES

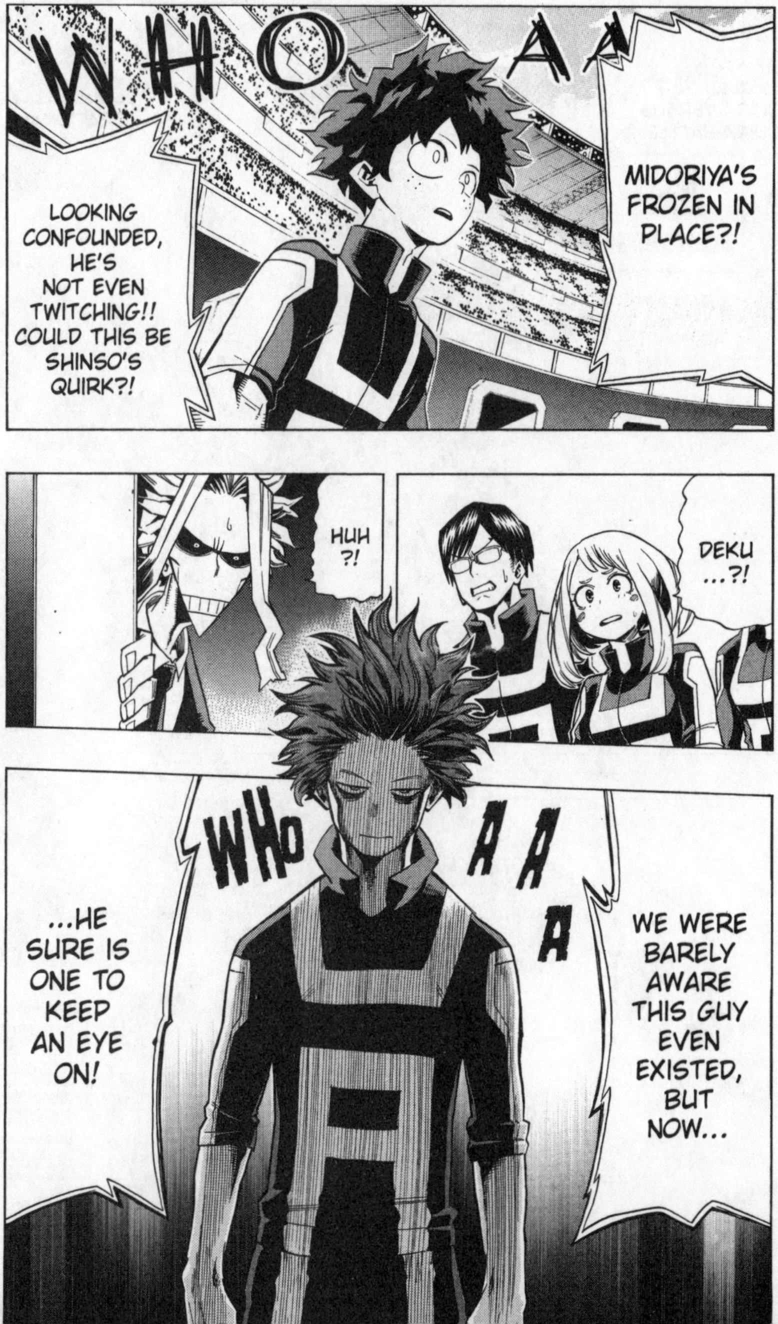
WHOA
MIDORIYA'S FROZEN IN PLACE?!
LOOKING CONFOUNDED, HE'S NOT EVEN TWITCHING!! COULD THIS BE SHINSO'S QUIRK?!
DEKU ...?!
HUH ?!
WHOAAA
WE WERE BARELY AWARE THIS GUY EVEN EXISTED, BUT NOW...
...HE SURE IS ONE TO KEEP AN EYE ON!

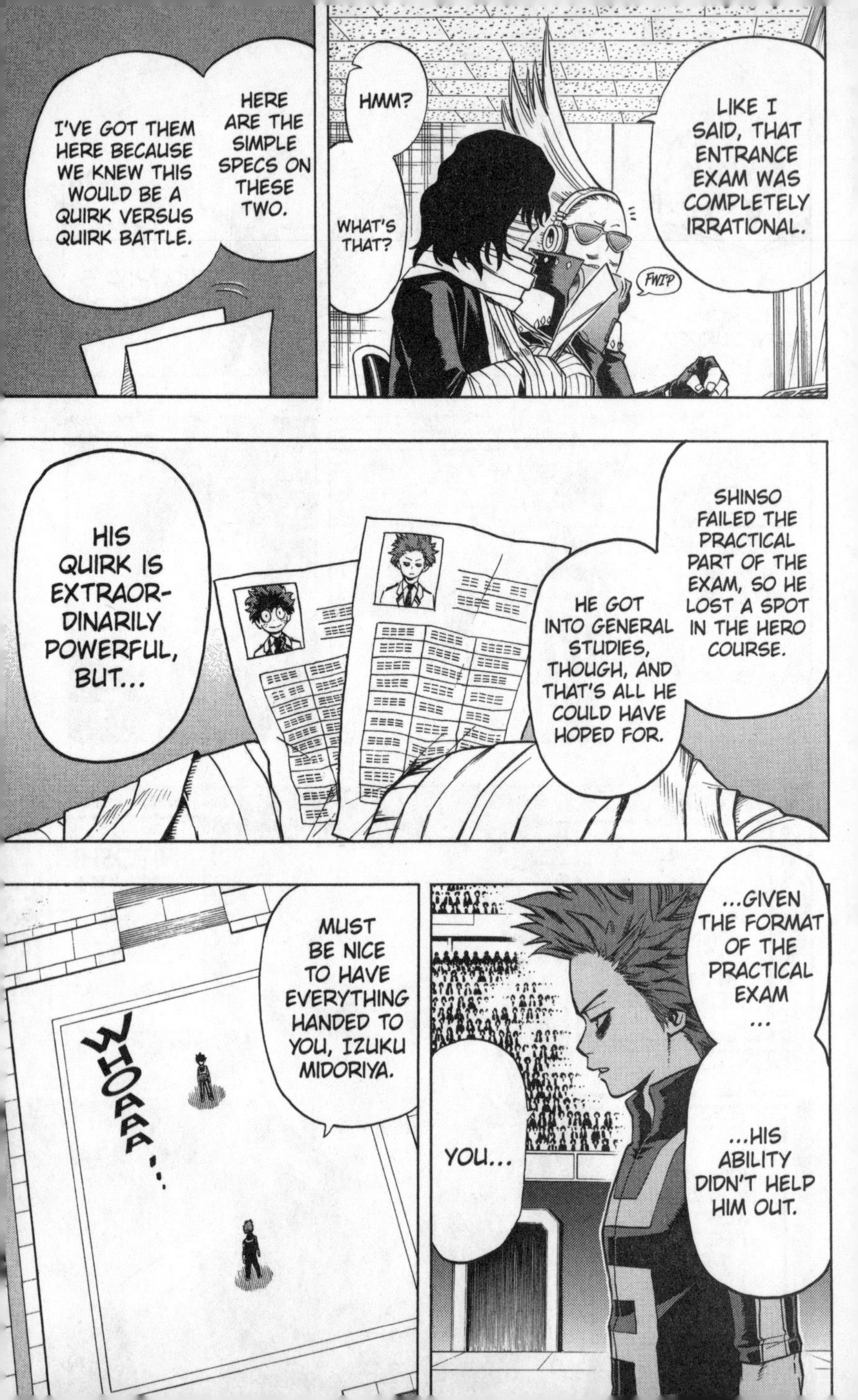
LIKE I SAID, THAT ENTRANCE EXAM WAS COMPLETELY IRRATIONAL.
FWIP
HMM?
WHAT'S THAT?
HERE ARE THE SIMPLE SPECS ON THESE TWO.
I'VE GOT THEM HERE BECAUSE WE KNEW THIS WOULD BE A QUIRK VERSUS QUIRK BATTLE.
SHINSO FAILED THE PRACTICAL PART OF THE EXAM, SO HE LOST A SPOT IN THE HERO COURSE.
HE GOT INTO GENERAL STUDIES, THOUGH, AND THAT'S ALL HE COULD HAVE HOPED FOR.
HIS QUIRK IS EXTRAOR-DINARILY POWERFUL, BUT...
...GIVEN THE FORMAT OF THE PRACTICAL EXAM ...
...HIS ABILITY DIDN'T HELP HIM OUT.
YOU...
MUST BE NICE TO HAVE EVERYTHING HANDED TO YOU, IZUKU MIDORIYA.
WHOAAA...

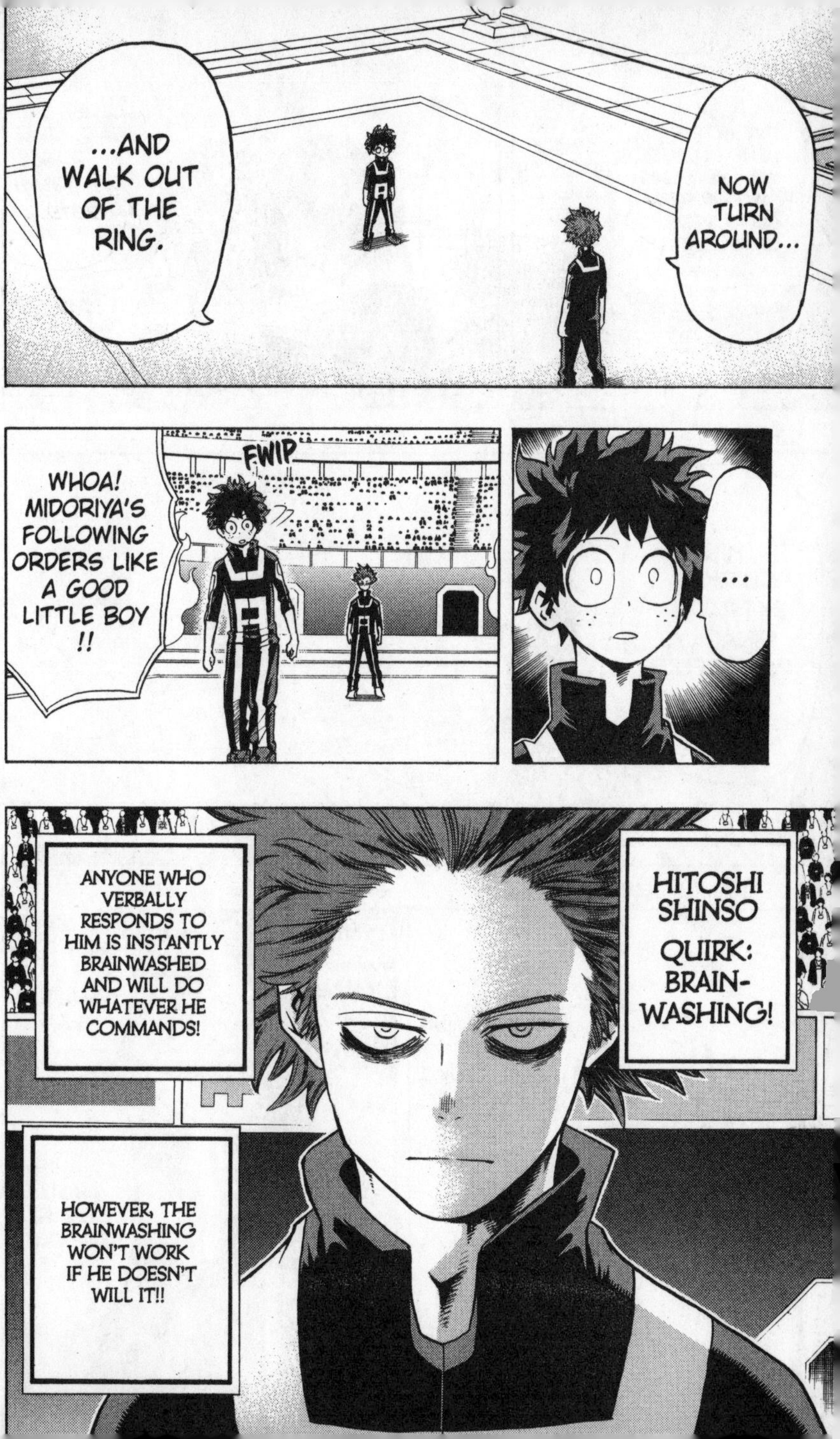
NOW TURN AROUND...
...AND WALK OUT OF THE RING.
...
FWIP
WHOA! MIDORIYA'S FOLLOWING ORDERS LIKE A GOOD LITTLE BOY !!
HITOSHI SHINSO
QUIRK: BRAIN-WASHING!
ANYONE WHO VERBALLY RESPONDS TO HIM IS INSTANTLY BRAINWASHED AND WILL DO WHATEVER HE COMMANDS!
HOWEVER, THE BRAINWASHING WON'T WORK IF HE DOESN'T WILL IT!!

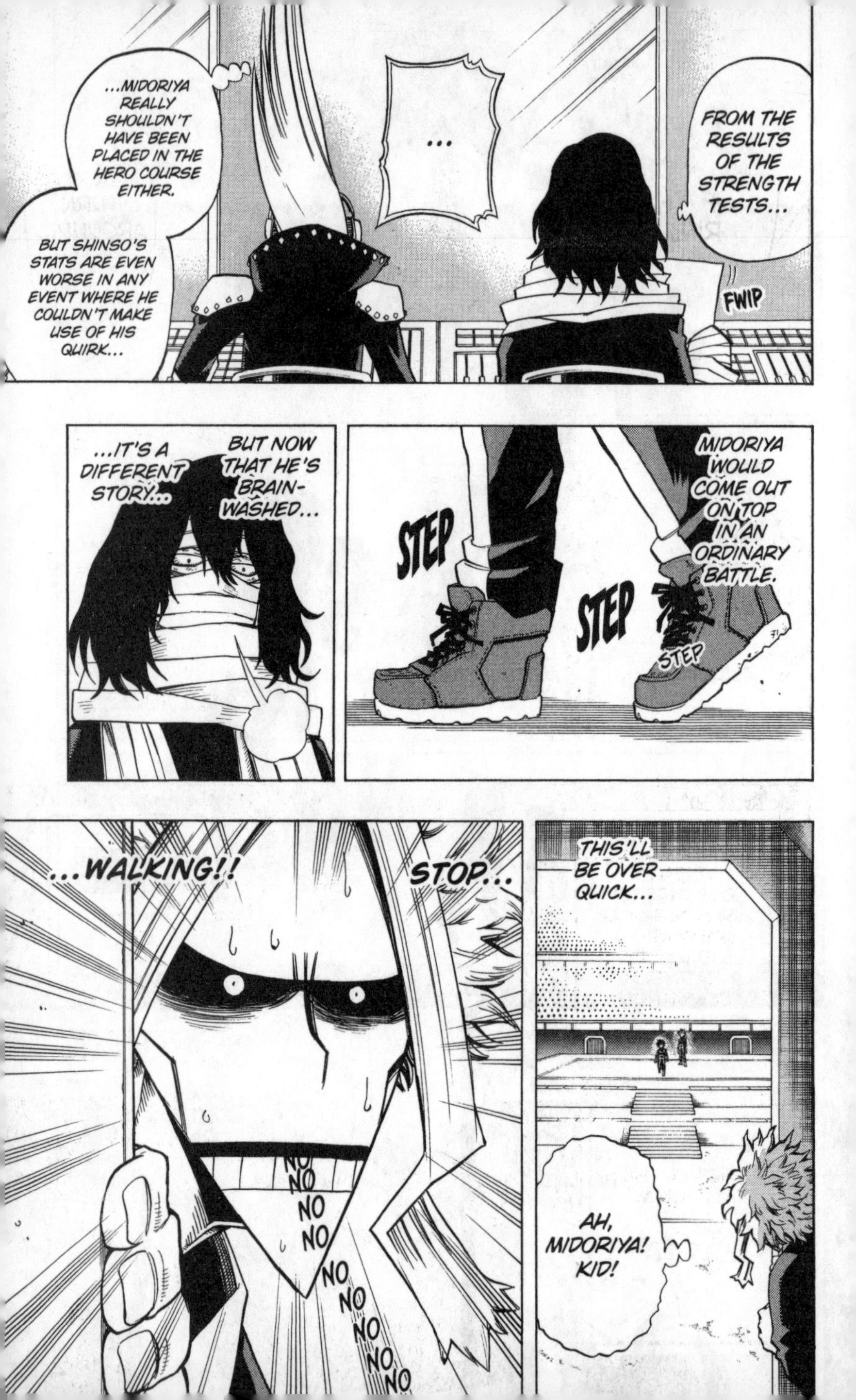
FROM THE RESULTS OF THE STRENGTH TESTS...
FWIP
...
...MIDORIYA REALLY SHOULDN'T HAVE BEEN PLACED IN THE HERO COURSE EITHER.
BUT SHINSO'S STATS ARE EVEN WORSE IN ANY EVENT WHERE HE COULDN'T MAKE USE OF HIS QUIRK...
MIDORIYA WOULD COME OUT ON TOP IN AN ORDINARY BATTLE.
STEP
STEP
STEP
BUT NOW THAT HE'S BRAIN-WASHED...
...IT'S A DIFFERENT STORY...
THIS'LL BE OVER QUICK...
AH, MIDORIYA! KID!
STOP...
...WALKING!!
NO NO NO NO NO NO NO NO NO NO

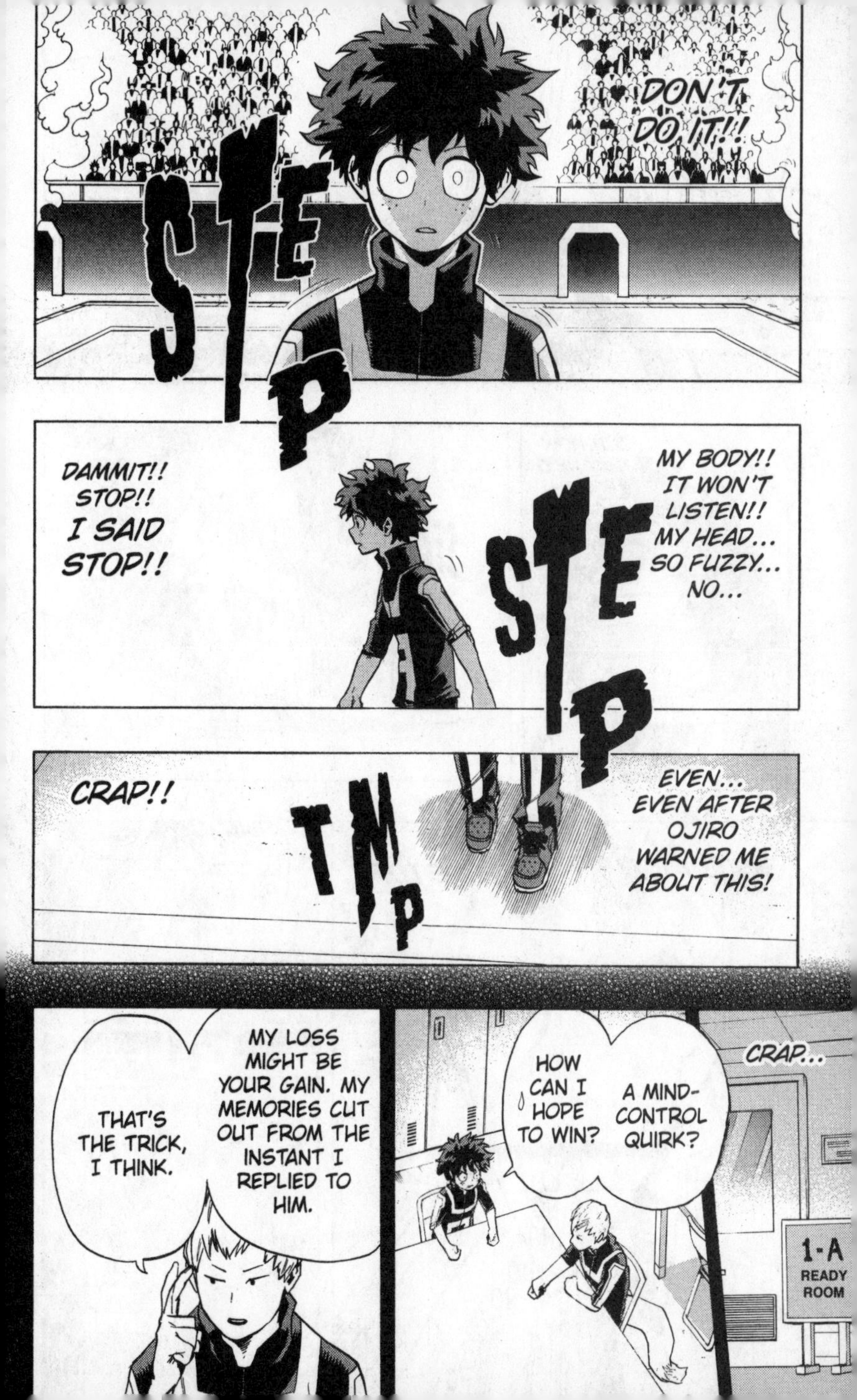
DON'T DO IT!!
STEP
MY BODY!! IT WON'T LISTEN!! MY HEAD... SO FUZZY... NO...
STEP
DAMMIT!! STOP!! I SAID STOP!!
EVEN... EVEN AFTER OJIRO WARNED ME ABOUT THIS!
TMP
CRAP!!
CRAP...
A MIND-CONTROL QUIRK?
HOW CAN I HOPE TO WIN?
1-A READY ROOM
MY LOSS MIGHT BE YOUR GAIN. MY MEMORIES CUT OUT FROM THE INSTANT I REPLIED TO HIM.
THAT'S THE TRICK, I THINK.

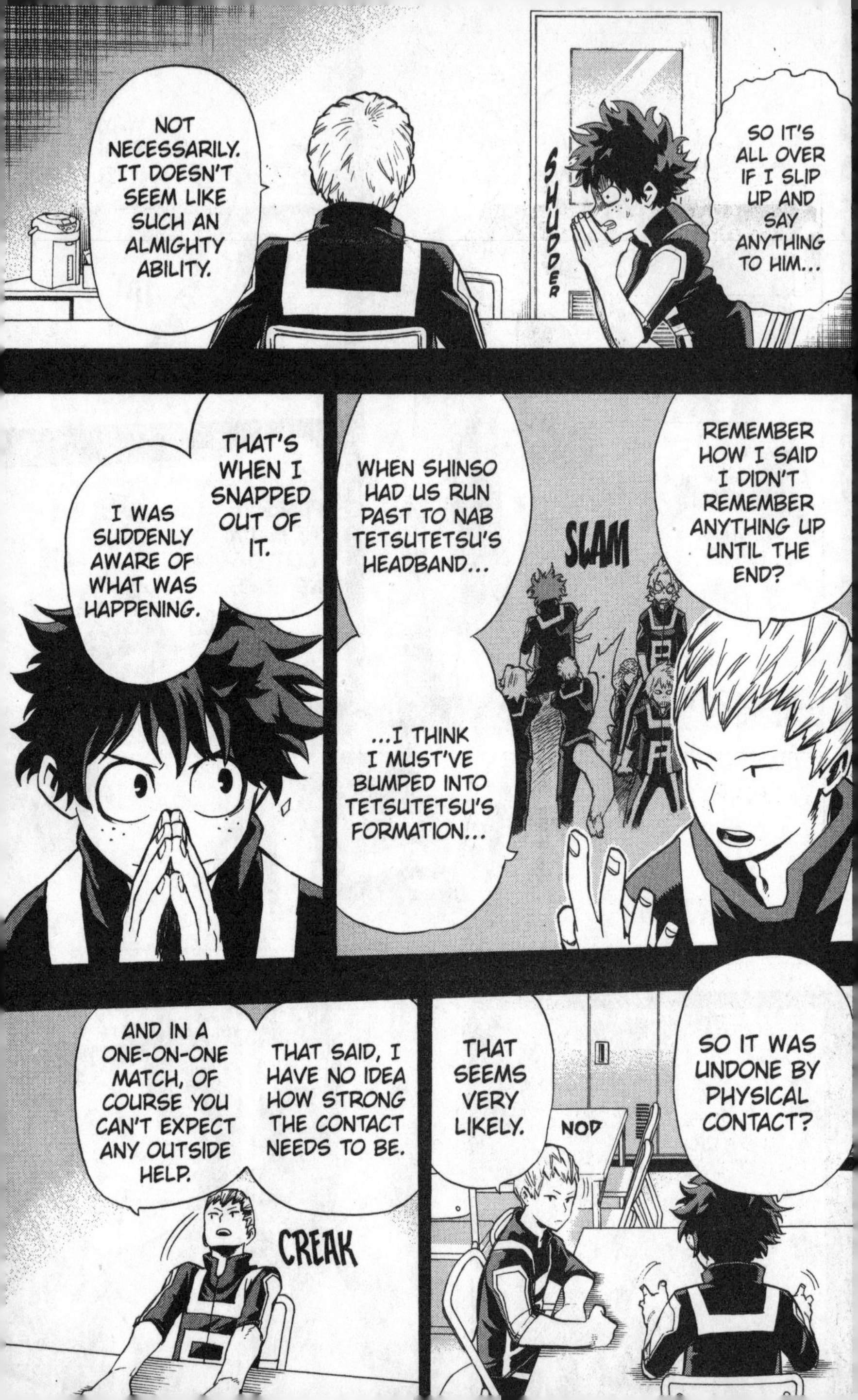
SO IT'S ALL OVER IF I SLIP UP AND SAY ANYTHING TO HIM...
SHUDDER
NOT NECESSARILY. IT DOESN'T SEEM LIKE SUCH AN ALMIGHTY ABILITY.
REMEMBER HOW I SAID I DIDN'T REMEMBER ANYTHING UP UNTIL THE END?
SLAM
WHEN SHINSO HAD US RUN PAST TO NAB TETSUTETSU'S HEADBAND...
...I THINK I MUST'VE BUMPED INTO TETSUTETSU'S FORMATION...
THAT'S WHEN I SNAPPED OUT OF IT.
I WAS SUDDENLY AWARE OF WHAT WAS HAPPENING.
SO IT WAS UNDONE BY PHYSICAL CONTACT?
THAT SEEMS VERY LIKELY.
NOD
THAT SAID, I HAVE NO IDEA HOW STRONG THE CONTACT NEEDS TO BE.
AND IN A ONE-ON-ONE MATCH, OF COURSE YOU CAN'T EXPECT ANY OUTSIDE HELP.
CREAK

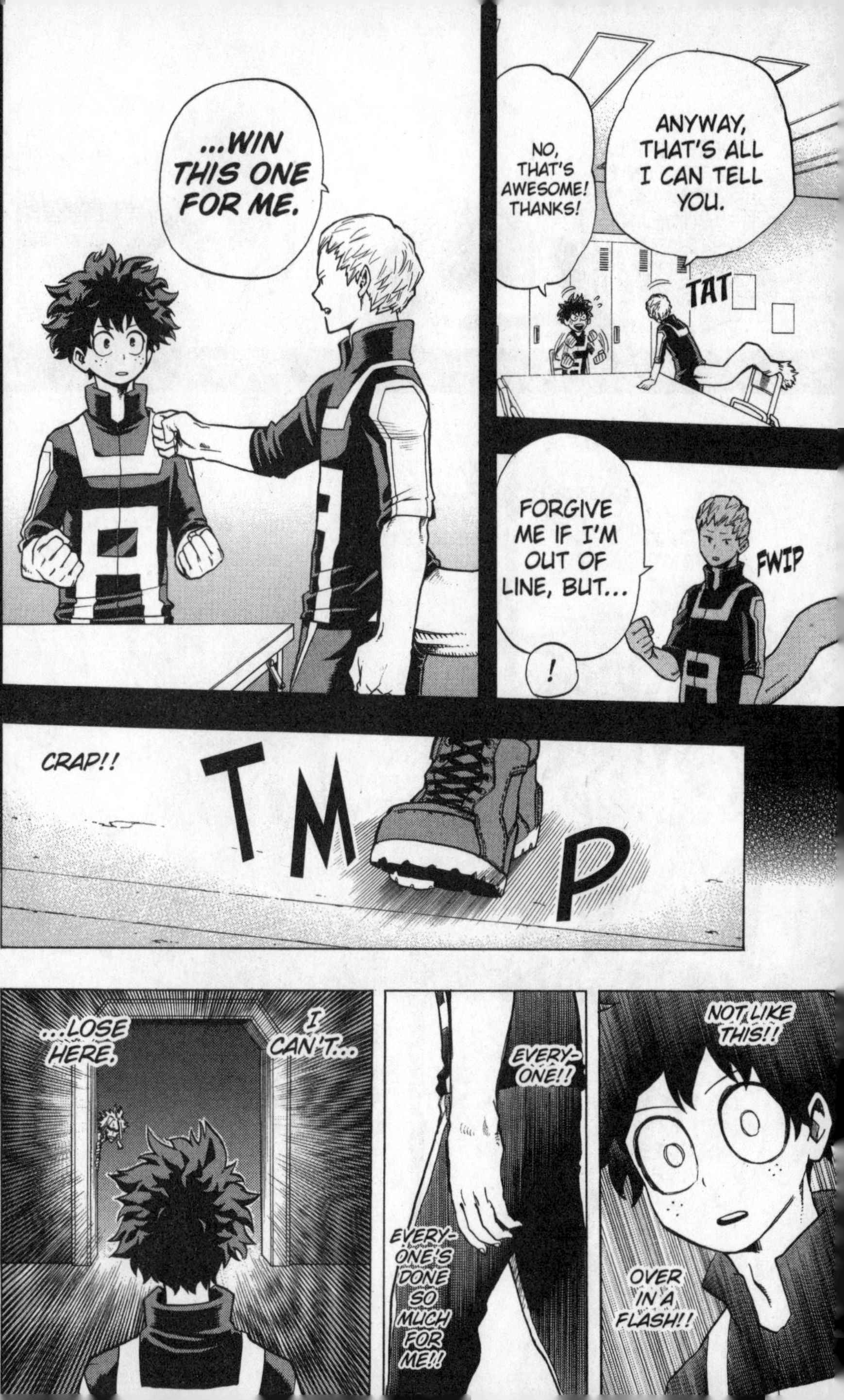
ANYWAY, THAT'S ALL I CAN TELL YOU.
NO, THAT'S AWESOME! THANKS!
TAT
FORGIVE ME IF I'M OUT OF LINE, BUT...
FWIP
!
...WIN THIS ONE FOR ME.
CRAP!!
TMP
NOT LIKE THIS!!
OVER IN A FLASH!!
EVERY-ONE!!
EVERY-ONE'S DONE SO MUCH FOR ME!!
I CAN'T...
...LOSE HERE.

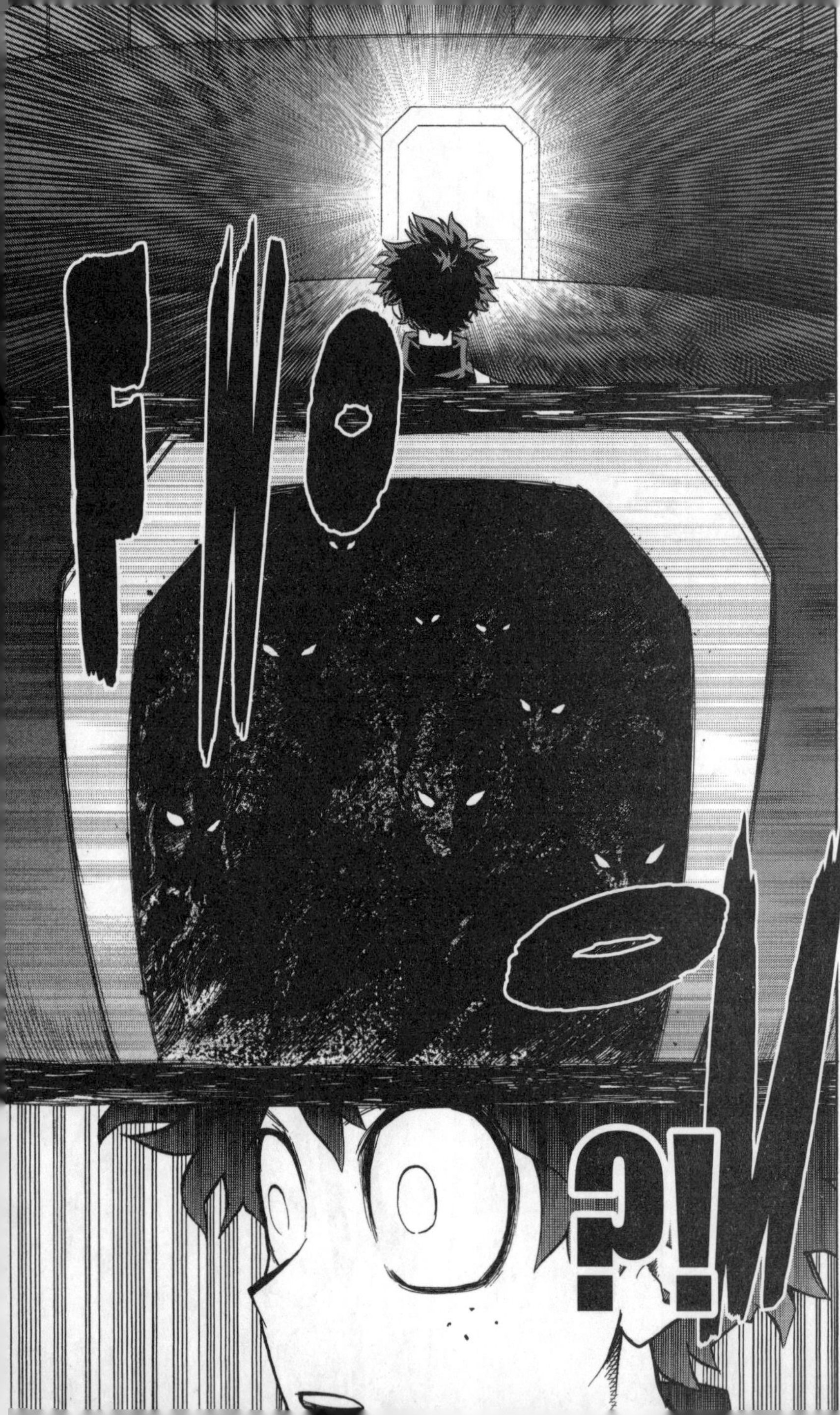
!?

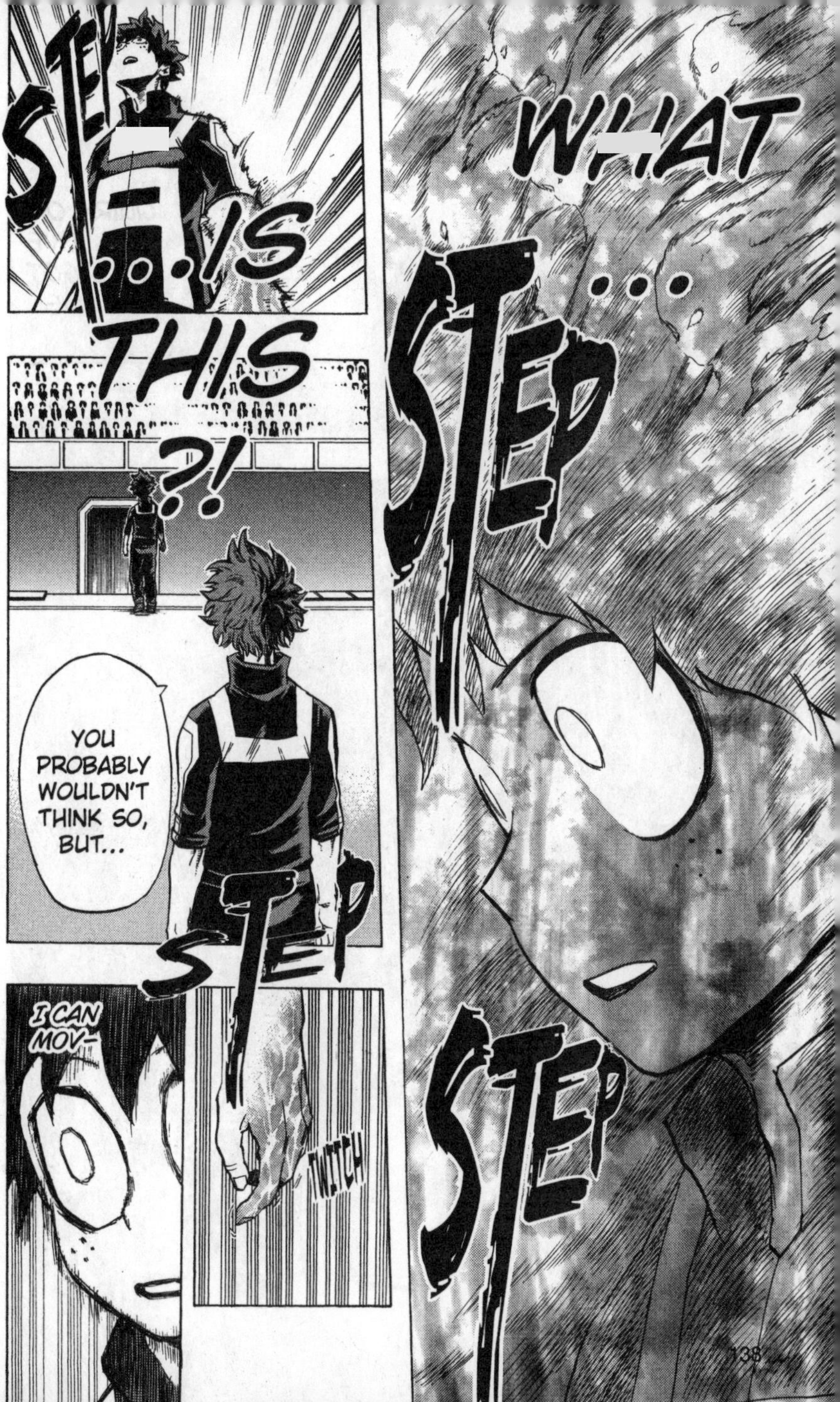
WHAT
STEP...
STEP
STEP
...IS THIS?!
YOU PROBABLY WOULDN'T THINK SO, BUT...
STEP
TWITCH
I CAN MOV-

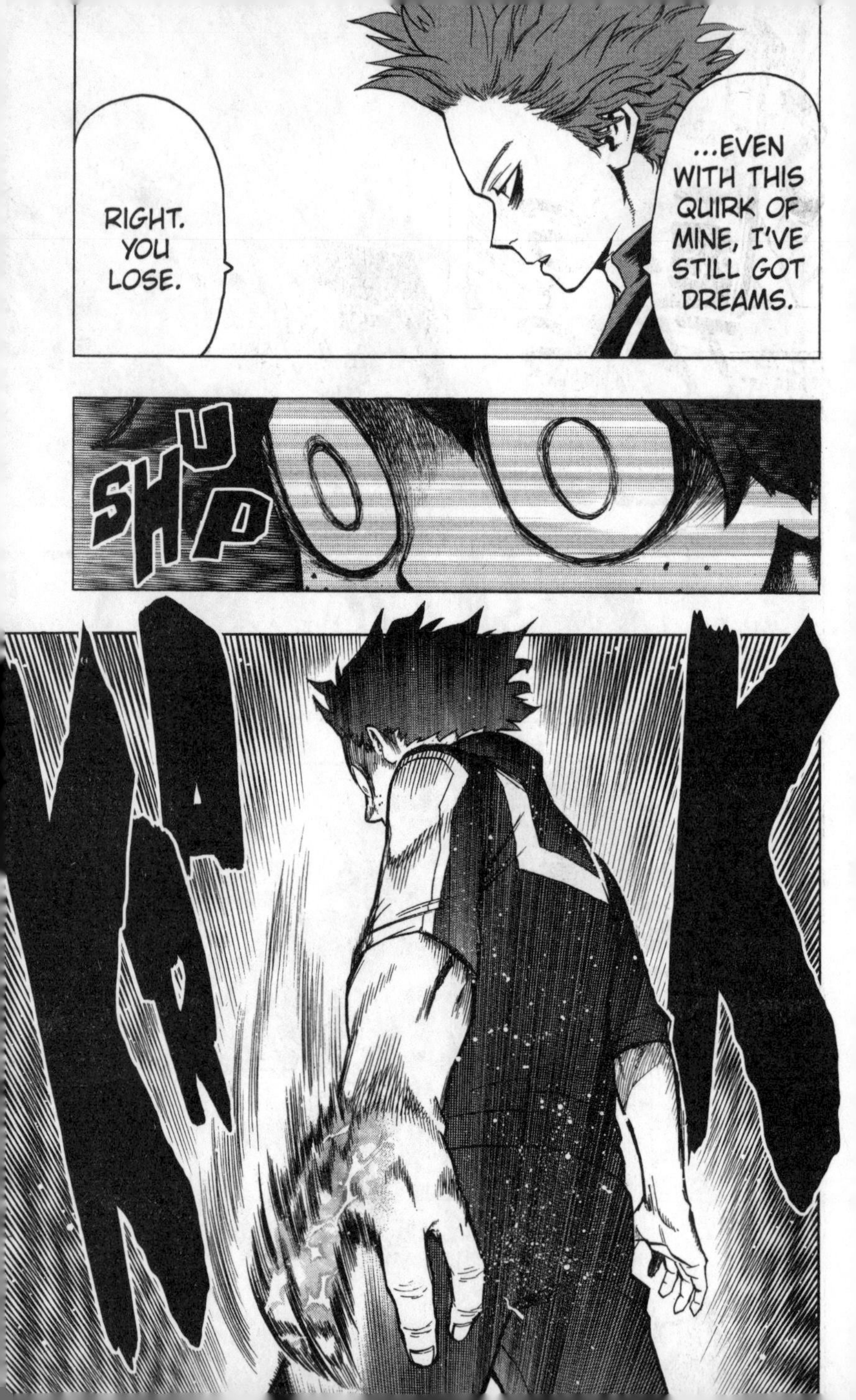
...EVEN WITH THIS QUIRK OF MINE, I'VE STILL GOT DREAMS.
RIGHT. YOU LOSE.
SHUP

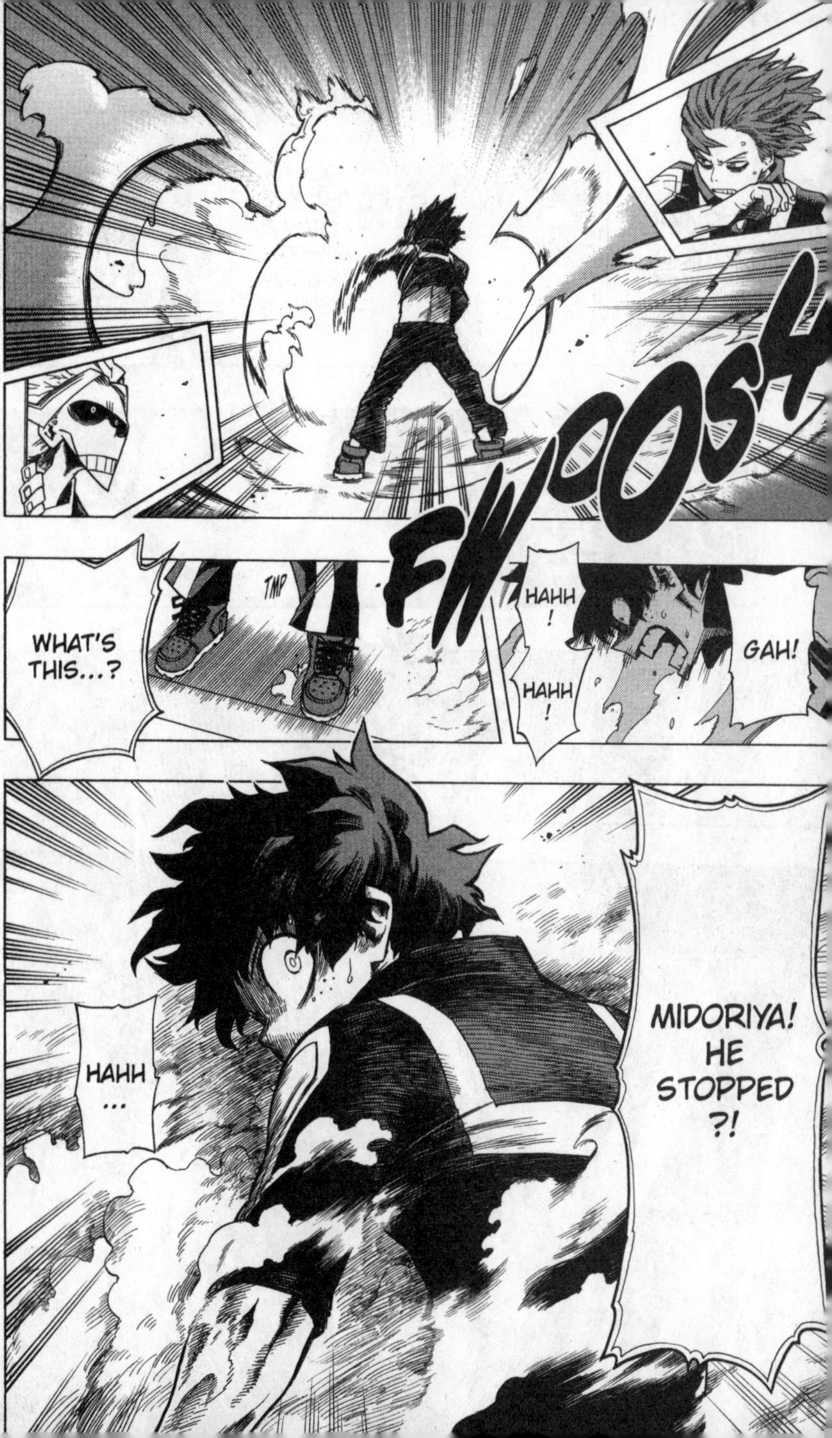
FWOOSH
HAHH! HAHH!
GAH!
TMP
WHAT'S THIS...?
MIDORIYA! HE STOPPED?!
HAHH...

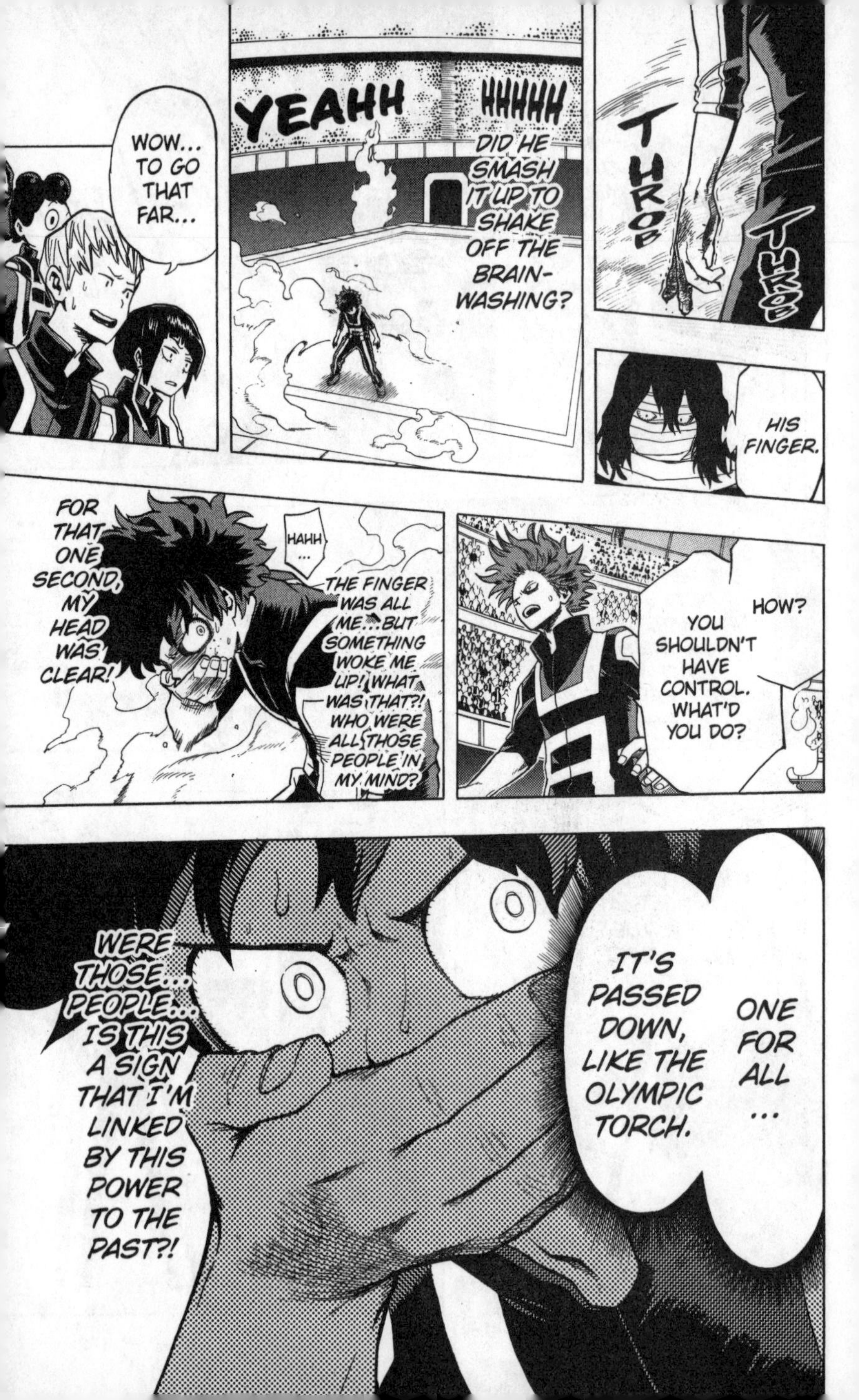

THROB
THROB
HIS FINGER.
YEAHH
HHHHH
DID HE SMASH IT UP TO SHAKE OFF THE BRAIN-WASHING?
WOW... TO GO THAT FAR...
HOW?
YOU SHOULDN'T HAVE CONTROL. WHAT'D YOU DO?
HAHH...
THE FINGER WAS ALL ME...BUT SOMETHING WOKE ME UP! WHAT WAS THAT?! WHO WERE ALL THOSE PEOPLE IN MY MIND?
FOR THAT ONE SECOND, MY HEAD WAS CLEAR!
ONE FOR ALL...
IT'S PASSED DOWN, LIKE THE OLYMPIC TORCH.
WERE THOSE... PEOPLE... IS THIS A SIGN THAT I'M LINKED BY THIS POWER TO THE PAST?!

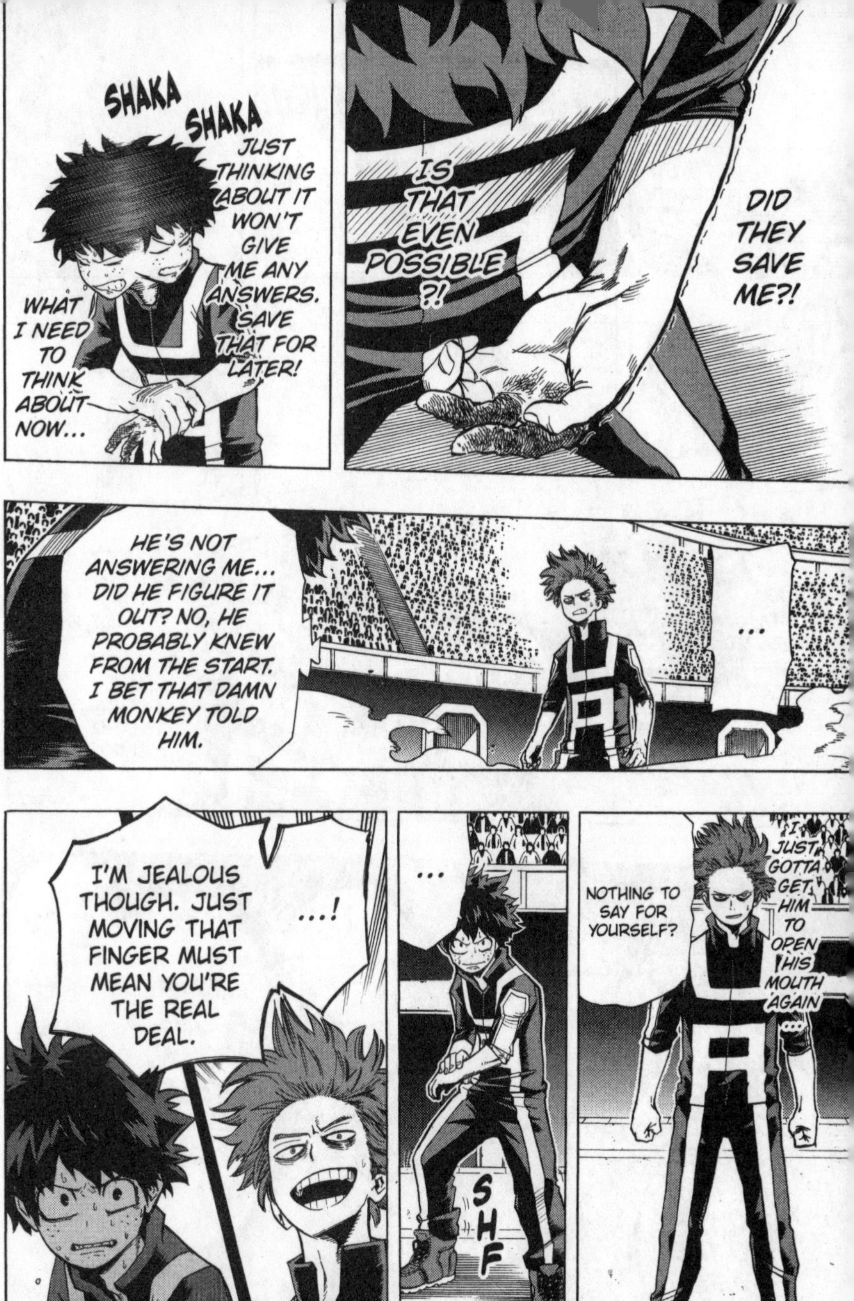
DID THEY SAVE ME?!
IS THAT EVEN POSSIBLE?!
SHAKA SHAKA
JUST THINKING ABOUT IT WON'T GIVE ME ANY ANSWERS. SAVE THAT FOR LATER!
WHAT I NEED TO THINK ABOUT NOW...
...
HE'S NOT ANSWERING ME... DID HE FIGURE IT OUT? NO, HE PROBABLY KNEW FROM THE START. I BET THAT DAMN MONKEY TOLD HIM.
I JUST GOTTA GET HIM TO OPEN HIS MOUTH AGAIN...
NOTHING TO SAY FOR YOURSELF?
...
SHF
I'M JEALOUS THOUGH. JUST MOVING THAT FINGER MUST MEAN YOU'RE THE REAL DEAL.
...!

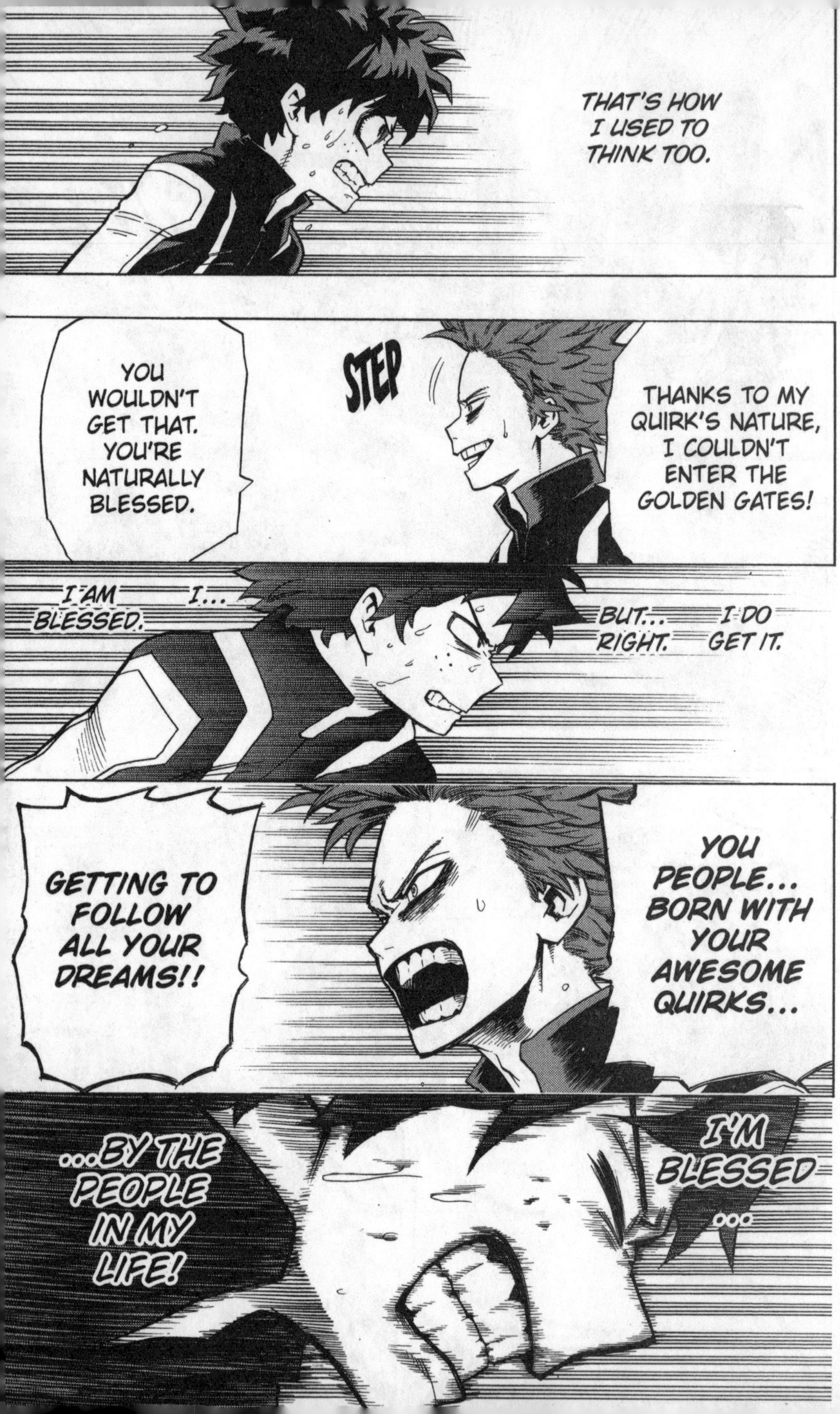
THAT'S HOW I USED TO THINK TOO.
THANKS TO MY QUIRK'S NATURE, I COULDN'T ENTER THE GOLDEN GATES!
STEP
YOU WOULDN'T GET THAT. YOU'RE NATURALLY BLESSED.
I DO GET IT.
BUT... RIGHT.
I...
I AM BLESSED.
YOU PEOPLE... BORN WITH YOUR AWESOME QUIRKS...
GETTING TO FOLLOW ALL YOUR DREAMS!!
I'M BLESSED...
...BY THE PEOPLE IN MY LIFE!

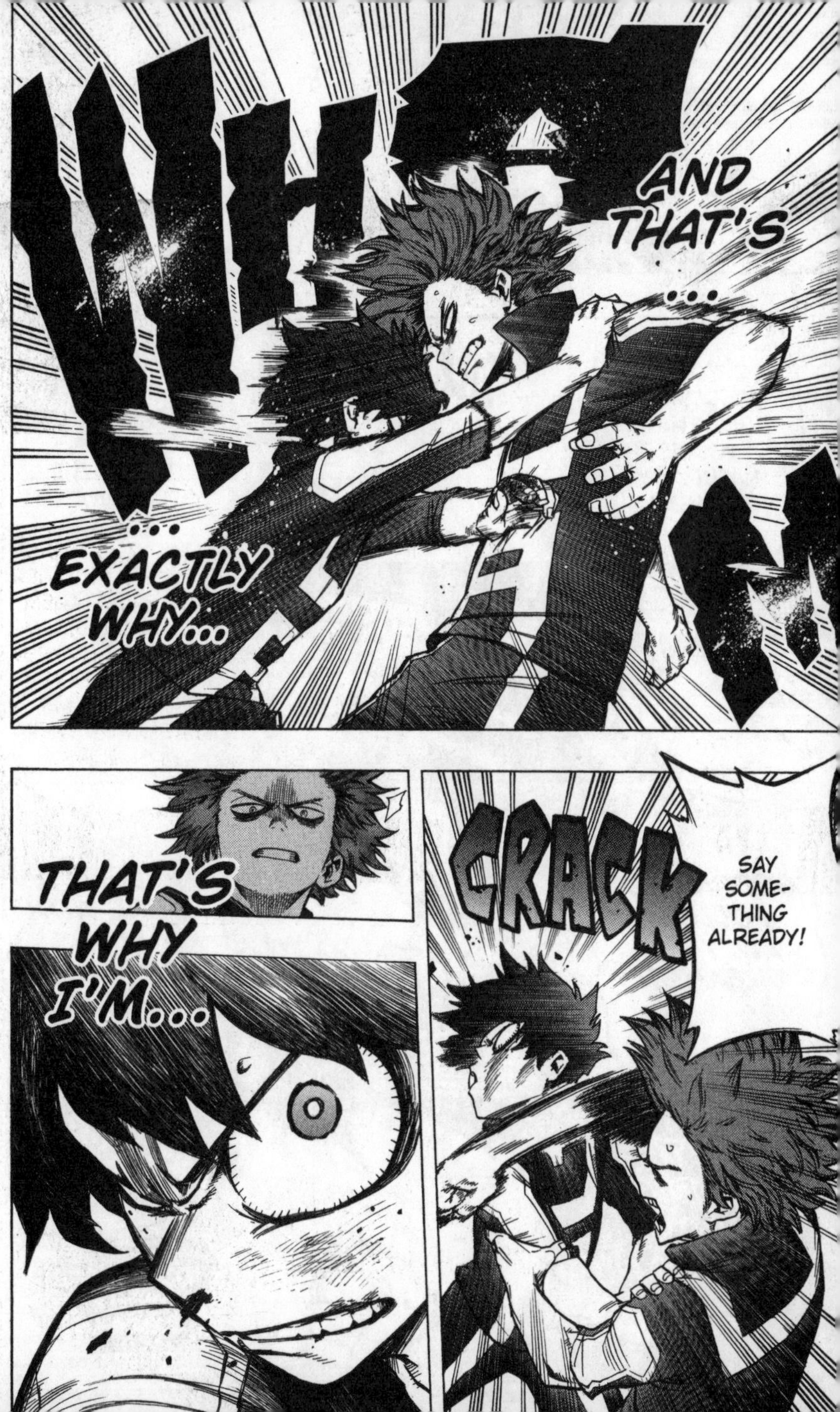
AND THAT'S...
...EXACTLY WHY...
CRACK
SAY SOME-THING ALREADY!
THAT'S WHY I'M...

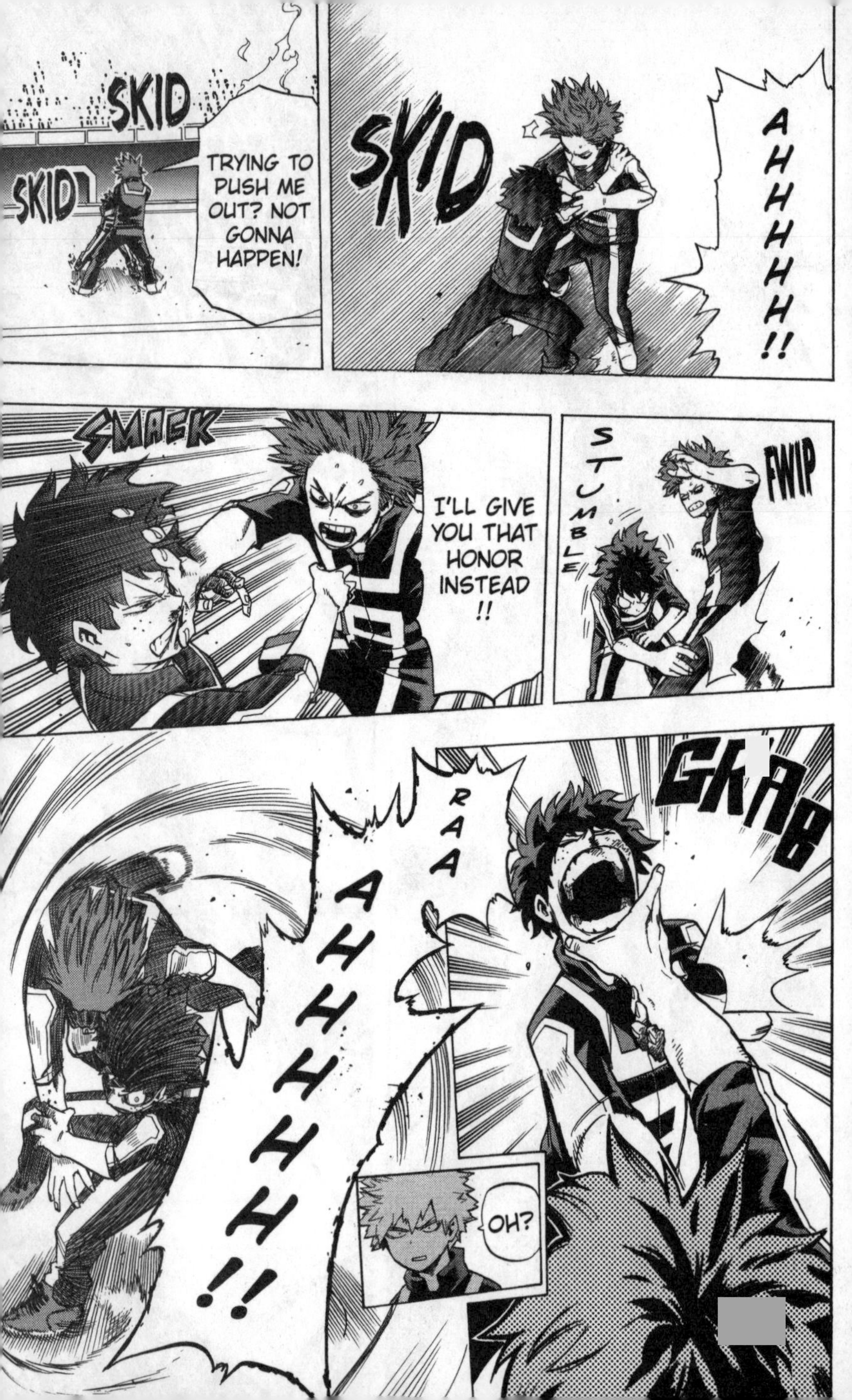
AHHHHHH!!
SKID
SKID
TRYING TO PUSH ME OUT? NOT GONNA HAPPEN!
SKID
FWIP
STUMBLE
I'LL GIVE YOU THAT HONOR INSTEAD!!
SMACK
GRAB
RAAAHHHHHHH!!
OH?

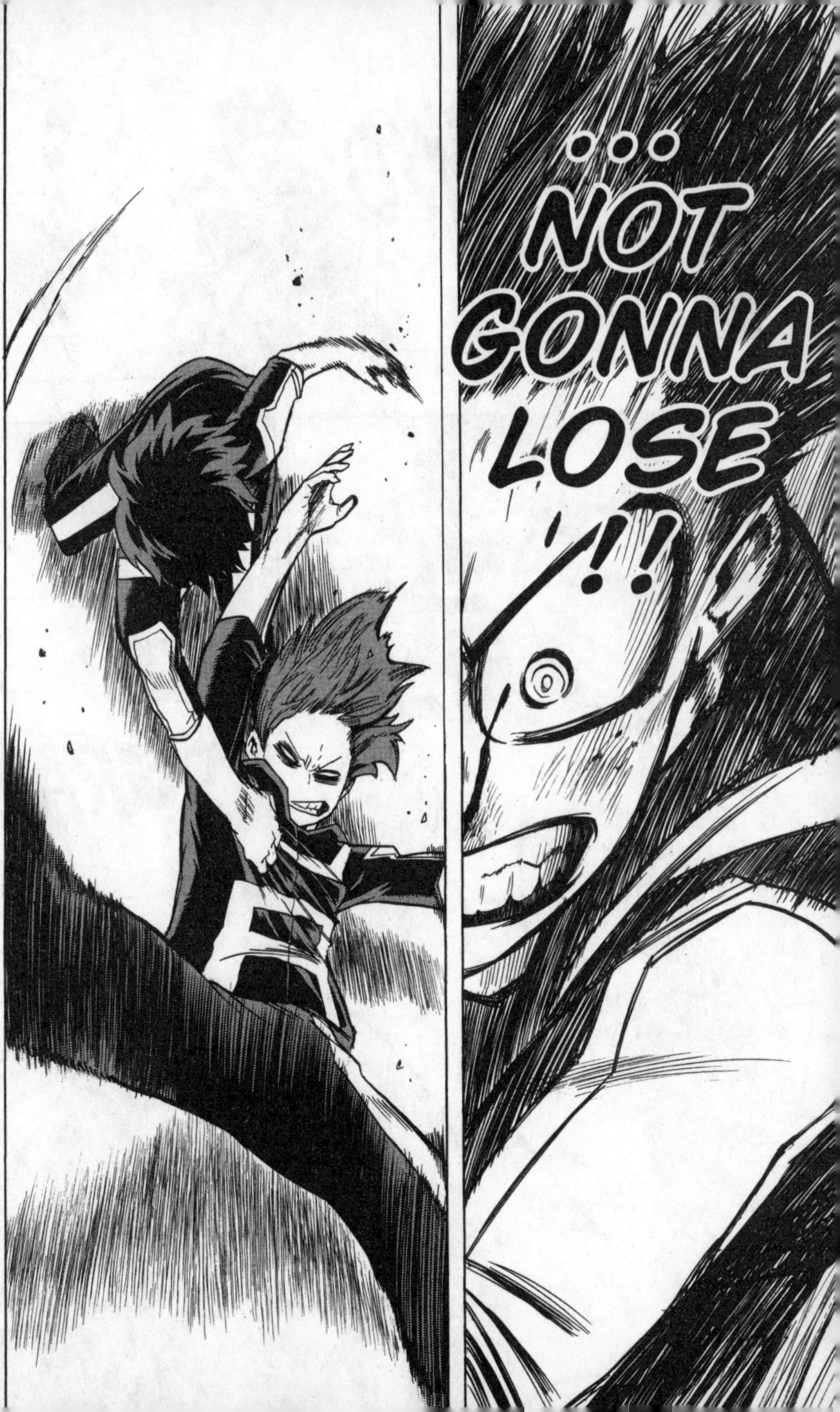
...NOT GONNA LOSE!!

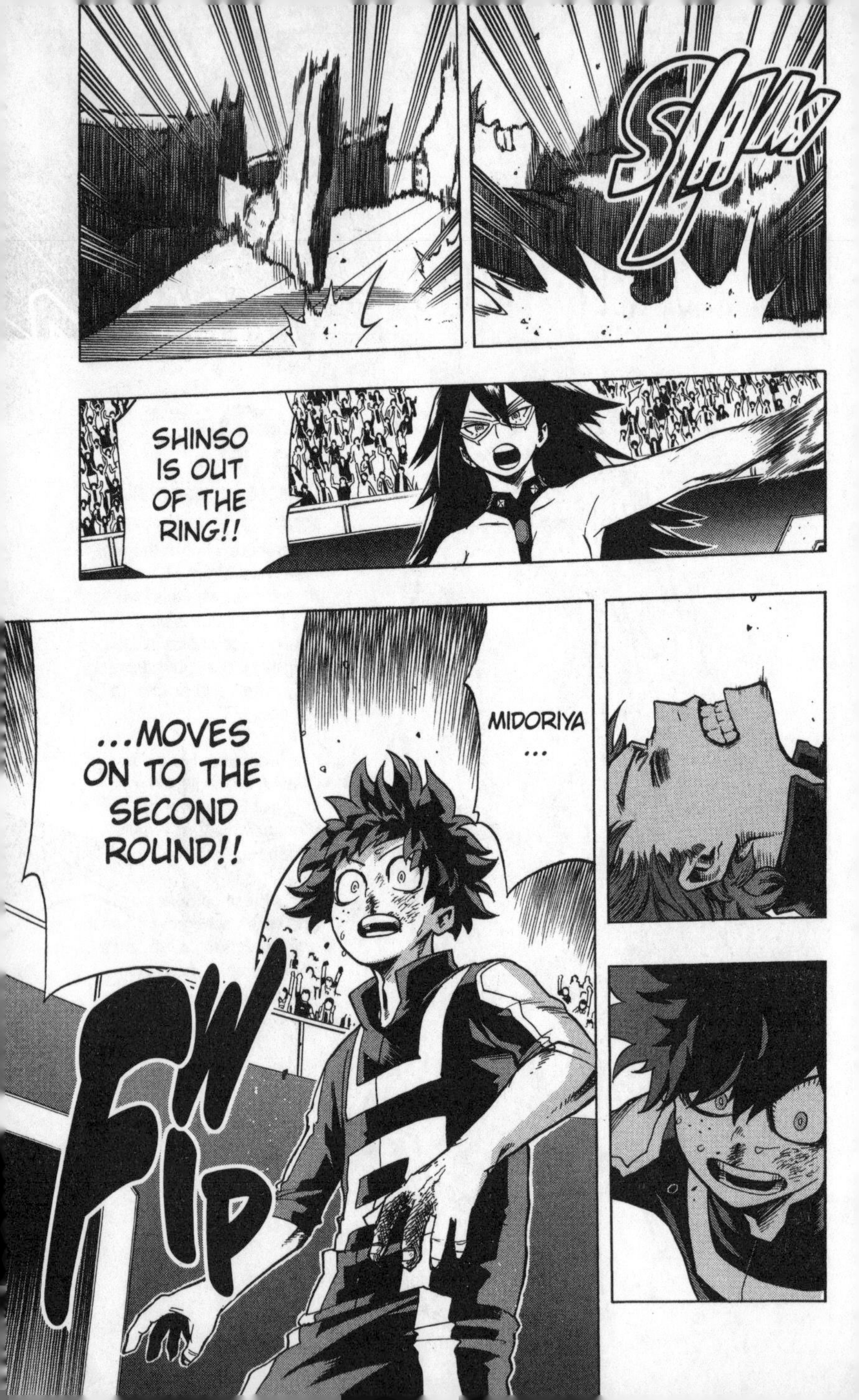
SFAM
SHINSO IS OUT OF THE RING!!
...MOVES ON TO THE SECOND ROUND!!
MIDORIYA ...
FWIP

IBARA SHIOZAKI (15)

STREET CLOTHES

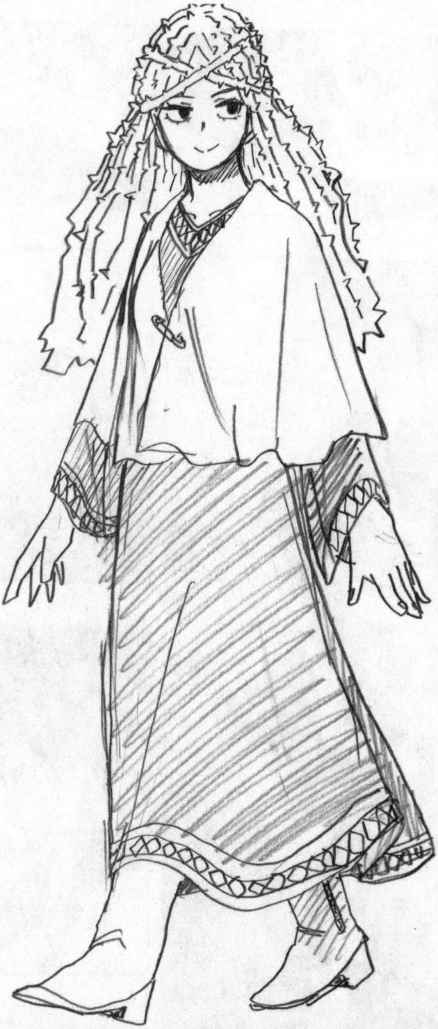

Birthday: 9/8
Height: 167 cm
Favorite Thing: Bread

BEHIND THE SCENES

When I drew her in the first draft, I said, "I really screwed myself over with this one." Her hair is such a pain. I didn't notice at first in the rough sketches, but drawing-wise, she's a character to be feared.

She was meant to be in Class A but switched over to Class B at some point. Wonder why. Can't really remember.

She's full of compassion. She hates scheming against or tricking people, so she's unexpectedly open and aboveboard.

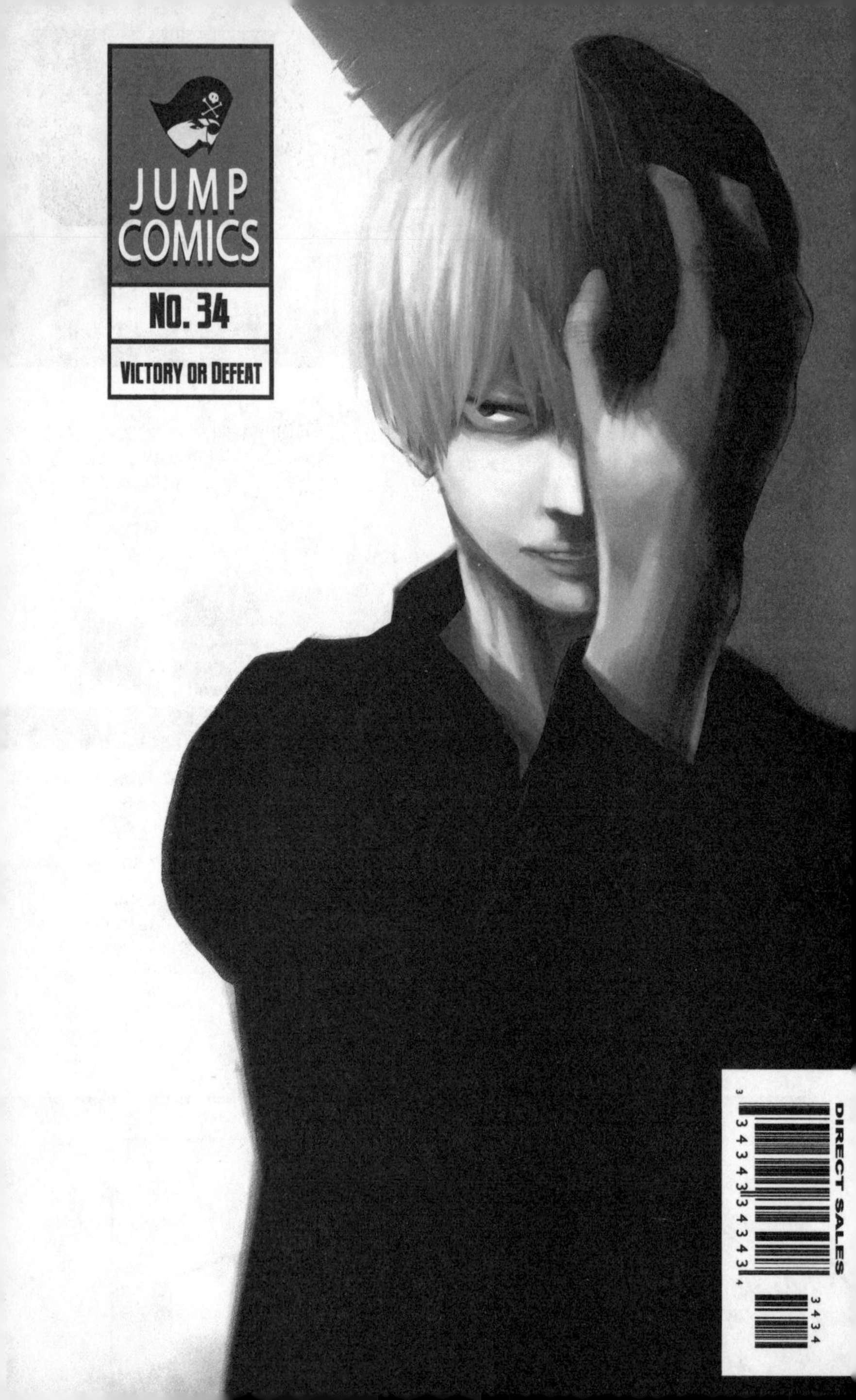
JUMP COMICS
NO. 34
VICTORY OR DEFEAT
DIRECT SALES

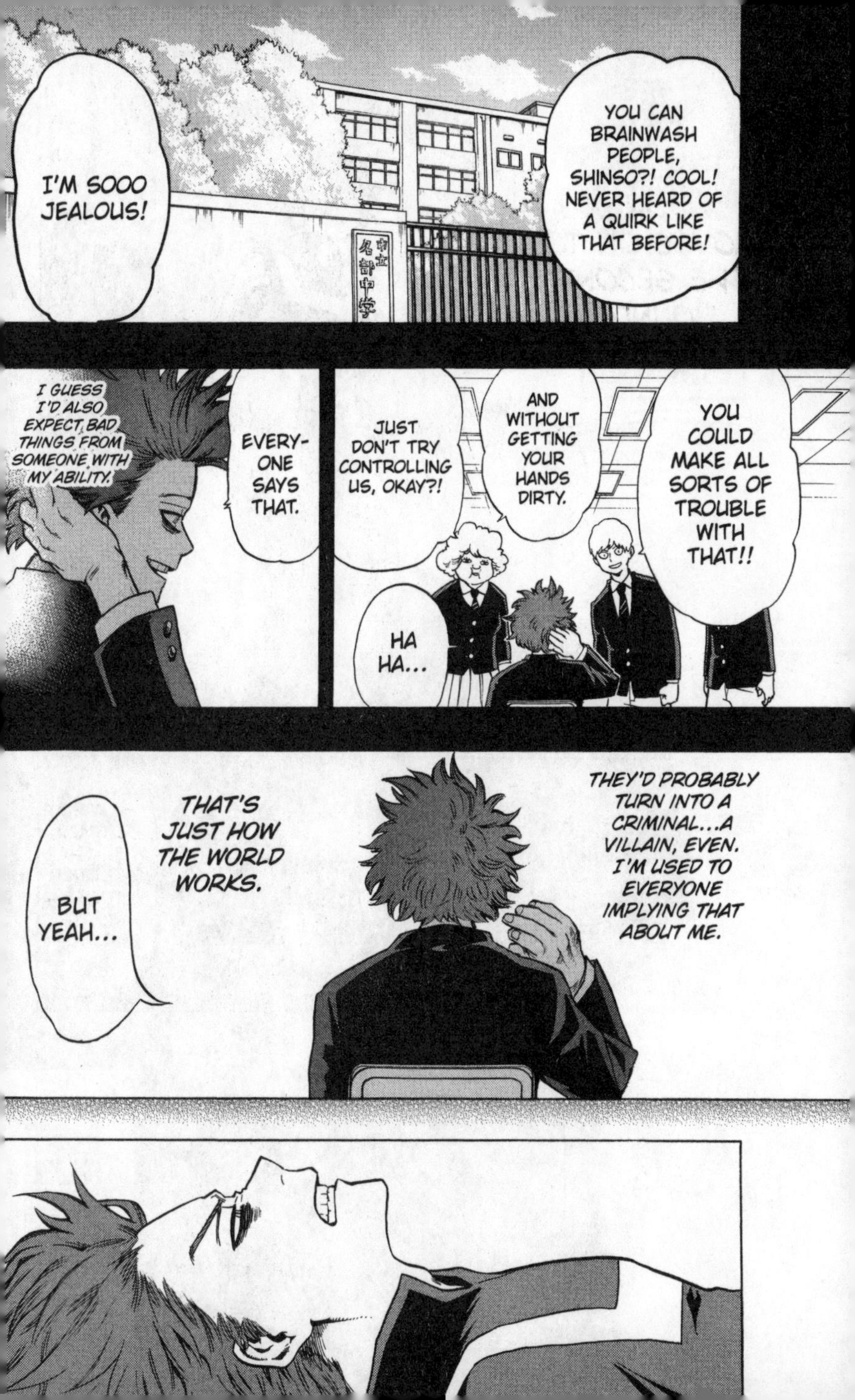
YOU CAN BRAINWASH PEOPLE, SHINSO?! COOL! NEVER HEARD OF A QUIRK LIKE THAT BEFORE!
市立名部中学
I'M SOOO JEALOUS!
YOU COULD MAKE ALL SORTS OF TROUBLE WITH THAT!!
AND WITHOUT GETTING YOUR HANDS DIRTY.
JUST DON'T TRY CONTROLLING US, OKAY?!
HA HA...
EVERY-ONE SAYS THAT.
I GUESS I'D ALSO EXPECT BAD THINGS FROM SOMEONE WITH MY ABILITY.
THEY'D PROBABLY TURN INTO A CRIMINAL...A VILLAIN, EVEN. I'M USED TO EVERYONE IMPLYING THAT ABOUT ME.
THAT'S JUST HOW THE WORLD WORKS.
BUT YEAH...

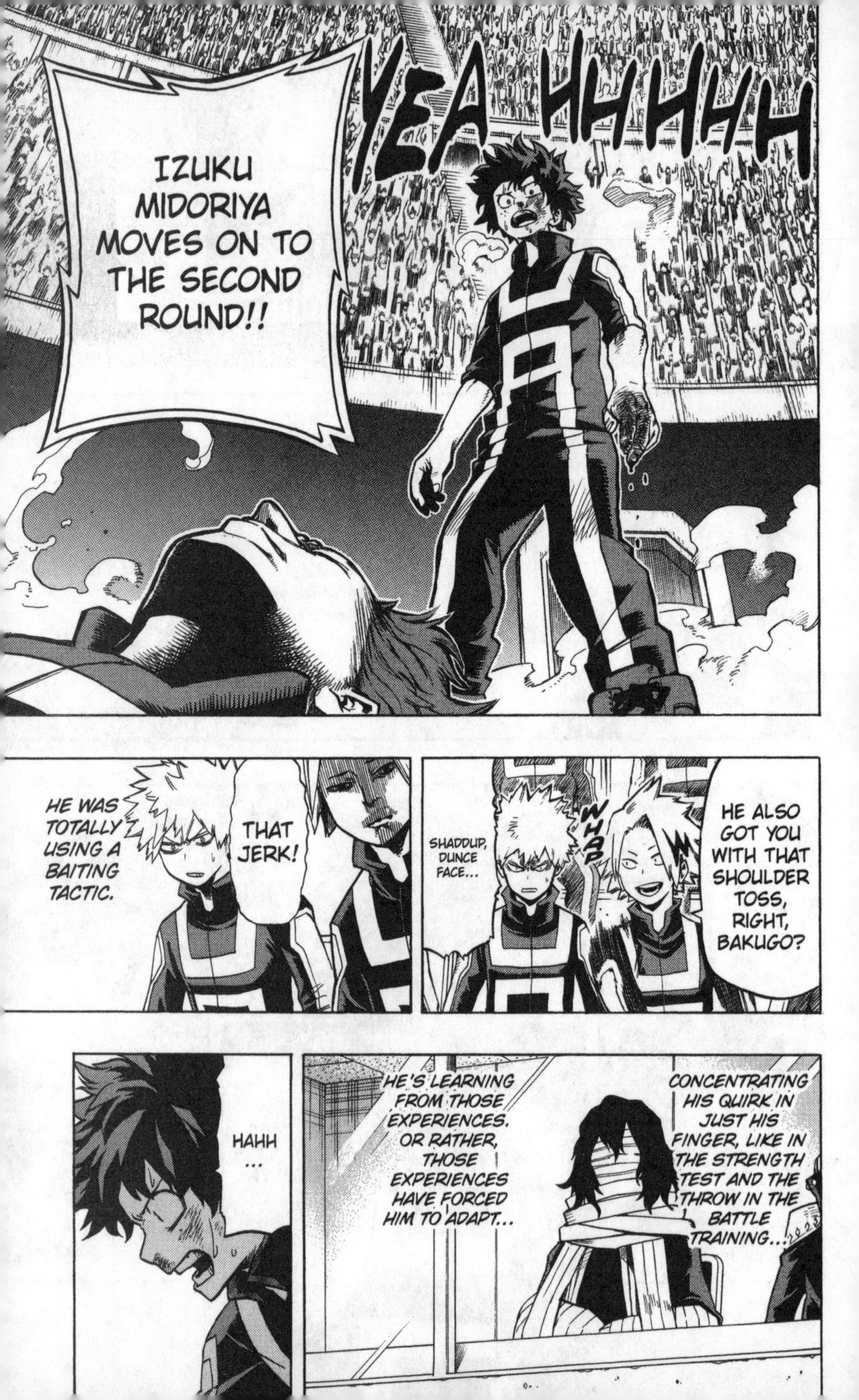
YEAHHHHHH
IZUKU MIDORIYA MOVES ON TO THE SECOND ROUND!!
HE ALSO GOT YOU WITH THAT SHOULDER TOSS, RIGHT, BAKUGO?
WHAP
SHADDUP, DUNCE FACE...
THAT JERK!
HE WAS TOTALLY USING A BAITING TACTIC.
CONCENTRATING HIS QUIRK IN JUST HIS FINGER, LIKE IN THE STRENGTH TEST AND THE THROW IN THE BATTLE TRAINING...
HE'S LEARNING FROM THOSE EXPERIENCES. OR RATHER, THOSE EXPERIENCES HAVE FORCED HIM TO ADAPT...
HAHH ...

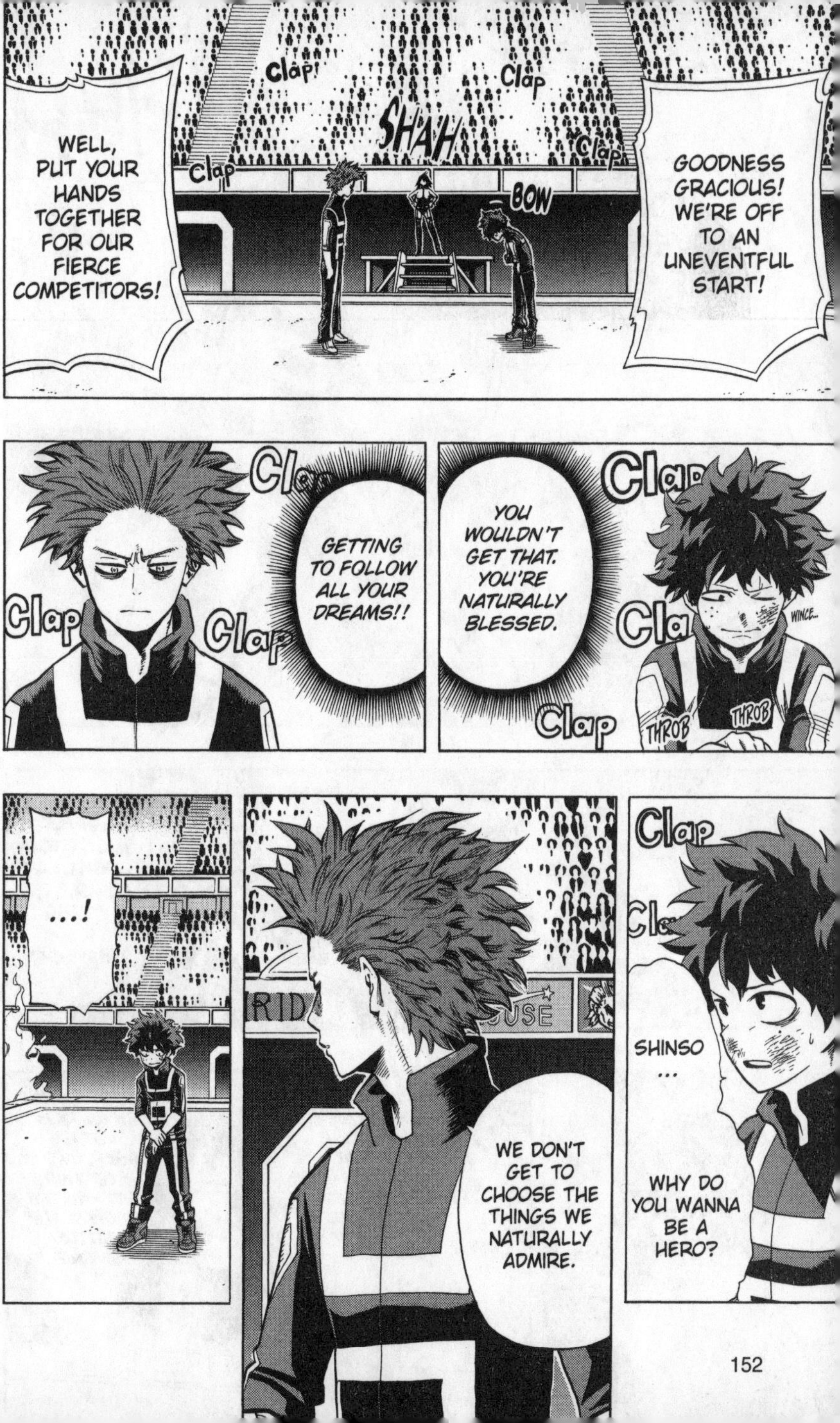
Clap
Clap
SHAH
Clap
GOODNESS GRACIOUS! WE'RE OFF TO AN UNEVENTFUL START!
BOW
Clap
WELL, PUT YOUR HANDS TOGETHER FOR OUR FIERCE COMPETITORS!
Clap
YOU WOULDN'T GET THAT. YOU'RE NATURALLY BLESSED.
Cla
WINCE...
THROB
THROB
Clap
Clap
GETTING TO FOLLOW ALL YOUR DREAMS!!
Clap
Clap
Clap
Cla
SHINSO...
WHY DO YOU WANNA BE A HERO?
WE DON'T GET TO CHOOSE THE THINGS WE NATURALLY ADMIRE.
...!

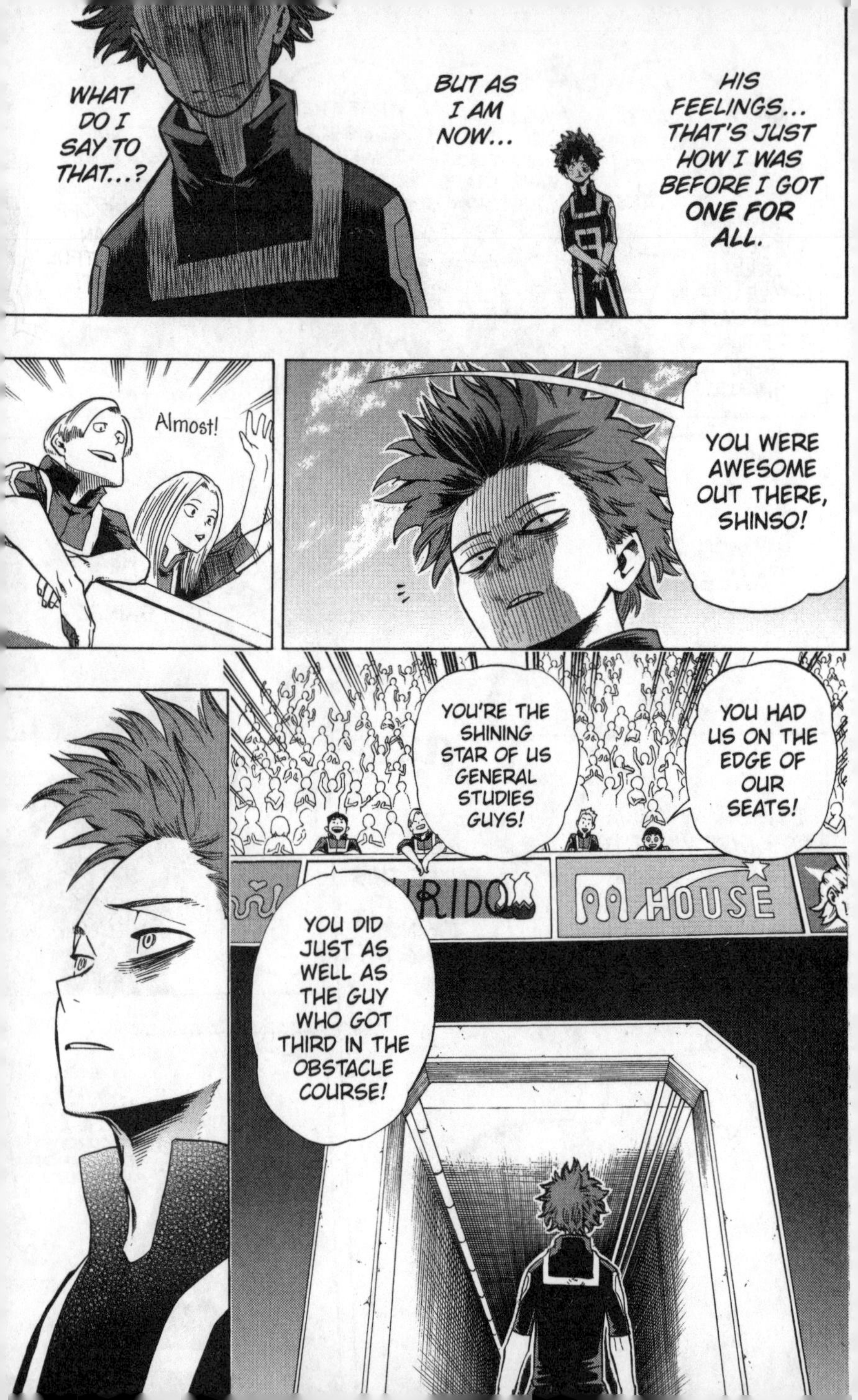
HIS FEELINGS... THAT'S JUST HOW I WAS BEFORE I GOT ONE FOR ALL.
BUT AS I AM NOW...
WHAT DO I SAY TO THAT...?
YOU WERE AWESOME OUT THERE, SHINSO!
Almost!
YOU HAD US ON THE EDGE OF OUR SEATS!
YOU'RE THE SHINING STAR OF US GENERAL STUDIES GUYS!
HOUSE
YOU DID JUST AS WELL AS THE GUY WHO GOT THIRD IN THE OBSTACLE COURSE!

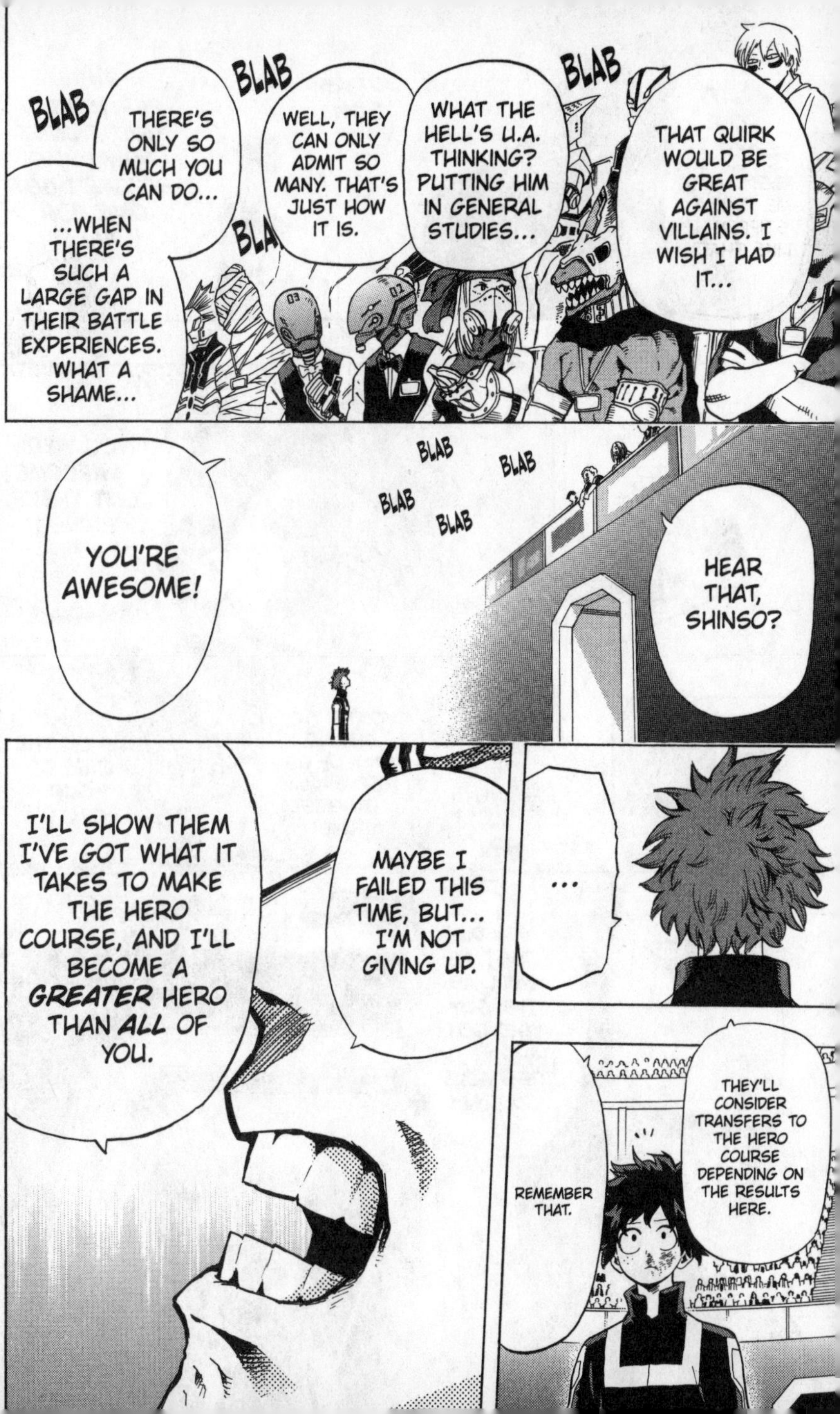
BLAB
THAT QUIRK WOULD BE GREAT AGAINST VILLAINS. I WISH I HAD IT...
WHAT THE HELL'S U.A. THINKING? PUTTING HIM IN GENERAL STUDIES...
BLAB
WELL, THEY CAN ONLY ADMIT SO MANY. THAT'S JUST HOW IT IS.
BLA
BLAB
THERE'S ONLY SO MUCH YOU CAN DO...
...WHEN THERE'S SUCH A LARGE GAP IN THEIR BATTLE EXPERIENCES. WHAT A SHAME...
HEAR THAT, SHINSO?
BLAB
BLAB
BLAB
BLAB
YOU'RE AWESOME!
...
THEY'LL CONSIDER TRANSFERS TO THE HERO COURSE DEPENDING ON THE RESULTS HERE.
REMEMBER THAT.
MAYBE I FAILED THIS TIME, BUT... I'M NOT GIVING UP.
I'LL SHOW THEM I'VE GOT WHAT IT TAKES TO MAKE THE HERO COURSE, AND I'LL BECOME A GREATER HERO THAN ALL OF YOU.

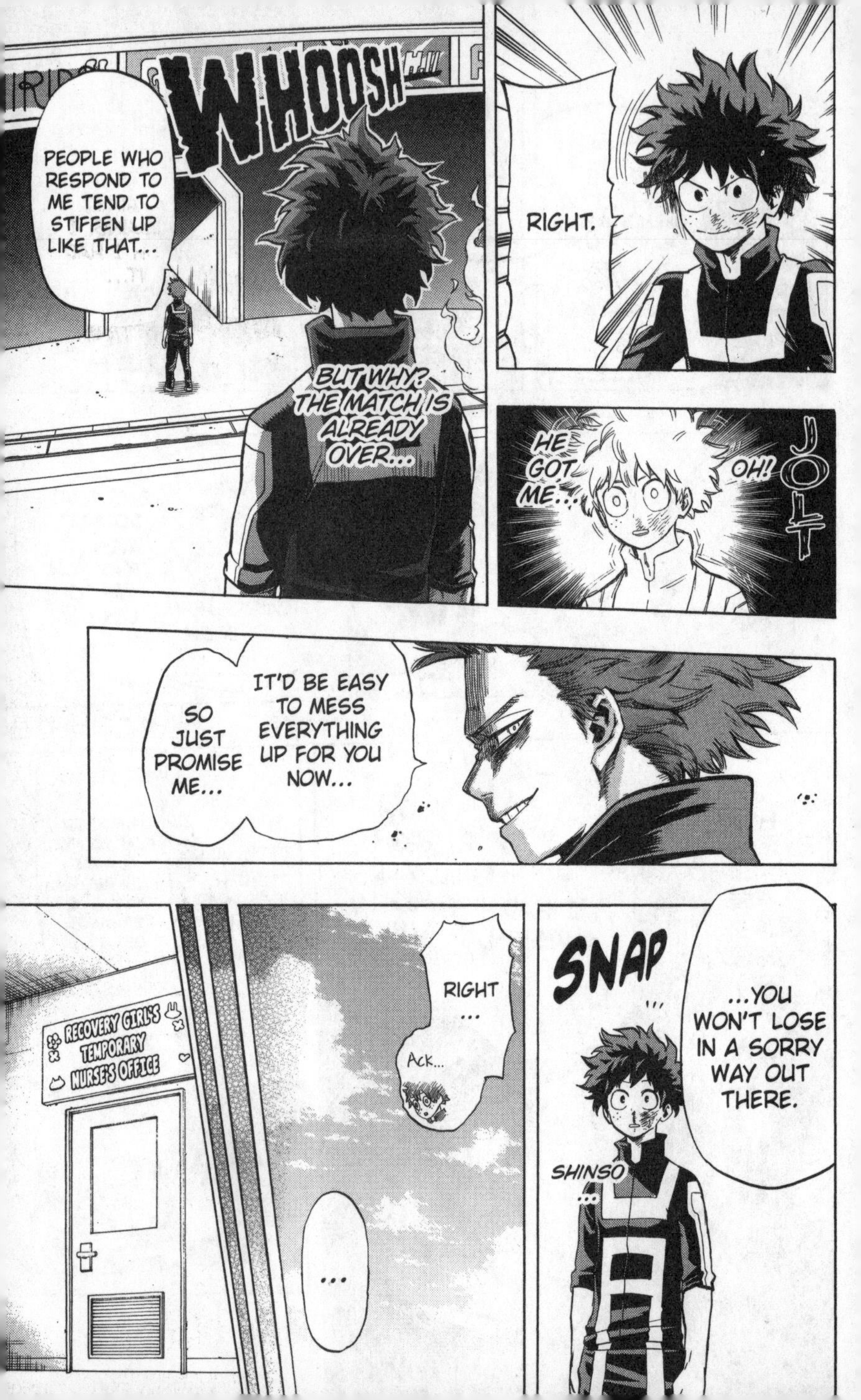
RIGHT.
JOLT
OH!
HE GOT ME...
WHOOSH
PEOPLE WHO RESPOND TO ME TEND TO STIFFEN UP LIKE THAT...
BUT WHY? THE MATCH IS ALREADY OVER...
IT'D BE EASY TO MESS EVERYTHING UP FOR YOU NOW...
SO JUST PROMISE ME...
...YOU WON'T LOSE IN A SORRY WAY OUT THERE.
SNAP
SHINSO...
RIGHT...
ACK...
...
RECOVERY GIRL'S TEMPORARY NURSE'S OFFICE

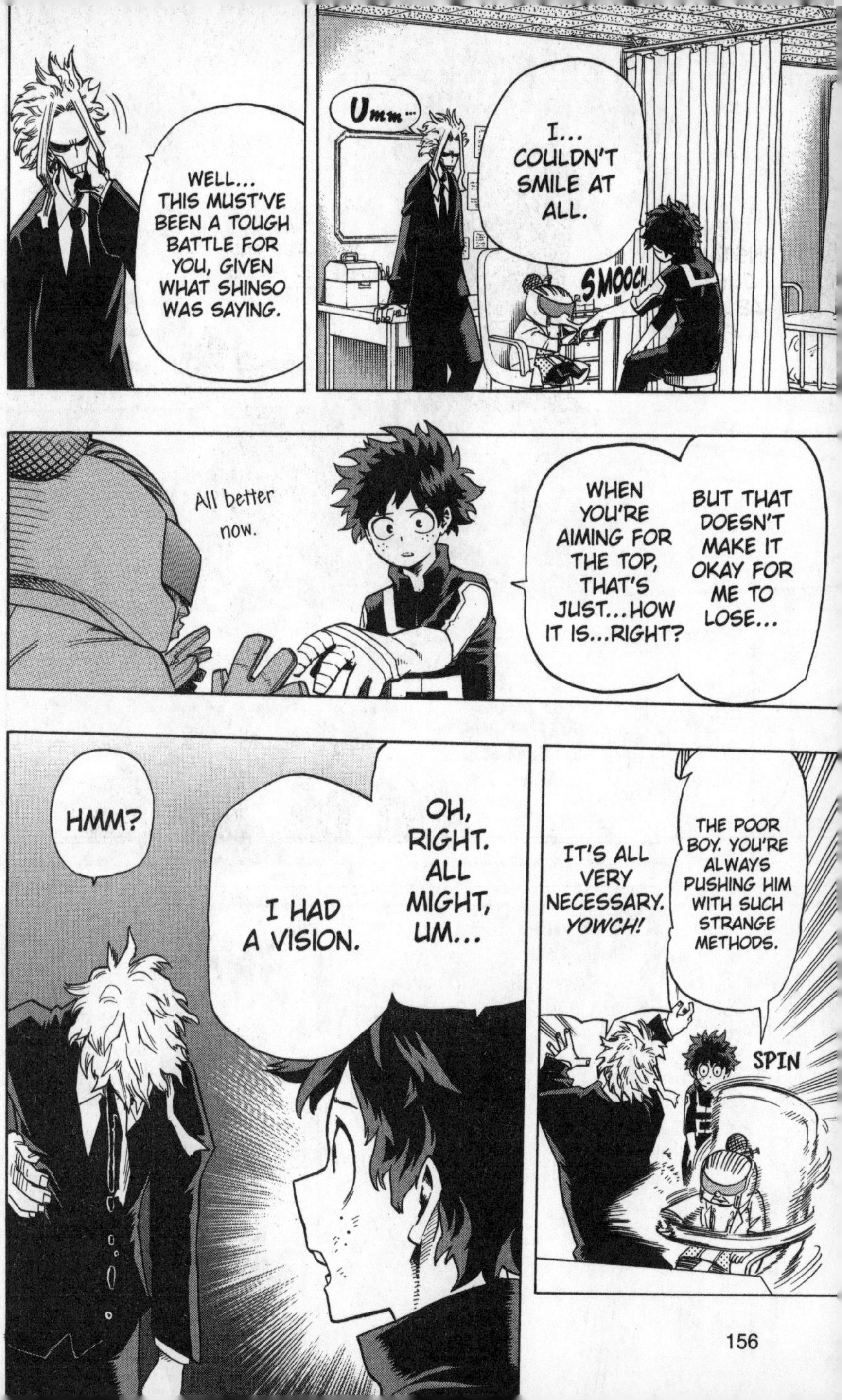
Umm...
I... COULDN'T SMILE AT ALL.
SMOOCH
WELL... THIS MUST'VE BEEN A TOUGH BATTLE FOR YOU, GIVEN WHAT SHINSO WAS SAYING.
WHEN YOU'RE AIMING FOR THE TOP, THAT'S JUST...HOW IT IS...RIGHT?
BUT THAT DOESN'T MAKE IT OKAY FOR ME TO LOSE...
All better now.
THE POOR BOY. YOU'RE ALWAYS PUSHING HIM WITH SUCH STRANGE METHODS.
IT'S ALL VERY NECESSARY. *YOWCH!*
SPIN
OH, RIGHT. ALL MIGHT, UM...
I HAD A VISION.
HMM?

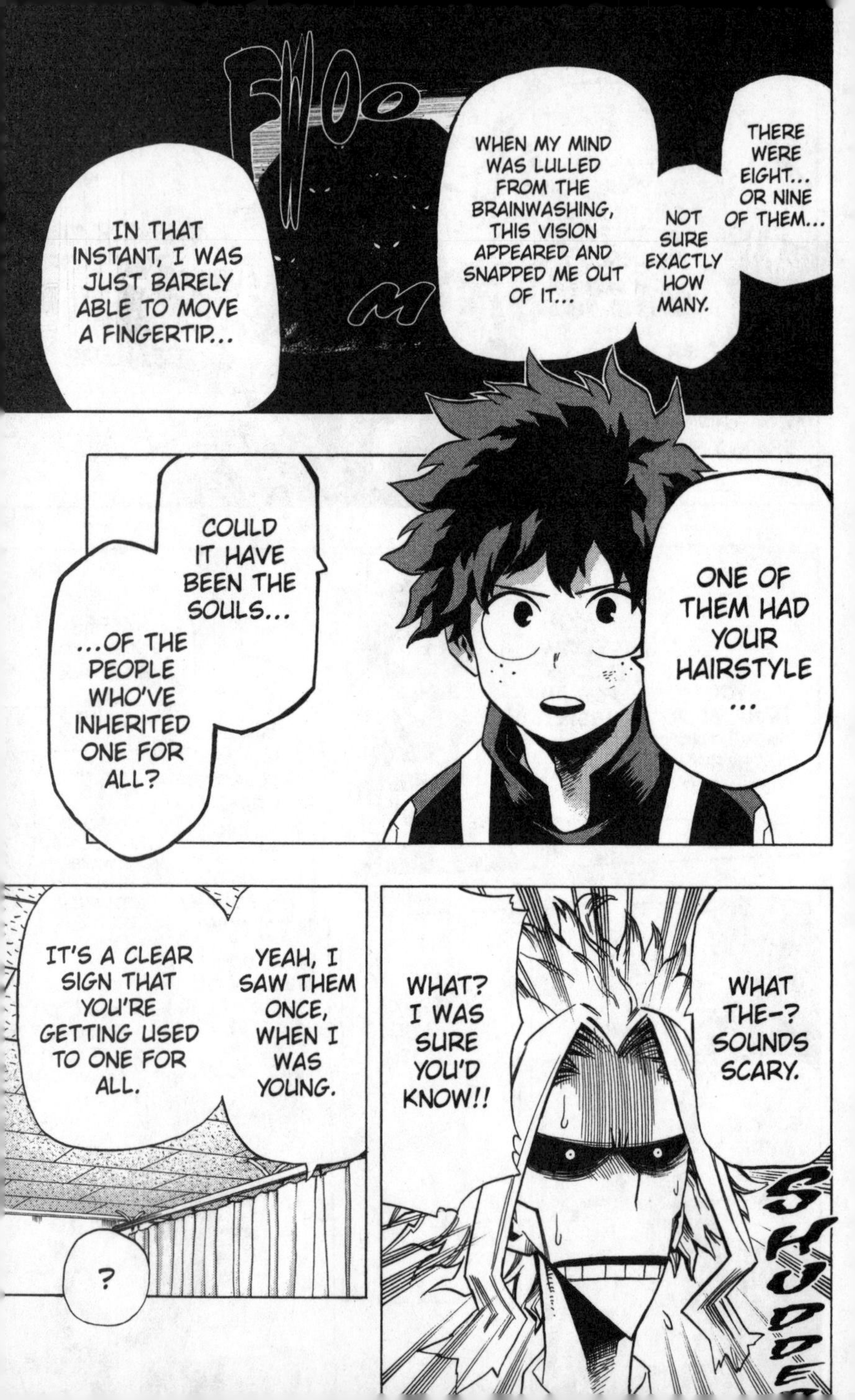
FWOOM
THERE WERE EIGHT... OR NINE OF THEM...
NOT SURE EXACTLY HOW MANY.
WHEN MY MIND WAS LULLED FROM THE BRAINWASHING, THIS VISION APPEARED AND SNAPPED ME OUT OF IT...
IN THAT INSTANT, I WAS JUST BARELY ABLE TO MOVE A FINGERTIP...
ONE OF THEM HAD YOUR HAIRSTYLE ...
COULD IT HAVE BEEN THE SOULS...
...OF THE PEOPLE WHO'VE INHERITED ONE FOR ALL?
WHAT THE-? SOUNDS SCARY.
WHAT? I WAS SURE YOU'D KNOW!!
SHUDDE
YEAH, I SAW THEM ONCE, WHEN I WAS YOUNG.
IT'S A CLEAR SIGN THAT YOU'RE GETTING USED TO ONE FOR ALL.
?

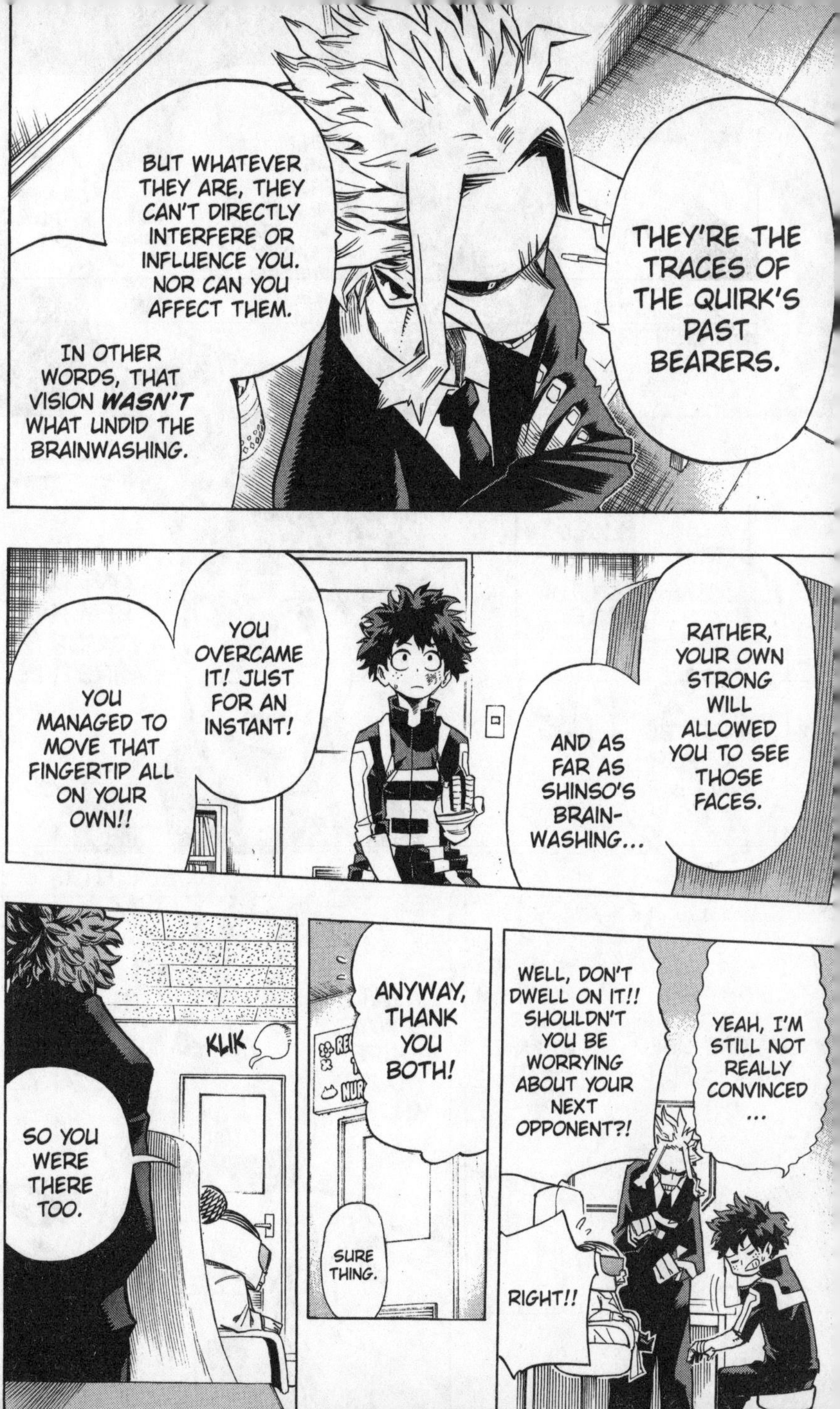
THEY'RE THE TRACES OF THE QUIRK'S PAST BEARERS.
BUT WHATEVER THEY ARE, THEY CAN'T DIRECTLY INTERFERE OR INFLUENCE YOU. NOR CAN YOU AFFECT THEM.
IN OTHER WORDS, THAT VISION ***WASN'T*** WHAT UNDID THE BRAINWASHING.
RATHER, YOUR OWN STRONG WILL ALLOWED YOU TO SEE THOSE FACES.
AND AS FAR AS SHINSO'S BRAIN-WASHING...
YOU OVERCAME IT! JUST FOR AN INSTANT!
YOU MANAGED TO MOVE THAT FINGERTIP ALL ON YOUR OWN!!
YEAH, I'M STILL NOT REALLY CONVINCED ...
WELL, DON'T DWELL ON IT!! SHOULDN'T YOU BE WORRYING ABOUT YOUR NEXT OPPONENT?!
RIGHT!!
ANYWAY, THANK YOU BOTH!
SURE THING.
KLIK
SO YOU WERE THERE TOO.

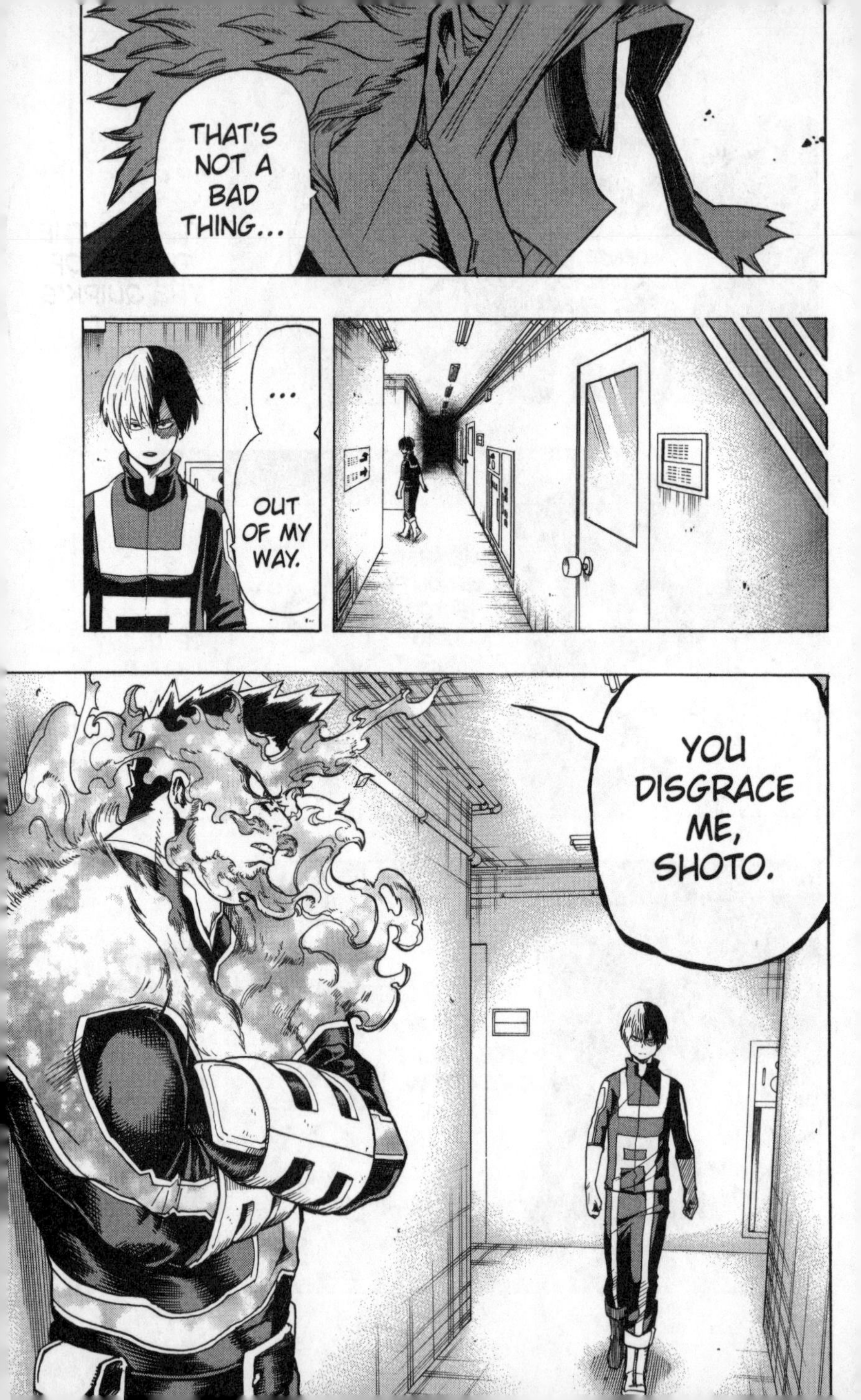
THAT'S NOT A BAD THING...
...
OUT OF MY WAY.
YOU DISGRACE ME, SHOTO.

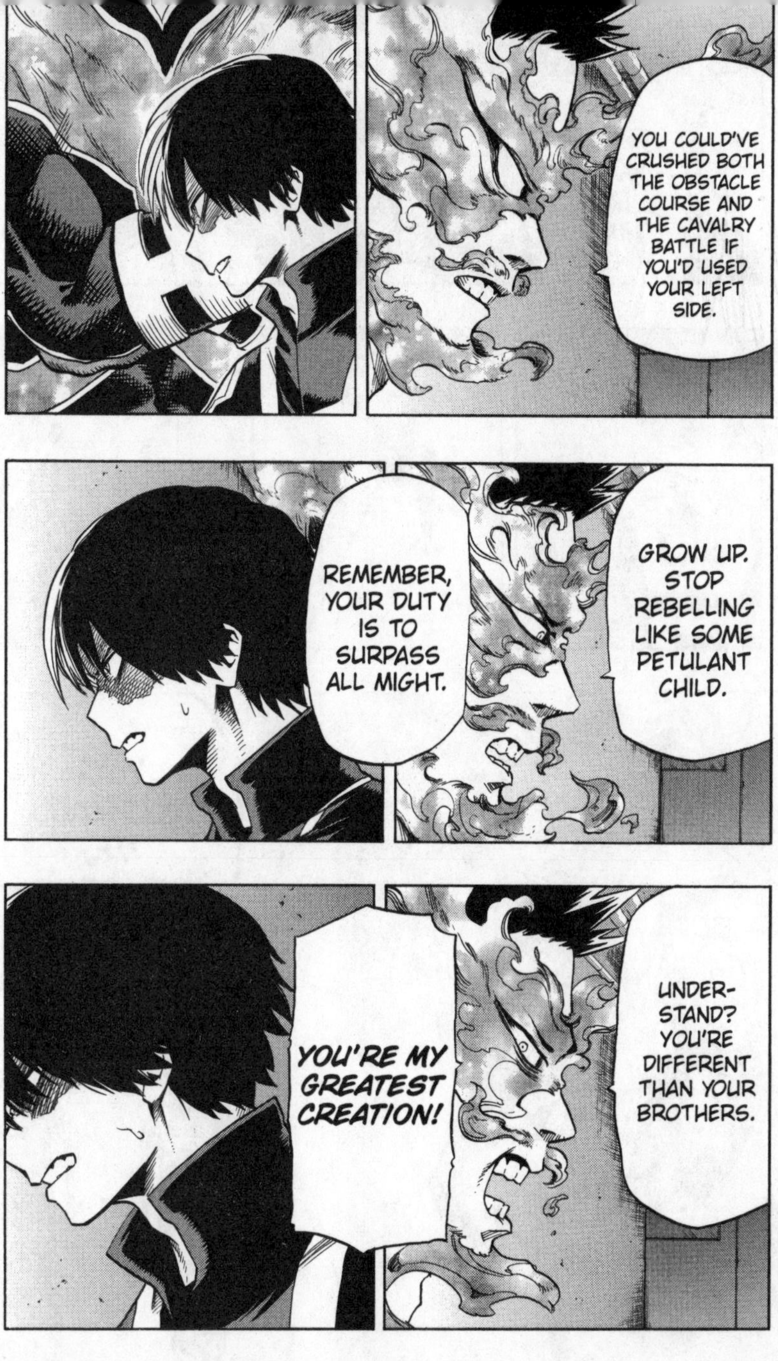
YOU COULD'VE CRUSHED BOTH THE OBSTACLE COURSE AND THE CAVALRY BATTLE IF YOU'D USED YOUR LEFT SIDE.
GROW UP. STOP REBELLING LIKE SOME PETULANT CHILD.
REMEMBER, YOUR DUTY IS TO SURPASS ALL MIGHT.
UNDER-STAND? YOU'RE DIFFERENT THAN YOUR BROTHERS.
YOU'RE MY GREATEST CREATION!

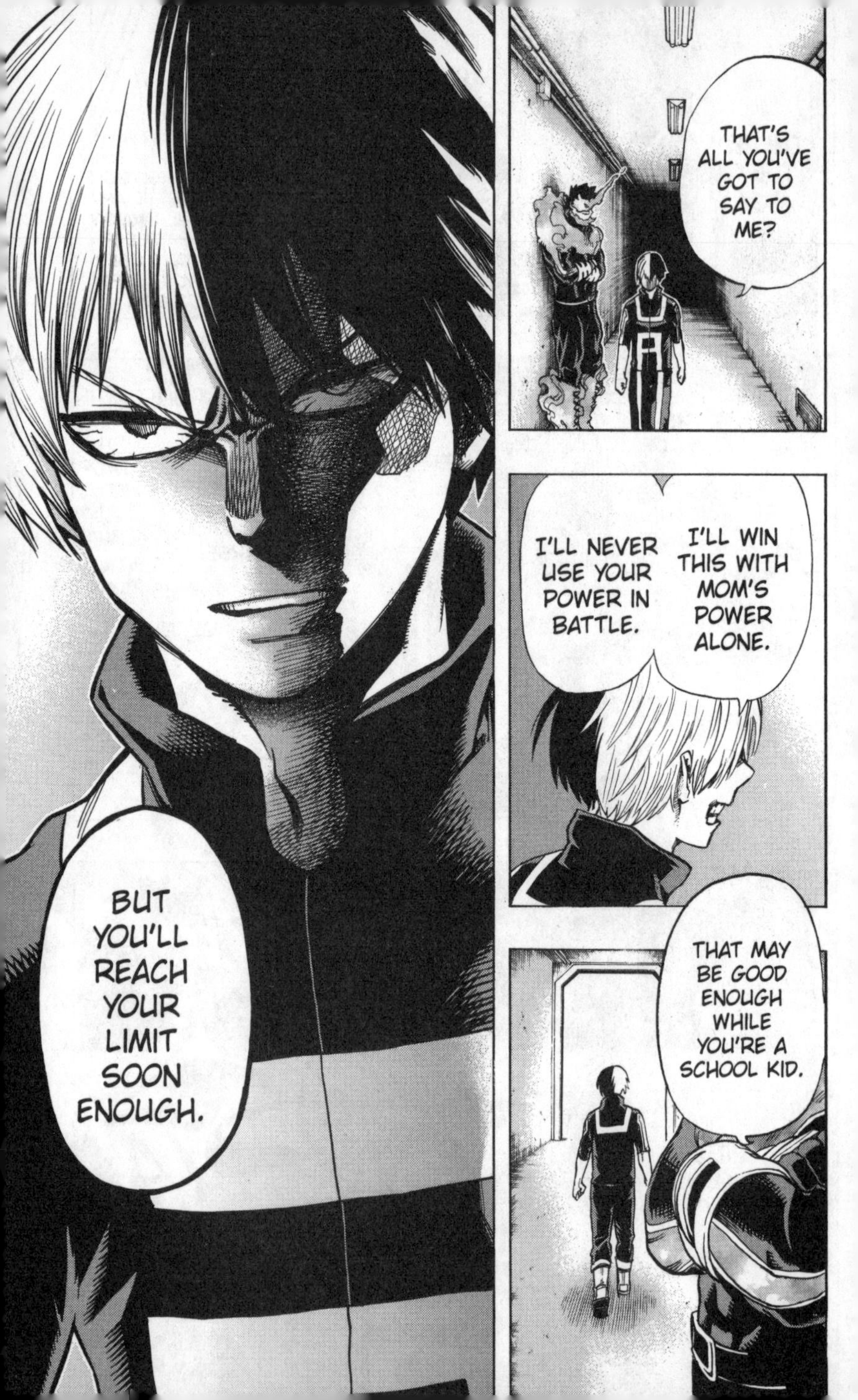
THAT'S ALL YOU'VE GOT TO SAY TO ME?
I'LL WIN THIS WITH MOM'S POWER ALONE.
I'LL NEVER USE YOUR POWER IN BATTLE.
THAT MAY BE GOOD ENOUGH WHILE YOU'RE A SCHOOL KID.
BUT YOU'LL REACH YOUR LIMIT SOON ENOUGH.

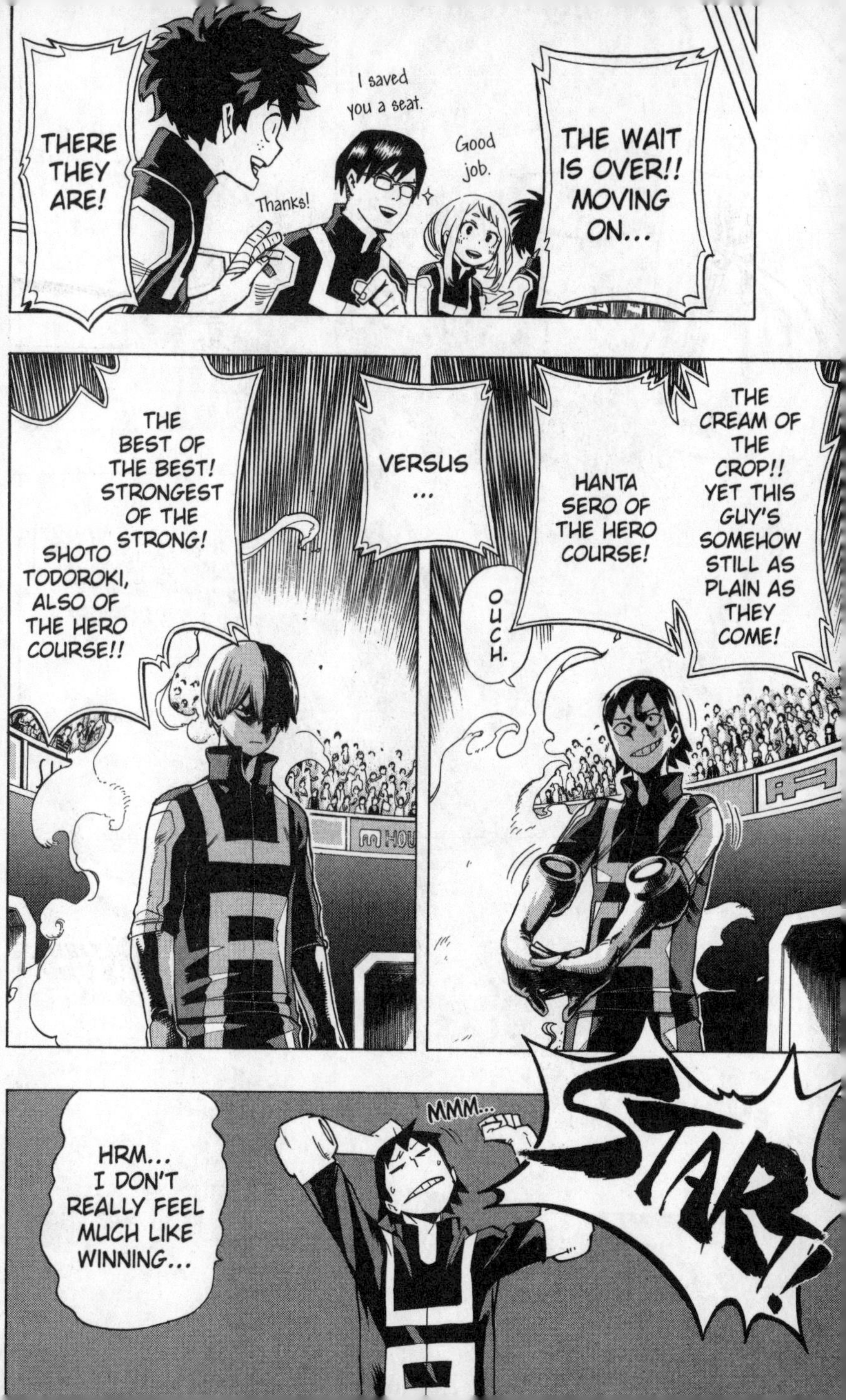
THE WAIT IS OVER!! MOVING ON...
I saved you a seat.
Good job.
THERE THEY ARE!
Thanks!
THE CREAM OF THE CROP!! YET THIS GUY'S SOMEHOW STILL AS PLAIN AS THEY COME!
HANTA SERO OF THE HERO COURSE!
OUCH.
VERSUS...
THE BEST OF THE BEST! STRONGEST OF THE STRONG!
SHOTO TODOROKI, ALSO OF THE HERO COURSE!!
STAR!
MMM...
HRM... I DON'T REALLY FEEL MUCH LIKE WINNING...

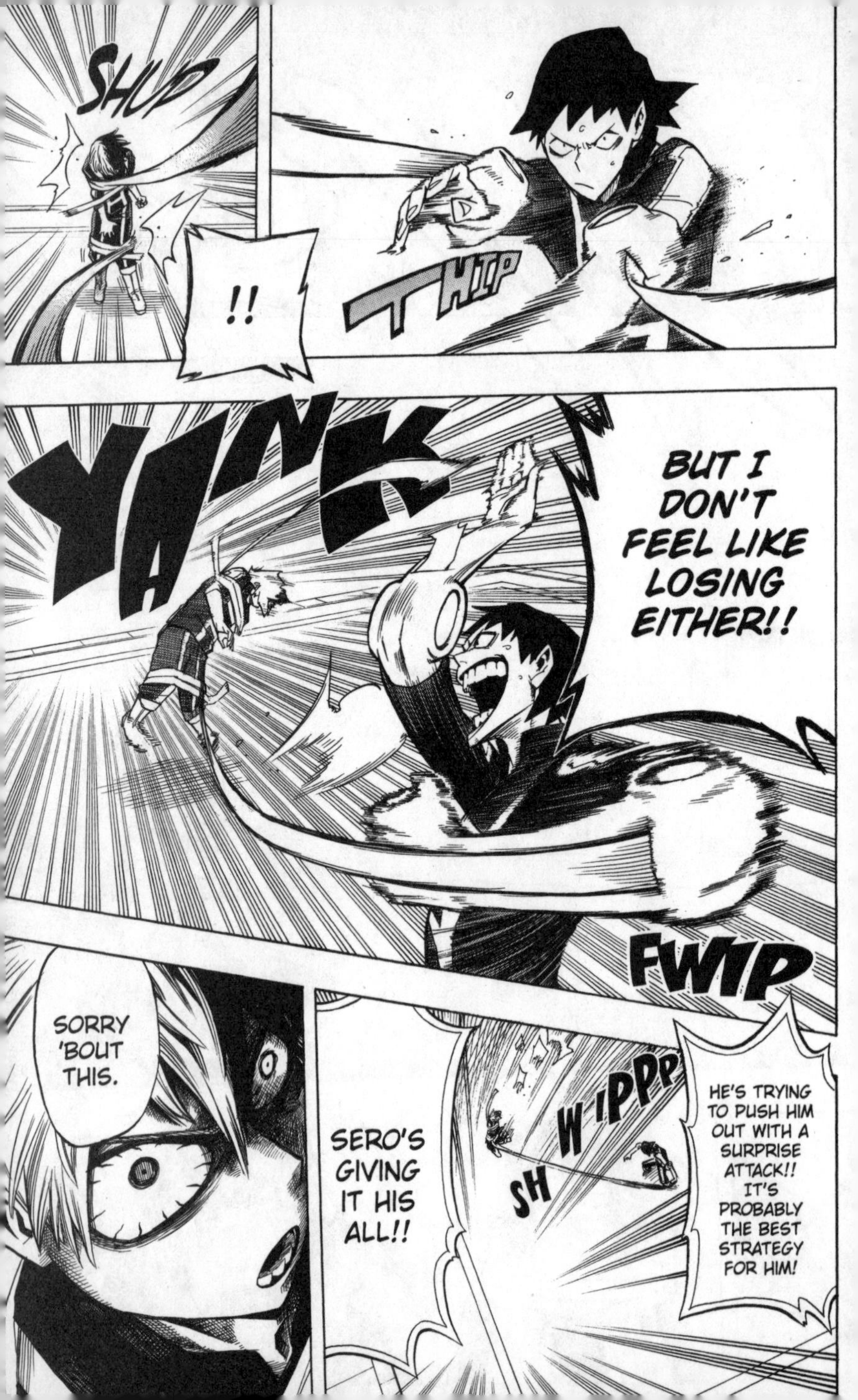
THIP
SHUP
!!
BUT I DON'T FEEL LIKE LOSING EITHER!!
YANK
FWIP
HE'S TRYING TO PUSH HIM OUT WITH A SURPRISE ATTACK!! IT'S PROBABLY THE BEST STRATEGY FOR HIM!
SHWIPPP
SERO'S GIVING IT HIS ALL!!
SORRY 'BOUT THIS.

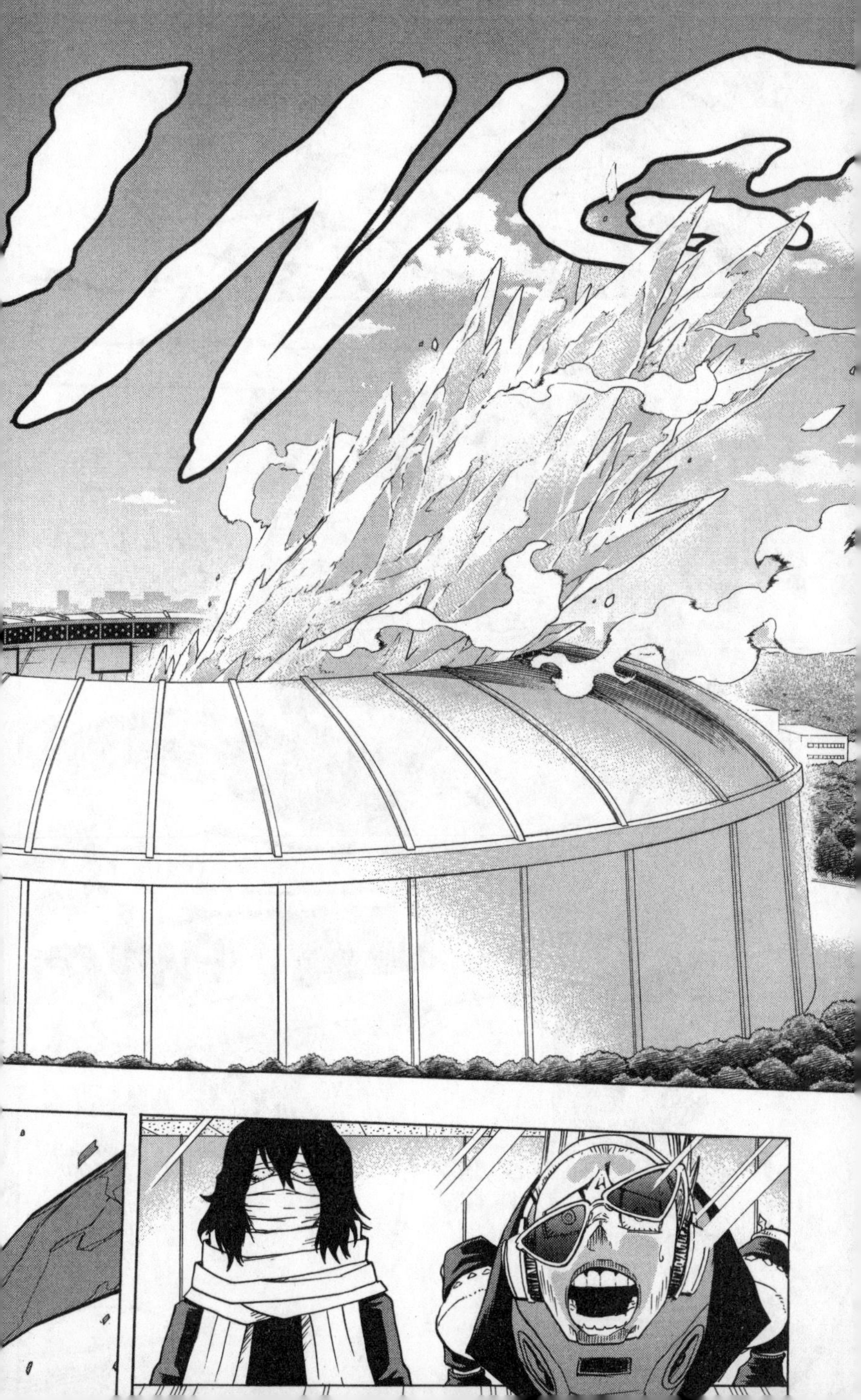

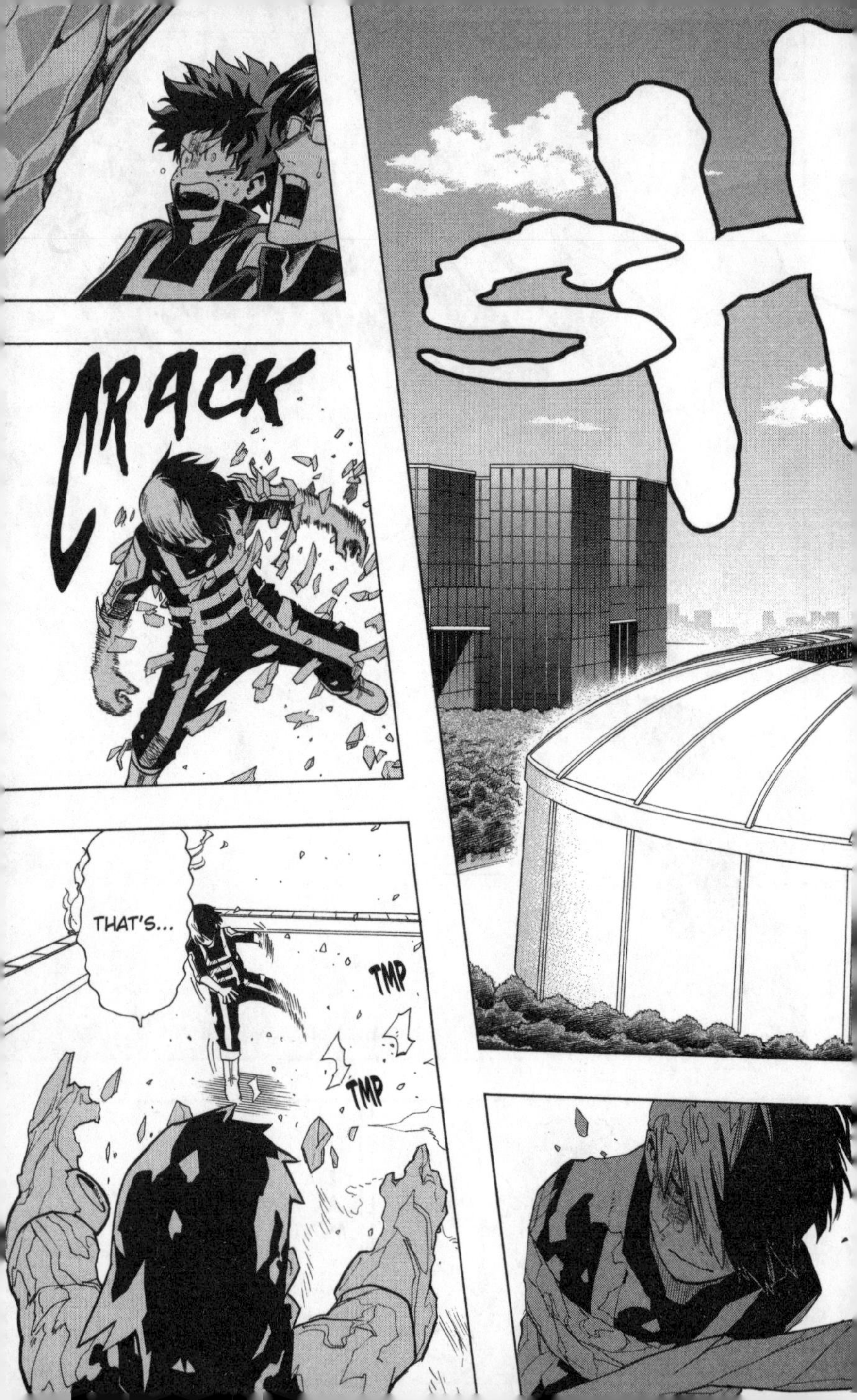
CRACK
THAT'S...
TMP
TMP

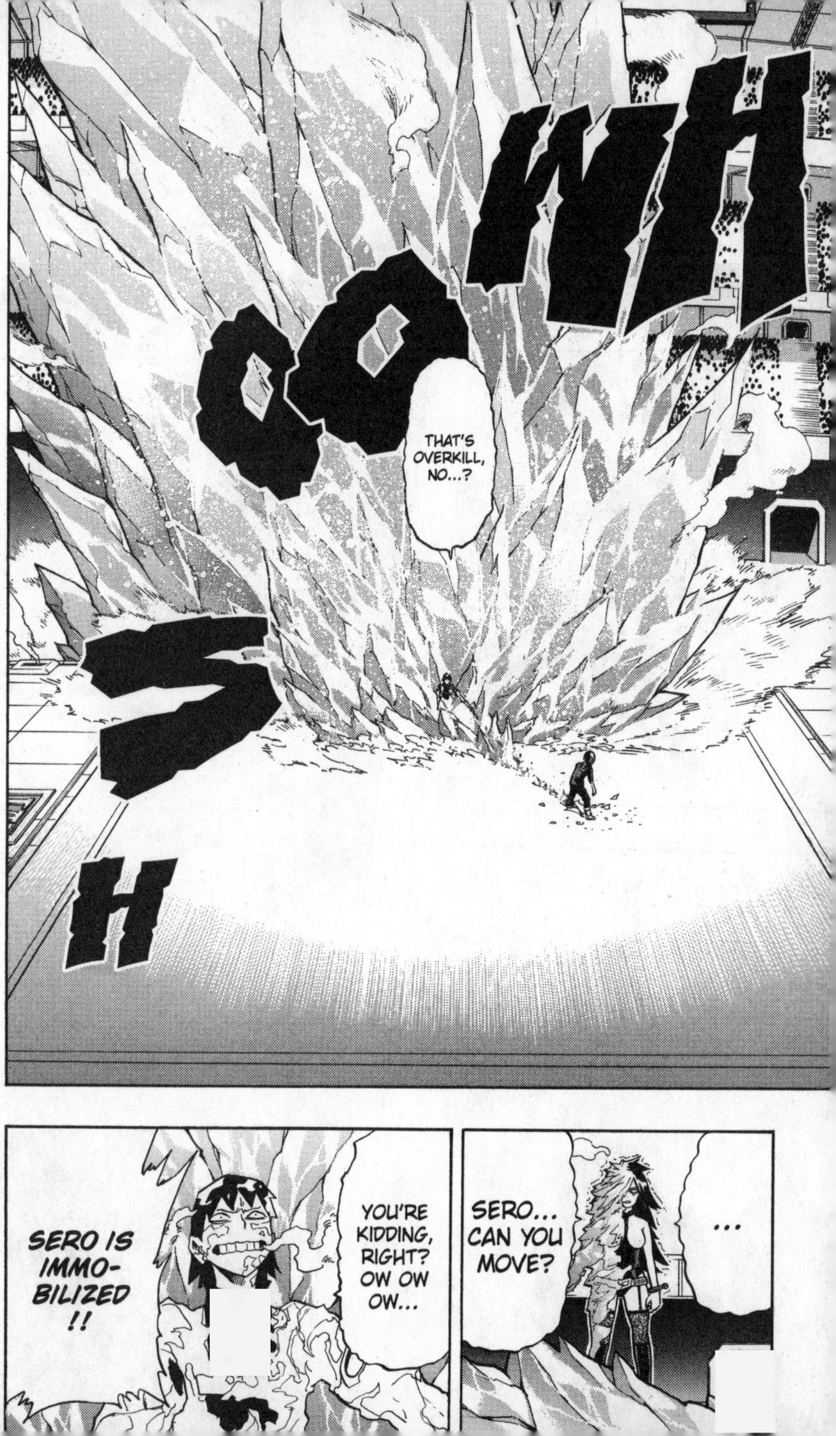
WHOOSH
THAT'S OVERKILL, NO...?
...
SERO... CAN YOU MOVE?
YOU'RE KIDDING, RIGHT? OW OW OW...
SERO IS IMMOBILIZED!!

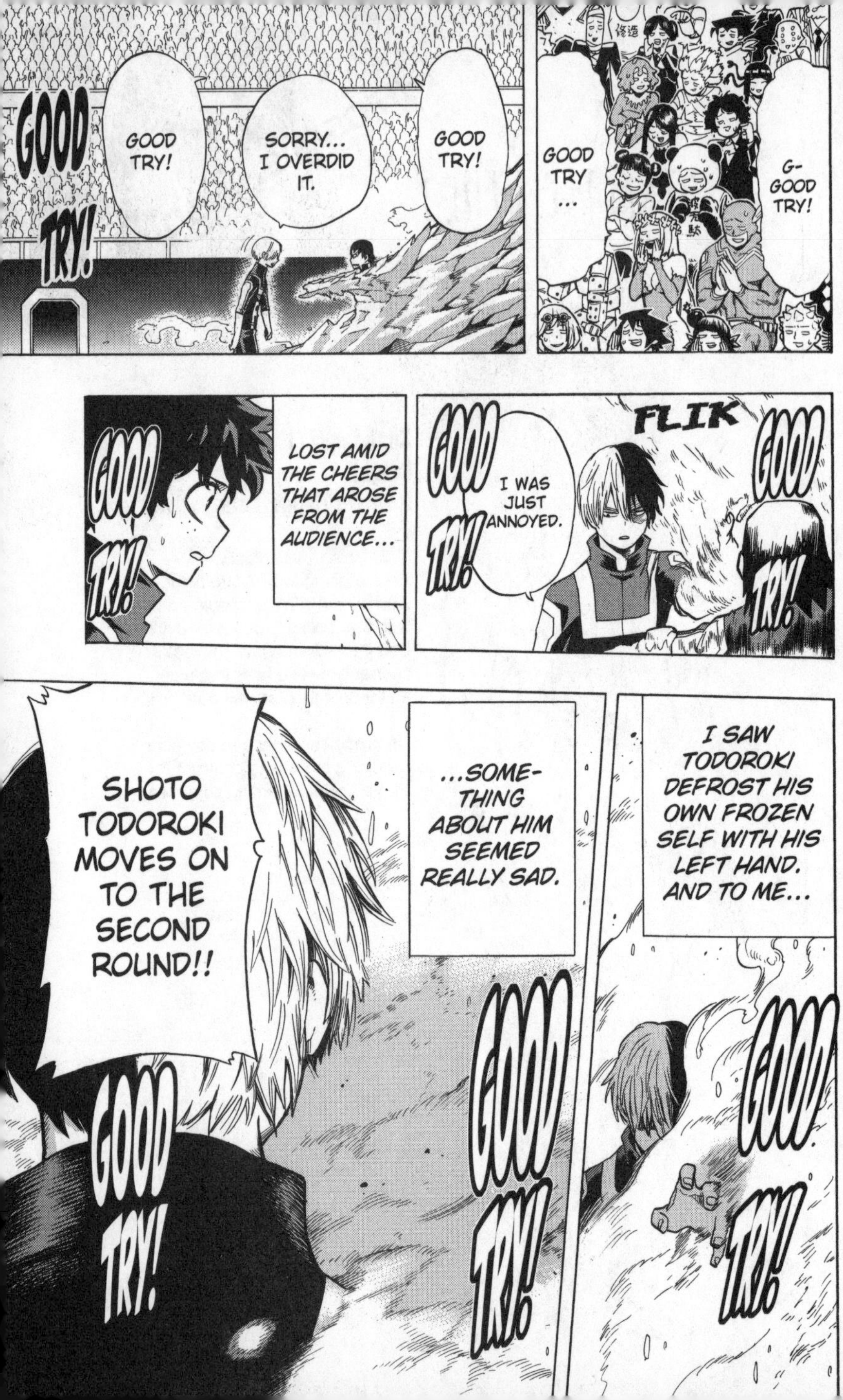
G-GOOD TRY!
GOOD TRY ...
GOOD TRY!
SORRY... I OVERDID IT.
GOOD TRY!
GOOD TRY!
FLIK
GOOD TRY!
I WAS JUST ANNOYED.
GOOD TRY!
LOST AMID THE CHEERS THAT AROSE FROM THE AUDIENCE...
GOOD TRY!
I SAW TODOROKI DEFROST HIS OWN FROZEN SELF WITH HIS LEFT HAND. AND TO ME...
GOOD TRY!
...SOMETHING ABOUT HIM SEEMED REALLY SAD.
GOOD TRY!
SHOTO TODOROKI MOVES ON TO THE SECOND ROUND!!
GOOD TRY!

HITOSHI SHINSO (15)

STREET CLOTHES

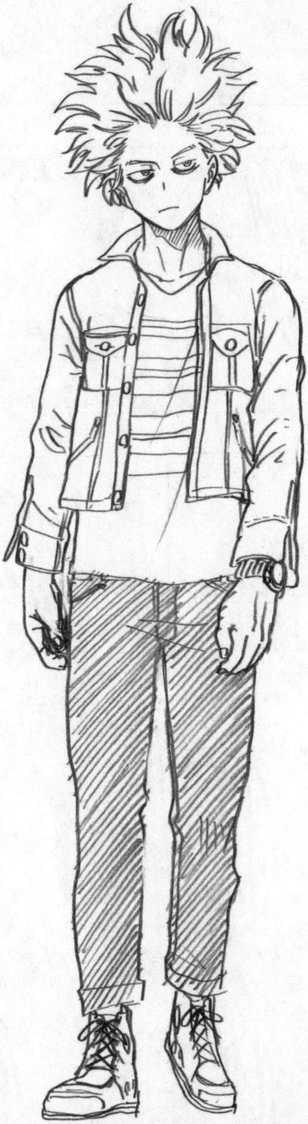

Birthday: 7/1
Height: 177 cm
Favorite Things: Cats, cycling

BEHIND THE SCENES

Before going to bed one night, I was thinking, "What would I do with that ability?" Use it for evil? Use it to skirt the law, maybe? I suddenly awoke later that night, and this character was born.

I'm pretty sure that one day soon, I'm going to have to confront my own ridiculous naming schemes.

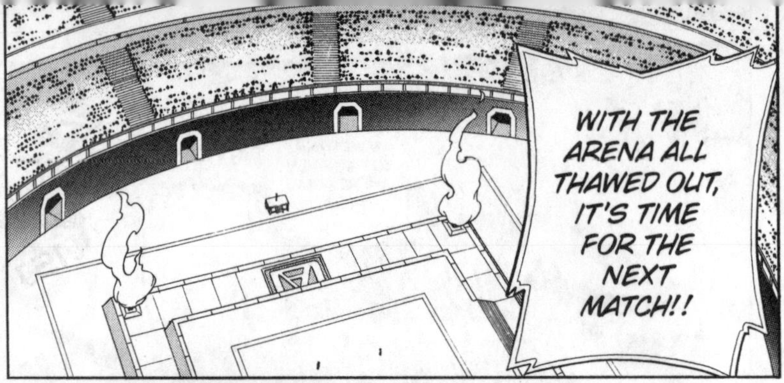
WITH THE ARENA ALL THAWED OUT, IT'S TIME FOR THE NEXT MATCH!!

NO.35 - BATTLE ON, CHALLENGERS!

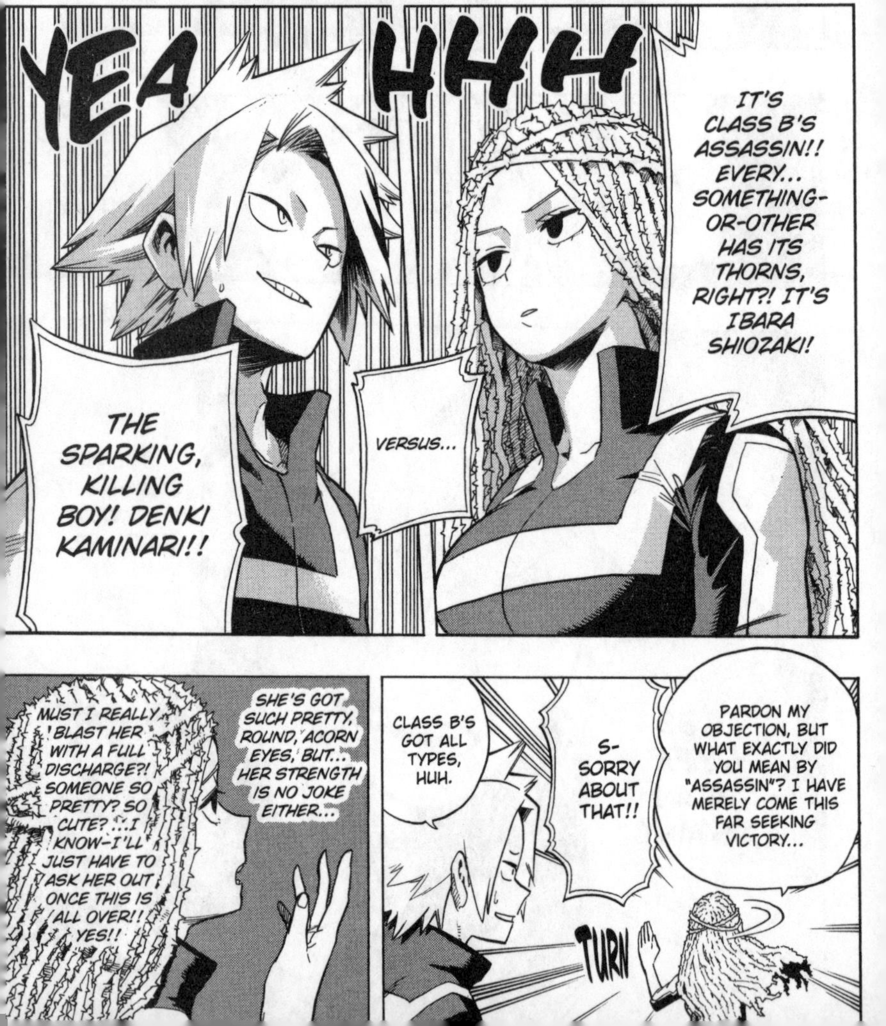
YEAHHH
IT'S CLASS B'S ASSASSIN!! EVERY... SOMETHING-OR-OTHER HAS ITS THORNS, RIGHT?! IT'S IBARA SHIOZAKI!
VERSUS...
THE SPARKING, KILLING BOY! DENKI KAMINARI!!
PARDON MY OBJECTION, BUT WHAT EXACTLY DID YOU MEAN BY "ASSASSIN"? I HAVE MERELY COME THIS FAR SEEKING VICTORY...
S-SORRY ABOUT THAT!!
CLASS B'S GOT ALL TYPES, HUH.
TURN
SHE'S GOT SUCH PRETTY, ROUND, ACORN EYES, BUT... HER STRENGTH IS NO JOKE EITHER...
MUST I REALLY BLAST HER WITH A FULL DISCHARGE?! SOMEONE SO PRETTY? SO CUTE? ...I KNOW-I'LL JUST HAVE TO ASK HER OUT ONCE THIS IS ALL OVER!! YES!!

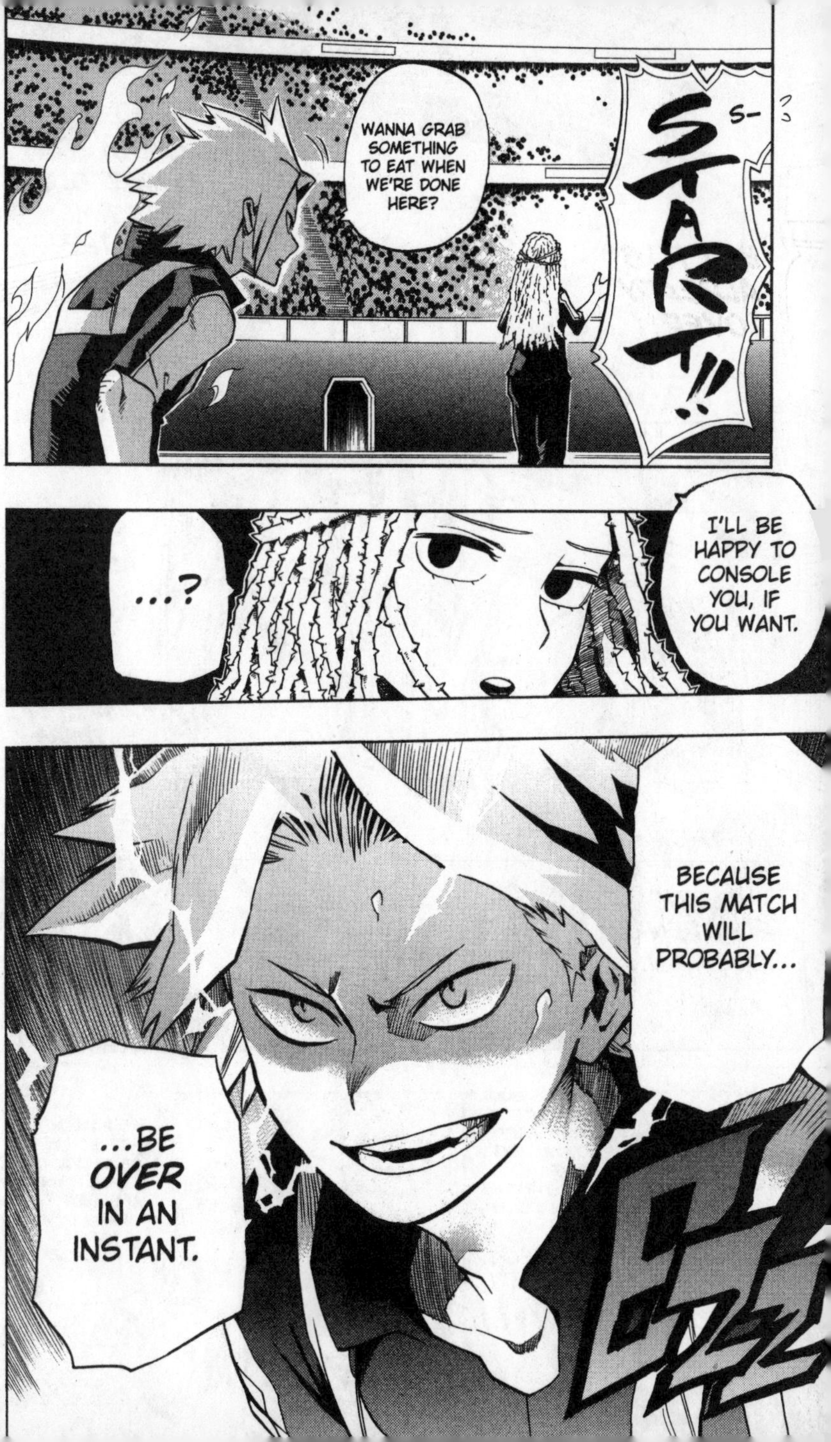
S-
START!!
WANNA GRAB SOMETHING TO EAT WHEN WE'RE DONE HERE?
I'LL BE HAPPY TO CONSOLE YOU, IF YOU WANT.
...?
BECAUSE THIS MATCH WILL PROBABLY...
...BE *OVER* IN AN INSTANT.

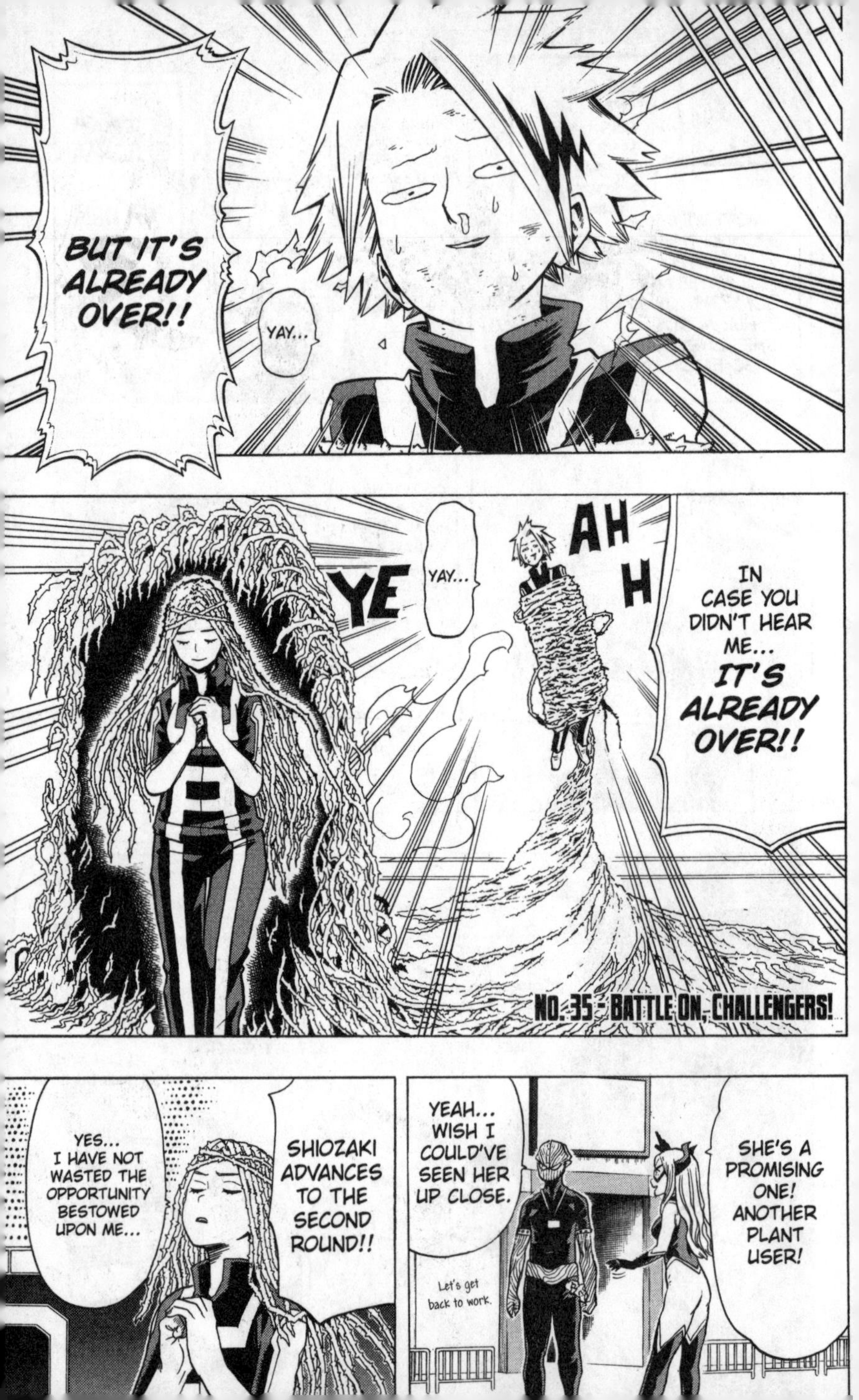
YAY...
BUT IT'S ALREADY OVER!!
IN CASE YOU DIDN'T HEAR ME... IT'S ALREADY OVER!!
AHH
YAY...
YE
NO. 35 - BATTLE ON, CHALLENGERS!
SHE'S A PROMISING ONE! ANOTHER PLANT USER!
YEAH... WISH I COULD'VE SEEN HER UP CLOSE.
Let's get back to work.
SHIOZAKI ADVANCES TO THE SECOND ROUND!!
YES... I HAVE NOT WASTED THE OPPORTUNITY BESTOWED UPON ME...

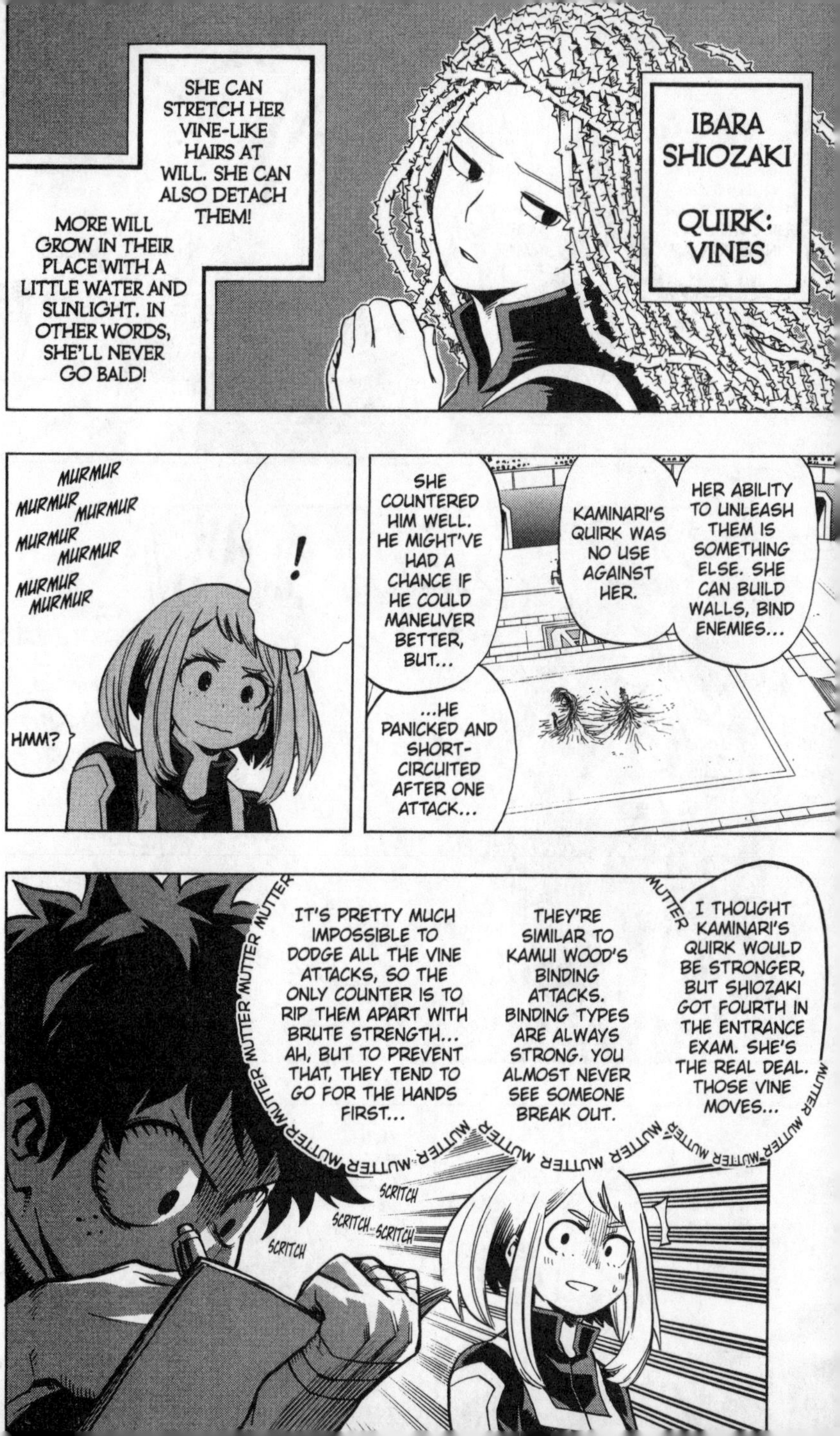
IBARA SHIOZAKI
QUIRK: VINES
SHE CAN STRETCH HER VINE-LIKE HAIRS AT WILL. SHE CAN ALSO DETACH THEM!
MORE WILL GROW IN THEIR PLACE WITH A LITTLE WATER AND SUNLIGHT. IN OTHER WORDS, SHE'LL NEVER GO BALD!
HER ABILITY TO UNLEASH THEM IS SOMETHING ELSE. SHE CAN BUILD WALLS, BIND ENEMIES...
KAMINARI'S QUIRK WAS NO USE AGAINST HER.
SHE COUNTERED HIM WELL. HE MIGHT'VE HAD A CHANCE IF HE COULD MANEUVER BETTER, BUT...
...HE PANICKED AND SHORT-CIRCUITED AFTER ONE ATTACK...
!
MURMUR MURMUR MURMUR MURMUR MURMUR MURMUR MURMUR
HMM?
I THOUGHT KAMINARI'S QUIRK WOULD BE STRONGER, BUT SHIOZAKI GOT FOURTH IN THE ENTRANCE EXAM. SHE'S THE REAL DEAL. THOSE VINE MOVES...
THEY'RE SIMILAR TO KAMUI WOOD'S BINDING ATTACKS. BINDING TYPES ARE ALWAYS STRONG. YOU ALMOST NEVER SEE SOMEONE BREAK OUT.
IT'S PRETTY MUCH IMPOSSIBLE TO DODGE ALL THE VINE ATTACKS, SO THE ONLY COUNTER IS TO RIP THEM APART WITH BRUTE STRENGTH... AH, BUT TO PREVENT THAT, THEY TEND TO GO FOR THE HANDS FIRST...
MUTTER MUTTER MUTTER MUTTER MUTTER MUTTER MUTTER
SCRITCH SCRITCH SCRITCH SCRITCH

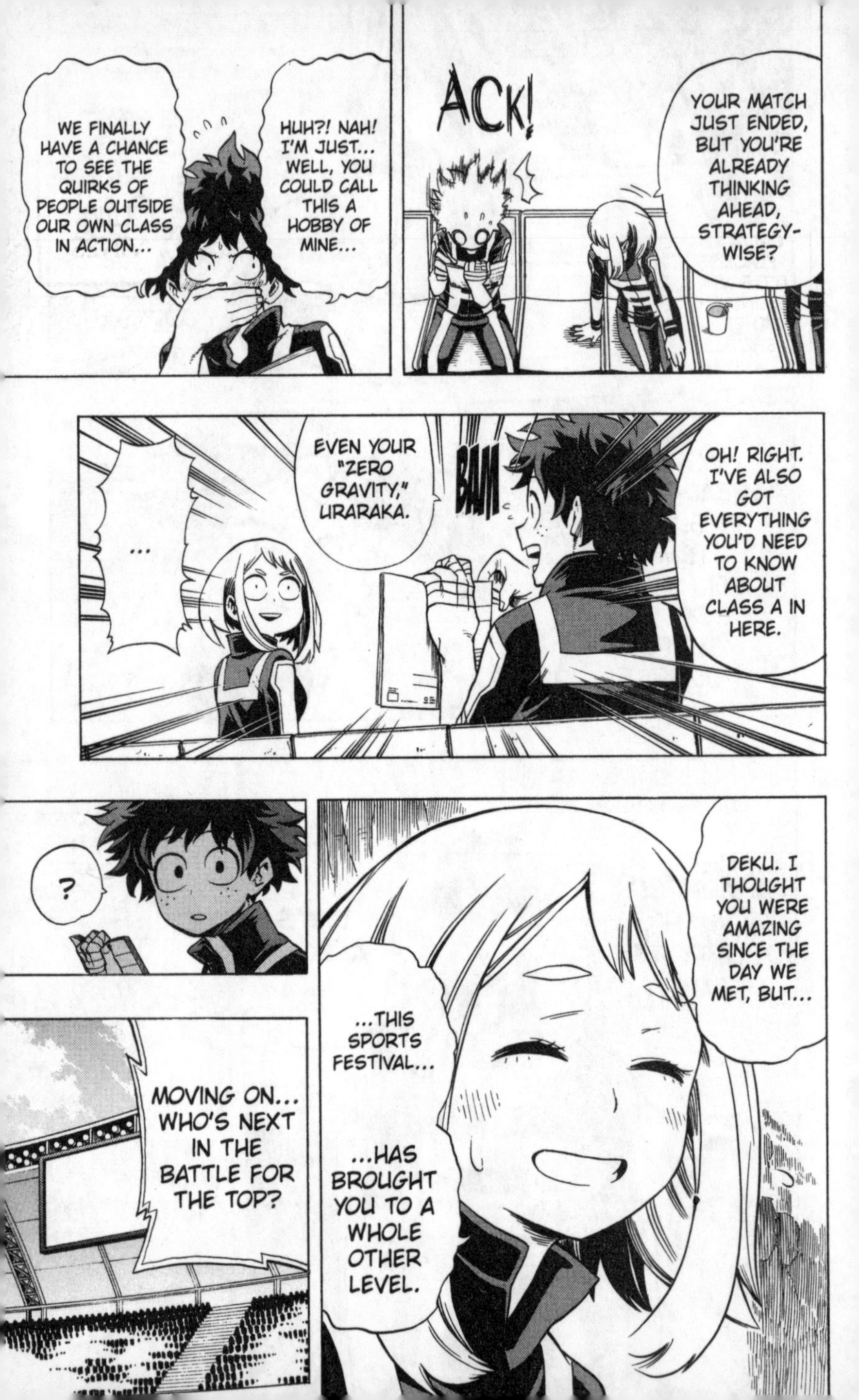
YOUR MATCH JUST ENDED, BUT YOU'RE ALREADY THINKING AHEAD, STRATEGY-WISE?
ACK!
HUH?! NAH! I'M JUST... WELL, YOU COULD CALL THIS A HOBBY OF MINE...
WE FINALLY HAVE A CHANCE TO SEE THE QUIRKS OF PEOPLE OUTSIDE OUR OWN CLASS IN ACTION...
OH! RIGHT. I'VE ALSO GOT EVERYTHING YOU'D NEED TO KNOW ABOUT CLASS A IN HERE.
BAM
EVEN YOUR "ZERO GRAVITY," URARAKA.
...
DEKU. I THOUGHT YOU WERE AMAZING SINCE THE DAY WE MET, BUT...
...THIS SPORTS FESTIVAL...
...HAS BROUGHT YOU TO A WHOLE OTHER LEVEL.
?
MOVING ON... WHO'S NEXT IN THE BATTLE FOR THE TOP?

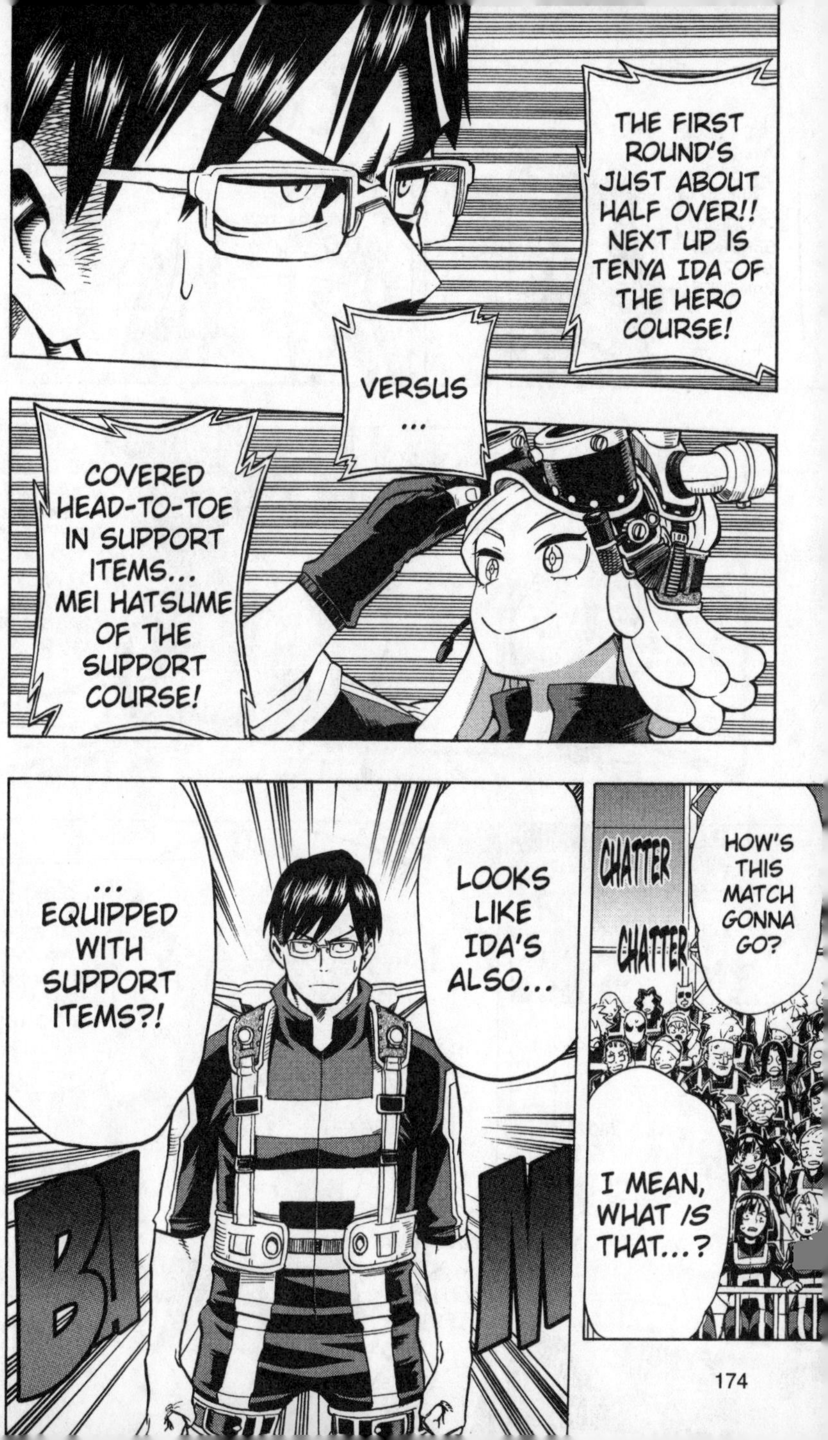
THE FIRST ROUND'S JUST ABOUT HALF OVER!! NEXT UP IS TENYA IDA OF THE HERO COURSE!
VERSUS ...
COVERED HEAD-TO-TOE IN SUPPORT ITEMS... MEI HATSUME OF THE SUPPORT COURSE!
HOW'S THIS MATCH GONNA GO?
CHATTER
CHATTER
I MEAN, WHAT *IS* THAT...?
LOOKS LIKE IDA'S ALSO...
... EQUIPPED WITH SUPPORT ITEMS?!
BAM

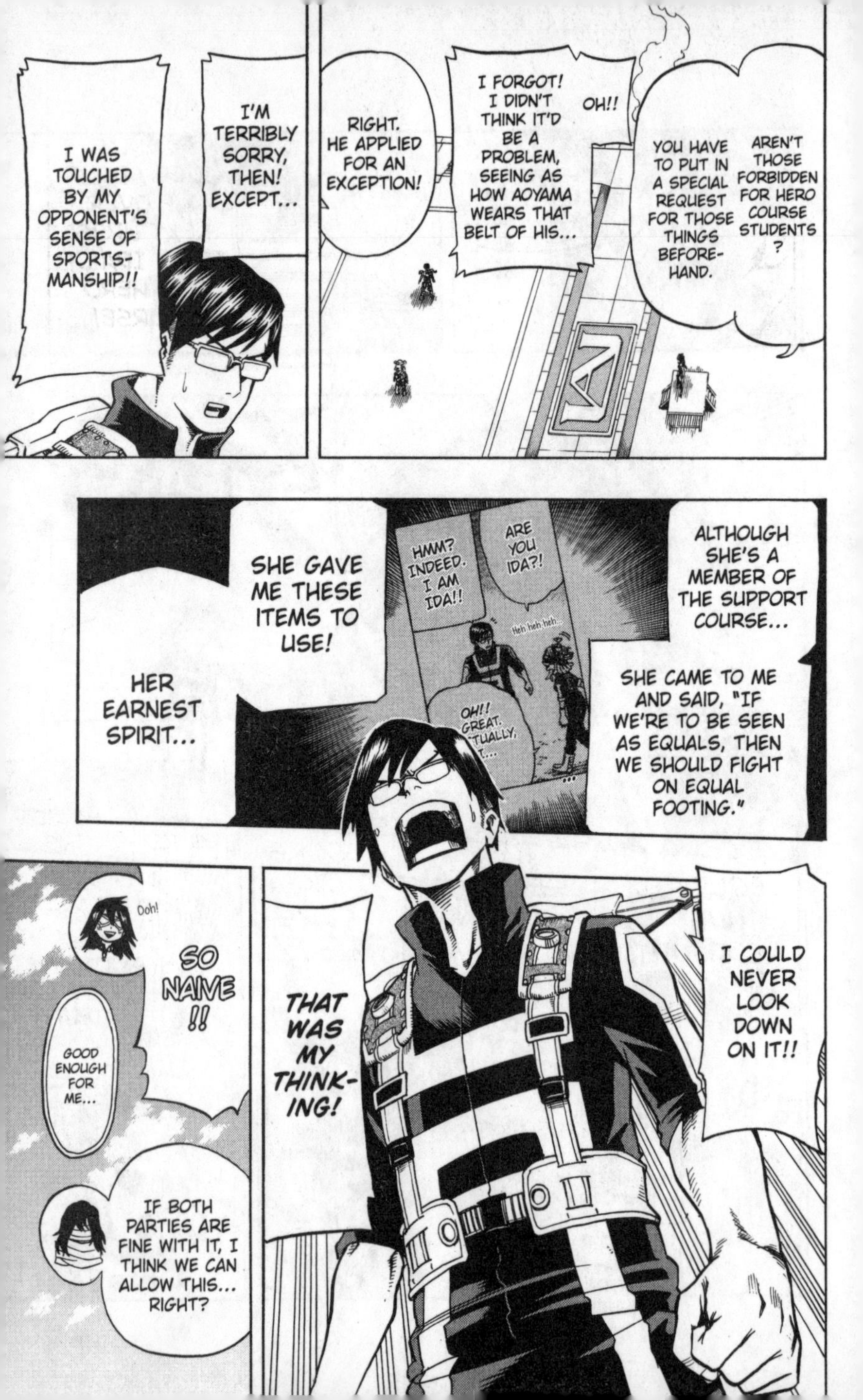
AREN'T THOSE FORBIDDEN FOR HERO COURSE STUDENTS?
YOU HAVE TO PUT IN A SPECIAL REQUEST FOR THOSE THINGS BEFOREHAND.
OH!!
I FORGOT! I DIDN'T THINK IT'D BE A PROBLEM, SEEING AS HOW AOYAMA WEARS THAT BELT OF HIS...
RIGHT. HE APPLIED FOR AN EXCEPTION!
I'M TERRIBLY SORRY, THEN! EXCEPT...
I WAS TOUCHED BY MY OPPONENT'S SPORTSMANSHIP!!
ALTHOUGH SHE'S A MEMBER OF THE SUPPORT COURSE...
SHE CAME TO ME AND SAID, "IF WE'RE TO BE SEEN AS EQUALS, THEN WE SHOULD FIGHT ON EQUAL FOOTING."
ARE YOU IDA?!
HMM? INDEED. I AM IDA!!
Heh heh heh...
SHE GAVE ME THESE ITEMS TO USE!
HER EARNEST SPIRIT...
I COULD NEVER LOOK DOWN ON IT!!
THAT WAS MY THINKING!
Ooh!
SO NAIVE!!
GOOD ENOUGH FOR ME...
IF BOTH PARTIES ARE FINE WITH IT, I THINK WE CAN ALLOW THIS... RIGHT?

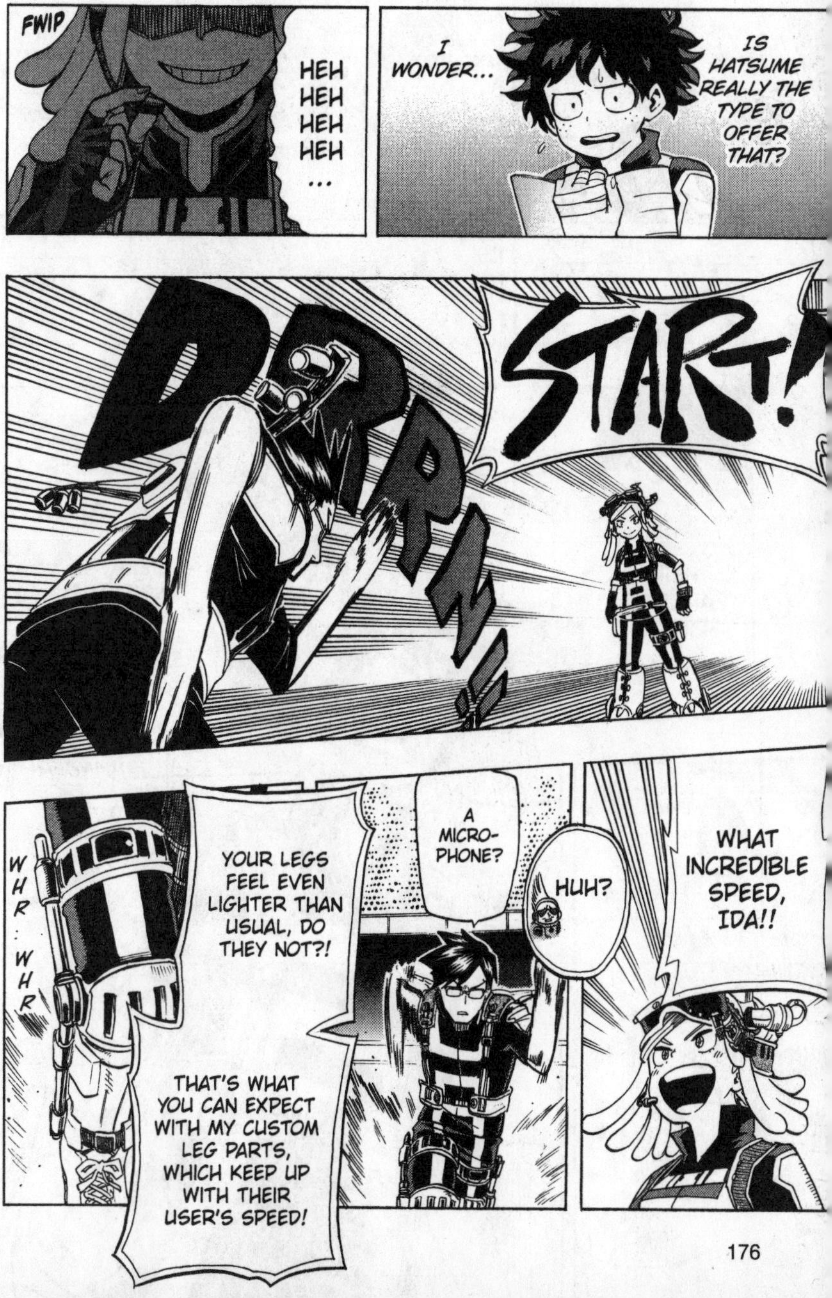
IS HATSUME REALLY THE TYPE TO OFFER THAT?
I WONDER...
HEH HEH HEH HEH...
FWIP
START!
WHAT INCREDIBLE SPEED, IDA!!
A MICROPHONE?
HUH?
YOUR LEGS FEEL EVEN LIGHTER THAN USUAL, DO THEY NOT?!
THAT'S WHAT YOU CAN EXPECT WITH MY CUSTOM LEG PARTS, WHICH KEEP UP WITH THEIR USER'S SPEED!
WHR WHR

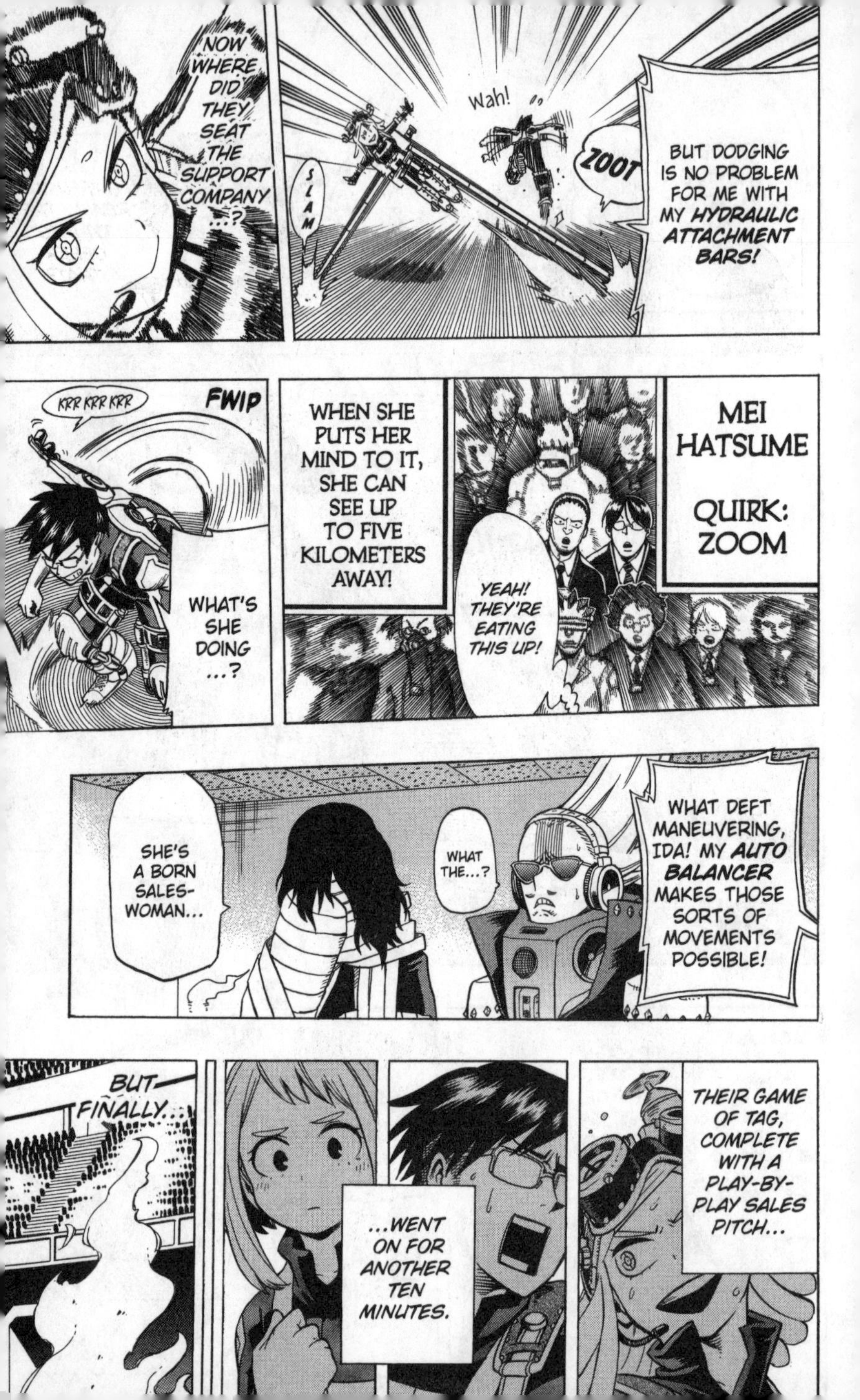
BUT DODGING IS NO PROBLEM FOR ME WITH MY **HYDRAULIC ATTACHMENT BARS!**
ZOOT
Wah!
SLAM
NOW WHERE DID THEY SEAT THE SUPPORT COMPANY ...?
MEI HATSUME
QUIRK: ZOOM
YEAH! THEY'RE EATING THIS UP!
WHEN SHE PUTS HER MIND TO IT, SHE CAN SEE UP TO FIVE KILOMETERS AWAY!
FWIP
KRR KRR KRR
WHAT'S SHE DOING ...?
WHAT DEFT MANEUVERING, IDA! MY **AUTO BALANCER** MAKES THOSE SORTS OF MOVEMENTS POSSIBLE!
WHAT THE...?
SHE'S A BORN SALES-WOMAN...
THEIR GAME OF TAG, COMPLETE WITH A PLAY-BY-PLAY SALES PITCH...
...WENT ON FOR ANOTHER TEN MINUTES.
BUT FINALLY...

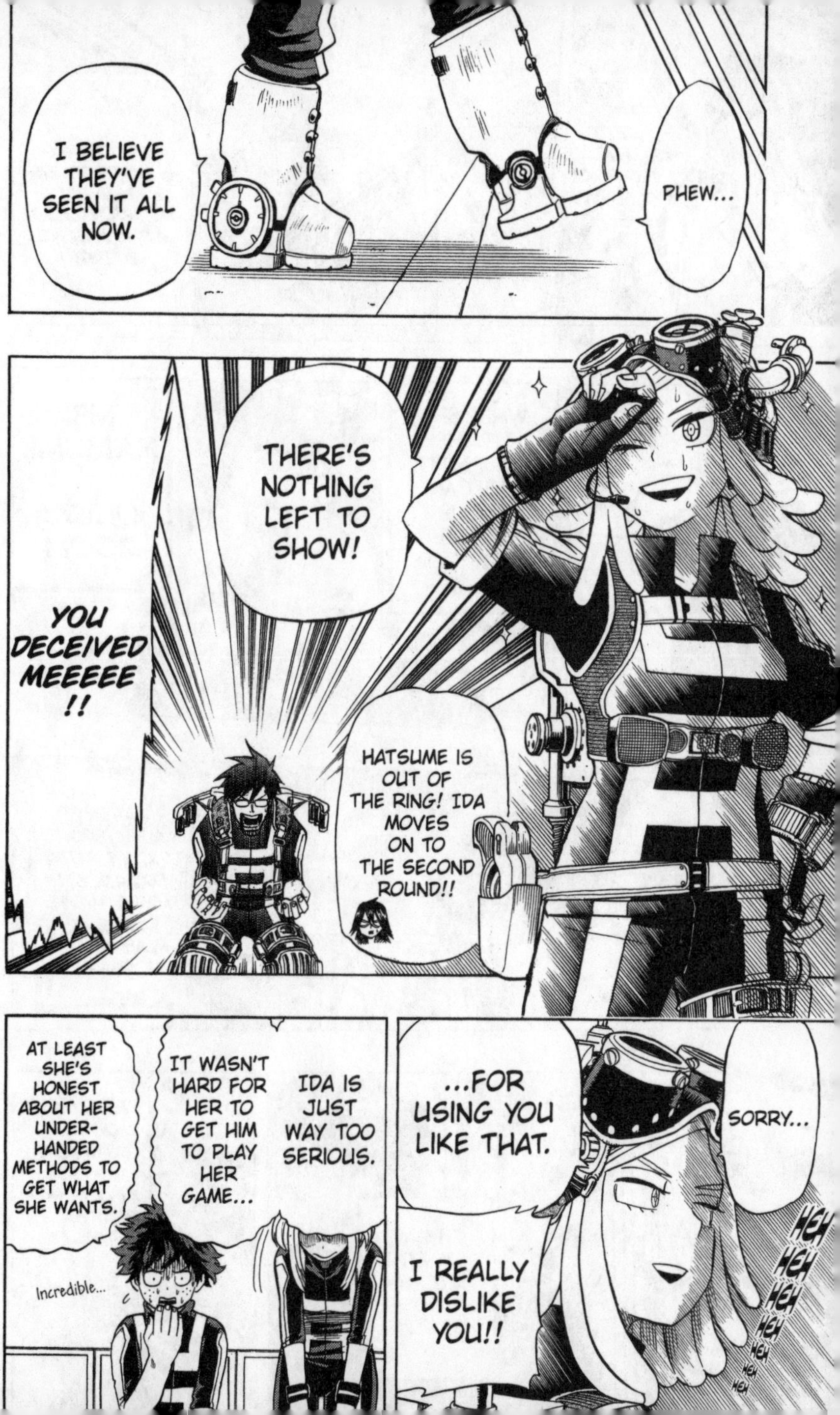
PHEW...
I BELIEVE THEY'VE SEEN IT ALL NOW.
THERE'S NOTHING LEFT TO SHOW!
YOU DECEIVED MEEEEE!!
HATSUME IS OUT OF THE RING! IDA MOVES ON TO THE SECOND ROUND!!
SORRY...
...FOR USING YOU LIKE THAT.
I REALLY DISLIKE YOU!!
HEH HEH HEH HEH HEH HEH HEH
IDA IS JUST WAY TOO SERIOUS.
IT WASN'T HARD FOR HER TO GET HIM TO PLAY HER GAME...
AT LEAST SHE'S HONEST ABOUT HER UNDER-HANDED METHODS TO GET WHAT SHE WANTS.
Incredible...

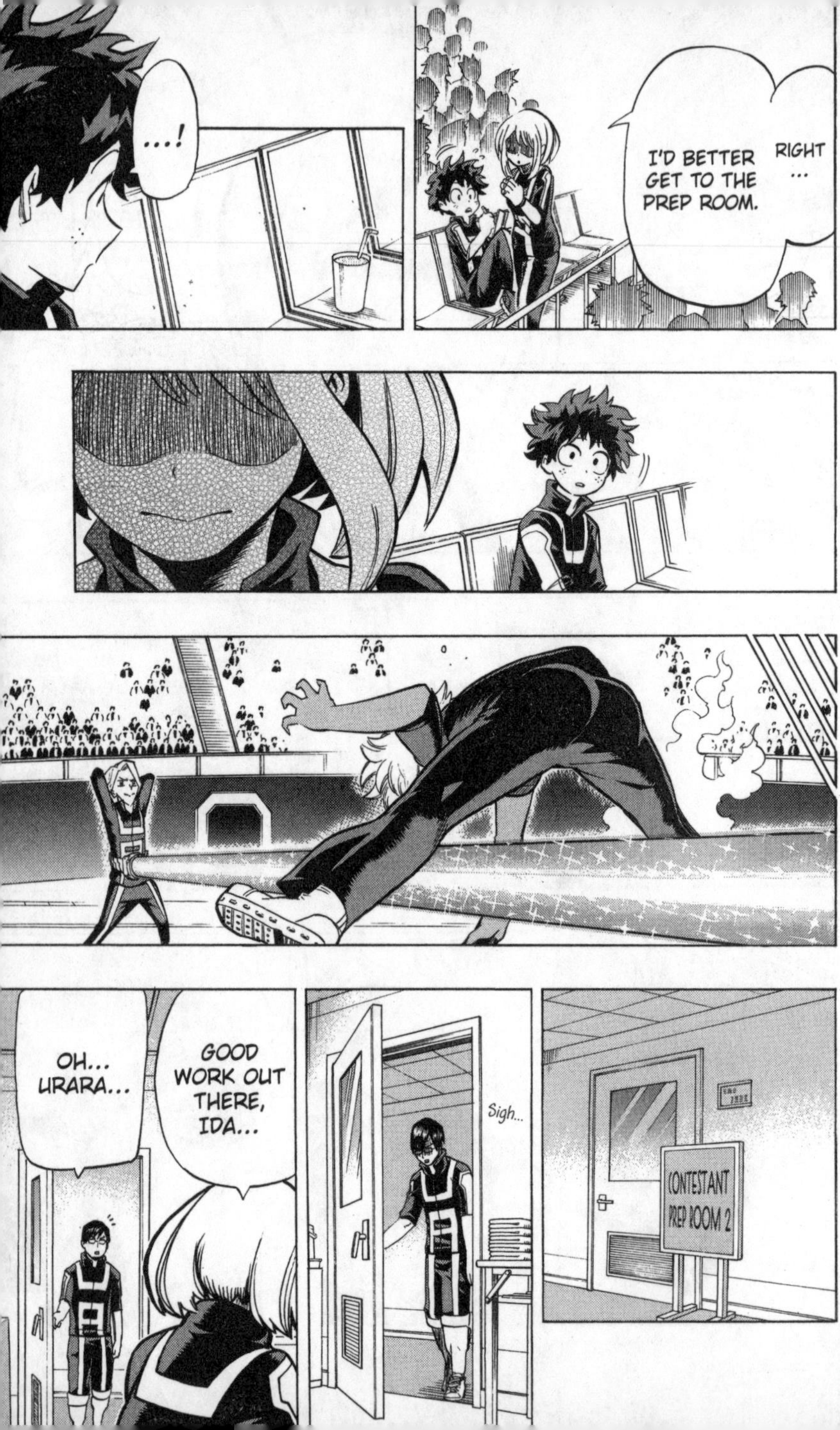
RIGHT ...
I'D BETTER GET TO THE PREP ROOM.
...!
CONTESTANT PREP ROOM 2
Sigh...
GOOD WORK OUT THERE, IDA...
OH... URARA...

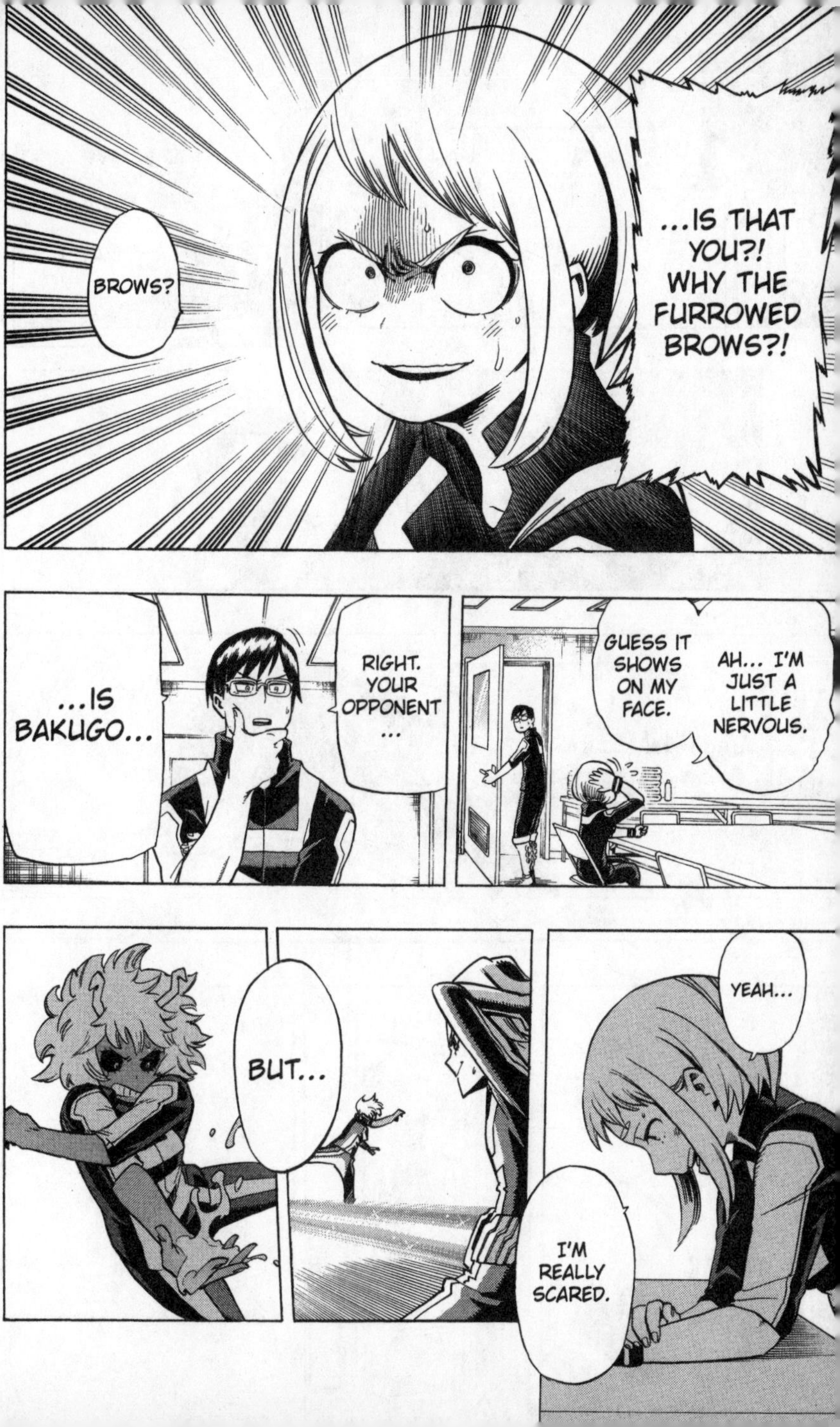
...IS THAT YOU?! WHY THE FURROWED BROWS?!
BROWS?
AH... I'M JUST A LITTLE NERVOUS.
GUESS IT SHOWS ON MY FACE.
RIGHT. YOUR OPPONENT ...
...IS BAKUGO...
YEAH...
I'M REALLY SCARED.
BUT...

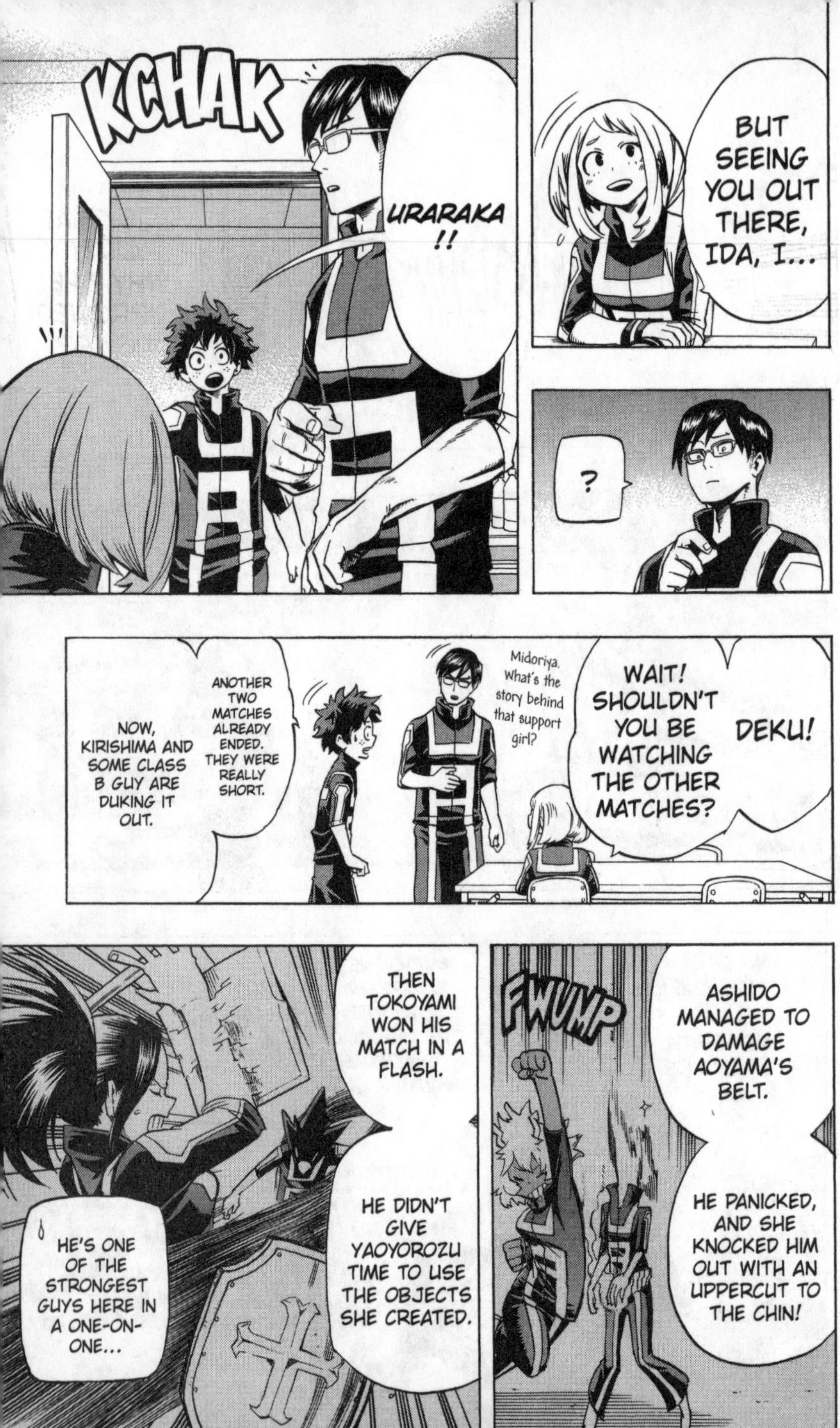
BUT SEEING YOU OUT THERE, IDA, I...
?
URARAKA!!
KCHAK
DEKU!
WAIT! SHOULDN'T YOU BE WATCHING THE OTHER MATCHES?
Midoriya. What's the story behind that support girl?
ANOTHER TWO MATCHES ALREADY ENDED. THEY WERE REALLY SHORT.
NOW, KIRISHIMA AND SOME CLASS B GUY ARE DUKING IT OUT.
ASHIDO MANAGED TO DAMAGE AOYAMA'S BELT.
FWUMP
HE PANICKED, AND SHE KNOCKED HIM OUT WITH AN UPPERCUT TO THE CHIN!
THEN TOKOYAMI WON HIS MATCH IN A FLASH.
HE DIDN'T GIVE YAOYOROZU TIME TO USE THE OBJECTS SHE CREATED.
HE'S ONE OF THE STRONGEST GUYS HERE IN A ONE-ON-ONE...

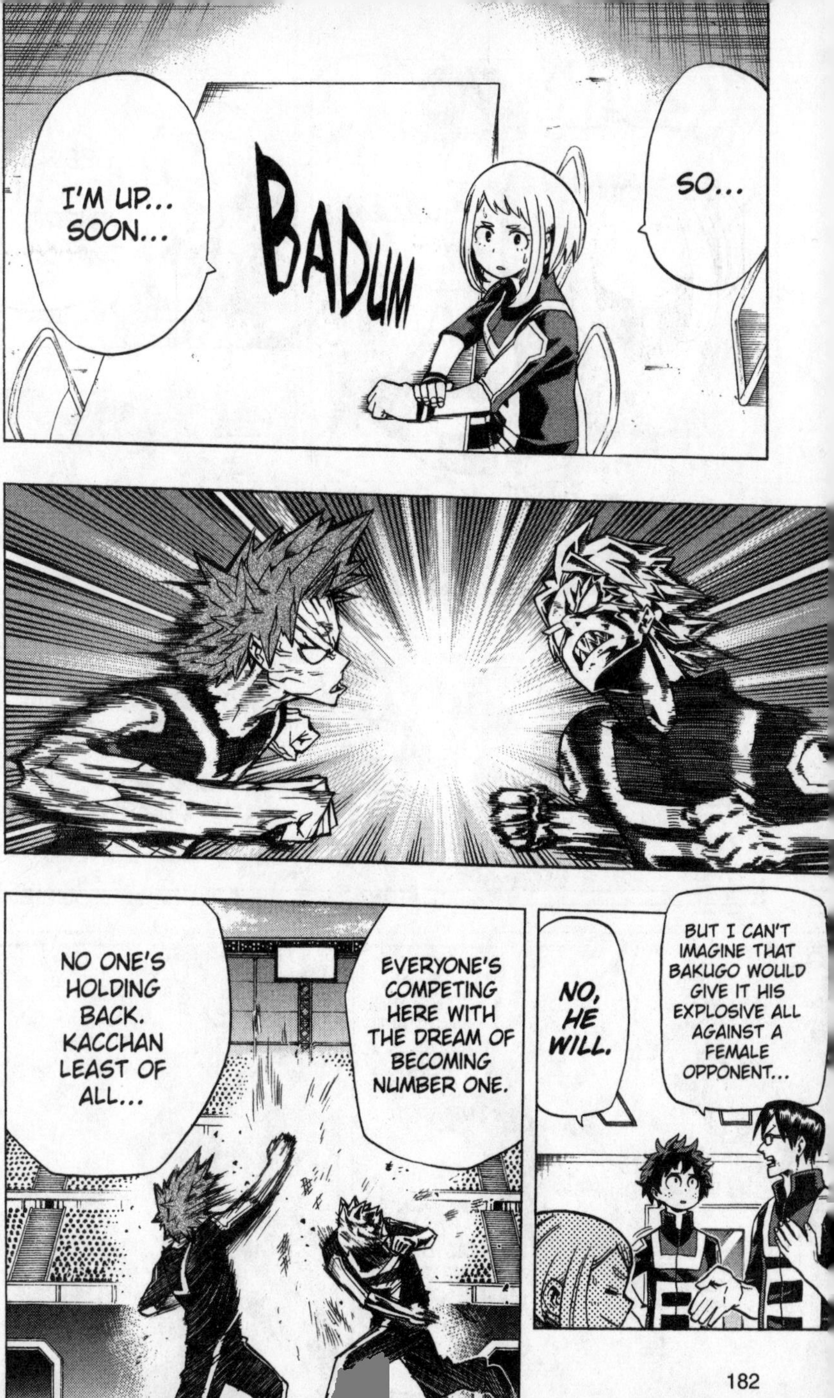
SO...
BADUM
I'M UP... SOON...
BUT I CAN'T IMAGINE THAT BAKUGO WOULD GIVE IT HIS EXPLOSIVE ALL AGAINST A FEMALE OPPONENT...
NO, HE WILL.
EVERYONE'S COMPETING HERE WITH THE DREAM OF BECOMING NUMBER ONE.
NO ONE'S HOLDING BACK. KACCHAN LEAST OF ALL...

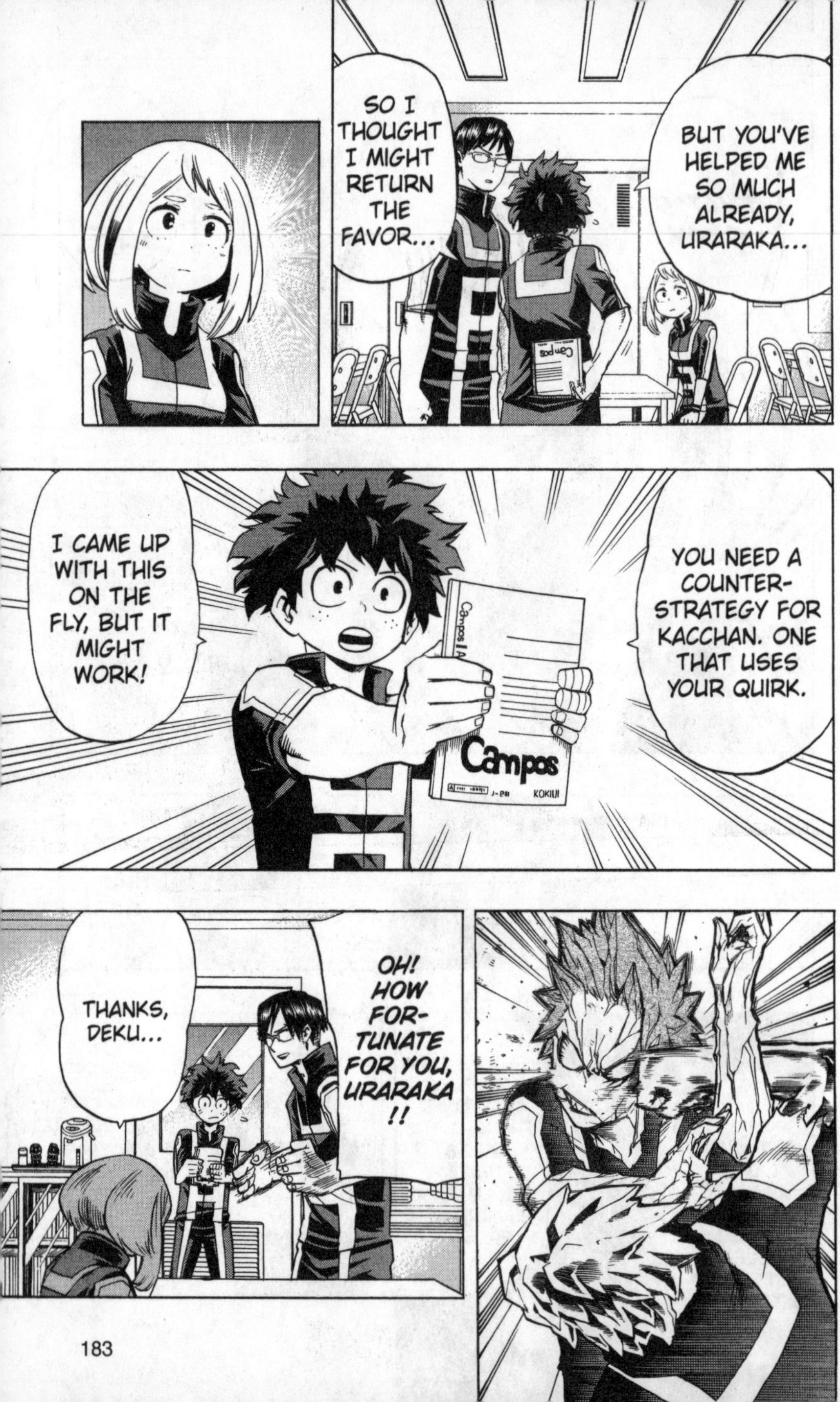
BUT YOU'VE HELPED ME SO MUCH ALREADY, URARAKA...
SO I THOUGHT I MIGHT RETURN THE FAVOR...
YOU NEED A COUNTER-STRATEGY FOR KACCHAN. ONE THAT USES YOUR QUIRK.
I CAME UP WITH THIS ON THE FLY, BUT IT MIGHT WORK!
Campos
OH! HOW FORTUNATE FOR YOU, URARAKA!!
THANKS, DEKU...

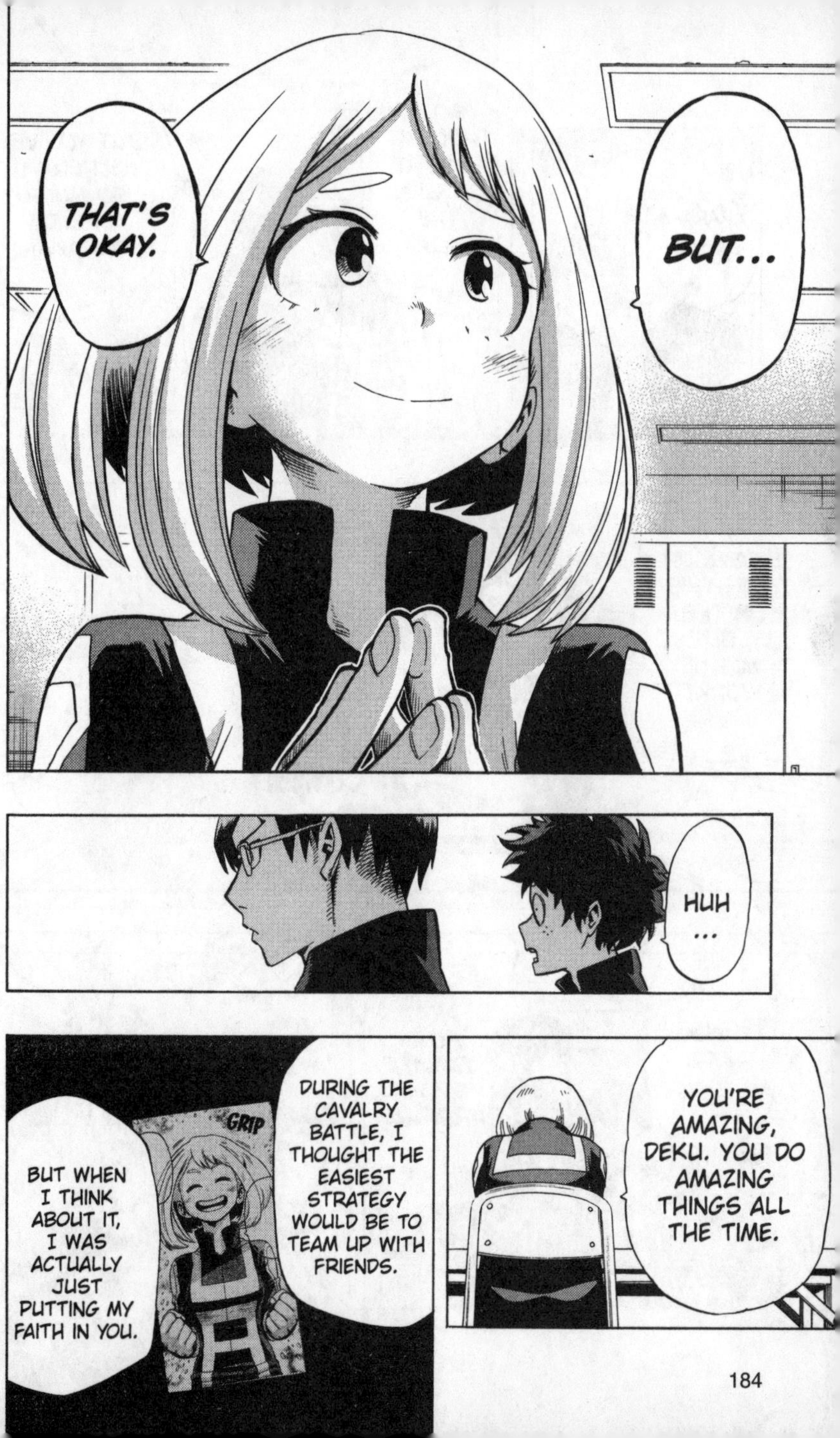
BUT...
THAT'S OKAY.
HUH ...
YOU'RE AMAZING, DEKU. YOU DO AMAZING THINGS ALL THE TIME.
DURING THE CAVALRY BATTLE, I THOUGHT THE EASIEST STRATEGY WOULD BE TO TEAM UP WITH FRIENDS.
GRIP
BUT WHEN I THINK ABOUT IT, I WAS ACTUALLY JUST PUTTING MY FAITH IN YOU.

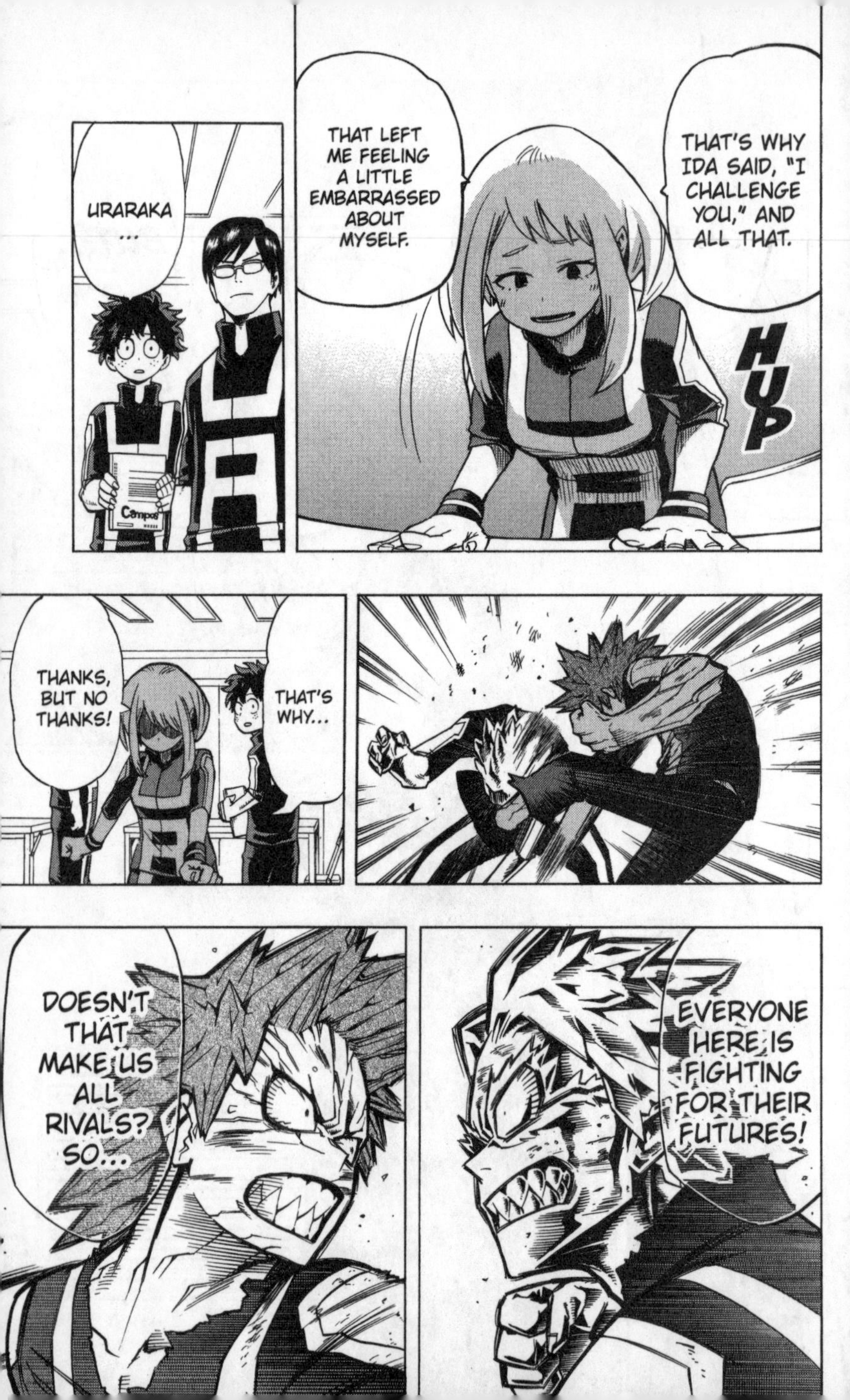
THAT'S WHY IDA SAID, "I CHALLENGE YOU," AND ALL THAT.
THAT LEFT ME FEELING A LITTLE EMBARRASSED ABOUT MYSELF.
HUP
URARAKA ...
THAT'S WHY...
THANKS, BUT NO THANKS!
EVERYONE HERE IS FIGHTING FOR THEIR FUTURES!
DOESN'T THAT MAKE US ALL RIVALS? SO...

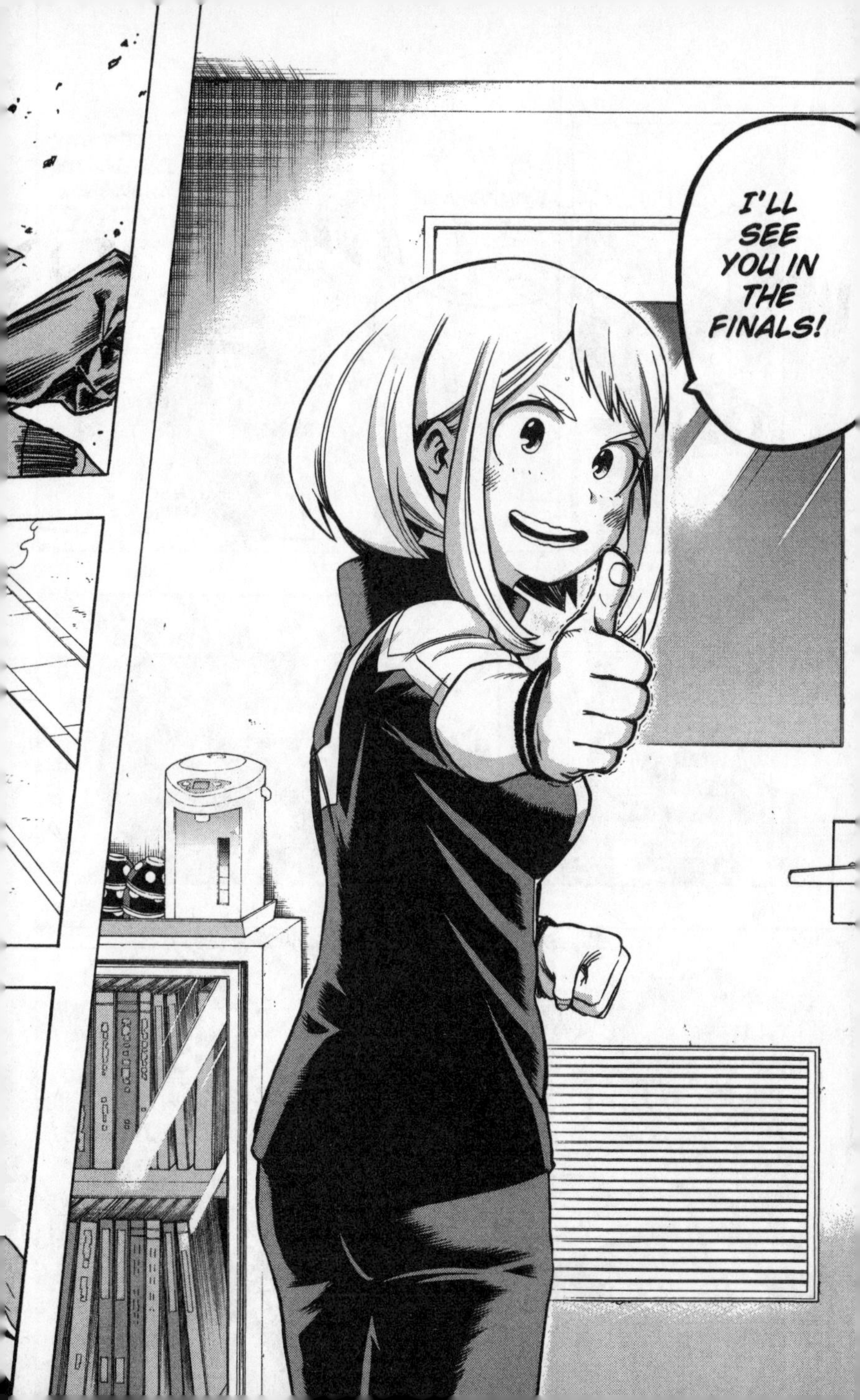
I'LL SEE YOU IN THE FINALS!

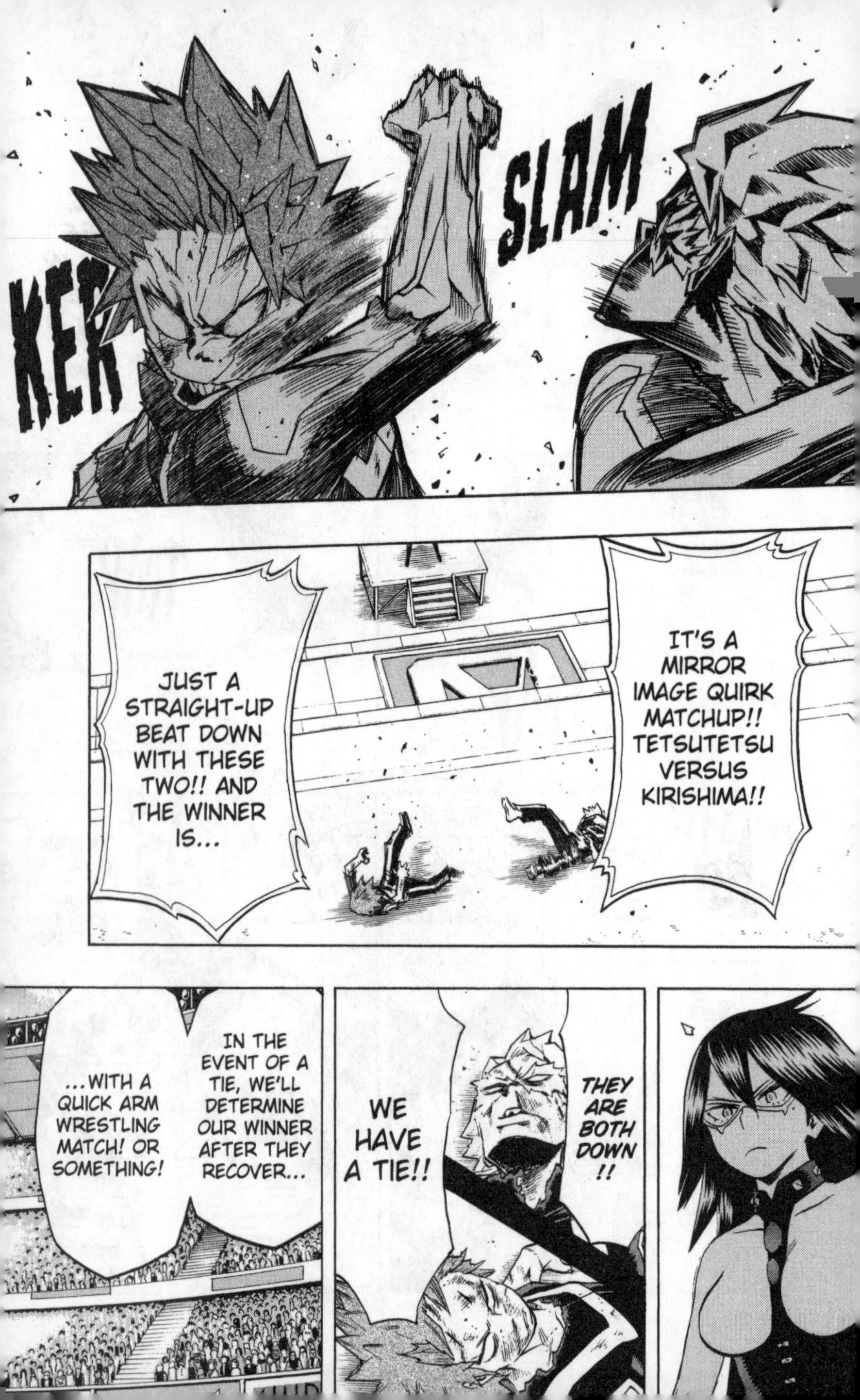
KER SLAM
IT'S A MIRROR IMAGE QUIRK MATCHUP!! TETSUTETSU VERSUS KIRISHIMA!!
JUST A STRAIGHT-UP BEAT DOWN WITH THESE TWO!! AND THE WINNER IS...
THEY ARE BOTH DOWN!!
WE HAVE A TIE!!
IN THE EVENT OF A TIE, WE'LL DETERMINE OUR WINNER AFTER THEY RECOVER...
...WITH A QUICK ARM WRESTLING MATCH! OR SOMETHING!

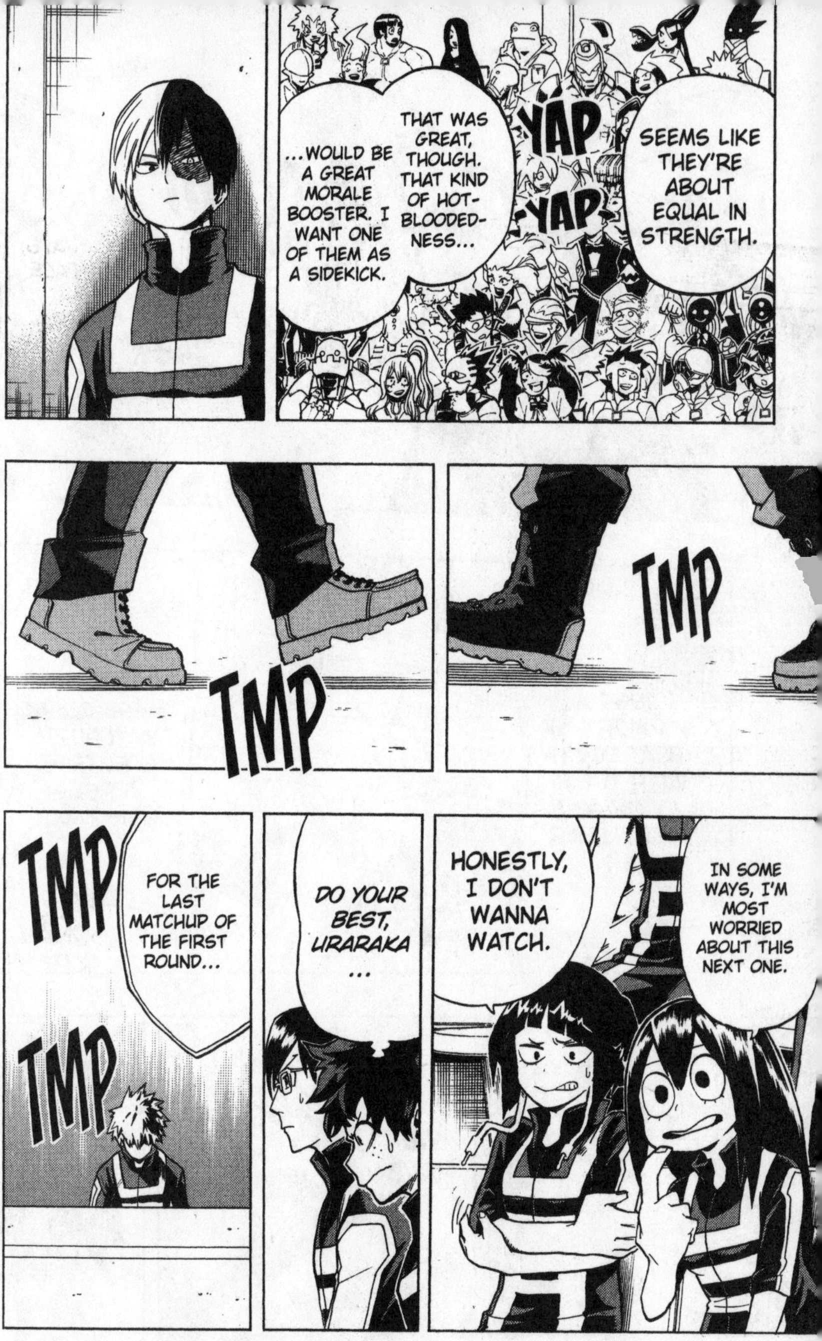
SEEMS LIKE THEY'RE ABOUT EQUAL IN STRENGTH.
YAP
YAP
THAT WAS GREAT, THOUGH. THAT KIND OF HOT-BLOODEDNESS...
...WOULD BE A GREAT MORALE BOOSTER. I WANT ONE OF THEM AS A SIDEKICK.
TMP
TMP
IN SOME WAYS, I'M MOST WORRIED ABOUT THIS NEXT ONE.
HONESTLY, I DON'T WANNA WATCH.
DO YOUR BEST, URARAKA...
FOR THE LAST MATCHUP OF THE FIRST ROUND...
TMP
TMP

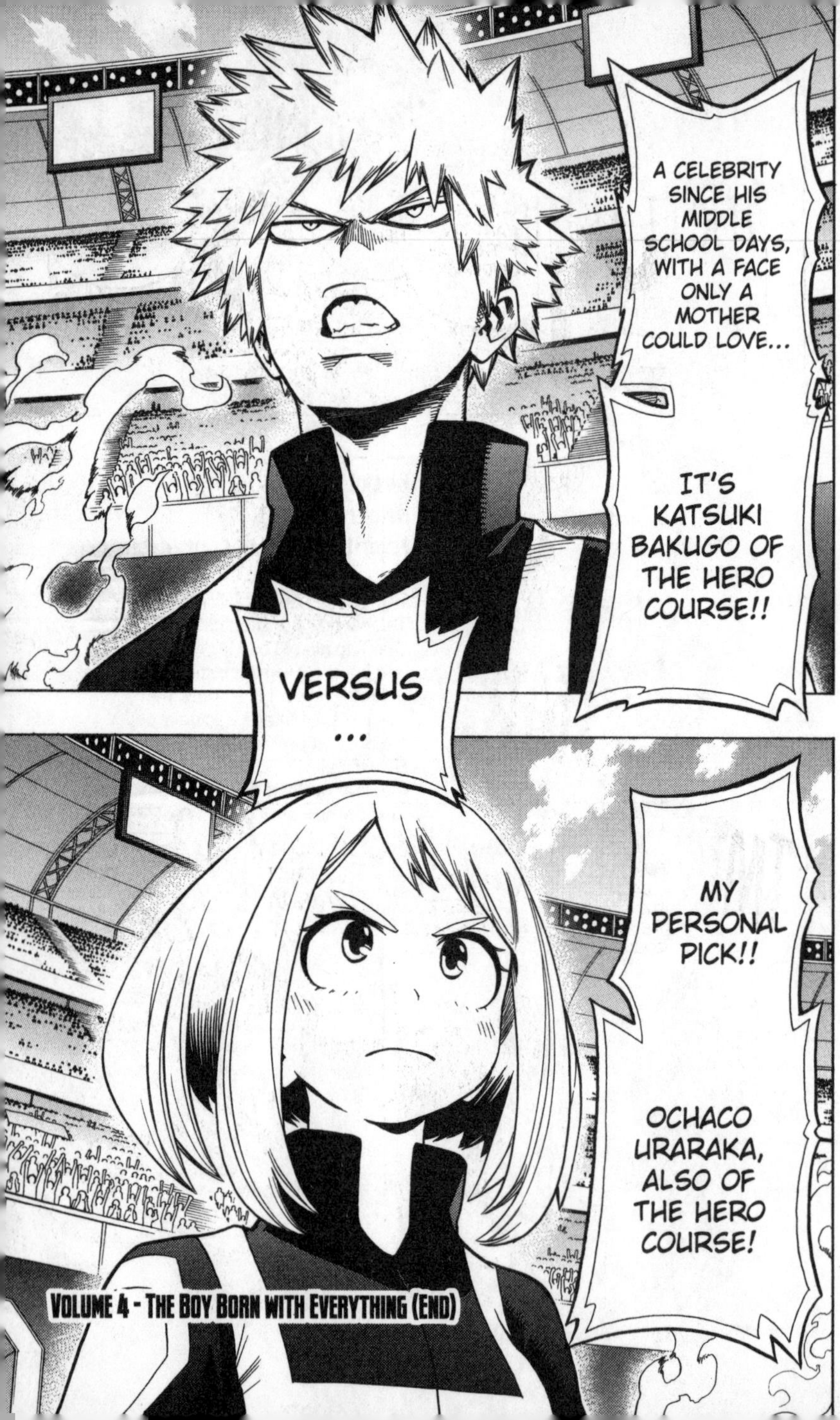
A CELEBRITY SINCE HIS MIDDLE SCHOOL DAYS, WITH A FACE ONLY A MOTHER COULD LOVE...
IT'S KATSUKI BAKUGO OF THE HERO COURSE!!
VERSUS ...
MY PERSONAL PICK!!
OCHACO URARAKA, ALSO OF THE HERO COURSE!
VOLUME 4 - THE BOY BORN WITH EVERYTHING (END)

MINA ASHIDO (15)

STREET CLOTHES

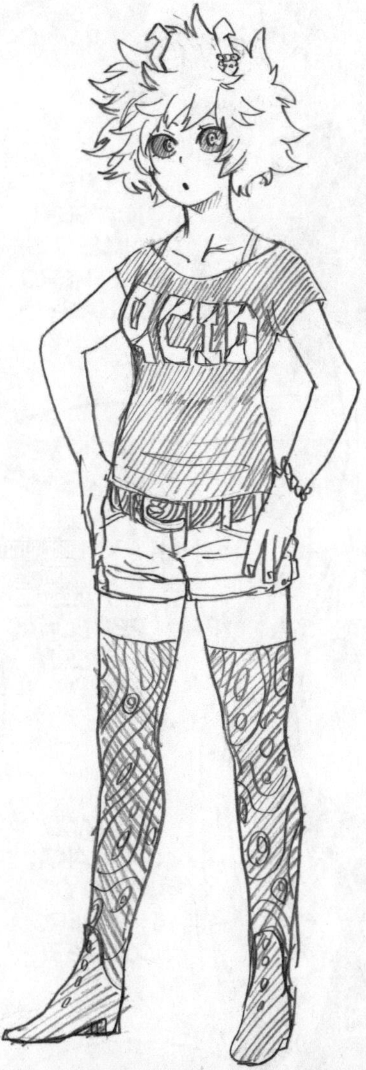

Birthday: 7/30
Height: 159 cm
Favorite Things: Dancing, natto, okra

BEHIND THE SCENES

Truly a victim of circumstance. Due to plain old bad luck, she's come this far without really getting to show off… I draw her really plain, but she's actually got the best reflexes among the girls. By which I mean she's a top-class member of Class A. I hope I get to show how strong she is sooner or later.

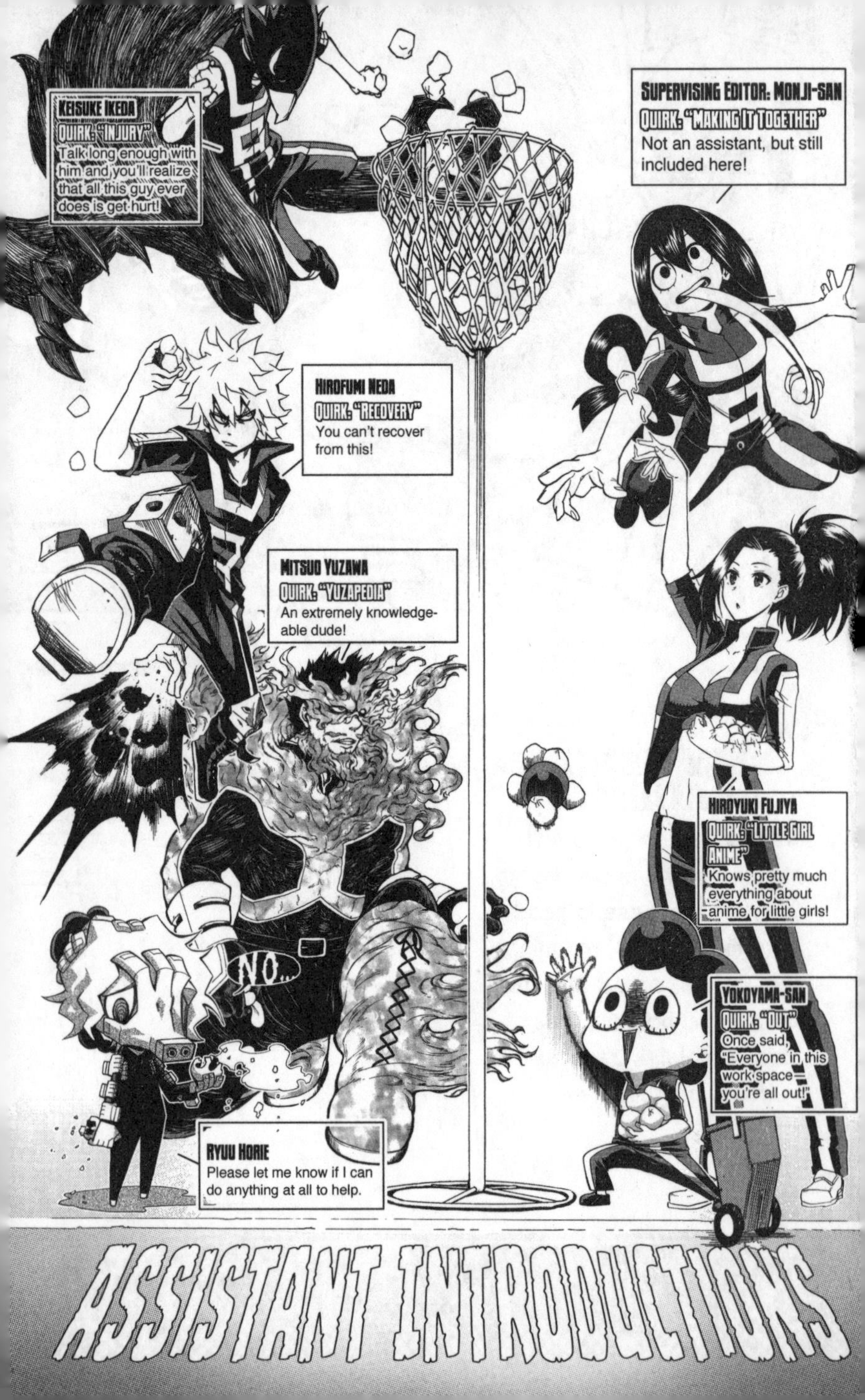

SUPERVISING EDITOR: MONJI-SAN
QUIRK: "MAKING IT TOGETHER"
Not an assistant, but still included here!
KEISUKE IKEDA
QUIRK: "INJURY"
Talk long enough with him and you'll realize that all this guy ever does is get hurt!
HIROFUMI NEDA
QUIRK: "RECOVERY"
You can't recover from this!
MITSUO YUZAWA
QUIRK: "YUZAPEDIA"
An extremely knowledge-able dude!
HIROYUKI FUJIYA
QUIRK: "LITTLE GIRL ANIME"
Knows pretty much everything about anime for little girls!
YOKOYAMA-SAN
QUIRK: "OUT"
Once said, "Everyone in this work space you're all out!"
NO...
RYUU HORIE
Please let me know if I can do anything at all to help.
ASSISTANT INTRODUCTIONS

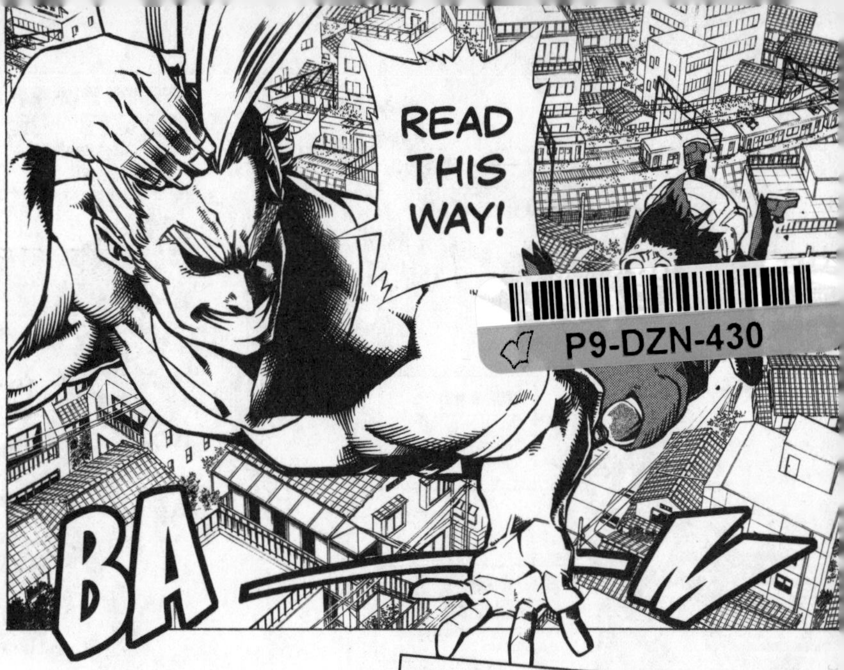
READ THIS WAY!
BA-M

MY HERO ACADEMIA

reads from right to left, starting in the upper-right corner. Japanese is read from right to left, meaning that action, sound effects and word-balloon order are completely reversed from English order.

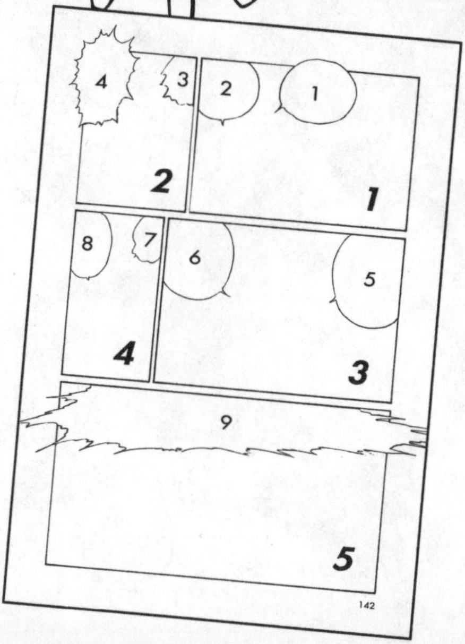
1
1
2
2
3
4
2
3
5
6
3
7
8
4
9
5
142